ABORTION AND THE LAW
From International Comparison to Legal Policy

ABORTION AND THE LAW

From International Comparison to Legal Policy

by

ALBIN ESER

and

HANS-GEORG KOCH

translated by

EMILY SILVERMAN

T·M·C· ASSER PRESS

The Hague

Published by T·M·C·ASSER PRESS
P.O.Box 16163, 2500 BD The Hague, The Netherlands
<www.asserpress.nl>

T·M·C·ASSER PRESS' English language books are distributed exclusively by:

Cambridge University Press, The Edinburgh Building, Shaftesbury Road,
Cambridge CB2 2RU, UK,
or
for customers in the USA, Canada and Mexico:
Cambridge University Press, 100 Brook Hill Drive, West Nyack, NY 10994-2133, USA
<www.cambridge.org>

ISBN 90-6704-197-1
(9789067041973)

PRINTED IN THE NETHERLANDS

Preface

This volume presents a compact summary of the results of a multi-staged criminal law research project devoted to a quasi-eternal problem of humanity: the preterm termination of a pregnancy aimed at preventing birth.

Although the practices engaged in to terminate pregnancies as well as the societal debates on the subject can be traced back to the far distant past, the phenomenon of illegal abortion and legal termination of pregnancy has apparently never before been as widely practiced or as intensely discussed as it is today. The destigmatization of a once inviolable prohibition has led, in recent decades, to an unparalleled wave of reform of traditional criminal laws regulating abortion all over the world, whereby the paths to reform chosen by the various legal systems are extremely diverse. This has led to a remarkable variety of regulations, a variety that cannot, however, be explained simply in terms of conflicting ideas concerning the best way to avoid terminations of pregnancy. Instead, the very goal to be set – namely, the fundamental question regarding the degree to which unborn life should be protected, especially in relation to the right of the pregnant woman to self-determination – is obviously highly controversial. Also the subject of controversy are the effects of various regulations on the methods by which pregnancies may be terminated in practice and on the frequency with which they are in fact terminated. Although one might assume that a more or less far-reaching retreat of the criminal law in this area would lead to a corresponding increase in the number of terminations performed, this widespread assumption appears to be precipitate; for as a superficial comparison of various regulatory models has already shown, greater criminal law permissiveness does not necessarily lead to a higher frequency of terminations. Similarly, rigid prohibitory norms do not automatically lead to a smaller number of abortions.

With the role of the criminal law in reducing terminations of pregnancy thus put into question, scholars who engage in comparative legal and empirical-criminological research should recognize and respond to the need to investigate this relationship more closely. This is especially true in a country such as the Federal Republic of Germany where, on the one hand, unborn life has a fundamentally recognized right to protection but where, on the other hand, criminal law is supposed to be the 'last resort' for the protection of legal values.

This leads us to pose the following questions:
- whether and if so to what extent and under what circumstances specifically criminal law regulations and their application in practice actually influence conduct,
- whether (and if so which) other norms (co-)influence the termination of pregnancy in practice, and finally
- whether and to what extent protective mechanisms located outside the criminal

law suffice and whether they may even be more suitable than criminal law instruments.

With its research project 'The Law of Abortion: An International Comparison',
the Max Planck Institute for Foreign and International Criminal Law in Freiburg
took on the task of resolving these questions. The project design encompassed
three stages: an international survey (1), a number of empirical-criminological
implementation studies (2) and an assessment of legal policy (3).

(1) All continents were considered in the decision of which countries to include in
the *international survey*. For the most part, the study was conducted on the basis of
reports covering a single country; in some cases, however, it made sense to address
several regionally- or culturally-related countries in one project report. The 40 reports ultimately submitted treat a total of 64 countries, 26 of them European. Thus,
coverage of Europe – in terms of the political structures as they existed in the 1980s
– is virtually complete. As far as the inclusion of non-European countries is concerned, we felt strongly that it was important to include representatives of all significant cultural and legal circles; a limiting factor here was the capacity of the
Institute, with the participation of both internal and external scholars, to prepare
country reports. In addition to a detailed overview of all relevant legal regulations,
each country report also includes a basic review of existing social conditions as
well as a section devoted to data on the prevalence of the termination of pregnancy
and the frequency with which illegal abortion is subject to criminal prosecution.
These country reports were published in two comprehensive volumes: A. Eser and
H.-G. Koch (eds.), *Schwangerschaftsabbruch im internationalen Vergleich.
Rechtliche Regelungen – Soziale Rahmenbedingungen – Empirische Grunddaten.
Teil* [Vol.] *1: Europa* (1744 pages), *Teil* [Vol.] *2: Außereuropa* (1353 pages), (Baden-
Baden, Nomos 1988 and 1989, cited in the following as E/K I and E/K II, respec-
tively).[1] At least with regard to the Max Planck Institute – and perhaps even
worldwide –, no other comparative legal project devoted to a single topic has ever
achieved comparable dimensions.[2]

---

[1] The introductory comments [*Geleitwort*]) to E/K I and II (pp. 5-9 in both volumes) contain
a description of the objectives and structure of the project as a whole.

[2] Even the otherwise still unique *Vergleichende Gesamtdarstellung des Deutschen und
Ausländischen Strafrechts* (edited by K. Birkmeyer et al.) from the beginning of the last century,
in which the discussion of 'abortion (§§ 218-220 RStrGB)' was undertaken by G. Radbruch (in
Vol. V, *Verbrechen und Vergehen wider das Leben*, Berlin, Otto Liebmann 1905, pp. 159-183), is
comparable to our project neither in scope nor in execution. The same is true for other comparative legal studies, such as the studies, published as monographs, by E. Ketting and Ph. Van
Praag, *Schwangerschaftsabbruch: Gesetz und Praxis im internationalen Vergleich* (Tübingen,
Deutsche Gesellschaft für Verhaltenstherapie 1985); S.J. Frankowski and G.F. Cole (eds.), *Abortion and Protection of the Human Fetus* (Dordrecht, Martinus Nijhoff 1987) and P. Sachdev
(ed.), *International Handbook on Abortion* (New York, Greenwood 1988).

(2) In the *empirical stage of the project*, the Max Planck Institute's Department of Criminology under the direction of Prof. Dr. Dr. h.c. mult. *Günter Kaiser* undertook the study of three particularly important issues concerning the implementation in the Federal Republic of Germany of the criminal abortion law reform of 1976: first, the prosecution and disposition of cases by law enforcement agencies; second, the ways in which women decide whether to continue or terminate their pregnancies; and finally, the attitudes and conduct of physicians with regard to § 218 StGB.[3]

(3) An important goal of the *comparative legal stage of the project* was to identify both the common features as well as the differences among the various national laws governing the termination of pregnancy; by proceeding in this fashion, we hoped to find regulatory alternatives for a possible reform. In addition, relevant legal developments that took place in the individual countries subsequent to publication of the country reports were documented and a detailed comparative analysis undertaken. Finally, from the point of view of legal policy, recommendations with detailed reasoning were made: A. ESER and H.-G. KOCH, *Schwangerschaftsabbruch im internationalen Vergleich. Teil* [Vol.] *3: Rechtsvergleichender Querschnitt – Rechtspolitische Schlußbetrachtungen – Dokumentation zur neueren Rechtsentwicklung* (932 pages), (Baden-Baden, Nomos 1999, cited in the following as E/K III).

At the time the project was planned, the sensitive nature of the topic in Germany, from a political perspective, was readily apparent. Therein lay the central impetus to dedicate comparative legal research efforts on an as yet unmatched scale to the problem of the termination of pregnancy and to integrate criminological-empirical studies focused on the German situation. During the planning phase of the project, however, there was no way to anticipate the direction that the general political developments in Germany and Europe would take. The dynamics on the national political level that were triggered by the Unification Treaty of 31 August 1990, particularly with regard to the termination of pregnancy,[4] led to a situation in which preliminary results of our studies were introduced at a quite early stage into the

---

[3] M. HÄUSSLER-SCZEPAN, *Arzt und Schwangerschaftsabbruch, Eine empirische Untersuchung zur Implementation des reformierten § 218 StGB*, Series 'Kriminologische Forschungsberichte,' Vol. 39 (Freiburg, Max-Planck-Institut für ausländisches und internationales Strafrecht 1989, 291 pages); B. HOLZHAUER, *Schwangerschaft und Schwangerschaftsabbruch, Die Rolle des § 218 StGB bei der Entscheidungsfindung betroffener Frauen*, Series 'Kriminologische Forschungsberichte,' Vol. 38 (Freiburg, Max-Planck-Institut für ausländisches und internationales Strafrecht 1989, 436 pages, 2nd unrevised edn. 1991); K. LIEBL, *Ermittlungsverfahren, Strafverfolgungs- und Sanktionspraxis bei Schwangerschaftsabbruch*, Series 'Kriminologische Forschungsberichte,' Vol. 40, (Freiburg, Max-Planck-Institut für ausländisches und internationales Strafrecht 1990, 189 pages).

[4] See Art. 31 para. 4 of the *Einigungsvertrag* [Unification Treaty] (*BGBl.* 1990 II, p. 885 ff.).

public discussion and indeed were reflected in parliamentary consultations.[5] At the risk of appearing immodest, it would appear that the legal comparative and criminological insights won in our project were not entirely without influence on the regulation of termination of pregnancy finally adopted by unified Germany. How and to what extent this influence was exerted must, in the interest of the greatest possible neutrality, be determined by an impartial historian. A welcome development would be the clearing up by such a scholar of misjudgments currently found in this area.

After the conclusion of the norm-finding process in reunified Germany regarding the termination of pregnancy, at least as far as federal legislation was concerned, it seemed as though the political topicality of this subject was a thing of the past. This was, however, not the case, as was soon shown by events such as the withdrawal – insisted upon by Pope John Paul II – of Catholic counseling centers from the counseling system, by the debates triggered by spectacular cases involving so-called 'late-term abortions' as well as by litigation in which parents sought to obtain child maintenance payments in cases where physicians failed to perform a termination. Also, more recent debates on the legal protection of embryos created in vitro show that the discussion of such fundamental issues as the right of unborn life to protection and the nature of appropriate legal instruments is by no means over.

In light of this, we decided to prepare an abridged English-language version of the three published volumes – which encompass a total of 4000 pages – and in so doing make the project's findings accessible to an international public. The compact volume is based on Volume 3 (E/K III), since this volume presented the country reports published in E/K I and E/K II in comparative form. In order not to exceed the capacity of a paperback, we have not included the documentation of more recent legal developments contained in the appendix to E/K III. Furthermore, the comparative legal cross-section was shortened considerably; at the same time, many of the individual citations to the country reports in E/K I and E/K II were removed. Readers in search of a detailed analysis or a specific source of information are referred to the original publications (E/K I-III). Reference to these volumes is simplified by the fact that the comparative legal cross-section – both in the original and in the shortened form presented here – conforms broadly to the outline followed by the country reports in E/K I and E/K II.

The first three chapters of this volume offer a *comparative legal cross-section*: Following a summary of social conditions and historical developments (I) is a de-

---

[5] The arguably most important texts containing these findings, statements of opinion and reform proposals can be found in A. Eser and H.-G. Koch, *Schwangerschafts-abbruch: Auf dem Weg zu einer Neuregelung, Gesammelte Studien und Vorschläge* (Baden-Baden, Nomos 1992) and in A. Eser, *Schwangerschaftsabbruch: Auf dem verfassungsgerichtlichen Prüfstand, Rechtsgutachten im Normenkontrollverfahren zum Schwangeren- und Familienhilfegesetz von 1992* (Baden-Baden, Nomos 1994, in collaboration with Chr. Hülsmann and H.-G. Koch).

tailed comparison of legal regulations (II), which is supplemented by statistics on the termination of pregnancy (III). The final chapter (IV) contains *concluding reflections from a legal policy perspective*. These reflections, first published in E/K III, are presented here in their entirety. Important findings, insights and trends are summarized and starting points and guidelines for possible reforms pointed out; the chapter ends with a proposed regulation intended to provide those interested in optimal regulation of the termination of pregnancy with food for thought. Results of the aforementioned empirical criminological studies were taken into consideration in the writing of this chapter. The *appendix* contains a list of the countries studied in this project (A) as well as a list of publications based on earlier relevant studies or prepared in connection with the project (B). It is apparent from these publications that the intensity and coordination of cooperation in the course of this project between criminal law scholars and criminologists reached a level rarely achieved anywhere.

Even if, as mentioned above, we have chosen not to include the more recent legal developments presented in the appendix of E/K III, both smaller and larger scale legislative changes implemented in the last 10 years in numerous countries were taken into consideration in the preparation of this abridged version of our research project. Thus, this volume conveys an impression of the current legal policy dynamic that made the termination of pregnancy a 'topic of the 20th century', both in Germany as well as in numerous other countries.

The concept for this book was developed by the two authors together. Each author wrote various sections of the book by himself, whereby the content of these sections was coordinated with the other author. Responsibility for parts II.1 to II.4 as well as for the legal policy reflections (chapter IV) lies with *Albin Eser*; *Hans-Georg Koch* is responsible for the rest of the text. We are deeply grateful to *Emily Silverman*, our translator, whose legal expertise, perseverance and feel for language enabled us to publish this work in English. Thanks are also due to *Ann Marie Ackermann* and *James Cohen* for their assistance in the translation.

Completion of our project does not mean the end of the discussion, and it certainly does not mean that all questions have been answered. This is especially true in the case of an issue that is as ideologically and politically charged as is the termination of pregnancy. If we have succeeded in revealing any misconceptions, in awakening any new insights for possible reforms or in giving impetus to additional studies, we will consider ourselves richly rewarded for the not insignificant amount of time and effort we have put into this project.

Freiburg im Breisgau, January 2005

Albin ESER
Hans-Georg KOCH

TABLE OF CONTENTS

Preface   V

Biographical Notes   XIX

Abbreviations   XX

Part I
Framework

I.1   Introduction   3

I.2   System and Standard of Social Services   4

I.3   The Position of Women in Society   5

I.4   Assessment and Significance of Family Planning and Termination of Pregnancy   7
    4.1   Preliminary remarks   7
    4.2   Sociopolitical and individual dimensions of family planning   7
    4.3   Governmental measures in the area of family planning   9
    4.4   The significance of the termination of pregnancy in relation to other
        methods of birth control   9
    4.5   Assessment of the termination of pregnancy from a religious perspective   10
        4.5.1   The Roman Catholic Church   11
        4.5.2   Protestant churches   12
        4.5.3   Other Christian churches   13
        4.5.4   Islam   13
        4.5.5   Judaism   13
        4.5.6   Hinduism   14
        4.6   The stance of the medical community regarding the termination
            of pregnancy   14
        4.6.1   Regulations on the termination of pregnancy in professional codes
            of ethics   15
        4.6.2   Other determinants of the legal position of the medical community   16
        4.6.3   Assessment   16

I.5   Remarks on Historical Developments   18
    5.1   'Abortion tourism'   18
    5.2   On the significance of case law and criminal prosecution practice   19
    5.3   On the relative importance of demographic policy   20

Part II
Current Laws Regulating the Termination of Pregnancy

Introduction   25

II.1 Legal Sources and Regulatory Methodology Behind the Law on the
      Termination of Pregnancy   26
      1.1   Regulatory scope: between criminal and social welfare law   26
      1.2   Classification into categories of crime: from homicide to moral turpitude 27

II.2 Basic Concepts in Legal Regulation   29
      Preliminary remarks   29
      2.1   Legislative intent: from semi-official proclamations to diffuse
            speculations   29
      2.2   Legal values: from the protection of individual life to general
            demographic policy and sexual ethics   30
      2.3   Constitutional foundations: from apparent absence to binding guidelines
            for the legislature   34
            2.3.1   Survey   36
            2.3.2   Ranking in light of guidelines for the legislature   40
      2.4   Basic regulatory models: from (virtually) absolute prohibition to
            (almost) complete permission   42
            2.4.1   Regulatory diversity – criteria for classification   42
            2.4.2   Classification   45
                    A. 'Prohibition Model'   46
                    B. Pure 'Indication Model'   46
                    C. Combined (successive) 'time limit – indication models'   49
                    D. Pure 'time limit models'   50
            2.4.3   Comprehensive assessment: disregarding extremes leaves three
                    distinct regulatory approaches   51
      2.5   Concept of termination of pregnancy: fluid borders – terminological,
            substantive and temporal   57
            2.5.1   Terminological evolution   58
            2.5.2   Varying scope of substantive coverage: from intervention during
                    the course of pregnancy to successful killing   59
            2.5.3   The varying temporal range of termination: from conception to
                    the end of the birth process   60

II.3 Permissible Termination of Pregnancy   69
      Preliminary remarks   69
      3.1   Overview of the essential prerequisites for and the varying scope of legal
            terminations   70
      3.2   Indications   72
            3.2.1   Significance and terminology   72
            3.2.2   Recognized indications: from life-threatening risk to reduced
                    standard of living   74
            3.2.3   Particulars regarding the 'medical' and 'medical-social' indication 76
            3.2.4   Particulars regarding the 'eugenic' indication   79

3.2.5   Particulars regarding the 'criminological' indication   81

3.2.6   Particulars regarding the 'social' indication   83

3.2.7   Overview of 'other' grounds recognized for the termination of pregnancy   86

    A. Termination grounds in the person of the pregnant woman   87

    B. 'Illegitimacy' of the expected child   87

    C. Unusual social factors   87

    D. The pregnant woman's status as a foreigner   87

3.2.8   Contraindications   87

3.3   Consent   88

3.3.1   Consent of the pregnant woman: significance – substitutability   88

3.3.2   Essential prerequisites of consent   91

3.3.3   Special problems associated with pregnant women who are underage and those with limited mental/psychological competence   92

3.3.4   Rights of the partner to participate in decisions on termination – involvement of the woman's social milieu   93

3.4   Procedural prerequisites: counseling – third-party review   95

3.4.1   Trends   96

3.4.2   A closer look at third-party review and determination of indications   97

3.4.3   Individual aspects of counseling   101

3.5   Performance requirements: physician – hospital – procedures   106

3.5.1   Personnel and institutional requirements   106

3.5.2   Requirements concerning performance   107

3.5.3   Issues of control and sanctioning   108

3.6   Subsequent obligations: documentation – reporting – notification   109

3.6.1   Scope and goals   109

3.6.2   Varying degrees of confidentiality   110

3.6.3   Analysis   111

3.7   The legal nature of exemptions of terminations from punishment   111

3.7.1   Disparate levels of discussion: from disputes regarding constitutionality to indifference   112

3.7.2   Express declarations of permissibility   114

3.7.3   Regulations that differentiate   116

3.7.4   Prohibition and permission in the sense of rule and exception   117

3.8   Legal claims of the pregnant woman   118

3.8.1   Claim to the performance of a permissible termination   118

    A. Claims when a medical indication is present   119

    B. Area of application of more broadly defined indications as well as of time-bound exemptions from punishment   120

    C. Other narrowly defined indications   121

    D. Limitations applying to foreign women   122

3.8.2   Compensation for the costs of termination   123

    A. Survey   123

    a) Medical indication as the sole ground for permissible termination   124

b) Models with a more broadly defined scope of
permissibility   124
B. Comparative observations   126
3.9   The right of medical personnel to refuse to participate in the termination
procedure   127
3.9.1   Concrete scope   128
3.9.2   Scope of applicability with regard to 'persons'   128
3.9.3   Procedural rules governing the exercise of the right to refuse   130

II.4   Impermissible Termination of Pregnancy   131
Preliminary remarks   131
4.1   The structure of the criminal offense: from the uniform model to the
tripartite model and beyond   131
4.2   Modes of commission: from an all-encompassing approach to special
preparatory, participatory and other related offenses   133
4.2.1   Modes of commission and instruments used to commit the
offense   133
4.2.2   Attempted termination of pregnancy   134
4.2.3   Parties to the termination of pregnancy   135
4.2.4   Supplementary crimes of preparation, participation and other
related offenses   137
4.3   Legal consequences of a punishable termination of pregnancy: from
fines to life imprisonment   139
4.3.1   General categories   140
4.3.2   Special grounds for reducing and enhancing punishment   142
4.4   Termination of pregnancy and international criminal law   143
4.4.1   Reasons why women go abroad to terminate their pregnancies   143
4.4.2   Principles of jurisdiction: from (limited) territorial application to
an (extended) extraterritorial approach   144
4.4.3   Discrepancies between the punishability of termination at home
and abroad   145
4.4.4   Limiting rules and procedural requirements   147
4.4.5   Summary   147

II.5   Special Role of the Physician   153
5.1   Requirement that terminations of pregnancy be performed by physicians   153
5.2   Functions of physicians in preliminary proceedings   154
5.2.1   Functions of the physician in preliminary proceedings   154
5.2.2   Division of responsibility between the preliminary and the
performing stages   156
5.3   Rules covering performance of terminations of pregnancy   156
5.4   Special criminal provisions and sanctions pertaining to physicians   157
5.4.1   Sanctions related to the performance of terminations   157
5.4.2   Criminal sanctions with respect to 'preliminary procedure'   159
A. In cases of exemptions from punishment based on some sort
of indication   159
B. In cases of exemptions from punishment based on time limits   160
C. Criminal provisions applicable to more than one model   161

	5.4.3	Other criminal sanctions	163
	5.4.4	Disciplinary and professional sanctions applicable to the termination of pregnancy	163
II.6	Preventive Measures		164
	6.1	Additional criminal offenses	164
	6.1.1	Independent preparatory and preliminary offenses	164
	6.1.2	Prohibitions against advertising and dissemination of information	165
	6.2	Government services	166
	6.2.1	Legislative intent	166
	6.2.2	Individual measures	167
II.7	Role of Termination of Pregnancy in the Prosecutorial Arena		171
	7.1	Duty to report terminations of pregnancy already committed	171
	7.2	Duty to report planned illegal terminations	172
	7.3	Special rules on the statute of limitations	173
	7.4	Special rules for prosecuting cases of illegal termination	173
	7.4.1	Prosecutorial discretion	173
	7.4.2	Features peculiar to the criminal process	174

Part III
Statistical Information

Introduction			177
III.1	Termination Statistics		178
	1.1	State of the data	178
	1.2	Comparative prevalence of terminations of pregnancy	179
	1.2.1	Frequency of the termination of pregnancy in various countries	179
	1.2.2	Comparison in the relationship to the respective regulatory model and counseling system	180
	1.2.3	Developments in the number of terminations over time	181
	1.3	Considerations regarding possible variables	182
III.2	Crime Statistics		185
	2.1	State of the data	185
	2.2	Comparison and evaluation	185
III.3	Judicial Statistics and Trends in Prosecution		187
	3.1	State of the data	187
	3.2	Comparison and evaluation	187

Part IV
Concluding Reflections from a Legal Policy Perspective

Preliminary Remarks   205

IV.1   Review: Findings – Insights – Trends   207
     1.1   Ideological prejudices   207
     1.2   The reality of the termination of pregnancy   209
         1.2.1   Termination of pregnancy: an ancient and worldwide
                phenomenon   209
         1.2.2   Frequency of termination and prosecutorial practice   210
         1.2.3   Attitudes towards contraception and termination   212
         1.2.4   Reform-inducing factors   215
         1.2.5   Effects of the (West) German reform of 1975   217
     1.3   On the ways of regulating the termination of pregnancy   218
         1.3.1   Variety of regulatory approaches   218
         1.3.2   The interdependence of regulatory diversity and social mores   222
         1.3.3   Model-building criteria   223
         1.3.4   'Medicalization' – 'proceduralization' 'socialization'   228
     1.4   On the role of criminal law – other leading factors   231
         1.4.1   Irrelevance of criminal law?   231
         1.4.2   Prevalence of psychosocial and socioethical factors?   237
         1.4.3   Determining conduct by means of proceedings?   241

IV.2   Outlook: Starting Points – Guidelines   244
     2.1   Regulatory maxims   244
         2.1.1   Clarity with regard to the regulatory goal and normative
                preconditions   244
         2.1.2   Norm-consciousness and social acceptance   247
         2.1.3   Transparence and consistence of the conduct-determining
                message   252
     2.2   Protected values and conflicting interests   255
         2.2.1   Plurality of rights and interests   256
         2.2.2   Relative nature of the protection of life   259
         2.2.3   The pregnant woman: autonomous yet bound by an obligatory
                weighing-up process   267
         2.2.4   Status-specific responsibilities   270
     2.3   Protection and legitimation through procedure   276
         2.3.1   Emergency indication: from third party evaluation to discourse   277
         2.3.2   Prevention through counseling   285
         2.3.3   Lawful termination of pregnancy   291

IV.3   A Proposed Regulation   295
Preliminary remarks   295
     3.1   Maxims and guiding principles   296
     3.2   Proposal of a law to regulate the termination of pregnancy   300

Appendix A: Country Reports 309

Appendix B: Publications 311

Index 319

Biographical Notes

Albin ESER was Professor of German, Comparative, and International Criminal Law at the Albert Ludwigs University of Freiburg and Director of the Max Planck Institute for Foreign and International Criminal Law. He earned his Dr. iur. from the University of Würzburg and his Master of Comparative Jurisprudence (M.C.J.) from New York University. He was a part-time judge at the Upper State Court of Appeal at Hamm/Westfalia and at Stuttgart/Baden-Württemberg. Since 2004 he is serving as Judge at the International Tribunal for the Former Yugoslavia in The Hague. In addition to his year at New York University, he has been a Visiting Professor at the University of California at Los Angeles, Columbia Law School, and the Institute of Medical Humanities at the University of Texas at Galveston. Although he has focused primarily on criminal law, he is also a specialist in law and medicine and is a member of the Board of Directors of the "Center for Ethics in Law and Medicine" at the University Hospital at Freiburg. In cooperation with Hans-Georg Koch, he led a comprehensive comparative and empirical research project on abortion in international perspective of which the manuscript in question is an abridged English-language version.

Hans-Georg KOCH earned his Dr. iur. from the University of Tübingen. As senior researcher since 1982 at the Max Planck Institute for Foreign and International Criminal Law, he is responsible for developing and directing the Institute's Medical Law section. He is a lecturer in medical law (University of Freiburg, University of Ulm) and a member of the Center for Ethics and Law in Medicine at the Albert Ludwigs University of Freiburg and of the Academy for Ethics in Medicine (Göttingen). In 2001, Hans-Georg Koch qualified as a university lecturer for the subject Medical Law with a paper entitled "Legitimation in Medical Practice." He has more than 200 publications (books and articles) in the fields of criminal and medical law. His special interests are relations between medical law and medical ethics, informed consent, medical responsibility, research on human subjects, abortion law, legal problems of genetics and artificial reproduction, euthanasia, and psychiatry and law.

Emily SILVERMAN earned her J.D. from the Boalt Hall School of Law (University of California, Berkeley) and her LL.M. from the University of Freiburg, Germany. She has lived and worked in Germany since 1991, during which time she was the recipient of fellowships from the German American Exchange Service and the Max Planck Society. She has been head of the United States section of the Max Planck Institute for Foreign and International Criminal Law in Freiburg since 2000 where, in addition to pursuing her own research, she has translated and edited numerous articles by German legal scholars that have appeared in English-language law journals in Europe and around the world.

ABBREVIATIONS

All ER	All England Law Reports
Art.	article
BGB	Bürgerliches Gesetzbuch ('German Civil Code')
BGBl.	Bundesgesetzblatt ('German Federal Law Gazette')
BGH	Bundesgerichtshof ('German Federal Supreme Court')
BGHSt	Bundesgerichtshof für Strafsachen ('decisions of the German Federal Supreme Court, criminal cases')
BT-Drs.	Bundestagsdrucksache ('printed matter of the Lower House of German Parliament')
BVerfG	Bundesverfassungsgericht ('Federal Constitutional Court')
BVerfGE	Bundesverfassungsgerichtsentscheidung ('decisions of the Federal Constitutional Court')
CCC	Canadian Criminal Cases
C.p.	Codice penale (Italy)
CP	Code pénal (Belgium, France), Código Penal (Spain)
CSFR	Czecheslovakian Federal Republic
CSP	Code de la santé publique
ČSSR	Czecheslovakian Sozialistic Republic
CTPA	Choice on Termination of Pregnancy Act 1996 (South Africa)
DÄBl.	Deutsches Ärzteblatt ('German medical journal')
D.C.	District of Columbia
DDR	Deutsche Demokratische Republik ('German Democratic Republic')
ECHR	European Convention on Human Rights
edn.	edition
eds.	editors
e.g.	for example
EHRR	European Human Rights Reports
E/K I, II,III	Albin Eser and Hans-Georg Koch (eds.), Schwangerschaftsabbruch im internationalen Vergleich,Teil 1: Europa (Baden-Baden, Nomos 1988), Teil 2: Außereuropa (Baden-Baden, Nomos 1989), Teil 3 Rechtsvergleichender Querschnitt – Rechtspolitische Schlußbetrachtungen – Dokumentation zur neueren Rechtsentwicklung (Baden-Baden, Nomos 1999)
E.R.	Queen Elizabeth (Elizabetha Regina); English Reports
esp.	especially
et al.	*et alia* ('and other persons')
etc.	*et cetera*
EuGRZ	Europäische Grundrechte-Zeitschrift ('European Journal of Fundamental Rights')

f., ff.	following
FACE	Freedom of Access to Clinic Entrances
FAZ	Frankfurter Allgemeine Zeitung (German newspaper)
Fed.Reg.	Federal Register
GDR	German Democratic Republic
ibid.	*ibidem* ('in the same place')
id.	*idem* ('the same')
i.e.	*id est* ('that is')
ILTR	Irish Law Times Reports
IR	Irish Reports
JZ	Juristenzeitung (German journal for jurists)
JuS	Juristische Schulung (German journal for jurists)
MMW	Münchener Medizinische Wochenschrift (German journal for physicians)
n.(nn.)	footnote(s)
No(s).	number(s)
NCP	Nouveau Code pénal (France)
NJW	Neue Juristische Wochenschrift (German journal for jurists)
nl	Dutch
Nr., No., N°	Nummer, Numero, Number
p.(pp.)	page(s)
par., para.	paragraph
Pos.	Position
Pub.L.	Public Law
RGBl.	Reichsgesetzblatt ('Law Gazette of the German Reich')
RGSt	Entscheidungen des Reichsgerichts in Strafsachen ('decisions of the Supreme Court of the German Reich in criminal cases')
RStGB/RStrGB	Strafgesetzbuch für das Deutsche Reich ('Criminal Code of the German Reich')
SCR	Canada Supreme Court Reports
S.Ct.	Supreme Court Reporter (USA)
SchKG	Gesetz zur Vermeidung von Schwangerschaftskonflikten (Schwangerschaftskonfliktgesetz) (German law for the prevention of conflicted pregnancies')
SchwAG	Schwangerschaftsabbruchsgesetz (German law governing the termination of pregnancy)
sect.	section
sent.	sentence
SFHÄndG	Schwangeren- und Familienhilfeänderungsgesetz (German law amending aid to pregnant women and families)

SFHG	Schwangeren- und Familienhilfegesetz (German law providing aid to pregnant women and families)
SGB	Sozialgesetzbuch ('Code of Social Law')
sic	Spelled or used as written
stat.	Statute
StGB	Strafgesetzbuch ('Criminal Code')
StPO	Strafprozessordnung ('Code of Criminal Procedure')
U.S.	United States
USA	United States of America
U.S.C.	United States Code
v.	versus
Vol.	Volume
ZRP	Zeitschrift für Rechtspolitik (German journal for jurists)
ZStW	Zeitschrift für die gesamte Strafrechtswissenschaft (German journal for jurists)

Part I

FRAMEWORK

I.1   Introduction   3

I.2   System and Standard of Social Services   4

I.3   The Position of Women in Society   5

I.4   Assessment and Significance of Family Planning and Termination
      of Pregnancy   7

I.5   Remarks on Historical Developments   18

I.1   INTRODUCTION

The countries included in this survey differ, in part considerably, with respect to the size and composition of their populations, social systems, cultural and religious traditions, general economic conditions, systems and standards of medical care and social services, the societal roles of women, the legal systems, and other key values. Several show considerable heterogeneity within their own borders, such as, for instance, the USA with its extremely disparate ethnic demographics and the multi-ethnic (former) Soviet Union. Both countries show that termination laws need not be uniform nationwide, but rather that each administrative subdivision of a country may pass its own, locally applicable termination laws.[1]

The various country reports endeavor to provide preliminary insights into the general conditions in the country under study in order to orient the reader to the current state of affairs. A systematic comparison of the data conveyed in the reports will be not be undertaken here; it would be more cumbersome than enlightening. Nevertheless, several aspects that appear significant with respect to the termination of pregnancy will be highlighted briefly, namely, the system and standard of social services (I.2), the position of women in society (I.3), as well as, most importantly, various aspects of the societal assessment and practical significance of family planning with special consideration paid to the relative importance of termination (I.4). Finally, some remarks concerning the historical development of the laws concerning the termination of pregnancy follow (I.5).

---

[1] This is valid regardless of whether the matter is understood as (primarily) falling under criminal or health law; see *infra* II.1.

I.2   SYSTEM AND STANDARD OF SOCIAL SERVICES

The foremost issue in the implementation of this study was to determine the general social conditions under which decisions for or against the termination of pregnancy are made. Both the law of termination and its practice exist – so we assume – not only in the context of specific ethically-based values and traditions but also, and probably not less importantly, in relation to the respective 'social climate'. Thus, one goal of the study was to identify sociopolitical factors that can contribute significantly in individual cases to the acceptance or rejection of a pregnancy and that, more generally, also contribute to the societal assessment of the decision for or against a child. Of course, this does not call into question the fact that, in many cases, women with problem pregnancies may well be unresponsive to any and all offers of assistance from third parties; in any event, it was not our intention to postulate strict causal relationships between specific social factors and specific manifestations of termination. Hence, a relationship between the organization of specific social services and the frequency of termination will only seldom be established in the country reports.

It should give one pause when – as for example in the Federal Republic of Germany – in spite of the availability of numerous financial subsidies for the benefit of families, the society is accused of being 'child-unfriendly'; this situation clearly indicates that the relationship of the older to the younger generation is not determined by monetary aspects alone. It also becomes clear that adequate social support is not merely a question of providing financial benefits: obviously, the social system that reflects, as a whole, the concerns of families, above all families with children, be a top priority. In this vein, the importance of sufficient numbers of part-time employment opportunities, a school system that provides after school care, as well as claims for unpaid leave in the interest of the family cannot be underestimated.

However, the following should also be taken into account: the less important children are for the financial well being (in the broader sense) of the family[2] – for instance as a (supplementary) form of retirement planning – the more (potential) parents may become conscious of children as a 'cost factor'. In other words, couples who are considering starting a family may be virtually forced to compare the career and earning opportunities they would have as parents with the opportunities they would have were they to remain childless.

---

[2] On the changing functions of the family, see also *infra* I.4.2.

I.3   THE POSITION OF WOMEN IN SOCIETY

The countries represented in this study differ already with respect to the position of women under constitutional law. Even in western Europe, express equality of men and women cannot be taken for granted, although the lack of a corresponding regulation alone does not necessarily result in a general legal or actual discrimination against women. On the other hand, the Irish constitution, for example, ascribes to women the traditional role of mother and housewife; thus, reports from this country about discrimination against women in the workplace are not surprising. Although an anti-discrimination act has been passed in the meantime, discrimination evidently continues – and on a not inconsiderable scale.

In the final analysis, it can be shown that, on a legal level, the *equality of men and women* has, throughout the course of the 20th century, become *the rule internationally*. Even where equality has not yet been (fully) realized (as for example in Islamic states), a legislative trend to strengthen women's rights is often apparent. Nevertheless, the ability of legislated equality to crack multiple traditional behavioral patterns is limited. Indeed, the effects – occasionally drastic – of some of these patterns continue to be felt. One example may be seen in the killing of newborn girls, a practice in the People's Republic of China that – abetted by rigid policies that favor limiting the numbers of births – appears to be an undeniable part of today's reality.

Above all, the *social situation of women who are mothers* is apparently highly problematic in many countries. Whereas to the extent that the practical implementation of gender equality for single women or married women without children is largely successful in the working world,[3] the assumption of the role of mother frequently remains linked with traditional role-expectations. Thus, even more than marriage, starting a family marks a more or less far-reaching turning point, especially in the social life of a woman, and her willingness to accept this change can no longer be seen as a given. This can certainly play a role, especially in the decision to have a first child or to terminate a pregnancy.

In conclusion, the discussion concerning the assessment of the termination of pregnancy recognizes two positions that, structurally, are diametrically opposed:

---

[3] Noteworthy in this context is the fact that in the USA it is married – not single – women who have conquered the job market.

- The first position focuses on the embryo/fetus. Supporters of this position are concerned solely with the question of the exceptional conditions under which an interference with or a thwarting of the embryo's chances of continuing to live, especially after birth, can be justified.

- The second position concentrates primarily on the role of the pregnant woman. Proponents of this approach give priority to the question of what could warrant interfering in her freedoms of choice and action, requiring her to perform the feat of carrying a pregnancy to term and, through birth, giving a child the 'gift of life' (sic!) – not to mention the child's care and upbringing after birth, responsibilities whose delegation is often only theoretically possible.

Ultimately, the termination controversy can be seen as a dispute between these two perspectives. For the position mentioned first, it stands to reason that the self-determination of the pregnant woman should be restricted from the beginning by means of 'indications' – however they may be designed; thus, the freedom of the pregnant woman to choose is viewed as an exception requiring justification. Under the second perspective,[4] it is the prohibition of termination that requires legitimation rather than the prerequisites for permitting it. An 'emancipated' understanding of social roles favors the second point of view: the more the role of women in society is seen (also) in terms of functions other than that of housewife and mother alone, the harder it is to take for granted that the mere fact of an incipient pregnancy can constitute a legitimate basis for expecting the woman to agree to the aforementioned performance, i.e., carrying the pregnancy to term and giving birth.

---

[4] This is clearly the basis for the US Supreme Court's position, but it is also found in the minority opinion of the second decision of the German Federal Constitutional Court (see *BVerfGE* 88, 203-366 at pp. 338 ff.).

I.4   ASSESSMENT AND SIGNIFICANCE OF FAMILY PLANNING AND TERMINATION OF PREGNANCY

4.1   Preliminary remarks

Presumably contributing to the fundamental framework surrounding termination and its legal regulation are the attitudes of the society under study towards termination, especially as seen in relation to other birth control measures. Of this complex of issues, the sociopolitical and individual dimensions of family planning will be addressed first (I.4.2). After a few remarks on the diversity of state measures in the area of family planning (I.4.3), the significance of terminations in relation to other methods of birth control will be discussed (I.4.4). The approaches taken by the major religions to contraception and termination of pregnancy as an aspect independent of national boundaries (I.4.5) as well as the attitude of the medical community (I.4.6) will be covered in somewhat more detail.

4.2   Sociopolitical and individual dimensions of family planning

As far as the social significance and the proliferation of family planning are concerned, many country reports describe a historic *process of change:* whereas previously the few initiatives dedicated to the idea of 'preventative' birth control[5] were almost always subject to religious reservations and political impediments, they experienced an undreamt-of, virtually uninterrupted upswing after the pill was introduced to a nearly worldwide market at the beginning of the 1960s.

   The social causes for this upturn can only be hinted at here. In addition to factors such as the *'emancipation'* of women,[6] the *'sexual revolution'*,[7] and the

---

   [5] The first relevant activities reported in European countries date, for instance, in the Netherlands to the year 1881, in France to the end of the 19th century and in Great Britain to the year 1921. It is noteworthy that initiatives in Egypt date back to the year 1937.

   [6] See *supra* I.3.

   [7] This catchword encompasses two phenomena: the one (more superficial) being a considerable increase in sexual relationships due to the freedom from worries about and consequences of unwanted pregnancy; the other (deeper) being a changed perception of human sexuality as having a value independent of reproduction. The one does not, of course, exclude the other.

'*changed functions of the family*', connections with *medical advancements* should not be taken too lightly: increased life expectancy, for example, works indirectly as a factor that should not be underestimated in support of the family planning concept. It stands to reason, but is also noteworthy, that the response to a scarcity of resources – how many people can a social system feed? – tends to be to reduce the number of births rather than to engage in a 'selection' of those already born.[8]

The long-term consequences of these processes on the composition and age distribution of society appear frequently not to have been noticed or in any case not to have been recognized in their full significance. In interplay with other far-reaching social changes such as have taken place in many countries in recent decades – in particular: dissolution of the extended family, entry of women into the work force – the *social function of providing for the next generation* has changed; in addition to its traditional, intangible meaning, it has attained – and dictates – an increasingly economic character, a factor whose proper price is apparently not easy to assess and which is made up of a number of mutually complementary contributions.

According to the structure of the society, *individual factors* that promote or discourage a restriction on the number of children one has are of varying importance. Having a large number of children is viewed in many countries as for example in Egypt and Ghana as well as in certain cultural circles with great respect – the mother especially is highly esteemed; contributions from the children may be needed to help feed the family and in some cases they serve as the 'best social security', that is to say, as an important element of the provision for old age. Family planning under such auspices can only mean the optimization of the interval between births in view of the health of the family, especially the mother; however, it cannot have as its primary goal the limitation of the total number of children born to one family. But among other 'more modern' portents, motivational factors that work against contraception can also be influential: insofar as sexual relationships with members of the opposite sex face moral objections, these objections must also apply to those measures whose goal is to avoid the unwanted consequences of such relationships; whoever violates the socially established maxim of chastity makes him or herself even more vulnerable to moral attack if he or she also endeavors to control the consequences of such actions, as in so doing it can be demonstrated that the person is acting on the basis of long-term reflection and not out of situational weakness.[9]

---

[8] These connections are clearly addressed, for instance, in Country Report Turkey (E/K II pp. 835-896 at p. 846).
[9] Instructive in this respect is the dilemma of teenagers in the USA.

Such considerations may occasionally even affect the assessment of the termination of pregnancy: the presumably 'isolated incident of sin', i.e., the undergoing of a necessary termination, could be viewed as the lesser evil in comparison to a (more reliable and) permanently manifested infringement of standards, such as the daily activity of taking the pill.

Finally, several special *'collective' issues* must be mentioned from which fodder for the rejection of the concept of birth control can be drawn: so, for instance, when – as in Australia with regard to the aborigines – a population group faces the danger of extinction or when – as contended with regard to the People's Republic of China in the 1950s – an entire nation faces an undesirable reduction in population; when family planning activities – supported not infrequently by industrial nations, but also heavily promoted by the United Nations – are understood as an expression of a new form of colonialism; or when concern about the influences of multinational pharmaceutical companies is expressed.

4.3   Governmental measures in the area of family planning

The country reports convey an impressive picture of the variety of measures with which the attempt is made in many – above all non-European – countries to influence the family planning decisions of individual citizens or to create the conditions necessary to convert such decisions into action. The relevant activities are not infrequently coordinated by state-sponsored family planning programs and supported by the authority of leading statesmen.

In the sense of a general categorization, these diverse measures differ in two respects, one being whether they tend more to promote or to discourage births prevention of births, the other being whether they are designed to achieve their stated goals directly or indirectly.

4.4   The significance of the termination of pregnancy in relation to other methods of birth control

Even if a few countries had already liberalized their legislation on the termination of pregnancy before the pill was introduced, a milestone in the spread of 'reliable' contraception, the overwhelming majority of such reforms did not actually take place until after its introduction. Thus, the triumphal procession of family planning through contraception proved to be the engine for fundamental reforms in termination law. Nevertheless, the opinion that it is better to use contraception than it is to abort is held almost universally – even among those who actively advocate the decriminalization of termination: termination of pregnancy is widely understood, independent of its type of legal regulation, as an *'ultima ratio'*, or at least it is not considered to be 'primarily a means of birth control'.[10] In family planning programs run or supported by the state, the goal of reducing the number of terminations is expressly pursued.

Empirical data on the attitude of the population towards the termination of pregnancy are available from a number of countries; of course, this information can hardly be used for comparative purposes. The data also indicate that even in places where a majority of the population supports a (more) permissive legal position, the termination of pregnancy is not viewed as just any method of birth control. The characterization of supporters of permissive regulation as 'abortion advocates'[11] is hence at the very least misleading.

Thus, the concern that the use of contraception will decidedly fall off when terminations are (widely) permitted is not confirmed by the findings of our project. Even for a country with very far reaching 'license' for termination such as the USA, the available data do not permit conclusive statements to the effect that this license has negatively influenced the willingness to use effective contraception on an appreciable scale; in Tunisia a clear increase in the use of contraceptive methods along with a concurrent decline in the number of terminations has been ascertained. However, in places where a 'family planning mentality' has gained acceptance, the outlook that (avoidable or unavoidable) lapses in planning can be 'corrected' through terminations also tends to be favored.

4.5 Assessment of the termination of pregnancy from a religious perspective

In the selection of countries for this project, the world's major religions were also taken into account. A cross-sectional analysis establishes that none of them views unborn life completely as a mere *'quantitée négligeable'*. Conversely – apart from the strict Catholic viewpoint – no position grants unborn life absolute preeminence over all the woman's interests, no matter how significant. On the contrary – to put it in legal terminology – the question of ethical-religious acceptance of the termination of pregnancy is ordinarily understood as a *balancing problem*. Because it is seen as a significant issue of protecting life, po-

---

[10] The 'in principle yes' to termination in the Netherlands must be interpreted in light of the empirically proven statement that there is no other country in which the use of dependable contraceptives is so widespread as in the Netherlands.
[11] See, e.g., H. BAUM, *Bannkreise des Tötens. Zur Kritik des utilitaristischen Standpunkts zum Schwangerschaftsabbruch* (Sankt Augustin, Academia 1995) p. 20. In comparison, the characterization 'pro-choice advocate' in the USA seems more appropriate.

litical representatives in countries where new legislation is being considered tend to feel obligated to take a legal policy stance on the matter.

4.5.1   *The Roman Catholic Church*

Around the world, the position of the Roman Catholic Church on the issue central to the termination of pregnancy appears to be quite uniform. This is not surprising, given that Rome retains ultimate authority in questions of church doctrine. The Church's position is characterized by the *principled rejection of the termination of pregnancy*: morally speaking, every intervention directed at ending unborn life is declared, without exception, to be impermissible from conception on; thus, whoever undertakes an abortion thereby excommunicates him or herself.[12] The state is considered to be responsible for protecting[13] unborn as well as born life, even through criminal law.[14] At most, vital medical indications – which today are very rare – might be excepted from the threat of punishment.

Of course, one must note that such strict viewpoints appear to have reached their limits in terms of their *ability to affect conduct*: in various countries – such as, for example, Belgium, France, the former Yugoslavia and the USA – there are reports of resistance against the official church position from the laity and even among clergy; in other countries – namely the Federal Republic of Germany, Austria, Portugal, Spain, Australia and the USA – the results of opinion surveys show that a considerable proportion of church members, on average, favor more liberal regulations. Additionally, it has been pointed out that the attitude of someone who belongs to a religious group towards the termination of pregnancy may depend on the person's 'proximity to the church'. Even in countries with a large Catholic population, such as Italy, Austria and Poland, terminations – legal as well as illegal – are reported to be quite widespread.

It might be due to the rigidity of the 'official' church position that, in the end, attempts by the church to have a decisive political *influence on modern termi-*

---

[12]   See the encyclicals '*Casti Connubii*' and '*Humanae Vitae*' as well as No. 2272 ff. of the new *Katechismus der Katholischen Kirche* (German edition, Munich, Oldenbourg 1993) with citations to the instruction '*Donum Vitae*' of the *Kongregation für die Glaubenslehre*, 22 February 1987. This official standpoint is not shared by all theologians with the same rigorousness. Even in official pronouncements, phrasing can occasionally be found that appears to tolerate certain exceptions to the prohibition of abortion.

[13]   According to the instruction mentioned *supra* n. 12, 'the law must provide for the appropriate punishment for each deliberate injury of its [the unborn's] rights' (translated from *Katechismus der Katholischen Kirche* (op. cit. n. 12), No. 2273.

[14]   Yet, not only through criminal law, but also through the expansion of social assistance, especially for the support of families.

nation legislation have been largely unsuccessful. Furthermore, in countries with a high proportion of Catholics, it appears that the encyclical '*Humanae Vitae*' has (unwittingly) contributed to the recognition of a basic separation of church (moral) and state (law). Thus, 'Catholic' nations such as Austria, France, and Italy have adopted quite permissive termination regulations.

On the other hand, it should not be overlooked that in some countries – Ireland, for instance – there is a virtual *consonance between Catholic dogma and state legislation* on the termination of pregnancy, and the degree of societal acceptance appears to be higher than in other countries with a comparably large Catholic population. In this context, it is important to remember that in Poland the State has become widely 'Catholicized' since the collapse of the communist system in the late 1980s, a development that has manifested itself in a new, clearly more restrictive law on the termination of pregnancy.[15]

4.5.2   Protestant churches

Given the diversity of the Protestant Church and its lack of central leadership, a uniform posture on the question of the termination of pregnancy cannot be expected. Moreover, according to the Protestant view, the personal conscience of the individual believer deserves greater emphasis, and the idea of a separation between the spheres of state and church meets with wider approval. Therefore, it is not surprising that even in countries with an overwhelmingly Protestant population, the institutions of this church do not participate as forcefully in the legal policy discussion on the termination of pregnancy as does the Catholic Church.

On the question of termination, the views within the Lutheran Church itself as well as among the other Protestant churches differ considerably. However, it is uniformly recognized that life from the beginning is fundamentally worthy of protection: the spectrum of the Protestant churches in South Africa as well as in the USA appears to cover the entire range of represented opinions on the termination issue. In other countries, such as Australia, deliberately restrictive positions of the indigenous Protestant churches are reported. In the West German reform discussion of the 1970s as well as in the corresponding Church circles in the Netherlands, various types of indication models as well as a 'time limit' solution were advocated. Especially noteworthy is the fact that in France, a

---

[15] See E. WEIGEND, 'Landesbericht Polen', in A. ESER and B. HUBER (eds.), *Strafrechtsentwicklung in Europa 4.2* (Freiburg, Max-Planck-Institut für ausländisches und internationales Strafrecht 1994) pp. 1087-1160 at pp. 1102 ff.; as well as E. WEIGEND and E. ZIELIŃSKA, 'Das neue polnische Recht des Schwangerschaftsabbruchs: politischer Kompromiß und juristisches Rätselspiel', 106 *ZStW* (1994) pp. 213-226.

traditionally 'Catholic country', the reform legislation on the termination of pregnancy was decisively influenced by the standpoint, developed essentially by French Protestant churches, that termination is the *'ultima ratio'* in conflict situations that must be viewed individually.

4.5.3   *Other Christian churches*

The posture of the *Greek Orthodox* Church appears to be comparable to that of the Roman Catholic Church, both in terms of its positions and in terms of its problems in achieving acceptance.

As far as the *Anglican* Church, at least in Great Britain, is concerned, it has adopted – in light of a permissively applied legal regulation, an increasingly restrictive posture in relation to termination. Currently, this posture deems termination morally justifiable only in cases of vital maternal indications, i.e., when the pregnant women's life is in danger. In contrast to the Catholic Church, there appears to have been no attempt made directly to influence believers in the formation of their opinions.

4.5.4   *Islam*

The view of Islam with regard to the termination of pregnancy is also far less uniform than that of the Catholic Church. Even among those countries where Islam is the state religion, there are serious differences in ethical standpoints. As described in great deal, both in the Country Report Egypt as well as in the over view of the Arab states, the religious sources lend themselves to divergent interpretations.[16]

4.5.5   *Judaism*

From the various standpoints taken by scholars, it is apparent that the attitude of Judaism to the termination of pregnancy is also characterized by a lack of uniformity. Accordingly, the status of the embryo is not incontrovertible, and its independent claim to protection can by no means be taken for granted. Put another way: according to the Country Report Israel, restrictions are not founded on the need to protect the embryo as such, but rather ensue from the consideration of a number of factors, such as the pregnant women's interest in integrity or the interest of the Jewish people in continued survival and propagation. In-

---

[16] See also D. ATIGHETCHI, 'The Position of Islamic Tradition on Contraception', 13 *Medicine and Law* (1994) pp. 717-725.

deed, protection of the embryo may in some cases come about as an indirect result of the treatment of these other factors. Attempts to derive a prohibition against the termination of pregnancy directly from the Torah have not succeeded in persuading the entire Jewish community. Thus, the attitude towards termination within Judaism varies: it encompasses everything from the Orthodox religious parties in Israel, which seek to equate the termination of pregnancy with murder, to the Reformed branches, probably best represented in the USA, which favor general latitude.

4.5.6 *Hinduism*

Unfortunately, the country reports on the south and east Asian countries participating in the project barely address the stance of the traditional religions of the countries on the termination of pregnancy.[17] Only the Country Report India contains a brief passage on the relatively strict posture of traditional Hinduism, according to which the termination of pregnancy was viewed as permitted only for a vital indication.[18] The inconsistency between this stance and the reportedly common practice, in light of the societal disregard for women, of killing or abandoning newborn girls is glaring. So seen, the practice of gender-selective termination following a preliminary amniocentesis,[19] evidently not infrequently encountered even today, does not represent a break from tradition.

4.6 The stance of the medical community regarding the termination of pregnancy

Every regulation of the termination of pregnancy is directed primarily at the pregnant women. To a great extent, however, physicians are also addressed. In the scope of existing prohibitions, this must be understood as a direct appeal to them not to use their professional competence to violate norms. But also in the

---

[17] For Japan, M. MURAMATSU, 'Japan', in P. SACHDEV (ed.), *International Handbook on Abortion* (New York, Greenwood 1988) pp. 293-301 at p. 294, notes 'strong support from certain religious groups' for political calls for stronger legal restrictions on the termination of pregnancy.

[18] On more recent developments in Hinduism, see also S. CHANDRASEKHAR, *Abortion in a Crowded World* (London, George Allen & Unwin 1974) pp. 40 ff.; S. CHANDRASEKHAR, 'The Hindu view on family planning and abortion', 28 *Population Review* (1984) pp. 7-44.

[19] See also 72 *Schweizerische Ärztezeitung* (1991) p. 1339: 'Indien: Ultraschall – Beihilfe zu Mord'; 132 *MMW* (1990) No. 46 p. 10: 'Indische Mädchen werden schon als Feten, selektiert'. A law has been enacted in India, with an effective date of 1 January 1996, that is supposed to prevent the misuse of prenatal gender determination for the purposes of aborting female fetuses.

framework of the respective regulations permitting termination, physicians are placed in a position of special responsibility: there are hardly any countries in which at least the actual performance of a non-punishable termination is not entrusted to physicians; frequently, physicians are integrated into the process in special ways prior to the procedure as well as during and after, by means of regulations regarding the evaluation of the need for the carrying out and the reporting of terminations.[20] The ability to implement restrictive normative programs as well as the practical realization of more or less permissive regulatory models are greatly dependent on the legal 'compliance' of the medical profession. Hence, its attitude definitely belongs to the more important aspects of every legal regulation of the termination of pregnancy.

4.6.1 *Regulations on the termination of pregnancy in professional codes of ethics*

It is a well known fact that the *Hippocratic Oath* itself already took a stand against termination. In numerous countries, professional codes of ethics assimilate this professional prescript, occasionally, to be sure, in a less categorical, more relative manner. Some codes, such as the relevant regulation in Spain, expressly stress the physician's freedom of conscience, especially that of a physician who is not prepared to take part in a termination. Indeed, numerous legal systems grant physicians the right to refuse to participate in the termination of pregnancy.[21]

A physician who violates his or her professional code may face specific *professional sanctions* – in addition to possible criminal liability.[22] Although the country reports are largely silent on measures taken against physicians by professional or disciplinary tribunals on account of professionally unethical behavior in connection with the performance of terminations – indeed, their omission, as for example in Belgium, is explicitly noted despite the obvious commission of violations –, this can be explained to a certain degree by the fact that the professional medical disciplinary system does not exactly seek public attention. However, this phenomenon also indicates that the ethical duties of professionals created by corresponding regulatory acts are primarily seen in terms of their programmatic character, and their implementation in practice as legal norms takes a secondary role.

---

[20] On these aspects see *infra* II.3.4.2-3, II.3.5, II.3.6.2-8 as well as II.5.2-3.

[21] For more details, see *infra* II.3.9.

[22] See *infra* II.5.4.4.

4.6.2 *Other determinants of the legal position of the medical community*

Professional medical organizations and associations in numerous countries participate in the legal policy discussion surrounding the issue of the termination of pregnancy. In contrast to stances following more or less in the Hippocratic tradition for example in Poland (positions not infrequently marked by religious influences), standpoints with a stronger pragmatic orientation – which must also be seen in terms of the discussion taking place in their respective countries – predominate. Probably influenced by their observations of the legal *status quo*, physicians repeatedly have argued in favor of – for the most part moderate – decriminalization, although the medical community by no means speaks with one voice in all places and at all times.

Especially where the various grounds for an exemption from punishment are concerned, medical indications as such appear to be widely accepted in the medical community. At the same time, views regarding the appropriate content of these indications diverge, and broad formulations, expressly preferred by some physicians, are emphatically rejected by others. Even the 'criminological' and embryopathic indication by no means find undivided approval in the medical community. This is clearly demonstrated, for instance, by the (implicit) rejection of the criminological indication by the French *Conseil national de l'Ordre des médecins* in a 1970 opinion or by an opinion of the Australian *Royal College of Obstetricians* that also dates from the 1970s. Even the embryopathic indication occasionally faces critique from medical circles.

The 'soft' indications and especially the 'go-ahead' for terminations based simply on the woman's request are highly controversial. The positions rejecting termination evidently stem in some cases from a general hesitation to recognize such a far-reaching right of self-determination. In countries such as the Netherlands and Canada in which the general law – not infrequently promoted by the relevant medical organizations – has developed into a for the most part permissive regulation, the resistance from physicians appears, to be sure, to be more the concern of a committed minority.

Calls have repeatedly been made for furnishing the profession with the most extensive freedom possible in order to remain exempt from the risk of criminal prosecution.

4.6.3 *Assessment*

The question as to the circumstances under which a termination appears to be ethically and/or legally acceptable is also hotly debated in the medical community. In light of this, it is not surprising that the efforts of the *World Medical Association* to develop a consensual statement regarding the rights of the un-

born, above and beyond the Oslo Declaration of 1970 on therapeutic termination,[23] was unsuccessful and that in the meantime these efforts have apparently
been abandoned.[24]

If, in the regulation of the termination of pregnancy in many countries, the
legislature gives the *medical community a key role*[25] – regardless of differences
in detail – in dealing with the potential conflicts of interest between unborn life
and the pregnant woman, and thereby delegates to it special responsibility, the
trust thereby placed in the professional might be justified on the whole by the
basic outlook of the medical community. However, various examples can be
used to show that a minority of especially permissive physicians is in a position
to make a lasting influence on the legal *status quo* as well as on the development of legal policy;[26] similarly, physicians who are opposed to the termination
of pregnancy or contraception feel justified in subjecting their patients to re-
prisals (as reported in Ireland) and, at least at a regional level (for example in
Mexico), actively prevent the implementation of regulations that are, in their
opinion, too permissive.

---

[23] Reproduced, e.g., in F.J. ILLHARDT, *Medizinische Ethik* (Berlin, Springer 1985) pp.
184 f.

[24] See E.D., '50 Jahre Weltärztebund', 94 *Deutsches Ärzteblatt* (1997) pp. C-1386-1387
at p. 1387; E.D., 'Ansätze zur Reform', 95 *Deutsches Ärzteblatt* (1998) p. C-1206.

[25] See *infra* II.5 for a thorough discussion.

[26] The Country Reports Belgium and Canada demonstrate this emphatically (E/K I pp.
432 ff., E/K II p. 618, respectively).

I.5   REMARKS ON HISTORICAL DEVELOPMENTS

For large parts of Europe, and for some non-European nations such as Turkey, Tunisia and to some degree Israel, the history of the legal regulation of the termination of pregnancy – in any case in the 20th century – may be an occasionally laborious[27] chronology of a *trend towards decriminalization*. In the majority of the surveyed countries, however, the withdrawal of the threat of criminal punishment and the establishment of the termination procedure as a 'service' covered by insurance within the framework of the health system cannot be equated with indifference on the part of the legislature towards unborn life. Even if a woman's right to self-determination is given priority in the ranking of the conflicting interests affected by a termination, and even if restrictions are still occasionally aimed only at abortions performed by lay people – because of the dangers they present to women's health, in the vast majority of countries surveyed in the course of this project, the termination of pregnancy continues to be portrayed, to this day, as an undesirable birth control measure.

In an attempt to identify the relevant *impetus leading to the liberalization of society* or *the factors influencing the development of legal policy*, the following points merit special emphasis, whereby no claim of comprehensive coverage is made: the phenomenon of terminations carried out abroad (I.5.1); the significance of case law and criminal prosecution practice (I.5.2); and the relative importance of arguments based on demographic policy (I.5.3).

5.1   'Abortion tourism'

It is clear from the legal developments in Germany that the so-called *abortion tourism* phenomenon (not a particularly sensitive term) created a not inconsiderable pressure to liberalize. It may come as a surprise to the German reader in particular when something similar is reported even from countries that are often regarded today as protagonists of permissive abortion legislation: noteworthy here is the Swedish 'Trip-to-Poland Affair' of 1965.[28] In another example, the procurement of abortions abroad appears to have attained a certain degree of significance in the Netherlands around 1970, before this country itself became for a time the leading European 'address' for women whose home countries continued to maintain restrictive legislation.

---

[27] It appears that it was especially difficult to codify modern regulations in Belgium, as indicated by the multitude of draft legislation submitted there.

[28] For more details, see E/K I pp. 1408 f.

Nevertheless, such phenomena cannot be understood in isolation; rather, their societal background must be examined. Evidently the changed role of women in society as well as changes in attitude concerning the role of sexuality and birth control have not failed to influence the attitude of the public towards the termination of pregnancy.[29] These developments may in fact have taken place practically simultaneously in many European countries; however, the adaptation of the various national laws to reflect these changes is a long way from completion. The willingness to travel abroad in order to terminate a pregnancy speaks for the gravity of the aforementioned societal changes. The countries whose reforms were implemented earlier have thus – unintentionally – influenced the legal policy of the 'slower' states.

5.2 On the significance of case law and criminal prosecution practice

There are many examples of the judiciary being called upon to determine the scope of permissibility where and as long as the legislature remained inactive.[30] It should not be forgotten, however, that attempts to demonstrate in more or less spectacular legal proceedings that the termination of pregnancy deserves to be punished have repeatedly led to reforms in exactly the opposite direction. In this context the legal policy developments in Belgium, Spain and the Federal Republic of Germany come to mind.[31]

In addition to such engines of reform as women's demands regarding self-determination (which received a boost from the spread of dependable contraceptives) and the issue of 'quacks',[32] problems associated with criminal

---

[29] On South Africa the different interpretation of the relationship between state and citizen is noted, which could call into doubt the authority of the state to protect the interests of the fetus.

[30] On these aspects see E/K III pp. 68 ff. From a German point of view it is particularly important to consider the decision of the *Reichsgericht* of 11 March 1927, *RGSt* 61, 243 ff. For a discussion of the significance of the case law of the *Bundesverfassungsgericht*, see. *infra* II.2.3.

[31] See H.-G. KOCH, 'Über Schwierigkeiten von Ärzten und Gerichten im Umgang mit § 218 StGB', in A. ESER and H.-G. KOCH, *Schwangerschaftsabbruch: Auf dem Weg zu einer Neuregelung* (Baden-Baden, Nomos 1992) pp. 69 ff., on the proceedings against the gynecologist from Memmingen, Dr. *Theissen* (see also the decision BGH 3 December 1991, *BGHSt* 38, 144 ff. = *NJW* 1992 pp. 763 ff.).

[32] Their significance is specifically noted in the case of such disparate countries as Italy, Poland, India, Japan and Tunisia. On the other hand, the practice of abortion by so-called 'irregular' doctors in the USA during the first half of the 19th century prompted their 'regular' colleagues into making demands, which were eventually successful, for the complete criminalization of the termination of pregnancy. To be sure, these actions were not only, and perhaps not even primarily, based on the motive of protecting life.

prosecution have also had a significant *liberalizing* effect in countries such as Belgium, France, Greece, Italy, the Netherlands and Sweden.[33] In Germany as elsewhere, women have resorted to organized self-incrimination in order to stress their reform concerns, thereby seeking to discredit criminal prosecution as it is practiced. Presumably influenced by these issues, the reform discussions in some countries (France, the Netherlands, Israel) have been accompanied by amnesties and moratoriums on criminal prosecution.

However, there are also reports of *opposition movements*, even where the existing laws are restrictive. Noteworthy in this context are the Turkish Penal Code of 1926 (in the version of 1936), which, along with an altered classification of offenses, also introduced more severe punishments, as well as the more recent constitutional reinforcement through a plebiscite of the existing, very far-reaching prohibition of the termination of pregnancy in Ireland.

In cases where the lawmakers charged with reform were seemingly uncertain of how best to proceed, as in France, they dealt with the situation by passing provisional legislation – possibly a probative method by which to allow the development over time of consensus on an issue as socially and politically controversial as this one.

5.3   On the relative importance of demographic policy

Considerations of demographic policy arise again and again in the course of reform discussions on the termination of pregnancy and may even be the basis of legal regulations.[34] Usually – namely in times of war or crisis – these policy arguments are pro-birth and supportive of population growth and thus are focused on establishing restrictive regulations.[35] The example of the People's Republic of China, in particular, illustrates how this subject matter was and still is instrumentalized – in a drastic manner – to further a policy of limiting population growth.[36] In a second example, a decrease in the disparity between the

---

[33] To what extent illegal terminations were performed by the pregnant woman herself, by lay persons or by physicians who were not very faithful to professional norms remains a subject for speculation; it is reasonable to assume that in a number of countries physicians themselves performed a considerable number of illegal terminations.

[34] One example is the German decree on the protection of marriage, family and motherhood of 1943. On the issue as a whole, see also *infra* II.2.2.

[35] Already in the first half of the 19th century, demographically and religiously motivated demands for the criminalization of the termination of pregnancy were made in the USA.

[36] See also TH. SCHARPING, 'Chinas Ein-Kind-Kampagne – politische, wirtschaftliche und gesellschaftliche Aspekte der Bevölkerungsentwicklung 1978-1994', in TH. SCHARPING

number of births and the number of deaths has been cited as lawmakers' secondary motivation for the Tunisian reform of 1965, with its 'abundance of children'-indication. However, the goal of not endangering the nation's economic advances by an excessive birth rate might have been better served through, for instance, the introduction at that time of regulations on the promotion and sale of contraceptive devices.

Formerly, demographic policy in Japan supported the establishment of restrictive termination regulations (1908); 40 years later – under changed conditions – demographic policy served as the basis for a quite permissive regulatory program.

Objectives of racial purity must also be mentioned in this context – a painful responsibility particularly for German authors.

---

and R. Heuser (eds.), *Geburtenplanung in China, Analysen, Daten, Dokumente* (Hamburg, Institut für Asienkunde 1995) pp. 27-230 at pp. 108 ff. as well as K.-F. Lenz, 'Deutsche Forschungen zum ostasiatischen Recht', in A. Eser and H. Nishihara (eds.), *Rechtfertigung und Entschuldigung IV* (Freiburg, Max-Planck-Institut für ausländisches und internationales Strafrecht 1995) pp. 45-63 at pp. 61 f.

Part II

CURRENT LAWS REGULATING THE TERMINATION OF PREGNANCY

Introduction   25

II.1 Legal Sources and Regulatory Methodology Behind the Law on
      the Termination of Pregnancy   26

II.2 Basic Concepts in Legal Regulation   29

II.3 Permissible Termination of Pregnancy   69

II.4 Impermissible Termination of Pregnancy   131

II.5 Special Role of the Physician   153

II.6 Preventive Measures   164

II.7 Role of Termination of Pregnancy in the Prosecutorial Arena   171

INTRODUCTION

The goal of this cross-sectional view of the intricate maze of widely divergent regulations of pregnancy termination around the world is to allow for the emergence of a profile of development and differentiation – be it spatial or temporal – from which similarities as well as differences and, last but not least, specific trends in the regulation of termination can be ascertained. This should make it possible for an individual country to determine where it stands within a larger spectrum of regulations and possibly to draw legal policy conclusions. Also, the cross-sectional view gives clear access to the whole range of existing solutions to any given question.

As dictated by the outline of the country reports,[1] this cross-section will examine – also in seven subsections – the extensive and varied material regulated by the termination laws of the countries included in the two previously published volumes of country reports is presented in six levels:

– First, through a more formal analysis of the various *sources of law and regulatory methodology* involving the termination of pregnancy (II.1),
– then, in a more structural-functional approach, through comparison of the *basic concepts in legal regulation* (II.2).
– Next, the prerequisites for and limits on *permissible terminations of pregnancy* are compared with each other more concretely (II.3),
– and then contrasted with the scope of application and the instances of *illegal terminations* (II.4).
– In light of the not insignificant role of *physicians* in approving as well as in sanctioning terminations, a summary of these aspects, previously handled in a piecemeal fashion, seems appropriate (II.5).
– These sections, primarily focused as they are on issues of legitimization and punishment, are supplemented by a comparison of *preventative measures* (II.6),
– and rounded off with a view towards the status of the termination of pregnancy in the prosecutorial arena (II.7).

---

[1] See E/K I pp. 13 f.

II.1 LEGAL SOURCES AND REGULATORY METHODOLOGY BEHIND THE LAW ON THE TERMINATION OF PREGNANCY

Even from an extremely formal perspective, the difference between the protections accorded unborn and those accorded born life is dramatic: While the killing of born life is handled virtually everywhere in the world in the criminal code or, where there is no criminal code (such as, for instance, in some common law countries), at any rate as part of basic criminal law, provisions concerning the protection or permissible killing of unborn life are found not only in the criminal law but also in other areas of the law, and, moreover, they exhibit widely differing regulatory techniques. These differences are most significant with regard to the sources of law (1.1) and in the classification of termination-related offenses into various categories of crime (1.2).

1.1 Regulatory scope: between criminal and social welfare law

With regard to the area of law in which the termination of pregnancy is exclusively or at least primarily regulated and the regulatory techniques utilized in this process, essentially five types of regulations can be identified:

- '*pure criminal law model*' (regulation of terminations exclusively in the criminal code or at least in the 'basic criminal law' of the country under study) – good examples can be found in the Arabic-Islamic legal system: (Bahrain, Egypt, Ghana, Tunisia), Brazil and, additional Latin American countries, Belgium, Ireland and Israel.
- '*supported criminal law model*' (prohibition and permission dealt with exclusively in the criminal code, but with supporting rules of a preventative-controlling or social-assistance nature in additional regulations) – examples include: Germany, Austria, Luxembourg, Portugal, Greece, England/Northern Ireland/ Wales, Poland (1993/1996); Lebanon, Syria, Jordan; Canada, USA, parts of Australia.
- '*supplemented criminal law model*' (basic norm of punishability located in the criminal code and supplemented by special termination regulations or by provisions located in other non-criminal legislation) – examples (with different emphases): France, the Netherlands, Norway, Switzerland, Turkey, (former) socialist countries, Peru, India, Taiwan, Japan, various Arab and Black African countries.

- *'extra-criminal law model'* (definitive regulation of termination in independent special legislation classified as health or social welfare law) – examples include: Denmark, Sweden, Italy, USA/Minnesota.
- Countries that *in the absence of special legal regulation* draw upon unwritten legal principles (e.g., Scotland) or religious law (e.g., Saudi Arabia).

An overview shows that the criminal code does indeed remain the main source of termination regulations but that this is no longer a foregone conclusion nor does the code carry the same exclusivity as was traditionally the case. Even if, on the one hand, the criminal code forms the starting point for the law on termination or, on the other hand, non-criminal regulations, in the final analysis, lead to criminal sanctions, there are nevertheless a growing number of legal systems that have shifted the regulation of termination to a greater or lesser extent from criminal law to health law or other social welfare laws. Indeed, the more the need for rules governing the granting of permission to terminate is acknowledged, the more this happens.

1.2 Classification into categories of crime: from homicide to moral turpitude

As far as the specific criminal classification of the termination of pregnancy within or in relation to other categories of offenses is concerned, the resulting picture – similar to that familiar from previous eras – remains highly variable, ranging from the systematic categorization of termination as equivalent to the killing of born life, to its classification as a violation of family order and public morals, and not infrequently ending up in its own independent section of the criminal code. Roughly speaking, six basic concepts are distinguishable, whereby, to be sure, uniformity is virtually never found, not even within a single cultural group:

- *Crimes (only) against life* (Germany, Greece, New York, several Latin American, African, and Arab countries);
- *Crimes against life and limb* (Switzerland, a conspicuously large number of Latin American and formerly socialist countries);
- *Bodily harm* (France [former law], Israel, and also, to a certain extent, Sudan and India);
- *Crimes against the person* (France [current law], Egypt, Ghana, Canada and the former USSR);
- *Crimes against the public interest* like youth and family (former German Democratic Republic, Bahrain, Algeria, Morocco), or family order and

public morals (Luxembourg, Belgium, Chile, Jordan, Lebanon, Syria);
• *Special offense category solely for the termination of pregnancy* (the Netherlands, Austria, Portugal, Spain, Turkey, Japan, Taiwan).

Clearly, those countries that have completely separated the termination of pregnancy from the criminal code itself and reclassified it under *health or social welfare law*, such as Denmark, Sweden and Italy, cannot be taken into account here. Insofar as their laws still contain threats of criminal punishment in order to safeguard certain duties, these threats have the character, usually perceived as less stigmatizing, of mere *supplementary criminal law.*

II.2   BASIC CONCEPTS IN LEGAL REGULATION

Preliminary remarks

While the preceding discussion dealt more with the formal, technical-legal features of the law on the termination of pregnancy and hence left the substance of its regulations unexamined, we now begin our inquiry into the actual content of the various regulations. The inquiry focuses on six aspects: the determination of more or less clearly articulated *legislative intent* (2.1); the identification of fundamental *protected values* (2.2); the ascertainment of *constitutional guidelines*, including any possible concretizations in constitutional jurisprudence (2.3); the characterization of the most significant *basic regulatory models* (2.4); as well as the *conceptual delimitation* of the termination of pregnancy (2.5). However, this comparison of various regulatory material focuses on basic representative comparisons of commonalities and differences in the laws of the individual countries: more detailed descriptions of the prohibition or permissibility of terminations will be considered in the following chapters.

2.1   Legislative intent: from semi-official proclamations to diffuse speculations

If an explanation is sought for why abortion regulations around the world are so diverse, one can easily be found in the great variety of expressions of legislative intent as well as in the diversity of interests identified as worthy of protection. As a result of the way in which legislative intent and protective interests have been articulated recently (in some cases self-contradictory), they may well come into conflict with one another. However, when viewed from this perspective the amount of information on this subject that can be derived from the country reports is not especially large; indeed, considering the to some extent spotty coverage of this area in the reports, it may be merely coincidental. This is not simply because only a few of the country reports explicitly discussed this point but also because in examining possible regulatory motives – i.e., in cases where the legislature has not provided a clear explanation for its actions – one moves to a great extent in the realm of speculation. Such speculations do not, however, necessarily forfeit all claim to reality, since, as a rule, the 'abstract' legislature is motivated and spurred to action by concrete individuals and/or political movements. Seen in this light, the following legislative aims are more or less clearly articulated in the country reports:

- Protection of unborn life;
- Avoidance of terminations;
- Woman's right to health and/or self-determination;
- Interests of the father/partner;
- Adaptation to societal changes;
- Demographic goals;
- Elimination of discrimination in the prosecutorial arena;
- Involvement of the woman's social milieu;
- Procedural simplification.

Although we are in no position to provide detailed commentary on this incomplete list of leading goals and interests, it can come as no surprise that the legal regulation of the termination of pregnancy varies depending upon which aspects are ascribed greater – and which lesser – importance.

2.2   Legal values: from the protection of individual life to general demographic policy and sexual ethics

The *legal values* protected by the regulation of the termination of pregnancy are not necessarily identical to the regulatory goals mentioned above, even if they are largely parallel. For if lawmakers, for instance, are persuaded to support reform legislation on termination in order to adapt to societal changes, no claims can be made on that basis about which interests requiring legal protection the regulation is (ultimately) intended to benefit: Hence, contrary to first impressions, a liberalization of termination laws need not necessarily intend greater respect for a woman's freedom of choice nor signify a weakening in the protection of life; rather, it might simply serve demographic interests in restrictive birth control, and the pregnant woman's individual freedom of choice could very well be of no interest whatsoever to lawmakers. Similarly, a conscious, limited relaxation of the criminal law may in fact be a strategic maneuver designed to provide more consistent protection to unborn life from the newly drawn frontline.

As these examples indicate, the central purpose of a termination regulation (and thus many of its secondary effects as well) cannot be understood until the interest(s) to be protected have been clarified. Depending on whether a regulation is meant to serve only a single legal value or several – possibly contradictory – values, the *consequences* for the form and interpretation of a particular regulation may be *quite different*. Hence, the question as to the role of the father, for instance, takes on completely different proportions, depending on whether or not his interest in the continuation or the termination of the pregnancy is also recognized as a legal value.[2]

As the legal values actually considered in regulations of the termination of pregnancy must be accorded significant importance, it is all the more surprising that a serious *discussion concerning these legal values* is found in only a fraction of the countries surveyed. With the noteworthy exceptions of Israel and Japan, in-depth discussions of the issues surrounding legal values are reported practically nowhere but in Europe (such as, in addition to the Federal Republic of Germany, Yugoslavia, Poland, Romania, the former Soviet Union).

Of course, the *identification* of the legal values inspiring such a regulation is not so simple. The central value behind a regulation is only rarely expressed as directly as it is in the French law, which contains a statement guaranteeing the sanctity of human life from its beginning, (a similar statement is part of) the new Polish regulation of 1993/96).[3] Furthermore, a glance at the systematic classification to a specific category of crime (*supra* II.1.2) is not always helpful; indeed, it may even be misleading. In Germany, for instance, termination of pregnancy is considered a 'crime against life.' Thus, it would certainly run directly counter to the statutory assessment to deny unborn life any attribute whatsoever of a legal value worthy of protection; fundamental affirmation of such attributes, however, still leaves open – among other things – the issue of whether unborn life is to be considered a value equal in every respect to born life and/or whether additional legal values – such as health and the pregnant woman's right to self-determination – should also be protected, which could be problematic if interests must be balanced.[4] Conversely, other countries – such as Belgium – classify the termination of pregnancy as an 'offense against family order and public morals';[5] nevertheless, it would indeed be a mistake, according to the Belgium interpretation, to view the 'interruption de grossesse' as an offense that is primarily or even exclusively against such a vague general interest as 'public morals'.[6] Therefore, one may neither restrict oneself to explicit procla-

---

[2] Apparently in order to prevent fathers from ever hindering a legal termination, the *High Court of Australia* found it necessary to deny fetuses, before birth (when existence independent of the mother begins), any rights of their own upon which fathers could rely.

[3] The relevant French provision is Art. 1 of the Law of 1975; the relevant Polish provisions are the Preamble and Art. 1 of the law on family planning of 1993/96. It is explicitly mentioned in the new German regulation of 1992/95 as well, at least as a goal of counseling (§ 219 StGB in the version of the SFHG and SFHÄndG).

[4] On this point, see also *infra* II.2.3 and IV.2.2.1-3.

[5] Indeed, this is true not only for the old version of the Belgian Penal Code [*CP*] of 1867 but also for the current version of the law of 1990 regulating the termination of pregnancy since the location of Arts. 349 ff. within the CP remains unchanged.

[6] In fact, Belgian legislative material indicates that an 'avortement' is also seen as an

mations nor rely solely on legal classifications of crime in the determination of legal values; rather, one must work with all available methods of interpretation in order to identify the values that regulations of the termination of pregnancy were meant to protect.

In light of the difficulties associated with the identification of legal values, which appear not to be fully recognized in some countries, the following *overview* can be nothing more than an attempt to structure information taken from the country reports according to specific criteria of protection, whereby one must of course remain aware of the possible distortions that may result simply from the various degrees of intensity of the discussions concerning legal values and from the more or less superficial nature of the corresponding findings.

First of all, with this reservation in mind, the (rather rare) regulations with a *single legal value*, such as *unborn life* (e.g., former South African law) or public morals (English-speaking countries of Black Africa) differ from those – more frequently encountered – with a *plurality of legal values*. Among the latter, the primacy of unborn life is recognized at least theoretically (although not necessarily in concrete individual cases) virtually everywhere (e.g. – with considerable differences in detail – the Federal Republic of Germany, Ireland, Spain, Czech Republic, Zambia). The health concerns of the pregnant woman including danger to her life and/or health (as in a number of Arab countries, England, Greece) or her freedom of choice (as in the Federal Republic of Germany, France, Italy, Spain, Poland [current law]) are designated as so-called 'secondary legal values', although the ranking among these legal values varies. Furthermore, additional interests, such as demographics, may also be protected, as in Spain and Turkey.

Although the fundamental primacy of unborn life can be assumed in the aforementioned countries, this can hardly be said of countries that accord the *health* of the pregnant woman such great significance that her health appears to be the primary legal value. In this respect, regulations of the termination of pregnancy in former eastern European socialist countries stand out rather conspicuously[7] because despite the fact that these countries stressed with emancipatory fervor a woman's right to terminate and consequently her freedom of decision, the exercise of this right was supposed to serve, above all, the protection of her health. Indeed, there appears to be a strong emphasis on the health interests of pregnant women outside the socialist legal system as well, such as in Australia, Israel, and probably also in Canada.

'offense against the person', whereby, in the meantime, the legal literature also views the physical integrity of the woman as a protected legal value.

[7] Although equally emphasizing demographic policy, the People's Republic of China must also be mentioned here.

Even further removed from the traditional understanding of the protection of life are those termination regulations that give precedence – at least for a certain period of time – to the *pregnant woman's freedom of choice* (e.g., Sweden, USA, South Africa [current law]). The regulations of the former East Germany as well as those of all countries that grant not only an exemption from criminal liability but also a right to terminate that requires no further justification may also be included here, although with reservations, because in the final analysis the health of the pregnant woman is decisive in these countries.[8] Even if, in principle, the pregnant woman's freedom of choice has not been accorded a priority higher than that of unborn life, at any event her freedom of choice has in the meantime found broad recognition as an additional legal value, and this, to be sure, not only under socialist-emancipatory conditions such as in Yugoslavia, Poland and the Soviet Union or under feminist influences as in Italy,[9] but also, oddly enough, in Latin American[10] and Arab countries,[11] where one would not traditionally expect a special respect for a woman's right to self-determination under normal circumstances.[12]

In comparison to the growing respect for a woman's right to self-determination, *consideration of the possible interests of the father and/or husband* is more uncommon. Only a few countries provide even a modicum of protection for the interests of the husband and/or father; this is the case, for example, in Mexico, where the husband has a – judicially substantiated – right to offspring, as well as formerly in Tunisia, where until the reform of 1965 the head of the family was to be assured a 'minimum number' of offspring. Moreover, one might assume the existence of a protective reflex in favor of the husband where termination is made contingent upon his consent, as, for example, in Japan, Taiwan and Turkey, as well as in Morocco if a termination is not indicated on the basis of vital medical reasons.[13] When one considers that, from a historical perspective, the right of the husband to offspring was once a primary – if not exclusive – legal value (e.g., under Roman law, for a time),[14] then this is in any case a

---

[8] On the countries with a 'right' to termination, see *infra* II.3.8.1.

[9] See additionally – where, although the reasons are different, the results are similar – the Federal Republic of Germany, France, the Netherlands and Spain.

[10] As in Costa Rica and Mexico within the meaning of a 'right to motherhood'.

[11] Primarily in Tunisia, but to a certain extent in Turkey, Libya and Sudan as well.

[12] See also Australia, Taiwan, Ghana, Israel and Canada.

[13] See additionally the overview of the requirement of the consent of husband/father, *infra* II.3.3.4.

[14] See A. ESER, 'Zwischen 'Heiligkeit' und 'Qualität' des Lebens. Zu Wandlungen im strafrechtlichen Lebensschutz', in J. GERNHUBER (ed.), *Tradition und Fortschritt im Recht. Festschrift zum 500jährigen Bestehen der Tübinger Juristenfakultät* (Tübingen, Mohr 1977) pp. 377-414 at pp. 383 f. with references.

noteworthy pendulum swing to the other extreme. However, in response – as, for instance, in the Federal Republic of Germany – the first counter demands for more inclusion of fathers, at least in conflict counseling, have already been observed.[15] We will return to this point later.

In traditional criminal abortion law, *demographic interests* have played a not inconsiderable role. Currently, however, the prohibition or permission of abortion as an instrument of demographic policy in Europe no longer plays anywhere near a comparable role; indeed, today these objectives of the past are expressly rejected[16] – if, that is, they are even considered worth mentioning at all.[17] In spite of this trend towards a decrease in importance, demographic policy has by no means totally disappeared from criminal abortion law, but rather plays – more or less openly – a virulent role in the law of a considerable number of countries. In extreme cases, one can even speak of a *pre-eminence of demographic policy* in relation to all other protected interests;[18] this may take the form of a *pro-birth* policy, as in the Romanian abortion law of 1966, or, in contrast, a policy intended to *lower the birth rate*, as in the People's Republic of China. Finally, the Taiwanese regulation can only be seen as a regulation specifically designed with eugenics in mind.

2.3   Constitutional foundations: from apparent absence to binding guidelines for the legislature

If one approaches the question of the constitutional foundations and boundaries of the termination of pregnancy from a German perspective, one might expect it

---

[15] See *infra* II.3.3.4.B-D. The failure to consider the interests of fathers has already been criticized in Austria. With regard to demands for reform, see also Italy, where the exclusion of the father from the pre-termination process if the mother does not want him to participate is considered a violation of the spouse's constitutionally guaranteed right to equal treatment. On these issue, see also the *Paton* case, which has made it all the way to the *European Court of Human Rights* (*infra* II.2.3 n. 20, 25) as well as the English case *C. v. S.* [1987] 1 *All ER* 1230, in which the question of the influence of the father on the decision whether to terminate in the case of an illegitimate child was addressed.

[16] This is the case in the Federal Republic of Germany, where although they are not accepted as a legal value, demographic policy arguments continue to be raised in the reform discussion, in the GDR (until 1972), Portugal (where demographic policy interests were recognized as late as 1955 as a protected legal value by the case law, Sweden and Hungary and, outside Europe, in Costa Rica.

[17] Demographics are not mentioned in Italy, Yugoslavia, the Netherlands, Austria or Switzerland, nor are they mentioned in South Africa, a number of Arab countries or Canada.

[18] Until its reform in 1983, the Turkish abortion law, under the heading 'offenses against the integrity and health of the race', could be included here. Also, a minority opinion sees even the current Spanish abortion law as protecting only the demographic interests of the state.

to be discussed almost as intensely in other countries as in Germany, where some remarks from politicians and organizations, and even from criminal and constitutional scholars, create the impression that the Basic Law has already so clearly and conclusively marked out the regulation of the termination of pregnancy that from the very outset there has been almost no leeway for legislative discretion in creating legal policy in this area.[19] A search abroad, however, for a comparable reduction of legal policy to mere constitutional interpretation would largely be in vain. In any event, proceedings before constitutional courts are apparently becoming more common, with the trend exhibited in the following countries in chronological order: Italy (1971/75), Austria (1974), Ireland (1974/92), France (1975/90), Federal Republic of Germany (1975/93), Great Britain (1980), Portugal (1984/85) and Spain (1985) and, after the fall of communism, in Hungary (1991) and Poland (1997) as well. Clearly, the focus of constitutional conflict over the termination of pregnancy is located in Europe, a point that is also underscored by the multiple appeals to European human rights authorities.[20] In addition, North America is of course prominently represented, with critical cases in both the United States (1973/89/92) and Canada (1975/88). From other continents, the only other countries with relevant constitutional decisions appear to be Israel (1980)[21] and Colombia (1994).

---

[19] On this point, see also *infra* IV.1.3.3, text accompanying n. 62 ff. as well as IV.2.1.

[20] Grounds for these appeals are provided by Art. 2 para. 1 of the European Convention on Human Rights (ECHR) 1950, according to which 'Everyone's right to life shall be protected by law'. The extent to which the termination of pregnancy is consistent with 'everyone's right to life' has already been the subject of a number of proceedings; as yet, however, for a number of reasons, these cases have not progressed beyond evaluation at the level of the *European Commission on Human Rights* (the Commission). Consequently, no judgments have been issued by the *European Court of Human Rights*. Following is a list of relevant cases: *Brüggemann & Scheuten*, B 6956/75 (5 *EuGRZ* (1978) p. 199), (complaint lodged by women against the restrictions placed on abortion by German law; question of extent to which the life of the unborn may be seen as life within the meaning of Art. 2 ECHR expressly left open by the Commission); *Paton* v. *United Kingdom* (1980) 3 *EHRR* 408 (a British father sought to prevent his wife from terminating her pregnancy, see *supra* n. 15); *Hercz* v. *Norway*, E 17004/90 (the permissibility of a termination in the 14th week of pregnancy does not violate Art. 2 ECHR, at least under the conditions provided by Norwegian law). On this subject as a whole – in addition to the study conducted by C.J. FORDER (cited *infra* n. 23) – see also D. HARRIS, 'The Right to Life under the European Convention on Human Rights', 1 *Maastricht Journal of European and Comparative Law* (1994) pp. 122-138 at pp. 126 ff. For a perspective that goes beyond – but still addresses – the abortion issue, see also M.K. ERIKSSON, 'The Legal Position of the Unborn Child in International Law', 36 *German Yearbook of International Law* (1993) pp. 86-130 at pp. 91 ff.

[21] *Cr.A.* 413/80, *Ploni* v. *Plonit*, Judgment 35(3) p. 69.

2.3.1 *Survey*

In the interest of brevity, the aforementioned jurisprudence can be summarized as follows:

- In its decision No. 49 of 16 March 1971, the *Italian* Constitutional Court declared Article 553 C.p., which criminalized public demand for birth control measures, unconstitutional; also, decision No. 27 of 18 February 1975 declared Article 546 C.p., which regulated abortion with the consent of the pregnant woman, unconstitutional to the extent that it did not permit termination in cases in which the health of the woman was seriously threatened and the threat could not be averted in any other way.
- In its ruling of 11 November 1974, the *Austrian* Constitutional Court rejected the action of the Salzburger state government to have the new time limit regulation of § 97 para. 1 No. 1 StGB declared unconstitutional.
- In two separate decisions, the *Irish* Supreme Court[22] determined incidentally that the right to life protected by Article 40.3.3 of the Irish Constitution of 1937 also included the right of the unborn life not to be destroyed. In the meantime, this guarantee of the protection of life has been qualified by the new para. 2 of Article 40.3.3 to the extent that the right to life of the unborn may not restrict freedom to travel and may not limit the freedom to obtain information relating to termination services. This amendment to the constitution followed a decision of the Supreme Court[23] in which the right of a 14-year-old to travel to England to terminate her pregnancy was at issue.
- In its decision of 15 January 1975, the *French* Conseil Constitutionnel held that the new and liberal regulation of the termination of pregnancy did not violate basic constitutional principles.[24] The Conseil d'État [the highest administrative court] ruled in its decision of 21 December 1990[25] on the compatibility of the reform law on the termination of pregnancy, No. 75-17 of 17 January 1975, and the supplementary law No. 79-1204 of

---

[22] *McGee* v. *Attorney General* (1974) *IR* 284 and *G.* v. *An Bord Uchtala* 113 *ILTR* 25, 1979.

[23] *Attorney General* v. *X* (13 *Human Rights Law Journal* (1992) pp. 210-229. For more on this point, see C.J. FORDER, 'Abortion: A Constitutional Problem in European Perspective', 1 *Maastricht Journal of European and Comparative Law* (1994) pp. 56-100 at pp. 57 ff.

[24] See also the decision of 27 July 1994 concerning prenatal diagnoses (No. 94-343/344 DC, *Recueil des décisions du Conseil constitutionnel* 1994 pp. 100-105 at pp. 103 f.).

[25] *Recueil Dalloz* 1991, Jurisprudence, p. 283 ff.

31 December 1979 with Article 2 of the European Convention on Human Rights and Article 6 of the International Covenant on Civil and Political Rights. These decisions rejected the complaints of various organizations against the approval of the abortion pill RU 486 issued by the French Ministry of Health on 28 December 1988.

- In the decision of the *German* Federal Constitutional Court of 25 Feb. 1975,[26] in a process initiated by the government of Baden-Württemberg (and joined by the CDU/CSU parliamentary group in the Bundestag as well as additional Länder governed by the CDU/CSU) to test the constitutionality of a law, the newly introduced time limit solution was declared unconstitutional. In its decision of 28 May 1993,[27] in a process initiated primarily by CDU/CSU members of the Bundestag and supported by a similar request from the Bavarian government to test the constitutionality of a law, the court declared the SFHG of 1992 unconstitutional to the extent that a termination following counseling in the first 12 weeks of pregnancy and performed by a physician, in accordance with § 218a para. 1 StGB in the version of the SFHG, was to be 'not unlawful'. In addition, the counseling regulation of § 219 StGB in the version of the SFHG was found to be 'insufficient' for the protection of unborn life.[28] The Federal Constitutional Court has also addressed aspects other than the limits of permissibility according to criminal law: In a ruling of 18 April 1984, a submission from a social security court, whose goal was the restriction of services provided by the health care system, was found to be inadmissible and dismissed.[29] In addition, a constitutional complaint raised by several physicians challenging the Bavarian implementing provisions aimed at preventing specialization in the performance of terminations was found, in substance, to be largely well-founded.[30]

- As far as *Great Britain* is concerned, there is no national court decision on point but rather, following exhaustion of internal legal procedures, a decision of the supranational European Commission of Human Rights: In this case, the claim of a father concerning his right to prevent an abortion was rejected, among other reasons, because the right of the fetus to life in the early phases of pregnancy is subject to an implied limitation in order to

---

[26] *BVerfGE* 39, 1 ff.

[27] *BVerfGE* 88, 203 ff.

[28] For additional details, see A. ESER in A. SCHÖNKE and H. SCHRÖDER (eds.), *Strafgesetzbuch: Kommentar*, 26th edn. (Munich, C.H. Beck 2001) introductory remarks 6 ff. to § 218.

[29] *BVerfGE* 67, 26 ff.

[30] *BVerfGE* 98, 265 ff.

protect the life and health of the woman, and thus the granting of permission to terminate according to the (broad) medical indication of English law does not violate the right to life guaranteed to 'everyone' in Article 2 of the European Convention on Human Rights.[31]

- In a decision of the *Portuguese* Constitutional Court of 19 March 1984,[32] in a process carried out on behalf of the president to establish the constitutionality of the partial legalization of termination, the partial legalization was found not to be contrary to the constitution; in a decision of 29 May 1985,[33] in a subsequent norm control process undertaken by an ombudsman for the legal system, the compatibility of the reform law with the constitution was confirmed.

- In its decision of 11 April 1985, the *Spanish* Constitutional Court, in a preventive proceeding to test the constitutionality of planned Article 417bis CP, held the introduction of an expanded indication regulation to be fundamentally admissible; however, the procedural regulations were insufficient to guarantee against improper expansion of the grounds for exemption from punishment, and thus the law, as a whole, was found to be unconstitutional. Although not directly related to the aborto-provisions as such, it appears at least indirectly relevant in the constitutional context that, in a judgment of 27 June 1984, the Spanish Constitutional Court found the reasoning of the Supreme Court requiring the embryo to be treated like a 'Spanish citizen' to be incompatible with the principle *nullum crimen/nulla poena sine lege*.

- In its decision of 9 December 1991,[34] the *Hungarian* Constitutional Court declared non-statutory provisions allowing terminations under certain conditions unconstitutional on (purely) formal grounds (i.e., a statute was required). As far as the (consequently) required regulation is concerned, the finding of the majority of the Constitutional Court – i.e., that it is within the responsibility and competence of the legislature to determine where the law draws a line between the unconstitutional extreme-solution of the prohibition of abortion, on the one hand, and the permission of abortion without justification, on the other, and what indications will be required – is no less significant. Furthermore, it must be noted that the fundamental

---

[31] *Paton v. United Kingdom*, Application No. 8416/78, Commission Decision of 13 May 1980 (8 *EuGRZ* (1981) pp. 20-22).

[32] 2 *Acórdãos do Tribúnal Constitucional* (1984) No. 25/84.

[33] 5 *Acórdãos do Tribúnal Constitucional* (1985) No. 85/85.

[34] 64/1991; XII.17; German version in G. BRUNNER and L. SÓLYOM, *Verfassungsgerichtsbarkeit in Ungarn – Analysen und Entscheidungssammlung 1990-1993* (Baden-Baden, Nomos 1995) pp. 256-305.

vow of the Hungarian Parliament to honor and protect the 'life of the fetus from conception'[35] is not a constitutional guarantee but merely a legislative statement of policy.

- By decision of the *Polish* Constitutional Court of 28 May 1997,[36] the amending law of 1996 – with which numerous restrictions introduced by the Law of 1993 were to be removed and the legal situation described in the country report was to be reestablished by the reintroduction of a social indication – was declared partially unconstitutional, since the constitutionally guaranteed protection of human life, which also extends to prenatal life, may not, according to the Constitutional Court, be constricted by simple statutory law.

- In the *Roe* v. *Wade* decision, the *United States* Supreme Court[37] placed restrictions on the individual state legislatures regarding the criminalization of termination. In the following years, due to not insignificant changes in the political climate in the US and in the policy of the Supreme Court, these restrictions have been – to some extent – withdrawn by decisions such as *Webster* v. *Reproductive Health Services*.[38] In its decision in *Planned Parenthood* v. *Casey*,[39] the Supreme Court reiterated its support for the core of the *Roe*-decision of 1973 – according to which the freedom of the woman in questions of family planning is a fundamental right that must be protected.

- In the first Morgentaler decision (*Morgentaler* v. *The Queen*, 1975), the *Canadian* Constitutional Court found that the abortion law in force did not violate the constitution. In the second Morgentaler decision (*R.* v. *Morgentaler*, 1988), however, the abortion law was declared unconstitutional on the basis of constitutional amendments undertaken in the meantime. In two additional decisions, the Constitutional Court denied the right of the father of an unborn child to prevent the pregnant woman from abort-

---

[35] Preamble to the Law LXXXIX of 17 December 1992.

[36] K 26/96; see also Dz.U. 1997, No. 157, Pos. 1040.

[37] 93 *S.Ct.* 705 (1973).

[38] 109 *S.Ct.* 3053 (1989); for details on these developments, see S. WALTHER, 'Schwangerschaftsabbruch in den USA: Neuere Rechtsentwicklungen', 19 *EuGRZ* (1992) pp. 45-60.

[39] 112 *S.Ct.* 2791 (1992). On this point, see (as well as with regard to the Canadian *Morgentaler*-decision of 1988, *infra* text accompanying n. 40) – in comparative perspective – S. WALTHER, 'Thou shalt not (but thou mayest): Abortion after the German Constitutional Court's 1993 Landmark Decision', 36 *German Yearbook of International Law* (1993) pp. 385-404 at pp. 399 ff., as well as CH. MORRIS, *Die Rolle von Verfassung und Verfassungsgerichtsbarkeit in der politischen Auseinandersetzung in den USA und Kanada am Beispiel des Schwangerschaftsabbruchs* (Berlin, Duncker & Humblot 1997) pp. 81 ff.

ing[40] and denied that a partially born child was a 'person' within the meaning of the criminal offense of negligent homicide.[41] In an additional decision,[42] the Constitutional Court refused in 1989 to consider the claim of an abortion opponent that the abortion provision of sect. 251 Criminal Code violated the Canadian Charter of Rights and Freedoms, since at the time the decision was made this provision was no longer valid.

2.3.2   *Ranking in light of guidelines for the legislature*

In an attempt to rank the constitutional status in the surveyed countries – regardless of whether it is a status guaranteed by the constitutional court or a status as seen through the lenses of the more or less compelling 'prevailing opinion,' or even of the author of the country report – with regard to guidelines for the legislature for the protection of unborn life, there are essentially five different levels of guarantee:

- The broadest possible legislative discretion for the regulation of the termination of pregnancy is found in those countries where there is neither an express nor an implied guarantee of the right to life, either for born or for unborn life (e.g., England, Egypt, Australia and, until 1996, South Africa). The constitutional status of the unborn is probably even weaker in countries where its protection is not only not expressly established but conversely the reproductive freedom of the pregnant woman – including her right to terminate – is exclusively, or in any case preeminently, guaranteed (e.g., former German Democratic Republic, India).
- At the next level are countries such as Belgium, the Netherlands, Switzerland, Turkey, Israel, South Africa (since 1997), Japan, Canada as well as several Latin American countries in which the protection of born – but not unborn – life is constitutionally guaranteed.
- In contrast, the fetus is already included within the right to life in a few countries where, however, no derivative, specific criminal law duty to protect it has been recognized. This is the case in Austria, Zambia, the Czech Republic and Poland, for instance.[43] In addition, various Latin American

---

[40] *Daigle* v. *Tremblay* [1989] 2 *SCR* 530.

[41] *Sullivan and Lemay* v. *R.,* [1991] 63 *CCC* 3d 97.

[42] *Borowski* v. *The Attorney General of Canada* [1989] 1 *SCR* 342. On this issue, see M.L. McCONNELL, 'Even by Common Sense Morality: *Morgentaler, Borowski* and the Constitution of Canada', 68 *Canadian Bar Review* (1989) pp. 765-796; Morris, op. cit. n. 39, at pp. 139 ff.

[43] See *supra* n. 34 and n. 36.

constitutions, such as those of Ecuador and Peru, where unborn life is expressly protected from the moment of conception, as well as the American Human Rights Convention of 22 November 1969,[44] ratified by several Latin American countries, likewise leave open the kinds of consequences this type of guarantee might have on the punishability of the termination of pregnancy.

• At the next level of protection are countries where unborn life is in principle granted protection under criminal law but where constitutionally based exceptions to this protection are recognized. This occurs through time-bound gradations, particularly with respect to the (individual) fetus's ability to survive outside the womb (as advocated by the U.S. Supreme Court) and/or by denying the equality of born and unborn life (e.g., the Italian Constitutional Court).[45] Occasionally – as in constitutional court decisions in France and Portugal – the attempt is made to avoid collisions with the fetus's right to exist by restricting terminations to emergency cases so that the right of human life to respect is not slighted; this indicates a tendency towards inherent limits on the right to life. With such a willingness to leave room from the very beginning, so to speak, for certain limitations on the constitutional protection of unborn life, it is not surprising that the aforementioned courts tended to be open to the liberalization of criminal abortion law.[46]

• Finally, the highest level of protection is achieved in those countries that view not only the fetus's right to life but also the corresponding state duty of criminal protection as principles embodied in constitutional law. As far as can be determined from our country reports, only the Federal Republic of Germany, Spain, and Ireland fall into this category – with an increase in binding guidelines on the legislature; however, even in these countries, the 'counter-constitutional rights' of the pregnant woman (such as her own right to life and health, her human dignity and self-determination over reproduction, or her honor), although they do not take absolute priority over the unborn's right to life, are at least incorporated to one degree or another into the balancing of interests when determining possible grounds for exemption from punishment and/or time limits.

---

[44] According to Art. 4 No. 1 of this Convention, 'Every person has the right to have his life respected. This right shall be protected by law and, in general, from the moment of conception'.

[45] Similar arguments can be found in Austria and, insofar as fetuses are considered to have basic rights of their own, in Greece.

[46] See *supra* II.2.3.1.

2.4   Basic regulatory models: from (virtually) absolute prohibition to (almost) complete permission

2.4.1   *Regulatory diversity – criteria for classification*

In looking for common trends and similar structures behind the existing regulatory diversity in the area of termination of pregnancy, appropriate criteria for classification must first be identified, namely, criteria that appear particularly significant with respect to the scope and severity of the prohibition of abortion, on the one hand, and to the permissibility of termination along with the accompanying conditions, on the other. The distinguishing features that should be accorded significance depends, of course, on the perspective from which the model is to be developed. For example, those who wish to see the various termination regulations grouped according to the benchmark of medical discretion and cooperation will arrive at other models than those who look first and foremost at the possibility of termination in accordance with time limits or dependent on certain indications. Hence, it is not surprising that, when viewed from the perspective of medical professionalization and medicalization, the 'abortion regimes' identified by *Petersen*, with their differentiation between the 'abortion reform' model, the 'judicial' model, and the 'elective' model, differ significantly from the models developed here.[47] This also shows that models neither arise of their own accord nor do they exist in a vacuum; rather, their creation depends on value judgments that, in the final analysis, can be – consciously or unconsciously – politically motivated. This is also true for the frequently polemic – and correspondingly biased – reduction of possible termination models to a choice between the 'time limit model' and the 'indication model' (see *infra* IV.1.1, IV.1.3.3). In order to avoid this narrow perspective, the creation of models in the following is not dependent on one single differentiating criterion, but rather is based on a multi-factored approach.

Even if none of the following individual criteria alone suffices for the characterization of a basic model (indeed, a model is shaped by a combination of various criteria), it might still be helpful to introduce the most significant of the parameters with a few characteristic variables.

A. With respect to *time limits and gradations*, the beginning and the end points of termination regulations (see *infra* II.2.5.3) are of interest as are, in some cases, possible intermediate cut-off points.

---

[47] K.A. PETERSEN, *Abortion Regimes* (Aldershot, Dartmouth 1993) pp. 99 ff.

Various *intermediate cut-off points* can be inserted between the beginning and end points of termination regulations' scope of applicability: While termination is allowed under relatively permissive conditions in most of the reformed legal systems either until the tenth week of gestation (as now in Switzerland, until 2001 in France and until 1990 in Bulgaria) or more frequently until the twelfth week (as in Denmark, Italy and Luxembourg and now also in Belgium and South Africa), in other countries the intermediate limits are even longer – such as 16 weeks in Portugal (until 1997), 18 weeks in Norway, and 22 weeks in Germany and Spain. Still other countries extend the limit for permissive termination to the 24th week, as for instance Great Britain,[48] Kuwait and Taiwan. Some countries recognize a number of different cut-off points, such as Hungary (12, 16, and 18 weeks), South Africa – since 1996 (12 and 20 weeks and 'after the 20th week'),[49] and Greece (12, 19, and 24 weeks).

B. Indicators that are at least as revealing of a regulatory model's basic character are the *type and degree of permission afforded termination*. In this respect, too, the range is very broad, although four basic constellations of regulations, differing in their propensity to make concessions, can be identified:

- On the stricter end of the spectrum are those regulations in which abortion is not only generally prohibited but in which, in addition, no express grounds for allowing termination are given, so that the only way for a termination to remain unpunished is if the exemption from punishment follows from general legal principles. This basic position can be described under the catch-word *'prohibition model'*.
- The opposite extreme is characterized by a situation in which, independent of an indication that must be established *ex ante* and/or is subject to scrutiny *ex post*, termination remains exempt from punishment – either within a specific time period or even throughout the entire pregnancy. This position can be referred to – various nuances aside – as the *'time limit model'*.
- Between these two extremes but closer to the 'prohibition model' is the *'indication model'*, in which terminations, basically prohibited, are decriminalized, justified or at least excused under exceptional circumstances (that are more or less broadly defined).
- Finally, more in the other direction and (because they contain elements from both) located between the 'indication' and 'time limit models' are those regulations that can be collectively entitled the *'combined (succes-*

---

[48] On the basis of the amendment to sect. 1 para. 1(a) Abortion Act 1967 by the Human Fertilisation and Embryology Act 1990 sect. 37.

[49] S. 2(1) of the new regulation.

sive) time limit – indication model'. In this model, a termination is exempt from punishment, more or less, within a specific period varying from ten to 24 weeks; during the same time period or in one or more subsequent stages of pregnancy, terminations may not only be exempt from punishment but may even be considered permissible if specific indications are ascertained or other substantive prerequisites fulfilled.

C. Furthermore, the practical significance of *procedural conditions* that must be met in order for a termination of pregnancy to be exempt from punishment should not be underestimated. In this respect, five variables appear especially noteworthy:

- On the one hand, there are countries in which there are practically *no procedural provisions* regulating the performance of a termination. The absence of such provisions is hardly surprising in countries with a 'prohibition model', but the failure to require confirmation of an indication and/or the absence of a requirement that terminations be performed by a physician have also been encountered in some countries with an 'indication model'.
- However, in countries that have adopted restrictive prerequisites for the procedure, the minimum requirements are that the termination be performed by a *physician* and/or in a *medical facility*; thus, an attempt to ensure a medical 'safety net' is made.[50]
- With respect to additional procedural requirements (such as prior counseling and/or third-party review), the picture becomes much more complicated because the requirements are determined by their respective regulatory models. Hence – to begin with a requirement typically considered by the pregnant woman to be particularly demanding – one may expect, from the outset, to find the requirement of *third-party review* (i.e., the ascertainment of the presence of the prerequisites for a permissible termination by one or more physicians, by a panel, or by some other person or authority authorized to 'second-guess' the pregnant woman's decision) only in places where the exemption of a termination from punishment depends on the presence of an indication or on the absence of a contraindication. However, the indication requirement does not necessarily require a

---

[50] A somewhat odd exception from this rule is found in Bahrain, where in order for self-termination to be unpunishable the participation of a physician is necessary insofar as the abortion may not be undertaken 'if a physician has not been consulted or without the physician's knowledge' (Art. 321 Penal Code); in contrast, a third-party termination is apparently punishable only if it is undertaken 'without the consent of the woman' (Art. 322).

third-party evaluation; rather, the existence of an indication can be left up to the responsible self-assessment of the pregnant woman, of the terminating physician or up to a possible *ex post facto* judicial review.[51]

- In addition to, or in lieu of, an indication requirement (with or without third-party review), *counseling* of the pregnant woman is a possibility. However, 'counseling' does not mean the same thing everywhere. Whereas it may be seen in some countries as a *duty* and in others simply as an *option*, the *goal* of counseling, too, may vary from a purely medical one to – more or less – directive social counseling to counseling regarding the use of appropriate contraceptive measures in order to avoid unwanted pregnancies in the future.

- In addition to, or in lieu of, third-party review or counseling requirements as discussed above, some countries also have *other procedural provisions* that can impede or facilitate termination. For instance, even in cases involving time limit regulations, the *bureaucratic course* that must be run in order to obtain a termination can work, without more, like an obstacle course with a controlling, restrictive effect; indeed, such an effect may even be intended. Furthermore, the provision for or absence of *reporting requirements* as well as the nature of such requirements can be an indicator of the seriousness of a country's attempt to take control of the problem of the termination of pregnancy.

D. Finally, a possible grant of *privilege to the pregnant woman*, in the sense of guaranteeing her a special exemption from or mitigation of punishment, can also affect significantly the character of a regulatory model. Because depending on whether and to what extent a country is prepared to differentiate between a termination performed by the woman herself or a termination performed by a third party, conclusions can be drawn about whether the approach taken is one of uniform, more victim-oriented severity or if it is more an offender-oriented approach that takes individual factors into consideration.

2.4.2   *Classification*

Given its bulk and diversity, it would certainly be possible to differentiate the regulatory material according to the regulatory criteria analyzed in detail in the following sections. However, as far as the elaboration of *basic models* is con-

---

[51] Whether this is actually done in practice in Austria – where no formal determination of the existence of an indication is required, even for the stage of pregnancy (beginning at the third month) in which termination is dependent on an indication (§ 97 para. 1 No. 2 StGB), – is not clear from the relevant literature.

cerned, which is the issue here, the parameters discussed above should suffice for certain classifications. It would appear most efficient to take the prohibitive and permissive patterns presented in (B) of the previous section as flexible, basic models and to keep in mind the parameters listed in (A), (C) and (D).

A. 'Prohibition Model'

Under this label fall those regulations in which abortion is not only generally prohibited but in which, in addition, no express exceptions are granted, so that the only way for a termination to remain unpunished is if the exemption from punishment follows from general legal principles.[52] Again, such *substantive exemptions from punishment* are not an express part of the 'prohibition model' – in contrast to the following regulatory models – but rather are only possible on account of unwritten exclusions or general grounds for exemption, specifically in the following three ways:

- first, by means of a *statutory definition of the crime* that excludes 'therapeutic terminations';
- second, through reliance upon general grounds of justification or excuse;
- third, by the fact that, in practice, termination is permitted on the basis of *other unwritten grounds* that have the status of quasi-customary law.

Incidentally, the following three factors seem to be characteristic of the 'prohibition model': First, it is encountered only very rarely today; second, it is located – which should come as no surprise – in the criminal code;[53] and third procedural regulations for terminations – if there are any at all – are found in the professional codes of medical associations.[54]

B. Pure 'Indication Model'

For this type of model, it is characteristic that, on the one hand (as in the case of the 'prohibition model'), abortion is generally subject to punishment, but that, on the other hand, express exceptions from punishment in the form of 'indications' are recognized. Unlike the combined or pure 'time limit models', however, no provision is made for a blanket exemption from punishment – even in the absence of an indication – during some pre-established time period subsequent to implantation.

---

[52] See *supra* II.2.4.1.B, first block.

[53] See *supra* II.1.1.

[54] As in Egypt and Iraq to determine whether the prerequisites are fulfilled, whereas in Ireland – probably on account of fundamental, primarily religious opposition – there are, in the non-state arena as well, apparently neither procedural nor counseling rules to be found.

Considerable variation can be found among regulations based on the indication model (so-called because of the basic indication requirement); five important areas of variation are mentioned below:

- First, the *narrowness or breadth of the indication,*[55] whereby the former may result from a more restrictive and/or minimalist description of the grounds for an indication and the latter from a greater number of grounds for termination or their more 'blanket' definitions.
- Second, variations are apparent from a *chronological perspective,* in that in some countries the indication(s) provided for apply continuously, *without graduation,* from the beginning of the pregnancy until birth, while in other countries cut-off points restrict the applicability of the available indication(s) more and more as the pregnancy progresses. This fundamental difference in the two approaches is reflected terminologically in their characterization as 'graduated' and 'non-graduated' indication models.
- A further chronological aspect subject to variation has to do with the *early phase of the pregnancy.* Some countries that prohibit abortion enforce the prohibition as soon as conception has occurred, whereas others do not enforce it until after implantation has taken place.[56] In the latter cases, a not inconsiderable window of opportunity is opened for contraception 'after the fact'.[57] Hence, this criterion, essential as it is for determining the start-

---

[55] Indicated in the following overview for the individual countries by N (for a comparatively narrow) or B (for a comparatively broad approach to indications).

[56] Either by definition, in that intervention in the development of an egg before implantation in the uterus is not covered by the offense 'termination of pregnancy' (as, for example, in § 219d – currently § 218 para. 1 sent. 2 – of the German StGB) or else by simply tolerating procedures and measures that inhibit implantation without requiring any special indication-like justification for their use.

[57] Consequently, it is incorrect, strictly speaking, to speak in such cases of a 'pure' indication model; instead, they should be referred to as a 'combination model'. For if conception is considered the beginning of human life and yet there is an exemption from punishment – without further justification – up to the point of implantation, we are in fact dealing with a 'time-limit' approach. However, since this early phase is very difficult to identify in practice and since the legal policy discussions concerning 'indication' and 'time-limit' solutions *before* implantation cannot compare in vehemence with the discussions concerning an indication-free period *after* implantation, an acceptable approach with regard to the creation of *basic models*, which is the issue here, would seem to be not to treat the early stages as decisive. This should not be taken to mean, however, that the early stage should not be considered at all; rather, this factor will be addressed separately within each individual model.

ing point of the prohibition against abortion, is also identified – where ascertainable – in the systematic overview.[58]

- From a *procedural perspective*, it appears significant for the development of models to determine the extent to which – beyond the general requirement that the termination be undertaken by a *physician* and/or in a *medical facility*[59] – specific procedural prerequisites (such as counseling and/or the formal determination of the presence of an indication by means of third-party review) are necessary for exemption from punishment.
- Finally, the possibility of a *personal exemption from punishment for the pregnant woman* is also indicated in the overview.

In the case of the '*non-graduated*' *indication model,* the following observations can be made concerning the various possible regulatory constellations (see Diagram II/2, p. 64):

- In the majority of cases, the prohibition of abortion begins at conception (F 1-8).
- Indications tend to be interpreted rather narrowly (F 1, 3, 5, 7, 11).
- While a formal determination of the presence of an indication, at least, is required in about half of the countries (F 3, 7), counseling apparently plays only a minimal role (F 8 or absence of regulation at F 2, 6, 10, 14). There is also a relatively large number of countries with no special procedural safeguards whatsoever (F 1, 5, 9).
- A general exemption from punishment for the pregnant woman is extremely rare (F 17).
- This model type is most prevalent in Latin America and in the Arabic-African region; its appearance in Switzerland (until 2002) is all the more noteworthy.

It is characteristic of the '*graduated*' *indication model* that specific indications are applicable only during certain stages of pregnancy and that the possibility of obtaining an indicated termination decreases incrementally as the pregnancy

---

[58] This is in fact not easy to ascertain because there is only a comparatively small number of countries in which the onset of the abortion prohibition is established by law – either at the time of conception (as in Ecuador, Mexico and Peru) or following implantation (as in the Federal Republic of Germany and the Netherlands). In some countries lacking this type of legislation, it may be possible to draw some conclusions by looking at case law and literature; in others, the issue may be ignored entirely. On the subject as a whole, see also *infra* II.2.5.3.

[59] See also *supra* II.2.4.1.C, second block.

progresses. With regard to existing regulatory constellations using this model, the following remarks can be made (see Diagram II/3, p. 65):

– Although in a large number of countries the starting point of pregnancy as far as regulations regarding the termination of pregnancy are concerned is not legally clarified (F 5-12), the tendency is for implantation to be recognized in this context (F 9-12); indeed, in the meantime implantation has been expressly adopted by several countries as the relevant starting point (F 15, 16).
– The scope of indications in some countries is narrow here as well; in comparison to the 'non-graduated' indication model (F 7, 11), however, the tendency towards a broader approach to the indication requirement is clear (F 3, 8, 12, 16).
– While the emphasis is more on third-party review in the 'non-graduated' indication model, counseling here is apparently of greater significance (F 8, 12, 16). Some new regulations even expressly substitute counseling for third-party review up until a certain point in the pregnancy, thus placing responsibility for the final decision about the existence of an indication with the pregnant woman herself.
– Consequently, there are hardly any countries in this group with no procedural regulations whatsoever (F 1, 5, 9).
– There are also multiple occurrences of a general exemption from punishment for the pregnant woman (F 17).

C. Combined (successive) 'time limit – indication models'
Grouped together under this term are those regulations in which termination – as in the 'time limit model' – is basically exempt from punishment if undertaken within a specific, initial period of time; it is only later, during one or more subsequent stages of pregnancy, that – similar to the 'indication model' – the exemption from punishment is made dependent upon the existence of a specific indication or fulfillment of other substantive prerequisites. Note that these indications may also play a role already during the initial 'time limit' stage.[60]

In summary, the following tendencies in the 'combination models' (see Diagram II/4, p. 66) are striking:

– There is, apparently, little need for a clear definition of when the regulations on termination attach, as almost all the regulations (with the exception of F 3 and 16) function with a legally ambiguous boundary zone: (F6-12).

---

[60] See *supra* II.2.4.1.B, fourth block.

–   The procedural safety net is accorded no little significance: the majority of the regulations require at least third-party review during the indication stage (F 3, 7, 11) and some also require counseling in the 'time limit' stage (F 8, 12, 16), even if only in the form of a thorough explanation of 'risks and alternatives' followed by a short waiting period (F 6).[61]

–   The transition point from the initial 'time limit' state to the indication stage is generally located in the 12th week.

–   Pregnant women are exempted from punishment relatively often (F 17).

–   The regulations can all be traced to reforms that have taken place since the middle of the 1950s.

D. Pure 'time limit models'

Grouped under this label are those regulations in which – similar to the 'combination regulations' – a termination is exempt from punishment within a specific time period, independent of an indication that must be ascertained *ex ante* and/or subject to scrutiny *ex post*; these regulations do not, however, recognize a subsequent stage during which an indication is required – differing, in this respect, from the 'combination regulations'. Within the framework of this basic model, which is, to be sure, adopted by comparatively few countries (see Diagram II/5, p. 67), two fundamentally different positions emerge:

–   As far as the protection of unborn life is concerned, an upper limit is placed on termination of pregnancy (at around 24 weeks) (F 1). This time limit is even earlier than in some traditional indication and combination regulations.

---

[61] The law on this point in the US, which is based on the US Supreme Court decision *Roe* v. *Wade* (1973) has become significantly more restrictive in the intervening years. As a result of restrictions placed by state legislatures on a woman's right to choose and found by the US Supreme Court since the late 1980s to satisfy constitutional muster, the individual states are now free to impose *procedural regulations* on permissible terminations undertaken prior to fetal viability. These regulations typically involve requiring women to attend information sessions at which 'risks and alternatives' are presented as well as the introduction of mandatory waiting periods (e.g., requiring 24-hours to pass between provision of information deemed necessary to informed consent and performance of termination). Additional regulations include the obligation of the physician to determine and document the age of the fetus before every termination and to inform the woman of fetal age (on these developments, see WALTHER, loc. cit. n. 38, at pp. 50 f.). Following the landmark decision *Planned Parenthood* v. *Casey*, these kinds of measures are permissible only if they do not place an 'undue burden' on the woman's free choice; that is, a state regulation may not have 'the purpose or effect of placing a substantial obstacle in the path of a woman seeking an abortion of a nonviable fetus.' 112 *S.Ct.* 2791, 2820 (1992).

– However, where there is no upper limit (F 2, 3), the regulations apparently
are not concerned with the protection of unborn life but only with the protection of the pregnant woman or even with general demographic policy.

2.4.3 *Comprehensive assessment: disregarding extremes leaves three distinct regulatory approaches*

The model-development process discussed above was primarily concerned with
formal-structural criteria: the relationship of prohibition and exceptions, the
reliance on indications and/or time limits, chronological cut-off points and, last
but not least, procedural requirements.[62] With the resulting picture – five basic
models with variations –, one can easily lose one's perspective with regard to
what a specific regulation signifies concerning the approach of the legal community in question towards termination of pregnancy and with regard to what
behavior is expected from a woman facing the decision whether to terminate:
what the 'legal-ethical' message is, so to speak, that emanates from a termination regulation. If one wants to find an answer to this leading question – socio-
psychologically key because of its importance with respect to legal consciousness
–, one should not restrict oneself to a discussion of structural similarities and
differences on a comparatively technical, regulatory level, but rather one should
also consider more substantive factors, such as the primary object of legal protection, the role of the pregnant woman in the decision-making process and,
finally, the degree of societal approval or disapproval. Moreover, one must reduce the diversity – as vast as ever despite the development of the previously
discussed basic models – among regulatory variations to those core statements
that appear especially significant in influencing people's general awareness.

From this perspective, two extreme positions that, *at present*, are virtually
nonexistent in the world are initially excluded (A and B). Hence, there are three
basic positions to consider that appear particularly significant for the legal assessment and treatment of termination of pregnancy today (C-E).

A. At one end of the possible regulatory spectrum, there is, apparently, *no country
with a complete prohibition against the killing of developing human life* at this
time. Because human life already begins to develop with the merging of the
female ovum and male sperm in the form of a new and definitively determined
genetic 'life program unit',[63] a truly 'absolute' protection of unborn life would

---

[62] Of course, if one were to start from a different perspective, it would be possible to
identify other kinds of models (on this point, see *supra* text at II.2.4.1).

[63] For more on this point, see B. HASSENSTEIN, 'Lebensbeginn', in A. ESER et al. (eds.),
Lexikon Medizin-Ethik-Recht (Freiburg, Herder 1989/92) column 673 ff., especially at 678 ff.

exist only if every procedure leading to the destruction of a fertilized human egg cell in the process of development were without exception punishable and also actually prosecuted. This is not, however, the case, even in the countries associated with the 'prohibition model' (Diagram II/1, p. 63). Not only that even in this 'strictest' category of countries the use of devices and procedures that prevent implantation of the fertilized egg are effectively tolerated (and in some cases even promoted for purposes of family planning), thus condoning what could be considered a 'time limit regulation' for the pre-implantation stage,[64] there are also, in addition to this time-bound withdrawal of the criminal law, other techniques with which an exemption from punishment for the destruction of unborn life can be obtained, whether it be through a statutory exclusion of a 'therapeutic' termination as a curative procedure for the benefit of the pregnant woman, or by enlisting general rules of justification and excuse.[65] Therefore, the protection of unborn life through criminal law has not been 'absolute' for a long time – if indeed it ever was;[66] instead, protection has at most been 'relative'.[67]

B. Similarly, at the other end of the spectrum, we found not a single country with *no termination regulations whatsoever.* Even countries that have no upper time limit and thus allow termination until birth – e.g., Bahrain and the People's Republic of China – maintain that they cannot completely forego regulations, if only in order to ensure the consent of the pregnant woman and to guarantee a medically professional procedure to protect her health.[68] Therefore, a complete

---

[64] See also *infra* II.2.5.3.A.

[65] See *supra* II.2.4.2.A.

[66] For even in the Catholic church, in accordance with the long accepted 'animation theory', abortion was not prosecuted as a killing of a human being unless it took place after the advent of the so-called 'ensoulment' (40 days for a male, 90 days for a female fetus): see ESER, loc. cit. n. 14, at pp. 386 ff., 400 f.; G. JEROUSCHEK, *Lebensschutz und Lebensbeginn. Kulturgeschichte des Abtreibungsverbots* (Stuttgart, Enke 1988) esp. pp. 14 ff., 33 ff., 80 ff., 141 ff., 276 ff.

[67] Incidentally, this is the case in Germany even for embryos produced in vitro but not yet implanted, for the Embryo Protection Act in principle provides such embryos more protection than it offers an embryo in the womb; for although the embryo in the petri dish is protected, to a large degree, from inappropriate *use*, its very *existence* is *not* protected: on this point, see R. KELLER et al., *Embryonenschutzgesetz* (Stuttgart, Kohlhammer 1992) 1st part B V margin No. 18 f. (p. 95) and § 7 margin No. 32 f. (p. 255); on other possible contradictions between § 218 StGB and the Embryo Protection Act, see A. ESER, 'Neuregelung des Schwangerschaftsabbruchs vor dem Hintergrund des Embryonenschutzgesetzes', in A. ESER and H.-G. KOCH, *Schwangerschaftsabbruch: Auf dem Weg zu einer Neuregelung, Gesammelte Studien und Vorschläge* (Baden-Baden, Nomos 1992) pp. 147 ff.

[68] See *supra* II.2.4.2.B.

removal, without more, of all termination regulations, leaving the killing of unborn life in all stages and in all respects completely up to the pregnant woman or other participants, is virtually unprecedented worldwide.

C. Between these two extremes, three basic positions can be identified. The one with a more *restrictive* tendency is reflected in the *'prohibition and indication on the basis of third-party review'* model.

- Characteristic of this basic position is that:
- unborn life has clear precedence as the object of legal protection,
- the disapproval of termination of pregnancy under criminal law is accorded decisive importance,
- exceptions to the prohibition on abortion, to the extent they are granted in the form of special 'indications', are oriented to the principle of the balancing of legally protected values, are formulated rather narrowly in keeping with medical standards, and tend to be hostile to all kinds of 'social emergency situations',
- the presence of an indication may only be ascertained by persons (or panels) other than the pregnant woman herself, and/or an *ex post facto* judicial examination of the prerequisites for a termination may also be required,
- counseling oriented toward the independent decision of the pregnant woman, insofar as such counseling is provided for at all, is nowhere near as important as third-party evaluation.

- Even though the above-mentioned criteria are not necessarily present in each of the following countries and in some countries still other factors appear, this basic position is found most frequently in the 'prohibition regulations' (*supra* II.2.4.2.A) as well as in the 'non-graduated' and 'graduated indication models' (*supra* II.2.4.2.B); however, as far as 'indication regulations' are concerned, this position is found only to the extent that the indication must be ascertained *ex ante* by means of third-party review and/or is subject to judicial scrutiny *ex post*. Accordingly, the following countries can be associated with this basic position:
- in Europe: Ireland, Belgium (until 1990), Portugal, Spain, and Switzerland (until 2002) as well as with – in some cases – less stringent restrictions the old versions of the law in Bulgaria, the ÈSSR, Hungary, Finland and (until the reform of 1992) the Federal Republic of Germany,[69]

---

[69] Whereby admittedly in the latter it is necessary to take into consideration the special privilege accorded the pregnant woman by exempting her from punishment through the 22nd week of pregnancy if the termination is performed by a physician following counseling (§ 218 para. 3 sent. 2 StGB, currently § 218a para. 4).

– in Latin America, virtually all of which belongs to this group: in particular Argentina, Brazil, Chile (until 1991), Costa Rica, Ecuador and Peru, as well as Uruguay (with reservations),

– in the especially strict Arabic-African region (where no indications are provided for): Egypt, Iraq and the United Arab Emirates; and those that at least foresee an indication, namely, Algeria, Jordan, Kuwait, Lebanon, Libya, Morocco, Oman, Qatar, Zambia, Senegal, South Nigeria, Sudan, Syria, South Africa (until 1996) and, with reservations, Ghana.[70]

D. As a counterbalance and with a more *permissive* tendency are those regulations where *exemption from criminal liability is subject to time limits and based on self-determination.*

• Characteristic of this basic position is that:

– the pregnant woman's right to self-determination is granted standing at least equal to that of the protection of unborn life, if not higher or even exclusive standing,

– accordingly, for a specific time period, termination is left completely up to the pregnant woman; it requires no further justification nor is it subject to judicial scrutiny; it may even be declared to be her 'right',

– consequently, an express assessment of termination of pregnancy as an 'exception', as something to be avoided, is lacking and as a demonstration of this abstention from disapproval the regulations on termination of pregnancy may be transferred from the criminal code to health or social welfare law,[71]

– any accompanying procedures within the provided time limit are seen more as a facilitation or acceleration of the termination and as promoting the professional nature of the termination rather than seen as an obstacle,

---

[70] Canada, too, with its regulation that has been declared unconstitutional – but not replaced – would belong to this category.

[71] Nevertheless, it is by all means possible that the reasoning behind the decision of a country with a time-limit solution not to take the health policy steps necessary for the practical implementation of permitted termination is that the termination of pregnancy, despite its decriminalization, should remain a taboo to as great an extent possible. In Austria, for example, where the reforming legislature consciously limited itself to an amendment of the criminal code and did without all 'flanking' or supporting measures entirely, an indirect 'tabooization' of termination can be seen in the fact that termination, if not medically indicated, is barred from receiving benefits offered by the health care system, in the fact that no organizational measures have been taken to ensure that the entire country has access to institutions in which terminations can be performed and in the fact that public information concerning such institutions has not been made available or, indeed, has even been forbidden.

– and counseling is seen less as a duty than as an opportunity for the pregnant woman.

• Without implying that the aforementioned criteria are present in all of the following countries, particularly because one or the other of the countries could be classified in a different manner, it is mainly countries with a 'classical' time limit policy (*supra* II.2.4.2.C and D) that adhere to this position, although this is not necessarily always the case: With the exception of the USA,[72] Tunisia, Turkey, and South Africa (since 1996), this position is primarily found in Europe and is especially pronounced in the former German Democratic Republic and in Sweden as well as, with some reservations, in Denmark, Austria and the former Soviet Union.

E. Between the aforementioned 'classical' positions of 'indications subject to third-party review' on the one hand and 'self-determination subject to time limits' on the other, there is yet another approach that can be summed up as an '*emergency-oriented discourse model*'.[73] Such 'catchword' descriptions are not immune to misinterpretation, however. Hence, it is all the more important – here as well as with the descriptive names given to other models – to remain cognizant of the models' constituent factors.

• Characteristic of this middle position is that:
– in recognition of the priority of unborn life as an object of legal protection, termination of pregnancy is seen as an exceptional event and as something to be avoided; accordingly, it is legally disapproved,
– permission to terminate is granted only in exceptional cases and is dependent upon a balancing of interests designed to remedy an emergency or conflict situation, whereby this balancing requirement can be based on an explicit indication or on a corresponding definition of the objectives of counseling,

---

[72] But on this point see also the contrary movement since the case *Planned Parenthood* v. *Casey* (1992), *supra* II.2.4.2 n. 61.

[73] Although not yet described in these terms, the existence of an approach located between the traditional 'indication' and 'time-limit' solutions was already recognized in the early comparative legal analyses by H.-G. KOCH, 'Recht und Praxis des Schwangerschaftsabbruchs im internationalen Vergleich', 97 *ZStW* (1985) pp. 1043-1073 at pp. 1056 ff.; however, the amount of notice taken of this approach in the public discussion was inadequate. Since a possible explanation for this lack of attention is that discussion cannot take place in the absence of 'catchwords', we have tried in more recent publications to give these basic positions a name (see ESER and KOCH, op. cit. n. 67, at pp. 92 ff., 167 ff.).

– in compliance with a certain time-frame for deliberation before the termination, the pregnant woman must or should be counseled and, in certain
circumstances, must also submit her reasons to the physician,
– however, the final decision for or against a termination remains a decision
in the personal responsibility (and subject to the conscience) of the pregnant woman herself, largely free of *ex post facto* judicial review.

*   As might be expected, this position, focused on conflict resolution and relying upon counseling and genuine, open-ended discourse, is found primarily in those regulations in which prohibitive norms have more of a
backseat role and adherence to specific procedures is promoted. Moreover,
since in the last analysis the technical-legal outfitting as an indication or
time-limit regulation or as a combination of both does not signify, this
moderate position can be found in all of these basic models. Because it is a
comparatively modern approach, it is found, naturally, only in those countries whose termination laws have been reformed:
– in Europe: France, Great Britain, Italy and Norway as well as Belgium
since 1990, the Federal Republic of Germany since 1992 and Switzerland
since 2002; in addition – although with varying (sometimes contradictory)
reservations – Luxembourg, the Netherlands, and (probably also continuing beyond 1993) Poland and the ÈSFR, and (until 1990) Bulgaria,
– in the rest of the world: along with the still pending reform bill in Canada,
probably also Israel and Mexico.

F. A *complete overview* can be found in Diagram II/6 (p. 68). The following
three remarks concerning this schematic summary are intended to help prevent
any possible misunderstandings:

*   While several countries that appear in Diagrams 1-5 are not listed here,
this is not because they have been overlooked but rather because they cannot be clearly and adequately classified to any of the aforementioned
groups: the countries in question are Bahrain, Japan, and North and South
Yemen (countries that, in the meantime, have reunited).

*   Insofar as a classification has indeed been made, this was only possible, in
some cases, with reservations: these doubts are expressed by means of a
question mark following the entry.

*   Although column C (prohibition model/indication model on the basis of
third-party review) may seem to stand out starkly in this diagram, one
should not, of course, draw any rash conclusions regarding legal policy.

Rather, in the interpretation of this overview, three items should be considered:

– First, representatives of this category are overwhelmingly non-European countries whose abortion laws have not yet been reformed.
– By the same token, when comparing European countries to each other, only a few of the countries where reforms have recently taken place belong to this model (C), namely Portugal, Spain and, latterly, Poland.
– On the other hand, both the other groupings involve countries with reformed termination laws, whereby, notably, the 'time limit on the basis of self-determination' regulations (D) tend to date back to the first stage of post-war reform and the 'emergency-oriented discourse model' regulations (E) tend to have more recent origins.

Without drawing any rash conclusions about legal policy based on when a reform was undertaken – such as, for example, the conclusion that more recent developments are *per se* better –, at least two lessons can be extracted from this comparative legal overview. One is the observation that between the extremes of a total prohibition on or a total deregulation of termination of pregnancy, there is a continuum of different basic positions with fluid boundaries. The other is the realization that it is too simple to hold up the 'indication approach' and the 'time limit approach' in the legal policy discussion as the sole and moreover irreconcilable alternatives; on the contrary, there is certainly room between the two for a middle-of-the-road approach, an approach that is being taken by legal reformers in increasing measure.

2.5 Concept of termination of pregnancy: fluid borders – terminological, substantive and temporal

When people speak of 'abortion', as it tended to be called earlier, or of 'termination of pregnancy', as it is now called with increasing frequency, they appear to be essentially in agreement about the meaning of what is referred to: it concerns an intervention in the development of human life *in utero*. But if one looks more closely, the boundaries of what still does not or what no longer falls within the scope of abortion or termination of pregnancy become so fluid that a generally accepted definition of these terms appears to be impossible.

In order to demonstrate this with the most innocuous definition possible (because it is normally free of ulterior legal policy motives) we turn to the definition given in '*Meyers Enzyklopädischem Lexikon*': As it defines abortion as 'killing of the fruit of the womb in the mother's body or inducement of the miscarriage of a not yet viable "fruit" from the mother's body',[74] the uncertainty over the concept already finds expression in the contrasting alternatives 'killing' and 'inducement of miscarriage'. This uncertainty dogs the question of whether a successful killing is necessary for an abortion to occur, whether this killing must take place while the fetus is still in utero or whether it can also occur after birth. Or if, on the one hand, people speak of 'killing of the fruit of the womb' and, on the other hand, of 'miscarriage of the not yet viable "fruit" from the mother's body', the question remains whether, in the first case, the killing of an already viable fetus is still considered an abortion; if so, then the consequence is that the absence of viability evidently is not an essential element of abortion – which incidentally completely ignores the question of when the 'fruit' is considered to be still or no longer in the mother's body. Additionally, the fact that people's conceptions of an otherwise 'natural' birth process influence where they perceive the boundaries of termination of pregnancy to be means that difficulties are inevitable when deciding whether to include or exclude modern prenatal and perinatal obstetrical measures, such as the inducement of artificial labor or even the surgical caesarian section.

Although an exhaustive examination of these definitional subtleties cannot be undertaken here, in order to 'round off' the basic conceptions and to provide an introduction to the following, more detailed remarks, three aspects of the commonalities and differences in the definitional understanding of abortion and termination of pregnancy will now be addressed: terminological (2.5.1), substantive (2.5.2) and temporal (2.5.3).

2.5.1   *Terminological evolution*

Whereas in Germany a particular ideological bent is sometimes imputed based on the use of one set of terms or another, our comparative legal analysis indicates that the issue of terminology has not risen to the same level of importance in other countries.[75] A study of today's common usage around the world reveals essentially five discrete terminologies:

- Even if they have experienced reforms in recent years, a comparatively large number of primarily Latin American and Arab countries continue to employ designations that come from the Latin *abortus* (such as *aborto*,

---

[74] *Meyers Enzyklopädisches Lexikon*, Vol. 1, 9th edn. (Mannheim, Bibliographisches Institut 1971) p. 182.

[75] Furthermore, this is difficult to evaluate since the country reports rarely indicate whether a comparable discussion of terminology has taken place. France, Yugoslavia and Portugal are exceptional.

abortion or avortement) or to use other terms that are comparable to the German *Abtreibung*.[76]

- In a similarly traditional fashion, some countries (e.g., Ghana, India, Ireland) use *causing miscarriage of a woman* in the sense of the German *Herbeiführung einer Fehlgeburt*.

- Expressing more generally the idea of an intervention in a developmental process, the term *Schwangerschaftsunterbrechung* ['interruption' of a pregnancy], as was used in the German Democratic Republic, and – with the same meaning – the term *interruzione della gravidanza* (Italy) are being used more frequently today.[77]

- In order to counter the misconception that after an 'interruption' the pregnancy might continue, the term *Schwangerschaftsabbruch* ['abruptis' or termination of pregnancy] has been used since the reforms of the 1970s in the Federal Republic of Germany and in Austria as well as since 2002 in Switzerland.

- Far larger, however, is the number of countries that in the meantime *differentiate* terminologically between illegal termination, using a term comparable to the German *Abtreibung* [abortion], and legal intervention, using the more traditional designation *inducement of a miscarriage* (Zambia) or the more 'modern' designation *Schwangerschaftsunterbrechung, Schwangerschaftsabbruch* or *interruption* or *termination of pregnancy* (Switzerland (until 2002), Bulgaria, France, Great Britain, Luxembourg and Hungary are examples of this in Europe).[78]

2.5.2 *Varying scope of substantive coverage: from intervention during the course of pregnancy to successful killing*

The differing nomenclature might in fact reflect broadly differing views of what acts should be covered by a termination regulation, although this need not necessarily be the case. Setting aside for the moment the temporal demarcations that will be considered separately (see *infra* 2.5.3), the following basic positions emerge with respect to the killing requirement:

---

[76] See also F. KLUGE, *Etymologisches Wörterbuch der deutschen Sprache*, 23nd edn. (Berlin, Walter de Gruyter 1995) p. 7, where 'abort' in the sense of 'wasting away, having a miscarriage' is derived from the Latin *aboriri*.

[77] In the same vein, in France since the reform of 1995, the term 'interruption de la grossesse' is used uniformly; on previous mixed terminology, see *infra* text accompanying n. 78.

[78] On current terminology in France, see *supra* n. 77.

A. On the one hand are countries in which more emphasis is placed on the act of *inducing a miscarriage*. In these countries, apparently, the elements of the offense may be satisfied regardless of whether a death actually occurs and regardless of whether a death was in fact intended. The English tradition with its focus on 'procuring a miscarriage' is a primary example of this category.

B. Much more frequent, however, is a result-oriented emphasis, namely on the *killing of the fruit of the womb*. In this context it is not always completely clear:

– whether the event of death necessarily fulfills the objective elements of the offense (as is the case, in Europe, in Belgium, the German Democratic Republic, Greece, Luxembourg, Portugal, Scotland, Switzerland and Hungary as well as in Brazil, Costa Rica, and Mexico and in Iraq and Israel), with the result, to be sure, that a caesarian section that unexpectedly leads to the death of the child could also fulfill the elements of the offense of termination of pregnancy), or
– whether not least in order to shield obstetrical interventions, a premature ending of pregnancy coupled with the intent to kill the fetus must be included as an element of the offense (such as is the case in the Federal Republic of Germany and Austria[79] as well as in Egypt, India, Taiwan and Turkey).

2.5.3   *The varying temporal range of termination: from conception to the end of the birth process*

A *statutory definition* of the beginning and end of pregnancy for the purposes of termination is found in only a very few countries: e.g., the *beginning* is seen in *implantation* in the Federal Republic of Germany, the Netherlands and Luxembourg; the *end* is seen in the *completion* of birth in Canada. Therefore, in most countries, it is necessary to rely on traditional practices. This is true both with regard to the moment at which life is first protected as well as with regard to the transition between termination and general homicide offenses. General homicide offenses may apply (in some cases) during the birth process itself or may not attach until after the process has been completed; the offenses of (late term) termination are correspondingly narrow or expansive.

A. Concerning the *beginning* of the prohibition on termination and, relatedly, the use of measures designed to prevent implantation (such as the 'morning-

---

[79] For Austria, see. D. KIENAPFEL and H.V. SCHROLL, *Grundriss des österreichischen Strafrechts, Besonderer Teil*, Vol. I, 5th edn. (Wien, Manz 2003) p. 240.

after pill,' intrauterine devices, douches) or other means of 'menstrual regulation' such as curitage,[80] the spectrum ranges from consistently strict to self-contradictory to consistently permissive regulations, whereby – as, for instance, shown by a Portuguese law on emergency contraception from 2001[81] – the international trend appears to be in the direction of at least tolerating measures that prevent implantation. Questions concerning the *extrauterine* protection of embryos, which arise with increasing frequency due to modern reproductive procedures, were not the object of the study.

Clear regulation of the *end of pregnancy for the purpose of the offense of termination*, decisive with regard to the transition to general homicide offenses, is also extremely rare. For even in places where the law expressly refers to the *completion of the birth* or where one can infer from the fact that the offense of infanticide attaches 'during' or 'in' the birth that the decisive cut-off point is to be set at the *onset of birth*, uncertainties remain because both the onset and the completion of birth themselves represent a process in which a certain stage or event must be identified as determinative. So far as prevailing judicial and/or academic opinion on this question – apparently rather controversial in many countries – can be identified, essentially the following picture emerges:

- European countries, primarily (such as Belgium, the Federal Republic of Germany, Greece, Yugoslavia, Luxembourg, Austria, Rumania and the former Soviet Union), as well as Iraq refer to the *beginning of the dilating contractions of the first stage of labor*, while some countries refer to the *expulsive contractions of the second, or delivery, phase of labor* (such as the German Democratic Republic, Sweden and the prevailing opinion in Hungary). Even if the decisive stage is not precisely identified, this group includes as well all those countries that refer at least *generally* to the *onset of birth* (such as Bulgaria, the ČSSR and France as well as Argentina, Brazil and Tunisia).
- On the other hand, some countries (such as Chile, Ecuador and Uruguay as well as Canada and Turkey) refer to the completion of birth in a *general* way. Most frequently, however, a still more specific event within the completion phase is named: mainly the *beginning of the departure from the mother's body* (as in England, Italy and Portugal as well as Costa Rica and Mexico) or the *partial departure from the mother's body* (as in India and Japan), while other countries fix the transition from termination of

---

[80] See namely the discussion in the Netherlands (see E/K I pp. 1028 ff.).
[81] Law No. 12/2001 of 29 May 2001, *Diàrio da Repùblica*, Part I-A p. 3148.

pregnancy to homicide first at the *complete departure* from the mother's body (as in Ireland, Ghana, Israel and Mali) or even first at *respiration outside* the mother's body (as in South Africa, South Nigeria, the People's Republic of China and Taiwan, as well as in Portuguese jurisprudence).

The overview of the temporal delineations of the termination of pregnancy would remain incomplete, however, if it did not also note certain *intermediate stages* that are found in some countries.

- Examples include the common law 'child destruction' offenses, which normally come into play starting with the increasing *viability of the fetus* in the 28th week of pregnancy.[82] In the Netherlands, too, the killing of a *viable fetus* outside the womb is considered manslaughter (Article 82a of the Dutch Penal Code).

That the Netherlands – a country otherwise considered particularly 'liberal' – has chosen this path to a time-bound limitation of termination to the first two trimesters of pregnancy could be food for thought in the future. This is the case not only because such a regulation takes recent medical advances into account; rather, this kind of regulation can also be seen as an expression of the increasing value of independent fetal viability, a value whose special significance has until now received too little attention.[83]

---

[82] India, too, is comparable, where – although not by means of an independent offense but still factually similar – an aggravating factor is seen in the case of a termination involving a heavily pregnant woman.

[83] See *infra* IV.2.2.2, text accompanying n. 76 f.

DIAGRAM II.1   63

DIAGRAM II/1

'Prohibition Model'

Punishability beginning at	Exemptions from punishment			
	none	statutorily defined	emergency cases	other
conception normative	1	2	3	4
↑ in fact	5	6	7	8
boundary unclear in fact ↓	9 Chile (since 1989)	10 Belgium (old) Ireland	11 United Arab Emirates	12 Egypt
implantation normative	13	14	15	16 Iraq

DIAGRAM II/2

'Non-Graduated Indication Model'
with a tendency towards a *narrower* (n) or *broader* (b) indication
with no explicit restrictions until birth

Punishability beginning at	Exemption from punishment for terminations performed by physicians				Pregnant woman exempt from punishment
	with no (only) counseling	*with* additional *procedural requirements*			
		(only) third-party review	Counseling volun.(CV)/ oblig. (CO) + third-party review		
conception normative	**1** Ecuador: n	**2**	**3** Peru: n South Africa (old): n- b	**4**	**17**
	5 Latin America: n Brazil: n Yemen (new): n Morocco: n Oman: n Qatar: n Sudan (old): n (new): n-b Ghana: b Costa Rica: b	**6**	**7** Chile (old): n Algeria: n Jordan: n Lebanon: n Libya: n Senegal: n South Nigeria: n Syria: n	**8** Poland (old): b/CO	Poland (old)
in fact *boundary unclear* in fact	**9** Argentina: n	**10**	**11** Switzerland (old): n-b Canada: n-b	**12** Israel: n-b CV	Israel
implantation normative	**13**	**14**	**15**	**16**	

DIAGRAM II.3   65

DIAGRAM II/3

'Graduated Indication Model'

with a tendency towards a *narrower* (n) or *broader* (b) indication
with *cut-off points* (W: weeks or FV: fetal viability) during the pregnancy
or at birth (B)

CV/CO: Counseling voluntary/obligatory; in p: in part

Punishability beginning at	Exemption from punishment for terminations performed by physicians				Pregnant woman exempt from punishment
	with no	*with* additional *procedural requirements*			
	(only) counseling	(only) 3rd-party review	counseling + 3rd-party review		
conception normative	**1**	**2**	**3** India: b W 12/20/B Mexico: b C 12/ B	**4** Poland (new): b W 12/FV/B in p CO	**17** Poland
(↑) in fact	**5** Uruguay: b W 12/B	**6**	**7** Kuwait: n W 16/B Zambia: n W 28/B Saudi Arabia (new): n Taiwan: b W 24	**8** Belgium (new): b W 12/B CO Finland: b W 12/20/24/B CV *Italy: med.-eug. Ind. B CV	
		*Italy: b until 12 - CO			
boundary in fact	**9** Japan: b W 23/B	**10** *France: b until 12 CV	**11** *France: med.-eug. Ind.: W 12/B Portugal: n W 12/24/B Spain: n W 12/22/B	**12** Bulgaria (old): b W 10/B CO ČSSR (old): b W 12/16/24/B CO Hungary: b W 12(16/18)20/24/B CO England: b W 24/B CV Australia: b in p W 14/23/28/B CV	Bulgaria ČSFR France
implantation normative	**13**	**14**	**15** Romania (old): n-b W 12/24	**16** Germany (old): n-b W 12/22/B CO Luxembourg: n-b W 12/B CO	Germany until 22 CO

DIAGRAM II/4

Combined (Successive) Time Limit – Indication Model

exemption from punishment for a s*et time period* combined with *indication(s)*
with cut-off points (W: weeks during the pregnancy) or at birth (B)
CO: Counseling obligatory; in p: in part

Punishability beginning at	Exemption from punishment for terminations performed by physicians				Pregnant woman exempt from
	with no (counseling only by physician)	*with* additional *procedural requirements*			
		voluntary counseling + voluntary 3rd-party review	voluntary counseling + obligatory 3rd-party review of ind.	obligatory counseling + obligatory 3rd-party review of ind.	
	1	**2**	**3**	**4**	**17**
conception normative			Bulgaria (new): W 12/B South Africa (new): W 12/20/B		Bulgaria South Africa (new)
	5	**6**	**7**	**8**	
↑ in fact		USA (until 1992): W 12/24/B	Tunisia: W 12/B Yugoslavia: W 10/B	GDR: W 12/B Demark: in p W 12/B Norway: W 12/18/24 Western Australia (new): W 20/B USA (since 1992): CO in p	GDR Denmark Norway
boundary unclear	**9**	**10**	**11**	**12**	
in fact ↓	Austria: W 12/B Romania (new): W 14/B Switzerland (new): W 10/B		Greece: W 12/19/24/B Turkey: W 10/B	Sweden (new): W 18/24/B CO ČSFR(new): W 12/24/B USSR: W 12/B	Sweden Yugoslavia Turkey (until 10) ČSFR USSR
	13	**14**	**15**	**16**	
implantation normative				Germany (new): W 12/22/B CO	Germany: until 22 CO

DIAGRAM II.5   67

Diagram II/5

Pure 'Time Limit' Model

physician-performed termination exempt from punishment
within a set time period, regardless of (additional) indication

upper limit at fetal viability (between 24th and 28th weeks)	no upper limit prior to birth		exemption of pregnant woman from punishment
1	**2**	**3**	**4**
			Netherlands
- beginning at implantation - counseling obligatory - otherwise insurmountable emergency situation	with counseling by physician	without counseling; termination punishable only in terms of resulting injury to pregnant woman	Bahrain PR China South Yemen
Netherlands	Bahrain	PR China South Yemen	

DIAGRAM II/6

Basic Positions on the Regulation of the Termination of Pregnancy

A	C	E	D	B
completely prohibited	prohibition / indication model based on third-party review	emergency-oriented discourse model	exemption subject to time limits and based on self-determination	completely permissible
	Belgium (old)	Belgium (new)	Bulgaria (new)	PR China (?)
	Germany (till 1992)	Bulgaria (old)	Denmark	
	Finland	ČSFR	GDR	
	Hungary (old)	Germany (new)	Greece	
	Ireland	England/Wales	Yugoslavia	
	Portugal	France	Austria	
	Romania	Hungary (new)	Sweden	
	Spain	Italy	USSR	
	Switzerland (old)	Jersey		
		Luxembourg (?)	Turkey	
	Argentina	Netherlands	Tunisia	
	Brazil	Norway	South Africa (new)	
	Chile	Poland (?)		
	Colombia	Switzerland (new)		
	Costa Rica			
	Ecuador	Mexico (?)	USA	
	Peru			
	Uruguay (?)			
	Algeria	Israel		
	Egypt	Western Australia		
	Iraq			
	Jordan			
	Kuwait			
	Lebanon			
	Libya			
	Morocco			
	Oman			
	Qatar			
	Senegal			
	South Africa (old)			
	South Nigeria			
	Sudan			
	Syria			
	United Arab Emirates			
	Zambia			
	Ghana (?)			
	Australia			
	India			
	China/Taiwan			

II.3   PERMISSIBLE TERMINATION OF PREGNANCY

Preliminary remarks

It is certainly possible to disagree strongly both with the terminology used here as well as with the decision to address so-called 'permissible' terminations (II.3) before addressing 'impermissible' terminations of pregnancy (II.4). For not only do these two attributes appear to turn the traditional view of the fundamental 'punishability' of abortion on its head, but the characterization of the exceptions from the prohibition as 'permissible' may give the impression of an undifferentiated 'stamp of approval' for what are possibly mere exemptions from criminal liability.

Despite these and other possible concerns, we have again chosen to take this approach, as we did in the country reports, primarily on the basis of the following considerations: First, it is practically impossible to impart an overall picture of the prerequisites for a termination that is in conformity with legal regulations and that, in this sense, is 'legal' and at the same time to show where the boundary between permissibility and punishability is located without first giving a detailed, comprehensive presentation of all the requirements essential for a termination 'in conformity with the law'. Second, as far as the presentation of the material is concerned, it would appear to be more efficient to discuss first how the citizen (particularly the pregnant woman and the physician) must act in order to avoid coming into conflict with the law before turning to the possible reactions to norm violation.

Moreover, the decision to characterize a termination 'in conformity with the law' as 'permissible' is admittedly the result of a compromise: to refer instead to such terminations as, for example, 'exempt from punishment' would not do justice to those legal systems in which, from the outset, terminations are not punishable or are, at least, justifiable. If, on the other hand, we were to refer to terminations as 'lawful' or 'justified', this might (although not necessarily) lead to the inference of a higher degree of approval than should result from the mere exemption from punishment. Additionally, in consideration of the fact that the number of legal systems that recognize various degrees of exemption from punishment, further-reaching decriminalization or even complete legalization is not insignificant, the term 'permissibility' appears to be the one most likely to express in a way understandable to lawyers and non-lawyers alike that the termination of pregnancy is allowed if the rules are complied with and that the participants in such a termination need not fear state intervention or criminal punishment. Finally, it is important to remember that the controversy regarding the legal nature of the exemption from punishment of a termination has no-where else achieved dimensions comparable to those achieved in Germany – not to mention the emotional nature of the German debate.

Following an overview of the essential prerequisites for and the varying scope of legal terminations (3.1), the various kinds of indications – prerequisites for exemption from punishment in many countries – will be scrutinized in detail (3.2). Furthermore, the consent of the pregnant woman and/or in some cases of other people as well (such as the father or husband) is a fundamental element of the exemption from punishment (3.3). In addition to these substantive prerequisites, procedural requirements are playing an increasingly important role, be it in the form of preconditions such as counseling and third-party review (3.4), be it in the form of special requirements in the carrying-out of the procedure, such as the requirement that terminations be performed by a physician or in a hospital (3.5) or be in through post-termination obligations, such as in the form of documentation, reporting or registration with particular authorities (3.6). In light of this great variety in substantive and procedural prerequisites, the question of what can be concluded with regard to the legal nature of exemptions from punishment arises (3.7). The answer to this question may, on the one hand, be of utmost importance with regard to the possible claims of pregnant women (3.8); on the other hand, questions may be posed with regard to the right of medical personnel to refuse to participate in the termination of a pregnancy (3.9).

3.1   Overview of the essential prerequisites for and the varying scope of legal terminations

As shown by the presentation of the basic regulatory models, virtually no two regulations in the area of the termination of pregnancy are exactly alike (*supra* II.2.4). Thus, it should come as no surprise that the variety of prerequisites that may be required for a termination in accordance with the law is enormous. Nevertheless, if one resists intimidation and is not dissuaded by this diversity from attempting to identify what is typical, the elaboration of various models depends decisively on the criteria that one sees as definitive in establishing the scope of the 'permissible' termination. Although we do not deny the importance of many other factors, for the purpose of traversing a continuum of 'permissible' terminations – tying in to II.2.4., *supra* – , the following parameters appear to us to be determinative:

- the *time* factor, in reference to which both the point at which termination is first prohibited[84] and the period within which the termination of pregnancy

---

[84] For more on this point, see *supra* II.2.4.1.A and *infra* II.2.5.3.

is permissible are measured, that is, the establishment of a window of time within which termination of pregnancy is, for all intents and purposes, permissible;[85]

- the *substantive* prerequisites, such as, for example, the requirement of a particular indication;[86] note, however, that another important requirement, that of consent, does not help us in the task at hand – the elucidation of regulatory types – because it is a basic requirement of all regulations;[87]

- also certain *procedural* prerequisites such as, for example, counseling prior to termination and/or third-party review of the indication by people or panels other than the pregnant woman herself or the physician performing the procedure;[88]

- finally, the *legal nature* of the time period during which termination is exempt from punishment and/or of the reasons given for why permission should be granted may be significant, whereby the emphasis on this criterion is admittedly problematic as only very few regulations explicitly refer to the legal character of the various grounds provided for that may give rise to a permissible termination.[89]

An attempt to classify 'permissible' terminations into various subgroups on the basis of the foregoing criteria gives rise – beginning with the more repressive regulations and proceeding to those that are more permissive – to the picture presented in Diagram II/7 (p. 73), whereby readers interested in a more in-depth discussion are referred to the individual country reports. Furthermore, in viewing this diagram it must not be forgotten that the judgments expressed in it are based principally on the legal regulations in force in each individual country. An assessment of actual practice in these countries is another question entirely and one for which the necessary empirical information is largely unavailable.[90]

Where the permissibility or prohibition of termination depends upon whether the pregnancy has progressed beyond or is still within a set time-period, the question of the *method of calculating the duration of the pregnancy* arises. This aspect is only rarely regulated explicitly, and even more rarely is its regulation unambiguous. Whereas, for example, the last *menstrual period* is determinative for regulations in the former ČSSR as well as for the South African regulation of 1996, in other countries (such as France, Yugoslavia and Taiwan) the *mo-*

---

[85] On this point, see also *infra* II.2.4.2.C, D.

[86] For more on this point, see *infra* II.3.2.

[87] But regarding certain variations, see also *infra* II.3.3.3.

[88] For a more detailed breakdown, see *infra* II.3.4.

[89] For more on this point, see *infra* II.3.7.

[90] For more on this point, see *infra* III.1.

ment of fertilization is considered determinative, although it is not clear how this moment is to be pinpointed. Some countries (such as Federal Republic of Germany, Sweden and Poland) that rely on the moment of fertilization seek to solve this dilemma by calculating back to the last *menstrual period*. In contrast, Bulgaria and Hungary look to the point in time at which the 'pregnancy can be established objectively,' certainly a later stage in the process, whereby, again, it is not clear how this stage is to be pinpointed.

3.2 **Indications**

3.2.1 *Significance and terminology*

In countries where the termination of pregnancy is not simply permitted within a certain time period (as it is by the extreme time-limit regulations in Bahrain, South Yemen and the People's Republic of China[91]) or its permissibility is not merely dependent upon compliance with certain procedural requirements (as it is in the Netherlands[92]) but where exemption from punishment requires – at a minimum – the presence of a conflict, we are dealing with at least a partial 'indication regulation'. This is absolutely clear with regard to the regulations of the 'non-graduated' and 'graduated' indication models[93] in which the relevant laws expressly list the circumstances under which a pregnancy can be terminated legally. But even when there are no express grounds for exemption from punishment, as in the 'prohibition model',[94] a kind of 'unwritten' indication regulation can be seen in the possibility of calling on general grounds of justification or excuse. On the other hand, where termination is permissible for a certain period of time and where, after that period has passed, it is still permissible under certain conditions (as in the 'successive time-limit – indication model'[95]) the at least partial indication-character of the model cannot be denied.

In light of this situation, it is not surprising, from a terminological perspective, that an indication model may exist even if the model is not explicitly referred to as such. Rather, an indication model exists if, in addition to a set time limit or to other more procedural requirements (such as, for example, the requirement that the termination be performed by a physician), the permissibility of termination depends upon the presence of certain 'substantive' grounds. In

---

[91] See *supra* II.2.4.2.B.

[92] See *supra* II.2.4.2.D.

[93] See *supra* II.2.4.2.B.

[94] See *supra* II.2.4.2.A.

[95] See *supra* II.2.4.2.C.

DIAGRAM II.7   73

Diagram II/7

Grouping of Countries According to the Type and Scope of Permissible Terminations

Indication-based exceptions from the prohibition on termination			
more narrow regulation		*more broad regulation*	
beginning at conception	*beginning at implantation*	*beginning at conception*	*beginning at implantation*
A Algeria, Jordan, Kuwait, Lebanon, Libya, Zambia, Syria, Senegal, South Nigeria, South Africa (old), Chile, Peru	**C** Luxembourg, Portugal, Romania, Spain (old)	**A** Belgium (new), Finland, Italy, Poland (old), India, Mexico, Taiwan	**C** Germany (old), England, France, Hungary, Switzerland (old), Egypt, Israel, Australia, Canada
B Morocco, Oman, Qatar, Sudan (old), Brazil	**D** Belgium (old), Ireland, Iraq, United Arab Emirates, Argentina	**B** Ghana, Costa Rica, Ecuador, Uruguay	**D** Japan

with ↓ procedural requirements ↑ without

Exemption from punishment for a set time period combined with indication-based exceptions from punishment			
more narrow regulation		*more broad regulation*	
beginning at conception	*beginning at implantation*	*beginning at conception*	*beginning at implantation*
A Tunisia	**B** Bulgaria CI, ČSSR (old) CI, Germany (new), Greece, USSR (old) CI, Turkey CI, Switzerland (new)	**C** Denmark CI, GDR CI, Yugoslavia CI, Norway CI, USA CI, South Africa (new)	**D** Sweden CI
			E Austria

with ↓ procedural requirements ↑ without

Exemption from punishment for a set time period with no indication-based restrictions	
with procedural requirements	*without procedural requirements*
A Netherlands	**B** Bahrain, PR China, South Yemen

CI = preclusion of termination in the presence of a counter-indication

fact, in the language of the law, the characterization of grounds for termination as 'indications' is rare (as exceptions, see, for example, the former regulations of Bulgaria, Poland and Hungary) since legislatures are generally satisfied simply by describing the ground for termination and do not see the need for giving these grounds a special name. This lack of terminology is so extreme that in many countries a term comparable to 'indication' is nowhere to be found, not even in the relevant literature. Even authors writing in Romance languages and in English are frequently stymied by the term 'Indikation' – which, in the meantime, has established itself in the German-speaking world – despite the fact that the term shares a Latin root with and is spelled practically the same as the word 'indication', which appears in their own languages.

Yet another comment concerning the German use of the term 'indication' is appropriate at this point: Whereas the underlying perception of the German observer might well be influenced by the constitutional debate concerning the new regulation embodied in the Act to Aid Pregnant Women and Families [*Schwangeren- und Familienhilfegesetz*] of 1992, it might also be influenced by the fact that, in Germany, the indication regulation mandates the existence of certain substantive grounds for termination and also provides for the prior ascertainment and subsequent judicial scrutiny of these grounds.[96] This approach is neither compelling nor is it common, as quite a few regulations outside Germany – as further comparison will show – do not address the formal side of an indication at all. In order to preserve the impartiality of this comparison and to prevent it from being compromised by a particular national perspective, the following remarks will concentrate first on the substantive legal issues surrounding the factual grounds for termination; the procedures for ascertaining these grounds and/or for reviewing them will be addressed separately.[97]

3.2.2 *Recognized indications: from life-threatening risk to reduced standard of living*

Our first goal is to present a general overview of the grounds typically recognized for the termination of pregnancy.[98] The itemization used in this process, based as it is on the usual breakdown in Germany, is admittedly not unproblematic, especially considering the complicating fact that the classifications undertaken here often do not simply follow from the letter of the law, without

---

[96] See *BVerfGE* 88, 203 ff. at pp. 204, 274.

[97] See *infra* II.3.4.2.

[98] On the procedural requirements for determining the existence of an indication in individual cases, see *infra* II.3.4.

more, but rather reflect the situation as it is found in practice, to the extent that it is known. Keeping this in mind,

- the *'medical' indication* comprises cases in which termination is permitted on account of risks to life or health, whereby this category can be further subdivided into the 'vital' indication (which only recognizes life-threatening risks) and the willingness to consider (only) 'physical' and/or (also) 'mental' risks,
- the *'medical-social' indication* comprises cases in which familial, economic and other social factors may (also) be considered in evaluating health risks,
- the *'eugenic' indication* comprises cases in which the child and/or its parents or relatives suffer from genetic anomalies, or other embryopathic damage or fears thereof may justify a termination,
- the *'criminological' indication* comprises cases in which the pregnancy is in fact or is suspected to be the result of a forced or otherwise illegal impregnation of the woman,
- the *'social' indication* comprises cases in which termination is permissible on the grounds of untenable social conditions or other conflicts of interest, regardless of proof of either physical or mental risks,
- the *'other' indications* comprise cases in which termination is permissible on the basis of grounds not mentioned above, and
- the *'contraindication'* comprises cases in which a termination cannot be undertaken despite the presence of one or more of the aforementioned grounds because of contrary interests (such as when the risk to the pregnant woman's health is too great or it has been determined that the fetus is already viable).[99]

Since these indications rarely show up alone but rather tend to appear in various combinations, the picture as presented in Diagram II/8 (*infra* p. 89) and supplemented by the following remarks emerges:

The spectrum of recognized indications is extremely broad. Whereas one country may limit termination to a woman whose pregnancy puts her life at

---

[99] Since these definitions – with the exception of the so-called contraindication, which is unknown in (West) German law – essentially emulate the German regulations and are influenced by German case law and scholarship, additional information can be found in the comments by A. ESER in A. SCHÖNKE AND H. SCHRÖDER (eds.), *Strafgesetzbuch: Kommentar*, 24th edn. (Munich, C.H. Beck 1991) § 218a margin No. 41 ff. (social indication) and id., 26th edn. (Munich, C.H. Beck 2001) 218a margin No. 26 ff. (other indications except the contraindication).

risk, another country may allow termination simply if the pregnancy causes a reduction in her standard of living. In this context, geographical and ideological influences are not coincidental: Whereas – as can be seen from Diagram II/8 (p. 89) – the indications become more numerous as well as more liberal the closer one comes to Europe (Db-Eb), a strict interpretation of indications comes more to the fore in those Arab and African countries that are dominated by Islam (Aa) (Ireland is, of course, the Catholic/European exception). The fact that the groups recognizing only medical indications (Aa-Ab) also include European and North American countries does not belie this assessment, for in countries where the indication phase is not preceded, in any case, by a period of exemption from punishment in which no express justification for a termination is required (as it is in the USA and in the former GDR and the Soviet Union), the medical indication is treated very liberally – as, for example, until 2002 in some regions of Switzerland.

As broad as the spectrum of individual indications around the world, so diverse are the various groupings and combinations of indications. Beginning with the classical 'medical' indication (Aa) and its expansion to include the medical social (Ab), there are combinations with the eugenic indication (Ba-Bd), the criminological (Ca-Cc) and the social (Db) up to and including other grounds for termination (Ea-Eb). Even if the boundaries within these combinations are fluid, it can be inferred from the types and diversity of combinations of indications that legislatures are willing to make allowances for certain untenable conditions or interests of pregnant women, at least until the pregnancy has reached a certain stage. At the same time, this reflects the attitude towards unborn life and the position of women in the respective legal systems. In this context, the divergences between various countries become greater, apparently, the more social factors are taken into consideration.

3.2.3 *Particulars regarding the 'medical' and 'medical-social' indication*

After this general overview, this section will focus on some of the typical characteristics and distinctive features of this 'most classical' of all indications for termination of pregnancy.

A. If the termination of pregnancy is to be permissible at all, the first place where concessions will be made is in medically indicated cases. To this extent the 'medical indication' – regardless of individual differences in expression – can be seen as both the historical starting point as well as the *legitimating core* of the exemption from punishment and the exemption from the prohibition of abortion. In any case, this approach appears to be recognized the world over to such an extent that among the countries studied here not a single one was found in which abortion was prohibited, without exception, regardless of the possible risk to the life of the pregnant woman that continuing the pregnancy might pose, even if the exemption from punishment was only achieved by means of such outlets as the exclusion in the 'prohibition model', by statutory definition, of the 'therapeutic abortion' from the abortion prohibition (as in Ireland and in the former Belgian regulation) or the possibility of relying on general provisions of justification or excuse (as in Iraq, the United Arab Emirates and in Egypt).[100]

B. Despite widespread recognition, the *practical area of application* of the 'medical indication' may vary in scope:

- The indication is truly *narrow* only in countries where, limited to the risk to the life of the pregnant woman, only the vital indication is recognized and no other indications are available (e.g., Ireland, Lebanon, Oman).
- In the majority of countries with the medical indication, *physical* and *mental health risks* may also be considered.
- If no other indications are available, the 'medical indication' may be interpreted so *broadly* as to include: eugenic factors (former Soviet Union), social factors (Switzerland [until 2002] as well as a number of Australian states), a combination of eugenic and social factors (Canada), a combination of criminological and social factors (Costa Rica) or a combination of all three of these factors (former GDR).
- A similarly *broad* interpretation of the 'medical indication' can also be found, occasionally, even in countries where the pregnant woman's conflicts of interest may also be accommodated to a great extent by *other recognized indications*: This is the case, for example, in a number of neighboring European countries (such as Italy, Luxembourg, Denmark, Norway and Sweden) as well as in the old and new rules of the Federal Republic of Germany, where in assessing the risks to the life and health of the pregnant woman, effects on the 'present and future circumstances of her life' are also to be considered; this approach can also be found in South Australia, India, Japan and Taiwan.
- It is noteworthy that some countries have established gradations within the scope of the medical indication such that prerequisites for a permissible ter-

---

[100] On these points individually, see *supra* II.2.4.2 and II.3.1. – The situation is, however, unclear in Colombia, where after a constitutional court decision (see E/K III p. 845 f.) the (merely mitigating) criminological indication was expanded to cover cases of non-consensuel embryo transfer and a new provision was added to the law according to which it is possible to refrain from punishment altogether in cases involving 'extremely unusual motivation' (Penal Code [*Código penal*] in the version of 24 July 2000).

mination become *more demanding* as the pregnancy progresses. For example, the 'medical-social' indication, quite broad at the beginning of pregnancy, becomes narrower and narrower so that, as the pregnancy progresses, first mental and then physical risks to the pregnant woman's health no longer suffice until finally termination remains permissible only if the pregnant woman's life is at risk. These kinds of *temporal increments* can be found – with differences in detail – in, for example, Belgium, Great Britain, Switzerland (since 2002), Japan and the USA.

C. The *time-factor* also distinguishes the medical indication from the others.

- On the one hand – this is true for all countries for which in the following discussion of time-related applicability nothing different is stated –, it is usually *open-ended*; in this case it can, generally speaking, provide grounds for a termination all the way through pregnancy. However, there are also *exceptions* to this rule (even if they are few and far between) such as in Romania and Taiwan, where a limit is set at 24 weeks, as well as in Norway, where permission to terminate may no longer be given once the fetus has attained viability (generally at 24 weeks). Sweden has taken a similar approach but has not ruled out all exceptions whatsoever.[101]
- On the other hand, the medical indication, even if applicable, in theory, from the beginning of the pregnancy, generally does not achieve its *practical significance* until – as in the 'successive time-limit model' – the indication-free time period has passed or – as in the 'graduated indication model' – other indications can no longer be considered, which, in most of the countries subscribing to these two models, does not happen until after the third month of pregnancy. Still, reliance upon the medical indication prior to this point in time can be advantageous for the pregnant woman herself as well as for her physician, be it because the procedural conditions are less strict (there is, for example, no counseling requirement for this indication[102]), or be it because a medically indicated termination is considered 'justified' (and thus the costs of the procedure may be recovered) whereas a termination that is exempt from punishment simply because it is undertaken within a particular time period may be denied 'justified' status.[103]

---

[101] Even if limited to cases involving somatic indications, a termination can be authorized in Sweden even after the fetus has attained viability.

[102] As, for example, according to the old version of § 218b para. 3 of the German StGB in the case of a vital or somatically indicated termination.

[103] As, for example, in the new version of § 218a para. 1 of the German StGB; on related follow-up problems, see ESER, loc. cit. n. 28, at § 218a margin No. 1 ff.

3.2.4 Particulars regarding the 'eugenic' indication

As was the case with the 'medical' indication (II.3.2.3), the goal here, too, is solely to point out the typical manifestations as well as occasional unusual features of this indication. The use of the term 'eugenic' is more a reflection of international than of German usage since outside the German-speaking world the indication at issue here is only rarely referred to as 'genetic', 'embryopathic' or 'kindlich' (i.e., conditioned on abnormalities of the child).[104] Indeed, some countries – Japan and Taiwan, to be precise – go so far as to regulate the termination of pregnancy within the framework of 'Laws Protecting Eugenics',[105] thereby giving the eugenic indication top priority.[106]

A. Already as far as its *fundamental recognition* is concerned, the eugenic indication remains in the shadow of the more widely recognized medical indication (see Diagram II/8, *infra* p. 89). However, there are a few countries in which eugenic factors, although not recognized as independent indications, are accorded recognition *within the medical indication*. This is the case in countries such as Egypt, Iraq and probably Canada, as well as currently in the Federal Republic of Germany's new regulation.[107]

B. Once the eugenic indication has been recognized, regardless of whether it has been recognized independently or as a part of the medical indication, the far-reaching uniformity of its *practical scope of application* is noteworthy, although there are several striking variations.

* Whereas the new regulation in Ghana contains an explicit limitation *to physical* anomalies, in all other countries, apparently, so far as the following positions do not yield a different result, both *physical* as well as *mental* anomalies or damage may indicate a termination.

---

[104] On terminology, see also E/K III p. 211 text accompanying n. 8; for a historical overview, see E/K III pp. 73 ff.

[105] The new Turkish regulation of termination, within the framework of the 'Population Planning Law', is similar.

[106] In *actual practice* in Japan, however, the eugenic indication apparently plays virtually no role at all, as more than 99% of all legal terminations are medically indicated. On this point, see also Y. SHIRAI, 'Japanese Women's Attitudes Toward Selective Abortion', in *Studies in Humanities* No. 23 (Shinsu University 1989) pp. 25-36.

[107] Where the 'genetic' indication is now treated as a subcategory of the medical indication and as such is not affected by time limits (for background information and specific details, see ESER, loc. cit. n. 28, at § 218a margin No. 20, 37 ff. with additional references).

- Whereas the vast majority of countries with a eugenic indication look only to the genetic disorders of or damage to the *child* and a legal regulation covering the so-called reduction of multiple pregnancy was recently introduced in Denmark,[108] some countries see grounds for termination in the genetic disorders of the *parents*. In this context, the various approaches taken differ in scope: Whereas in Scandinavian countries (Denmark, Norway and Sweden) apparently only the genetic disorders of the *pregnant woman* signify,[109] in Romania genetic disorders of *either parent* may be relevant, and in the Asian countries of Taiwan and Japan a termination on eugenic grounds can even be indicated on the basis of the genetic disorders of *relatives*.[110]
- The *demographic policy* goals that are undeniably embodied in these broad applications of the eugenic indication and that can be pursued on the basis of other regulations (as, for example, in the former GDR and in Bulgaria) are expressly rejected in other countries, where, in the final analysis, a genetic indication depends upon the *intolerability of the burden on the pregnant woman* of continuing to carry a damaged child (as in England, Greece, Italy and especially clearly in the old regulation of the Federal Republic of Germany).
- From a *technical legal perspective*, most countries are satisfied with a *blanket clause*. However, more or less exclusive *catalogs of illnesses* can occasionally be found, such as in Bulgaria, the ČSSR and Romania as well as in Turkey and Taiwan.
- The following selection of *special guidelines* for determining the existence of a eugenic indication seems to be noteworthy: As far as deficits on the part of the *child* are concerned, the child's ability to support him- or herself in the future is apparently of importance in India. As far as *parental* deficits are concerned, their inability to shoulder responsibility for supporting the child is treated as an indication in Taiwan and Denmark.[111]

C. With regard to the *time factor*, there are, in addition to the mainstream approach, a great variety of other approaches. Whereas in the majority of countries that recognize a eugenic indication, the indication is *open-ended* and continues to be *applicable until birth*, eugenic indications can be found subject

---

[108] §§ 3a, b Law on the termination of pregnancy in the version of Law No. 435 of 10 June 2003.

[109] Also true within the framework of the medical indication in Canada.

[110] n 1996 these indications largely ceased to apply in Japan.

[111] As far as the latter is concerned, it is noteworthy that, despite adopting a nearly identical regulation, Norway did not follow the Danish lead in this regard.

to time limitations as diverse as the 12th week of pregnancy (former Romanian law) and the 28th week of pregnancy (Zambia, South Australia) as well as those subject to graduated *time-bound limitations* (e.g., in Luxembourg, Hungary, Japan and, as far as the outcome is concerned, as of late in Denmark[112]).

3.2.5 *Particulars regarding the 'criminological' indication*

It is important to remember, from a *terminological* perspective, that the use of the term 'criminological' to characterize the grounds for the termination of pregnancy summarized here has no basis in legal terminology but rather is a reflection of common usage in German-speaking countries.[113] In this context it should also be noted that this term is neither the oldest known characterization nor is it one used with complete satisfaction. For although in the cases addressed here the pregnancies at issue are the result of a criminal offense (or at least arose in a criminal context) and thus have some relationship to 'crime', they do not necessarily have anything to do with criminology. However, as previously used descriptions (some still in use in a number of countries today) such as 'ethical', 'moral' or 'humanitarian' are no better suited to communicating the specific nature of this indication both succinctly and comprehensively, we will stand by the term 'criminological', in the meantime the accepted term in Germany.

A. As far as its *fundamental recognition* is concerned, this indication, like the eugenic indication, also remains in the shadow of the more widely recognized medical indication (see Diagram II/8, *infra* p. 89). To be sure, a criminologically indicated termination need not necessarily be impossible even in the absence of express legal recognition, as such a termination would be permissible without further justification in countries employing either the 'successive time-limit-indication model' or the 'pure time-limit model' if undertaken *within the established time period* (as in the USA and in Sweden). It is also possible for a pregnancy with criminal overtones to fall within the scope of a broadly drawn *medical indication* or *blanket clause*; this has been reported in England, Italy and Switzerland as well in Costa Rica and India.

To the extent that the criminological indication has achieved *express legal recognition*, the following picture – taking possible form requirements into consideration – emerges:

---

[112] See § 3 sect. 3 Law on the termination of pregnancy in the version of Law No. 435 of 10 June 2003.

[113] See again E/K III p. 211; for more on the evolution of this indication, see E/K III pp. 75 ff.

- The combination of a *narrow medical indication and a narrow crimino-logical indication* can be found in Brazil, where termination in the case of rape is permissible and legally justified until birth (apparently without any special form requirements), and in Mali, where, in addition to rape, incest is also considered.[114]
- A similar combination, again offering the possibility of termination until birth but this time involving a *narrow medical indication and a broad criminological indication,* can be found today in Argentina and Ecuador and was found in South Africa as well until 1996, whereby the regulation in South Africa posed various form requirements but also offered the pos-sibility of legal justification.[115]
- The combination of a *broad medical and/or other indication with narrow criminological grounds* limited to the first 12 weeks of pregnancy and with additional form requirements can be found, apparently, only in Eu-rope (in Luxembourg, Portugal and Spain). A modified example of this combination (no form requirements and permissible until the 23rd week of pregnancy) can be found in Japan.
- The most frequently encountered combination consists of a *broad medical and/or other indication combined with broad criminological grounds* (as, for example, in Finland, Romania, Hungary, Greece and, Uruguay).

B. As regards the *crime-related prerequisites* upon which termination may be based, countries with blanket clauses (e.g., Turkey beginning in 2005) are less frequent, countries with a catalogue of crimes more frequent.

- In countries where *certain criminal offenses* must be present, the crimino-logical indication may be limited to *rape* (as in Luxembourg, Brazil and Japan), or to *rape and incest* (as in Finland and Romania as well as Argen-tina, Ecuador and Ghana); more frequent, however, is *rape in a broad sense* (as in Spain, Mexico and Uruguay and, until 1995, in Portugal) or – comparable in scope – *sexual offenses* (as in both the former and current German regulations as well as in Norway and, recently, Portugal), whereby in some countries *incest* is also a factor (as in Denmark, the former Yugoslavia and Taiwan), and (as in Israel) the fact that the preg-nancy is the result of an *extramarital relationship* may be grounds for ter-mination.

---

[114] Art. 13 Law No. 02-044 of 24 June 2002 on reproductive health.
[115] The new South African regulation of 1996 introduced a time limit of 20 weeks (sect. 2(1)(b)).

- On the other hand, even if the requisite criminal background has been established, a termination may still be prohibited on the basis of a *contraindication* such as, most importantly, disproportionate risk to the pregnant woman: this is the case in Denmark as well as in the former regulations of the GDR, Poland and Yugoslavia.

C. As far as the *time factor* is concerned, the criminological indication is subject to limits based on the duration of pregnancy more frequently than is the eugenic indication (12-24 weeks), but there are countries in which it remains applicable until *birth*.[116]

D. As far as *form requirements* are concerned, it is not surprising that, given the widespread apprehension that women with unwanted pregnancies could employ devious methods in order to obtain recognition of a criminological indication, some countries have established special procedural hurdles in order to prevent abuse. Such efforts are, however, rare:

- According to the new Turkish law, the procedure must be carried out by a specialist in a hospital.
- In any case, a *criminal complaint* is required in Spain; this requirement was removed in Portugal by the 1995 reform of the criminal code.
- Finland, Mexico, Poland as well as the former regulations in the GDR and Hungary go one step further, requiring an *investigation undertaken by police and/or prosecutor*.
- The strictest requirements – involving both *confirmation by a physician* as well as *corroboration by the district judge* – were found in the pre-reform version of the law in South Africa.

3.2.6 *Particulars regarding the 'social' indication*

Concerns regarding appropriate terminology – familiar from the foregoing discussion – are even greater in this context, as the characterization 'social' is a quite unspecific, collective term for grounds for a termination that are based less on medical factors, eugenic aspects or criminal activities and more on individual or interpersonal conflicts or other untenable familial, societal or (even) economic conditions. The question of whether we should instead refer to a 'general emergency indication', as used to be the custom in light of the Federal Republic's former § 218a para. II No. 3 StGB, is of secondary importance as

---

[116] On this point, see *supra* II.3.2.4.C.

long as it is clear that a 'social' indication, a term that is more common outside Germany, is by no means restricted to 'poverty cases' but rather – except where a narrower statutory regulation is involved – can encompass all kinds of individual or interpersonal conflict. Thus, depending upon the point of view taken, some of the cases presented in the following section as 'other indications' (II.3.2.7) could also have been included here.

A. As far as its *fundamental recognition* is concerned, the number of countries in which the 'social' indication is expressly permitted is small when compared to the indications discussed above (see Diagram II/8, *infra* p. 89). However, it must be kept in mind that social factors are even more likely than are eugenic or criminological grounds to be indirectly considered in the discussion of other indications – primarily the medical-social indication. It is, of course, easier to do without a special 'social' indication in countries where pertinent conflict situations can be accommodated within the framework of a (successive or pure) time-limit regulation; moreover, in such countries, a 'social' indication (although not recognized) may even be accommodated after the established time period has passed by a broadly interpreted 'medical-social' indication as, for example, in the former GDR or, since the reform, in the Federal Republic of Germany.[117]

In countries where the 'social' indication is *expressly recognized*, it never appears alone with the medical indication; rather, it always *supplements* other additional indications.

B. The description of *substantive prerequisites*, particularly difficult when dealing with an indication as unspecific as the 'social' indication, has been approached in various ways. Of these, three methods are of particular interest:

- Most countries are satisfied with a *blanket clause* that refers, as, for example in France and in the new Belgian regulation, to a 'cas de nécessité' or a 'situation de détresse' or to the 'economic, social or familial conditions' of the pregnant woman, as in Italy and, since 1996, in South Africa. Similar formulations are also found in Mexico ('serious and justified economic grounds'), Uruguay ('economic distress'), Denmark, Finland and Norway (significant burden for the woman in light of familial circumstances and support obligations) and in the new Hungarian regulation ('serious crisis in the mother's life'). Some countries seek to simplify the handling of this indication by providing a specific *standard* as, for ex-

---

[117] This is the case under the expanded § 218a II StGB in the version of the Schwangeren- und Familienhilfeänderungsgesetzes (see ESER, loc. cit. n. 28, at § 218a margin No. 26 ff.).

ample, in England and Zambia, where the risks associated with continuing the pregnancy must be greater than the risks posed by termination, or in the old regulation of the Federal Republic of Germany, where the severity of a general emergency indication had to be 'congruent' with a health risk.

- Other countries take the opposite route, instead allowing termination only in *certain cases* such as, for example, if the woman is unmarried, divorced or widowed or has a living child and is older than 40 (Bulgaria) or, as in Romania, if the woman has borne five children that she herself is raising.

- Yet other countries have tried a middle-of-the-road approach in which a *blanket clause is supplemented or clarified with examples:* The former is the case in Finland, where in addition to the blanket clause-like consideration of the life circumstances of the woman and her family, it is considered a special ground for termination if the woman has not yet reached the age of 17 or has passed the age of 40 or if she has already borne four children. Even more detailed are the former Czechoslovakian and Hungarian regulations, with their catalogue-like listing of grounds related to the pregnant woman's age, marital status, living situation and number of children.[118]

- As far as the *factors that may be considered* are concerned, the living conditions of the pregnant woman are of primary importance: comparable to consideration of the 'present and future circumstances in the life of the pregnant woman' as in the regulation of the Federal Republic of Germany (§ 218a para. 2 StGB) are the regulations in Denmark, Finland, Norway, Luxembourg and Poland as well as in South Africa since 1996. In addition to the interests of the pregnant woman herself, *familial* circumstances are also mentioned occasionally (in Denmark, Italy, Norway and in Taiwan), whereby the *children* are, on occasion, specifically mentioned (as in England and Mexico). The differences in these regulations may, however, be quite striking: Whereas Denmark, for example, focuses its attention on the support of older children, in Norway, a neighboring country, just the opposite is the case, with the uncertainty regarding the support of the expected child serving as the benchmark. Even the relevance of *economic* factors – which other countries are loathe to mention – is expressly stated in some countries (Italy, Mexico and Uruguay).

C. As far as the *time factor* in concerned, the scope of application of a statutorily recognized 'social' indication is usually limited in time. Whereas in a few countries is permissible only until the 10th week of pregnancy (as in Bulgaria

---

[118] On this point, see also the listing of 'other' indications *infra* II.3.2.7.

and until 2001 in France), such an indication can, as a rule, be applied until week 12 (as in Finland, France [since 2001], Italy, Romania, Hungary as well as the former regulation of the Federal Republic of Germany and the current Belgian regulation). In a few countries the indication is permissible for a longer period, such as in Norway (18 weeks), in South Africa since 1996 (20 weeks) and in England and Sweden (until viability of the child, set at 24 weeks). Occasionally, as in the Russian Federation, there is a kind of graduated approach whereby, in the weeks between the limit set by the time-limit model and the 22nd week, a detailed list of social indications applies.[119] In countries with a 'non-graduated indication regulation', as used to be the case in Poland, termination is possible, at least theoretically, up until birth.[120]

D. As far as *formal criteria* are concerned, requirements for the ascertainment of a 'social' indication are rarely tougher than for the ascertainment of other indications. The former Polish regulation was a notable exception, however; there, if a woman's statements concerning the circumstances of her life seemed to be manifestly untrue, and termination depended upon these circumstances, the physician was required to engage in an exacting *inquiry* into her life circumstances.[121] Furthermore, for some countries, of all the indications, the 'social' indication is the one whose ascertainment belies third-party assessment: similar to Polish regulations (now repealed), where the practically unreviewable '*self-assessment* of the pregnant woman' was determinative in establishing the presence of a social indication, the Italian regulation, too, is satisfied if a pregnant woman 'invokes' untenable circumstances, and does not subject this decision to yet another, formal indication determination.

3.2.7   Overview of 'other' grounds recognized for the termination of pregnancy

Finally, while the indications discussed above could be described, in some sense, as 'classical,' since – despite variations in their level of acceptance around the world – each embodies a particular type of indication, still other time-bound

---

[119] See Decree No. 485 of 11 August 2003 on the list of social indications for induced termination of pregnancy.

[120] Unless, that is, it would appear from the weighing-up process that a time limit would be appropriate (see ESER, loc. cit. n. 28, at § 218a margin No. 34, 42); in this regard see Norway, where the requirements for authorization become more difficult to fulfill as the pregnancy progresses (E/K I p. 1422).

[121] See *infra* II.3.4.2 describing other requirements that may have to be fulfilled in order for an indication to be recognized.

grounds for terminating a pregnancy exist, which, although they may display a certain affinity to one or another of the 'classical' indications, are themselves too diverse to be summarized within a single indication type. It is also characteristic of these grounds, in some countries, that they can be considered within the framework of other indications, although this is generally not clearly stated in the statutory text of the indications. The following criteria from a small circle of countries are presented here despite the fact that, under certain circumstances, they may already be an element or contributing factor of another, 'classical' indication. No claim is made as to their comprehensiveness:

A. Termination grounds in the *person of the pregnant woman*

- Especially young age (<14-17 years), occasionally also seen as an element of the criminological indication (e.g., Austria, Finland, Israel),
- More advanced age (>35-45 years) or the pregnant woman herself thinks she is 'too old' (e.g., Hungary, Finland, Israel, previously Romania, Sweden),
- Serious physical and/or mental illnesses/infirmities (e.g., Norway, Canada),
- Inability to rear children (e.g., Denmark, Finland) or
- Pregnancy while still breastfeeding another child (Saudi Arabia, former North Yemen).

B. *'Illegitimacy' of the expected child,* e.g., on account of incest (Israel, formerly South Africa), extramarital sex (Israel), violation of a marital prohibition (Taiwan) or involuntary artificial insemination (parts of Mexico).

C. Unusual *social factors* such as the marital status of the pregnant woman (single, divorced or widowed), the number of children (formerly in Bulgaria in combination with the advanced age of the pregnant woman), housing problems or familial disruption, or even the extended imprisonment of the pregnant woman or her husband or his long-term military or police service (formerly in Hungary).

D. The pregnant woman's status as a *foreigner* (formerly in Bulgaria).

3.2.8   *Contraindications*

A termination of pregnancy, in principle permissible, may, under certain circumstances, be prohibited by a so-called contraindication. This is the case– as can be seen in Diagram II/7 (*supra* p. 73) – in countries with time-related exemptions of punishment.

As far as the *kinds of grounds* are concerned that can stand in the way of a termination, the most frequent are *general clauses* of a type that prohibit a termination if it itself poses a serious risk to the health or life of the pregnant woman (this is the case in Denmark, Norway and Sweden as well as in the former ČSSR, GDR and Yugoslavia, and in Turkey and the USA). Some countries, such as Bulgaria and the former Soviet Union, have special *catalogues of illnesses*.

In some countries, in addition to or instead of the above limitations, a *termination in the previous 6-12 months* may prevent a subsequent termination (e.g., former GDR, ČSSR).

3.3 Consent

If there is one sound and uncontested prerequisite for the permissibility of termination of pregnancy (apart from the relatively modern requirement for performance by competent medical personnel), it is the necessity that the pregnant woman consent. Nevertheless, this presumably self-evident rule is neither everywhere clearly manifested in the law – indeed, the consent requirement can be derived indirectly from the general rules governing medical treatment by physicians- nor does the concept apply without exception. In addition, in this area numerous written and – perhaps even more common – unwritten prerequisites of both a substantive and a procedural nature have developed as have various limitations on the scope of consent itself. There are also rules to be found that regulate third-party (surrogate) consent when for one reason or another the pregnant women herself cannot be asked. Since the question here is admittedly most often less a matter of principle than of the particular details involved, the following comparison can be limited to a discussion of the basic positions with regard to the consent requirement (II.3.3.1), its essential prerequisites (II.3.3.2), special issues that arise in the case of minors and mentally incompetent pregnant women (II.3.3.3) and finally to a discussion of whether, in addition to the pregnant woman's consent, the consent of the husband, father or other third party should be required (II.3.3.4).

3.3.1 *Consent of the pregnant woman: significance – substitutability*

A. In most countries, we find an *explicit requirement of consent*. Some, though not all, of the countries with comparatively detailed consent regulations are Portugal, Turkey and (in particular for minors) Italy, as well as in unusual form

DIAGRAM II.8   89

Diagram II/8

Recognized Indications[1]

Aa[2]	(only) medical			Ab	medical-social
(only) threat to life	(also) threat to health phys.	psych.			(also) consideration of social, and some cases eugen. and/or crim. factors
Belgium (old)→ B[3]	Morocco→ B	Algeria→ B		Switzerland (old)→ B	
Ireland→ B	Jordan→ B	South Nigeria→ B		Egypt→ B	
Lebanon→ B	Peru→ B	Chile (old)→ B		United Arab Emirates→ B	
Libya→ B		Australia (partly)→ B		Costa Rica→ B	
Omar→ B				Australia (partly)→ B	
Qatar→ B		USA (TIM)[4]→ B		Canada→ B	
Senegal→ B				GDR (TIM) → B	
Sudan (old)→ B				Switzerland (new) →(TIM) B	
Syria→ B				USSR (TIM)→ B	

Combinations

Ba	med.+eugen.	Bb	med.+eugen.+crim.	Bc/Da	med.+eugen.+soc.	Bd	med.+eugen.+other
Iraq→ B		Luxembourg→ 12 W/B		Belgium (new)→·12 W/B		Zambia→·28 W/B	
Kuwait→·16 W/B[5]		Portugal→ 12/16 W/B		England→·24 W/B			
India→·12/20 W/B		Spain→ 12/22 W/B		France→·10 W/B		Austria (TIM)→ 12 W/B	
Australia (partly) → 14/23 W/B		Botswana→ 16					
		Ghana→ B					
Tunisia (TIM)→ 12 W/B		South Africa→ B					
Turkey (old)(TIM)→ 10 W/B		Japan→ 23 W/B					
		Taiwan→·24 W/B					
		Mexico (partly)→·12 W/B					
		Greece (TIM)→ 12/19/24 W/B					
		Yugoslavia (TIM)→·10 W/B					
		Turkey (new)(TIM)→·10/20 W/B					

Ca	med.+crim.	Cb	med.+crim.+soc.	Cc	med.+eugen.+crim.+other
Argentina→ B		Poland (old)→·/B		Israel→ B	
Brazil→ B		Uruguay→ 12 W/B			
Ecuador→ B					
Germany (new) (TIM)→ 12 W/B					

Db	med.+eugen.+crim.+soc.	Ea	med.+other	Eb	med.+eugen.+crim.+soc.+other
Germany (old)→·12/22 W/B		Sweden (TIM)→ 12/18/24 W/B		Finland→·12/20/24 W/B	
Italy→·12 W/B					
				Romania→·12/24 W/B	
South Africa (new)→·12/20 W/B				Hungary→·12/16/18/20/24 W/B	
				Bulgaria (TIM)→ 10/20 W/B	
				ČSSR (TIM)→ 12/24 W/B	
				Denmark (TIM)→ 12 W/B	
				Norway (TIM)→ 12/18/24 W/B	

---

1   This overview shows only those indications that are independently recognized; however, this does not preclude the consideration - within such an indication - of factors other than those expressed by the indication s primary characterization. This is, for example, the case for the group designated (Ab).

2   The positions Aa, Ab, etc., refer to the corresponding groupings explicated in the text.

3   → B = Applicability of this indication until birth (B) in the sense of the prohibition model (PM; see II.2.4.2.A) or the non-graduated indication model (NIM; see II.2.4.2.B).

4   → W-G = applicability of the indications only until quoted week (W) or continued applicability under more narrow circumstances until the next cut-off point (W) or until birth (B) in the sense of the graduated indication model (GIM; see II.2.4.2.B).

5   TIM = on the basis of a combined (successive) time-limit indication model (see II.2.4.2.C), indication applicable until the quoted week (W) or under more narrow circumstances until birth (B).

Brazil[122] and the former South Yemen. Countries where requirements for consent are discussed in detail are Germany and Switzerland, Costa Rica, Mexico and the USA.

Whereas the consent requirement remains a fundamental principle of permissible terminations, a great variety of *exceptions or at least of limitations* can be found:

- In certain *medically extreme situations,* usually described in greater detail, the consent of the pregnant woman is regarded as completely unnecessary and no provision is made for any kind of surrogate consent. This is the case, for example, with the so-called 'vital' indication in Spain and in the regulations of the former German Democratic Republic and in Iraq, Morocco, Qatar and Turkey; furthermore, in Brazil termination of a pregnancy against the will of the pregnant woman may even be justified in cases where her life is endangered. In some countries, as in Sweden, Southern Nigeria and Kuwait, the consent requirement may even be dropped in order to prevent damage to *the woman's health.* The possibility of a termination independent of consent in emergencies and *cases of extreme urgency* has a similar scope in Senegal and (until 1996) in South Africa. Whereas in these cases, however, the presumed interests of the pregnant woman are of primary importance, demographic considerations may also play a role, at least in places where the consent of the pregnant woman is regarded as dispensable in cases involving *eugenic indications,* as well; this is apparently the case in Ghana.[123]

- In some countries, consent of the pregnant woman is not considered indispensable under the conditions mentioned above, but rather the requirement can be *satisfied by alternative means,* in particular by the *presumed consent of the pregnant woman.* In some countries, although few in number, this is even established by law, as for example in Austria in the case of the vital indication and in Portugal with regard to both the vital as well as the strict medical indication, whereby in Portugal the circumstances from which the presumption of consent is derived must be contained in the physician's statement.[124] Otherwise, it is clear that consent can not be presumed when the

---

[122] The limitation of the consent requirement to the criminological indication can probably be explained by the fact that no need for consent is seen for the (sole remaining) case of the vital indication (see also *infra* text at B.).

[123] A conclusion drawn from the fact that the consent of the pregnant woman is expressly required in the context of both criminologically as well as medically indicated terminations, but in the case of eugenically indicated terminations there is no such requirement The same is also presumed in some parts of Mexico on account of an inadequate regulation.

[124] This regulation was dropped as part of the total revision of the Portuguese Penal Code (15 March 1995). It is part of the regulation concerning presumed consent (now: Art. 142 L.4).

pregnant woman has expressly stated her opposition to termination. Reports to the contrary come only from Turkey, where even the fundamental objection of the woman is apparently not generally regarded as relevant.

B. Finally, an *alternative to the consent of the pregnant woman* also comes into play when the decision can be made on her behalf by her legal representative or other substitutes. This comes into play primarily when the pregnant woman lacks the capacity to consent due to minority and/or limited mental competence.[125]

3.3.2   *Essential prerequisites of consent*

Of the wide range of individual criteria that could be applied to ascertain the validity of consent, the following will discuss only three particularly fundamental issues: The capacity to consent (A), the information necessary for informed consent (B) and the form of the declaration of consent (C).

A. There are essentially four basic models for judging the *capacity to consent*:

- A small group of legal systems has chosen to rely on a *set age limit*. For example, several countries simply require that the pregnant woman have reached the age of majority, while in other countries the law itself contains a reference to a particular age (e.g., 18 years in the previous regulations in Poland or – even younger – 16 years in the Australian Northern Territory and 14 in New South Wales).
- In contrast, another group of countries forgoes any age-based determination whatsoever and instead relies on the *individual capacity to consent* in each particular, concrete case (as, for example, in Austria, Sweden and Switzerland).
- A mixture, to some extent, of the two models mentioned above is found in countries where more or less *set age limits are combined with flexible criteria*: an example of this is when the age of majority is the fundamental criterion but the capacity to consent can be ruled out if certain mental or psychological disorders are present (as is the case in Taiwan or Turkey).
- Even more flexible is the approach found in those countries that rely primarily on inherent abilities of reasoning and judgment and that, by referring to various *age groups,* merely attempt to simplify the process of practical application; this is, for example, the case in England, where the

---

[125] Details concerning this special problem appear *infra* II.3.3.3.

statutes recognize age limits at 16 and 18 years of age, and in the Federal Republic of Germany, according to prevailing opinion, where limits at 14 and 16 years of age are recognized.[126]

B. As far as the *information* required for the procurement of valid consent is concerned, as yet many countries appear to be rather 'unenlightened' – after all, there are comparatively few legal systems in which the duties of the physician are mentioned at all. To the extent that these duties are mentioned, efforts can be observed, primarily in European countries with reformed laws, not to limit the information provided by physician to purely medical issues, but also to include the discussion of alternatives to the termination of pregnancy and/or future birth control. The group of countries where this is the case includes, in addition to the Netherlands, the Federal Republic of Germany and (since 1990) Belgium.

C. As far as the form of information is concerned, *specific* requirements are for all intents and purposes non-existent; such requirements exist, at most, with regard to consent. In this context, the Federal Republic of Germany is one of a relatively small number of countries that accept any form of consent, including oral consent; elsewhere, consent must at least be in writing and often a particular written form is required.

3.3.3 *Special problems associated with pregnant women who are underage and those with limited mental/psychological competence*

A comparatively varied picture emerges with regard to the special problems concerning pregnant women who are minors or who have limited mental/psychological competence. Speaking in purely geographical terms, the awareness of the problem appears to be particularly acute in Europe. This also holds for the Federal Republic of Germany, which is nevertheless somewhat behind some of its neighbors inasmuch as there is still absolutely no legal regulation of these questions in this country. In terms of practical application, Germany is not among those countries that use a sort of 'consensus model' to determine cumulative consent on the part of the pregnant woman (who is underage or otherwise limited in her capacity to consent), as in Denmark and Italy. Even less can Germany be counted among those countries that allow the will of the pregnant woman to prevail regardless of her age (as in the Netherlands and apparently in Sweden as well); rather, it is one of a shrinking number of countries that allow

---

[126] According to the South African regulation of 1996, a pregnant minor *should* consult with her parents, guardian, family members or friends.

for surrogate consent by a legal representative if the pregnant woman lacks the capacity to consent and that do not differentiate among pregnant women who are underage and those whose capacity is limited in another way – in contrast to a number of other countries. Significantly, however, the Federal Republic is among the countries in which the introduction of a veto right for the pregnant woman, depending on the individual degree of maturity and capacity for insight, is at least under discussion.

3.3.4 *Rights of the partner to participate in decisions on termination – involvement of the woman's social milieu*

To the extent that we are concerned here with the degree to which other parties, in addition to the pregnant woman capable of consent, can participate in the decision on termination of pregnancy, we naturally do not mean the physician or any of the personnel participating in the termination procedure nor do we mean any of the authorities who may have a role in determining whether the termination is permissible. Rather, we refer only to the question of the degree to which other parties from the social milieu of the pregnant woman, such as the husband or father of the child, can make decisive contributions to the decision-making process. Here, three basic approaches – differing with regard to the degree of participation – can be distinguished:

A. One of the most extensive forms of participation occurs when the express *consent of the partner* or other third party is required in addition to the consent of the pregnant woman in order to terminate a pregnancy.

- Such an extensive concurrent right to decide on the part of the husband or father of the child – with the corresponding encroachment on the pregnant woman's right to self-determination – is found only outside of Europe and even then only with certain limitations. The most extreme case is presented by Japan, where the law requires the consent of the husband or, in the case of a '*de facto* marriage,' the consent of the father of the child, naturally with the exception of the criminological indication (i.e., where the pregnancy is the result of a rape). Similarly, in Turkey – where interests of the husband must be respected primarily by virtue of his *status* – the consent of the husband is still required, whereby this requirement has been the subject of vehement criticism. The same is true in Kuwait, Morocco, Syria and Saudi Arabia (with differences in detail), although in these countries the termination of pregnancy is out of the question except in cases of strict medical indication, and in Jordan, which restricts third-party consent to those cases where the pregnant woman herself cannot write or speak. Other interests, i.e., *familial* interests, appear to take priority in Lebanon, where in addition to the husband, relatives also have the right to object to a termination; the physician can apparently ignore such objections only in cases of a vital indication.

- In contrast to these legal systems, we find, in the meantime, an almost equal number of countries that expressly *reject* this type of full, concurrent right of the husband and/or father to participate in the decision-making process. In Europe this is the case in the United Kingdom, Italy, Austria and in previous regulations in Bulgaria, the German Democratic Republic, Czechoslovakia and Hungary as well as in the Federal Republic of Germany.[127] It is also true for Australia, India, South Africa and the USA and, in the Arab world, in Iraq and (new regulations) in Tunisia. Despite the somewhat unclear legal situations in Mexico and Ecuador, these countries can also be listed here.

B. Instead of a positive consent requirement, participation in the decision-making process can be granted in negative terms through the creation of a *veto right*. A father's right to prevent a termination of pregnancy in this manner appears to have been granted only by South Africa until 1996 and only in cases involving a eugenic indication.[128]

C. The *hearing* appears to be gaining in prevalence: Instead of granting the husband or father of the child a concurrent right to decide that is equal to that of the pregnant woman, thereby de facto rescinding her right to self-determination, the husband or father should be allowed – according to the laws of various countries – to participate in the counseling and decision-making process, the goal being either to allow his interests to be taken into account or to involve him in the development of a feasible alternative to termination. A primary example of this trend is the new regulation in the Federal Republic of Germany, according to which, in agreement with the pregnant woman's wishes, the father and close relatives, in addition to professional counselors, are to be involved in the counseling process.[129] The Netherlands is almost as progressive as far as the involvement of persons from the social milieu of the pregnant woman is concerned. Somewhat less comprehensive is the opportunity to express himself

---

[127] Where this question has already lead to adjudication: see also A. BERNARD, *Der Schwangerschaftsabbruch aus zivilrechtlicher Sicht unter besonderer Berücksichtigung der Rechtsstellung des nasciturus* (Berlin, Duncker & Humblot 1995) pp. 69 ff.; M. v. KALER, *Die Rechtsstellung des Vaters zu seinem ungeborenen Kind unter der Geltung einer Fristenregelung* (Frankfurt/Main, Lang 1997). But see also text accompanying C and D.

[128] The South African regulation of 1996 appears to have put an end to this kind of veto-right of the father.

[129] § 6 III Schwangerschaftkonfliktgesetz.

given to the husband in Italy, Yugoslavia, the ČSSR and Hungary and to the father in Finland and France; the subject is under discussion in Israel.

In this context we should also mention the many years of judicial and legislative efforts in the USA to allow the husband to participate in the decision whether to terminate or continue the pregnancy by means of *notification requirements*. The attempts on the part of several US States to prescribe the notification of the husband by law (the so-called spousal notification requirement) was ultimately rejected by the US Supreme Court in 1992, since such a notification requirement would represent a substantial hindrance and thus an unacceptable, excessive burden on the woman's freedom of choice.[130]

3.4 Procedural prerequisites: counseling – third-party review

In order to complete the portrait of a 'permissible' termination of pregnancy, it is necessary to consider, in addition to substantive and time-bound prerequisites, various procedural prerequisites, as the permissibility of a termination – or at least its exemption from punishment – can be contingent on the fulfillment of more formal requirements. For the forthcoming, detailed examination of these procedural criteria, it was found to be expedient to distinguish among conditions that must be fulfilled *before the beginning* of a termination (such as counseling or determination of indications), those that must be fulfilled *in the context of the performance* of the termination (for example performance by a physician or in a hospital), and those that must be fulfilled *after termination* (such as obligations to document or report the termination). This section will address only the 'pre-termination procedural prerequisites'; the discussion of the 'performance requirements' and the subsequent 'post-termination obligations' will appear in the following two sections.[131]

---

[130] *Planned Parenthood* v. *Casey*, 112 *S.Ct.* 2791, 2826 ff. (1992). This decision was heavily influenced by empirical data concerning the frequency of domestic violence, particularly that occasioned by pregnancy – a circumstance that results in the transformation of a spousal notice requirement into an effective veto-right of the husband over his wife's decision. According to studies relied upon by the Court, in an average 12-month period in the US, approximately two million women were the victims of severe assaults by their male partners. Furthermore, the Supreme Court used this issue as an opportunity to confirm its view of marriage – in line with earlier decisions – based on the Constitution and to reiterate its rejection of the common-law understanding of a woman's role. Accordingly, the marital couple is not an independent entity with a mind and heart of its own, but rather an association of two individuals, each of whom retains a full complement of constitutional rights of 'privacy' – as an 'individual'.

[131] See *infra* II.3.5 and 3.6.

3.4.1   *Trends*

The wide range of variations already evident from the discussion of the substantive prerequisites for consent and for indications is hardly smaller in the context of procedural prerequisites for a permissible termination. Here four major groups can be identified: First, countries with no requirements for counseling or third-party review whatsoever; second and third, countries that consider either counseling, alone, or third-party review, alone, to be sufficient; and fourth, countries that require counseling as well as third-party review. Without going into detail, we can nevertheless *identify several trends:*

A. The older a regulation and the greater its support for a strict prohibition of abortion, the less likely the existence of procedural prerequisites for permissibility, since the implementation of procedural criteria could weaken the strictness of the prohibition. Conversely, the less reliance the legislature places on a criminal prohibition, the greater the likelihood that it will rely on the availability (or even the compulsoriness) of counseling; thus, the 'counseling model' is found primarily in association with reformed regulations. Between these extremes we find, on the one hand, countries with a more traditionally prohibitive stance, whose only established procedural regulation is in the form of a requirement for third-party review regarding the existence of an indication as well as, on the other hand, an increasing number of reform-oriented countries that couple the controlling impetus of third-party review with the motivational impetus of counseling.

B. To the extent that third-party review is required, whether alone or in connection with counseling, the actual manifestation of the requirement is extremely varied: This is true even with regard to the degree to which the procedure itself has been formalized, with the range extending from the complete absence of any special rules at all to regulatory systems with precise specifications governing the evaluating instance (i.e., a physician or a commission) and the procedure to be followed (such as the necessity of an application or the form of the response). Although the Federal Republic of Germany is generally distinguished by a high degree of formalism, this is especially true with regard to the subsequent judicial verifiability of the existence of the indication: While various neighboring countries accept the pregnant woman's own self-assessment and/or the judgment of the physician without providing for any further inquiry, Germany is one of a comparatively small number of countries with regulations that seek to give the (criminal) courts the final say with regard to the existence of an indication. The consequences associated with the requirement for third-party review can also be varied: If no attempt is made to ascertain the existence of an indication and the pregnancy is nevertheless terminated, the termination *as such* remains punishable in most countries. In contrast, in other countries, including the Federal Republic of Germany, there is a separate sanction for the failure to engage in the ascertainment process. Conversely, if the existence of an indication has been ascertained, its very existence, in most countries, is seen as legitimizing the termination of pregnancy. The German regulation, however, does not go this far: in Germany, the existence of an indication is seen as only one of the many factors to be considered by the terminating physician.

C. *Counseling*, required sometimes instead of and sometimes in addition to third-party review, is a comparatively new instrument for curbing termination of pregnancy. Given its newness, the effect on legal policy resulting from the German Federal Constitutional Court's fundamental recognition of the 'counseling concept' is all the more innovative. At present, the combination of third-party review and counseling is prevalent, whereby admittedly the advances made by the 'successive time limit-/indication-model' have pushed the requirement for third-party review further and further back into the later indication phase, while the time-bound exemption during the first trimester of pregnancy or before the viability of the fetus (USA) is becoming more and more dependent on counseling requirements.

To be sure, not all counseling is alike. As further detailed below (3.4.3), counseling can range from a restriction to medical aspects, on the one hand, to the consideration of social aspects, to the facilitation of an ultimately independent decision by the pregnant woman. It can also place particular emphasis on future birth control measures. Methods of counseling also differ from country to country, ranging from complete openness to direct attempts to influence the outcome. As far as counseling personnel is concerned, a trend away from physicians to special counseling centers can be observed.

3.4.2 *A closer look at third-party review and determination of indications*

Regarding the models that require a special third-party review, a number of commonalties and differences can be mentioned in summary, whereby in addition to several general observations (A), six aspects appear especially noteworthy: The transfer of the task to certain persons or bodies (B), the degree to which the procedure is formalized (C), the types of procedures and the methods of decision-making (D), procedures for possible complaints (E), the legitimizing effect of the indication and its determination and, finally, the sanctions in cases where no indication is found (F).

A. *In general* it can be said up front that the varying degree of detail already observed in connection with the substantive prerequisites for permissibility is found in a much wider range in the context of the formal ascertainment of indications. The countries with a comparatively in-depth formalization of the ascertainment process, or where related issues are at least discussed, include the Federal Republic of Germany and the former German Democratic Republic and France, the Scandinavian countries Denmark, Finland, Norway and Sweden, the former socialist countries Bulgaria, Czechoslovakia, Rumania and Hungary as well as Turkey (in Europe), Iraq and India (in Asia) and South Africa and with some reservations Tunisia (in Africa).

Furthermore it must be taken into account that in some countries requirements for third-party review are not uniform for all cases of permissible termination of pregnancy: some countries *differentiate* according to the duration of the pregnancy; others according to the type of indication.

B. Even the question of who is to be assigned the duty of performing the review and what (minimum) qualifications should be fulfilled reveals a broad spectrum:

- *In terms of personnel,* the options found vary from reliance solely on the pregnant woman's self-assessment to reliance on the opinion of the terminating physician to the (probably most frequent) obligatory involvement of a second physician, who is then prohibited from performing the termination, to the transfer of responsibility for the decision to several physicians or to a committee of physicians or even (as was the case in the former socialist countries of Eastern Europe) to a commission of greater or lesser size. In most Scandinavian countries, permission from an official instance is required for certain cases. A law enforcement agency may be also brought into the evaluation process, especially if a criminological indication is involved – as for example in Poland, Spain and Hungary.
- As far as the formal *authorization to determine the existence of an indication* is concerned, the requirement that the determination be made by a physician is usually not further specified, but occasionally (as in Greece, Switzerland [until 2002] and Turkey) an additional qualification depending upon the type of indication is required. Even more extreme was the requirement in South Africa (since repealed) of confirmation by the hospital's chief medical officer of an indication already determined by two physicians.

C. The *procedures* for review and determination of indications are apparently so strongly dependent on national administrative procedures that it is difficult to identify special factors pertaining to termination of pregnancy. In general, the procedure followed will involve the pregnant woman expressing her desire to terminate the pregnancy – directly or via her consulting physician – to the instance charged with making a decision and her being informed subsequently of the decision by that instance either orally or in writing, depending on the degree of formalization.

While in the case of a positive *decision*, the former German Democratic Republic, Denmark and Sweden apparently provide(d) for the immediate transfer of the pregnant woman to a hospital without formal requirements, the course of action when the termination is rejected varies: In the Scandinavian countries, a written explanation justifying the decision to reject is required. In contrast, in the former German Democratic Republic the only requirement was that the negative decision of the physicians' commission be conveyed to the pregnant woman orally and that the decision be explained in a suitable manner; the woman herself, however, was required to acknowledge this transaction in writing.

D. With regard to *procedural methods and the decision-making process*, the extent to which the physician or committee responsible for the review can or must conduct *investigations* above and beyond the information provided by the pregnant woman is of primary significance along with the extent to which other experts can or must be involved. This applies to differing degrees in Finland, Norway and Sweden, for the former socialist countries Yugoslavia, Romania and (in cases of criminological indications) for Hungary as well as for the head of the hospital in South Africa (at least until the new regulation of 1996). If the physician or the committee responsible for determination of indications is required to perform such investigations and at the same time to retain transparency, as is the case in the Federal Republic of Germany and to some extent in South Africa, the physician ultimately functions as the representative of third-party state control. However, on the other hand, if it is within the discretion of the physician to decide whether to engage in investigations above and beyond the information provided by the pregnant woman, final responsibility remains either with the physician or with the pregnant woman, depending on the model. The regulations in Portugal and Japan, which clearly rely on the responsibility of the physician, can probably be included in the latter variant.

E. The greater the legal significance of an indication and the more formalized the determination procedure, the more we could expect to find the *right to submit a complaint* against the non-recognition of an indication. This is indeed the case in that those countries that require an application for the authorization of a termination,[132] with the exception of Romania, all make provisions for due legal process to contest the non-recognition of an indication.[133] If the pregnant woman has no formal possibility to contest the negative decision, she may still be able get around it simply by consulting another physician; this is, for example, the case in the Federal Republic of Germany where no rules have been passed conferring competence in this area on any particular authority.[134]

F. A positive or an inadequate determination of indication followed by a termination may have the following consequences:

- On the one hand, in most European countries a *positive* determination of indication has – at least in practice, if not explicitly – a *legitimizing effect* on the termination; country reports from other areas and especially those from the Afro-Arab region are not clear on this issue.[135]
- As far as the consequences of the *inadequate determination of an indication* are concerned, three major approaches can be distinguished: The strictest of these is when the failure to comply with the required determination process leads to the *punishability of the termination of pregnancy*. This approach, where the positive determination of an indication constitutes a genuine prerequisite for permissibility, is taken in Denmark, Portugal, Spain and Israel as well as – apparently – in Mexico and (until 2002) in Switzerland. The second approach, taken in Greece, apparently allows an inadequate review to go *unpunished* when the indication in fact exists. Finally, in a third approach, the termination of a pregnancy remains legal if, despite the fact that the formal determination of indication is lacking, an indication is in fact present, but the failure to produce an adequate review is *penalized separately*. This approach, where the provisions of procedural control and the termination of pregnancy as such are subject to two separate assessments, can be found in the legal systems of the Federal Republic of Germany, Finland and Italy.
- Although the Federal Republic of Germany was in a small minority as far as the separate penalization of the formal indication-determination process

---

[132] As, for example, in France, Italy, Denmark, Finland, Norway, Sweden (after the 12th week) as well as in the former socialist regulations of the GDR, ČSSR, Yugoslavia, Poland, Soviet Union and Hungary.

[133] Insofar as the country reports of Iraq and South Africa contain no pertinent information on this subject, no claim can be made about how this situation is dealt with in these countries.

[134] See ESER, loc. cit. n. 28, at § 218b margin No. 11.

[135] For additional details, see the comments regarding the 'legal nature' of exemptions from punishment, *infra* II.3.7.

was concerned, it is absolutely alone in viewing the determination of an indication as a mere '*decision-making aid*' for the terminating physician. This is because the German approach, which does not release the terminating physician from taking direct responsibility for the actual existence of an indication even when the reviewing physician has already made a positive determination,[136] has yet to be pursued by any other country.

3.4.3 *Individual aspects of counseling*

As implied earlier, not all counseling is alike. This is evident in that in some countries, such as Austria and Greece, where counseling is a prerequisite for permissibility, all more specific regulation is absent. On the other hand, in some countries counseling plays an important practical role even without legal regulation, as apparently in the United Kingdom, Sweden and Israel as well as in South Africa before the new regulations of 1996. Otherwise, although based on varying legal foundations, we find comparatively informative reports on counseling regulations primarily from the European area, i.e., in addition to the East and West German regulations especially for Denmark, Finland and Norway as well as France, Italy and the Netherlands.

If we attempt to derive a profile of the various manifestations of counseling, the following characteristics appear worthy of emphasis: Content and goals of counseling (A), its manner and procedures (B), the persons and instances authorized to counsel (C), the possible involvement of third parties (D), whether there are time limits that must be observed (E), the type of confirmation and documentation required (F) as well as the legitimization or penalization in the case of completed or omitted counseling (G).

A. As far as the *content and goals of counseling* are concerned, only rarely do we find statements as explicit as the ones found in the old West German regulation, in which the primary goal was continuation of pregnancy, and in the new § 219 StGB of 1995, in which the protection of life is emphasized as part of an effort to support the making of a responsible and conscientious decision.[137] Thus, the following comparison cannot be more than an attempt to distill from the country reports a few of the common characteristics of laws that are occasionally ambiguous. Moving from one-dimensional to multi-dimensional counseling concepts, the following spectrum emerges:

---

[136] The reform of 1995 did not change this construction: see ESER, loc. cit. n. 28, at § 218b margin No. 1 f., 16.

[137] § 219 StGB in the version of 1995; for additional details, see ESER, loc. cit. n. 28, at § 219 margin No. 4 ff.

- Limitation of counseling to purely *medical* aspects, such as the risks associated with the termination or continuation of pregnancy, appears to obtain solely in France (since 2001) and in Bahrain.
- Similarly one-dimensional is the situation in Canada, where counseling is limited to a discussion of *future birth control* and in the People's Republic of China, where counseling is limited to cases involving *embryopathic or medical indications*.
- The combination of *medical and social* counseling is relatively common in the sense that the pregnant woman is to be counseled on social and legal problems of the pregnancy conflict in addition to health aspects as well as on the availability of public or private assistance for pregnant women, mothers and children. Counseling focuses on – and is apparently limited to – this medical/social objective in countries such as Denmark,[138] France (until 2001), the United Kingdom, Italy and – with special regulations concerning the counseling of young women under the age of 16 – in Switzerland (since 2002) as well as in the former socialist countries of Bulgaria, ČSSR and Hungary, in parts of Australia and in Taiwan (whereby in Taiwan information concerning the possible deformation of the fetus is apparently accorded special emphasis).
- In addition to the *medical/social* aspects mentioned above, counseling in several former socialist countries (Yugoslavia, Poland and the Soviet Union) is also supposed to address *birth control* (this is apparently also the case in Finland).
- In addition, it is remarkable that so many countries see counseling ultimately as a way to enable the pregnant woman to make an *autonomous decision*, although this is not always so clearly stated as in Norway, where 'the woman (has) the right to counseling so that she herself can make the final decision.'[139] However, this objective is seldom found alone, but rather it frequently appears in combination with *medical disclosure*, as in Luxembourg and Austria, and even more often in combination with both *medical/social* counseling and counseling emphasizing *birth control*, as in Norway, Sweden, the Netherlands, the German Democratic Republic and Israel; the new regulation in Belgium (1990) can also be counted here.

Despite its different vantage point, it is possible that the USA has recently joined this group as well. This is because state interest in the protection of life is currently given a higher priority than was the case in the 1970s and early 1980s, and thus in the USA, too, elements of medical dis-

---

[138] According to § 8 Abs. 4 of Law No. 430 of 31 May 2000 the physician must expressly offer the pregnant woman counseling in the sense of helping her reach a decision.

[139] § 2 para. 1 sent. 2 Norwegian Abortion Law.

closure and social counseling are coming together to enable the woman to make the most 'informed' and independent decision possible.[140]

In addition, *subsequent counseling*, which can include both post-terminative care as well as assistance with future birth control, is becoming increasingly important. This is true, in various forms, for France, the United Kingdom, the Netherlands and Israel as well as for the new regulations in the Federal Republic of Germany, Denmark[141] and South Africa.

B. Of course, the specific goals pursued can significantly influence the *method of counseling*. The more counseling is meant to encourage protection of life, the more directive it will need to be. On the other hand, the more the pregnant woman is to be empowered to make an independent decision, the more open the nature of the discussion. As far as can be inferred from the country reports, this goal-oriented approach to counseling can be divided into three major groups:

- *Directed* counseling aimed at the protection of life is expected in the former socialist countries of Bulgaria, ÈSSR and Yugoslavia as well as in Italy and apparently in the United Kingdom and, until the new regulation of 1996, in South Africa.
- In contrast, *neutral* counseling is prescribed by the former regulations of the German Democratic Republic and Hungary as well as the Netherlands, Sweden, Israel and (since 2001) France.[142]
- Between these two positions we find the new position (and perhaps even the old position) of the Federal Republic of Germany, according to which *one of the goals* of counseling is to urge the continuation of the pregnancy,

---

[140] In this vein, in *Rust* v. *Sullivan*, 111 *S.Ct.* 1759 (1991), the US Supreme Court upheld federal regulations limiting the granting of federal funds to family planning projects that engaged exclusively in preventive family planning and subjected grantees to a so-called 'gag-rule', according to which they were prohibited from engaging in counseling concerning the use of termination as a 'method of family planning' or from engaging in activities that in any way encouraged termination as a method of family planning (see WALTHER, loc. cit. n. 38, at pp. 46 f.). Subsequently, the political controversy surrounding this regulation led first to exemptions for physicians and finally, soon after President *Clinton* took office in January, 1993, to suspension of the regulation, removal of the gag-rule, and reinstatement of the previously operative regulations governing the funding of family planning projects. According to these regulations, projects are required, in the event of an unplanned pregnancy and where the woman so requests, to provide non-directive counseling on options relating to her pregnancy, including termination, and to refer her to termination, if that is the option she selects. However, projects are not permitted to promote or encourage termination; see 58 Fed.Reg. 7462 (1993).

[141] Law No. 430 of 31 May 2000 (§ 8 sect. 4).

[142] Art. L 2212-4 CSP in the version of 4 July 2001.

but counseling must remain *neutral* with regard to the pregnant woman's forthcoming decision.[143]

C. The type and success of counseling also depends on the persons and instances authorized to act as *counselors*. Depending on whether the goal is to simplify matters for the pregnant woman or whether more weight is to be placed on the neutrality of the counselors or on their expertise, the terminating physician, a physician other than the terminating physician or special counseling centers may be considered. All of these options are found in various combinations in the countries studied here; however, most of the countries exclude the terminating physician from engaging in (obligatory or optional) counseling.

D. The possibility of *involving third parties* in the counseling process can be of particular importance for the illumination of the pregnancy conflict and for the arrival at a universally satisfactory solution. This applies particularly to the father of the child, who in principle bears the same responsibility for the conception of the child as does the pregnant woman; also, the pregnant woman's husband (not necessarily the father of the child) as well as her parents can influence her decision in one way or the other, depending on their attitudes and willingness to help. Finally, other relatives or experts can also support the pregnant woman in the decision-making process. In this context, it is understandable that in a growing number of countries the involvement of third parties in counseling – at least if requested by the pregnant woman – is supported to varying degrees.

E. Any required *waiting period* can be important for the effectiveness of counseling. However, this requirement is comparatively rare, and even when it is used, the time periods employed are not uniform: While Germany considers a three-day waiting period between social counseling and termination sufficient, the Netherlands requires five days, the new Belgian law provides for six days, and in Italy and Luxembourg seven days are required. A seven-day period is also required in France between initial consultation with the physician and termination, and two days must pass between counseling and termination (these two waiting periods may run simultaneously).[144]

---

[143] This expression goal-oriented but open-ended counseling, which is found in no other country, is based primarily on a Federal Constitutional Court decision (*BVerfGE* 88, 281 ff., 301 ff.) and has since been codified at § 219 para. 1 StGB of 1995 in combination with § 5 para. 1 Schwangerschaftskonfliktgesetz (SchKG) [*Law on Conflicted Pregnancy*].

[144] Note that the 7-day-waiting period need not be complied with if compliance would cause the 10-week limit for a non-indicated termination to be exceeded.

F. At the conclusion of counseling, the pregnant woman is presented with a *certificate confirming that she has undergone counseling*. Whereas in the Federal Republic of Germany, content and timing of the counseling certificate are regulated by law,[145] a process that, in the meantime, poses an existential problem especially for Catholic counseling centers,[146] only a few other countries, such as France, Italy and the former German Democratic Republic, have taken a position on these issues. The distinction between anonymous counseling and the presentation of a personalized counseling certificate appears to be unique to Germany. Occasionally – as in Switzerland since 2002 – written information must be distributed.

G. As far as the *consequences* of sufficient or insufficient counseling are concerned, questions arise similar to those concerning third-party review:[147]

- If the counseling procedure is carried out (and confirmed) according to the law, exemption from punishment or even justification, depending on the underlying regulatory model, may result. This kind of 'legalizing effect' is also ascribed to the counseling process when the other prerequisites for permissibility have also been fulfilled in Denmark, Italy, the Netherlands and apparently also in France.[148]
- However, if termination is carried out *without the required counseling*, it can be sanctioned in different ways: While on the one hand in Greece up to now there has been absolutely no sanction for the failure to engage in counseling, which thus goes *unpunished*, in Austria this failure leads to the *punishability of the termination*. The same can be said for the criminal law in the Federal Republic of Germany, now that disregard for mandatory counseling is no longer dealt with as a separate criminal offense, but rather as a constitutive element for *exemption from punishment* under § 218a para. 1 No. 1 StGB of 1995. In contrast, other countries have preferred to take the approach used in case of insufficient determination of indications

---

[145] See on the reform of 1995 § 219 II sent. 2 StGB in combination with § 7 SchKG.

[146] According to a communique from Pope *John Paul II* to the Catholic bishops in Germany on 11 January 1998 (published in 52 *Herder-Korrespondenz* (1998) pp. 122 ff.), Catholic counseling centers should discontinue providing counseling certificates for decriminalized terminations. In the meantime in response to continued papal pressure (see most recently *Frankfurter Allgemeine*, 9 March 2002, p. 41) – the German dioceses have followed this communique. For a personal assessment, see A. ESER, 52 *Herder-Korrespondenz* (1998) p. 178 ff.

[147] See *supra* II.3.4.2.E.

[148] For details on this point, see *infra* II.3.7.3.

by providing for a *special penalty* for the termination of a pregnancy without the required counseling, although the termination may otherwise be in
full accordance with the law. As was the case with previous law in West
Germany, this also obtains in Finland, Italy and the Netherlands.

3.5   Performance requirements: physician – hospital – procedures

Requirements placed on the *performance* of the termination of pregnancy deal
primarily with *personnel* and *institutional factors*, such as the requirement that
the termination be performed by a *physician* (under certain circumstances with
the involvement of additional personnel) and/or is to be performed in such a
way that the termination may not take place just anywhere, but rather only in
certain *medical facilities* (such as hospitals or specially certified organizational
units).

Even more so than with the procedures preceding termination (II.3.4) and
those following the termination (II.3.6), the requirements regarding the performance of a termination of pregnancy are to a great extent dependent on the
medical standard of the country in which the termination takes place. Whereas
in one country a pregnancy may only be terminated by a specialist, in another
country even a general practitioner may be better qualified. Similarly, out-patient termination may be less risky for the pregnant woman in one country than
treatment in the gynecological ward would be in another. Therefore, the performance requirements discussed here may not be considered without taking the
medical standards of the respective countries into account.

3.5.1   *Personnel and institutional requirements*

Although today legal regulations almost everywhere require a termination of
pregnancy to be performed by a physician, some countries regard this risk-
reducing precaution as contrary to their 'prohibition model.' Also, regulations
that require a physician but not a hospital are quite common – primarily in Arab
and Latin American countries – as well as (irrespective of geography and regulatory model) regulations placing requirements on the respective medical facilities. Other alternatives include special regulations on the physician or on the
type and quality of the facility, such as the requirement, on the one hand, of
performance by a specially certified physician, a gynecologist or surgeon, or
the requirement that an anesthetist participate, or, on the other hand, the requirement that termination take place in specially equipped facilities, public
hospitals or institutions capable of providing the necessary post-procedural care.
Occasionally a distinction is made between 'early' procedures and those performed at an advanced stage of the pregnancy, and stricter requirements may

apply to the performance of medically indicated procedures – apparently due to worries about increased risks.

Exceptions to the physician requirement are found primarily in emergency situations as well as under circumstances where midwives are authorized to perform terminations. Although the express requirement that the performance of a termination of pregnancy be technically competent is comparatively rare, the explanation for this absence may be simply that it is taken for granted.

Well-aware that generalization leads inevitably to some loss of precision, the overall picture can be seen as follows:

3.5.2 Requirements concerning performance

Regulations concerning the method as well as the location and time at which a pregnancy is terminated can be of significance for the health risk faced by the pregnant woman as well as for control purposes.

A. As far as the *type and means of termination* is concerned, a great degree of freedom seems to prevail. Occasionally we find special requirements regarding anesthesia (as in Greece and Turkey) as well as regarding the possibility of post-procedural care (as in the law of the former German Democratic Republic and in the Federal Republic of Germany today[149]).

The introduction of the 'abortion pill' (RU 486, mifegyne®) in France, Sweden and the United Kingdom and now also in Germany has led to the need for special regulations aimed at clarifying the scope of application, which is limited to particularly 'early' terminations, as well as for the establishment of precautionary measures against improper distribution of the medication. Also noteworthy is the recent public controversy in the USA surrounding the permissibility of '*partial birth abortions*', which has, in the meantime, led to the introduction of special rules (with indication-like exceptions) forbidding the procedure.[150]

B. The question of whether terminations of pregnancy may be performed only on an *in-patient* or whether they may also be performed on an *out-patient* basis is an important one, as the answer may be of substantial and at the same time ambiguous significance both for the pregnant woman and for the interests of control. This is because while termination on an in-patient basis may guarantee the pregnant woman the highest quality of medical care, this type of treatment may be more time-consuming and may lead to the need for the woman to ex-

---

[149] See currently § 13 SchKG as well as *supra* II.3.5.2.
[150] See The Partial-Birth Abortion Ban Act 2002 (Public Law 108-105) of 5 November 2003 (codified at 18 *USC* § 1531).

plain the matter to members of her social circle (specifically her family or employer). Additionally, while public curbing and controlling interests are certainly easier to realize in connection with in-patient treatment, out-patient terminations may be less expensive for the public health system than the in-patient approach.

It is thus quite surprising that this question is only rarely addressed in the country reports. Occasionally a *phase-specific differentiation* is made, as for example in Sweden and the People's Republic of China; here it will hardly be surprising that early termination (until the 12th week) is usually performed on an out-patient basis while later terminations are performed on an in-patient basis. Instead of such phase-oriented differentiation we also find, for example in Poland, *indication-specific* differentiation between stationary termination in cases of medical indication and out-patient termination in cases of social and criminological indication.

C. The time factor in the form of a *requirement of prompt termination* can also be of importance for the pregnant woman, given the fact that the earlier a pregnancy is terminated, the smaller the associated risk. Thus we find primarily in the former socialist countries that decision-making bodies and physicians must perform a legal termination of pregnancy as quickly as possible. This type of promptness requirement also exists in Scandinavian countries in the sense that in case of approval the pregnant woman is to be transferred immediately to a facility appropriate for the performance of the termination or in case of rejection the request is to be forwarded immediately to the next higher instance. Sweden even attempts to emphasize this concern by anchoring the requirement for immediate forwarding of the matter in criminal law.

3.5.3 *Issues of control and sanctioning*

As already mentioned, medical requirements placed on the termination of pregnancy can also serve state interests in curbing and controlling termination, be it only due to the simple pragmatic fact that the pregnant woman has no alternative than to find a physician for the termination and to turn to certain facilities (in this way placing as many obstacles as possible in the path of women seeking to terminate), be it by means of a policy of selection, in which the restriction to certain physicians and/or facilities simplifies the monitoring process, or be it with the mid- to long-term goal of better ascertaining the reasons for termination of pregnancy in order to improve prevention. There are essentially three ways to achieve such goals:

- *Professional criteria,* according to which – via either the state or professional organizations – only certain physicians are permitted to perform terminations (e.g., Japan, Taiwan).
- *Quotas* on the number of terminations that can be performed by a given physician or facility within a particular period of time or in proportion to other medical operations (e.g., France, Italy and in some Canadian provinces). However, we also find the converse tendency towards approving certain medical facilities exclusively for termination of pregnancy in order to relieve the general hospitals (e.g., Israel).
- *Geographical restriction* in the sense that the pregnant woman for example can only have a pregnancy terminated in the area in which she resides (e.g., former German Democratic Republic, Canada, to some extent also Sweden). On the other hand, such geographic restriction is explicitly rejected as, for example, in Switzerland and, in light of the special relationship between a woman and her physician, in the former Polish regulations as well.

3.6 Subsequent obligations: documentation – reporting – notification

For a substantial number of countries, procedural preconditions such as counseling or third-party review (see above II.3.4) and/or certain performance requirements such as those regarding physicians or hospitals (see above II.3.5) are not seen as sufficient but rather the taking of additional procedural steps after the pregnancy has been terminated is required. Although the scope of these requirements varies, and they are sometimes limited to the internal documentation of the termination, they often include reporting to external authorities and occasionally include other types of notification.

3.6.1 *Scope and goals*

Generally, the tendency is that the fewer the procedural requirements the less likely reporting will be required. Accordingly, we find 'reporting-free' zones primarily outside of Europe, as well as in southern Europe. Thus, documentation and reporting requirements are primarily found in Europe and in countries with reformed regulations: the less restrictive the abortion regulations, the greater the probability of reporting requirements.

The intended *goal* can also differ. Whereas purely internal documentation is primarily concerned with the needs of the pregnant woman, especially regarding the provision of post-procedural care that might be necessary,[151] the docu-

---

[151] These kinds of records can be a source of information for subsequent hospital treatment, as determined in Iraq.

mentation of findings required of the physician can also serve to bring the physician to reflect on the reasons for his or her decision (this appears to be the goal of the detailed documentation requirements in the Netherlands). On the other hand, external reporting requirements are primarily concerned with the state interest in control. External reporting requirements may be undertaken with prevention in mind, in which case they tend to be limited to the identification of the grounds for the termination of pregnancy (so they can be addressed and perhaps remedied);[152] however, they may also be undertaken with the repressive goal of prosecuting illegal terminations of pregnancy.[153] In some countries, as now in Belgium, a physician's refusal to participate must be reported.

A small number of countries (Romania, Switzerland [until 2002])[154] have special notification requirements that apply only to emergency situations in which the otherwise required third-party review could not be performed. To this extent the subsequent notification requirement apparently is seen as an opportunity to make up for the absent third-party review. It may also be used to counteract an improperly extensive interpretation of such emergency situations.[155]

3.6.2   Varying degrees of confidentiality

The range of objectives in requirements for documentation, reporting and notification requirements is perhaps most easily recognized in the degree to which confidentiality is guaranteed to the immediately affected parties. The more this is the case, the greater the interest in the concerns of the affected individual or – in the case of purely statistical reports – in the identification of factors which may lead to or counteract termination of pregnancy. These primarily preventive control objectives can take on more repressive characteristics as the pregnant woman is offered less confidentiality; certainly repression is more of a factor when regulations require that the pregnant woman herself and/or the terminat-

---

[152] As presumably the case in countries where reporting is anonymous or takes place for the purpose of gathering statistics as in the countries listed *infra* at II.3.6.2, which include France, Italy, the Netherlands and Sweden as well as the Federal Republic of Germany.

[153] This is the case, according to the country report, in India; it is also the case – by law – in Zambia. Failure to comply with the requirement under previous law to name both the pregnant woman and the physician who performed the termination could lead to the imposition of criminal sanctions on the physician. In contrast, under sect. 7(3) CTPA of 1996 the name and address of the pregnant woman are no longer to be included in the prescribed information.

[154] See also *infra* II.7.1.

[155] The situation under the Israeli rule governing exceptions would appear to be similar (see n. 156).

ing physician be identifiable. In this context we find essentially two contrasting groups of countries:

- Countries in which documentation and/or reporting is to take place *anonymously* and/or only statistical information is required: This is true in Germany, France, Italy, the Netherlands, Sweden, Spain and under the new Belgian and Swiss regulations, as well as in Uruguay, the USA, Senegal and under the new South African regulation and with some reservations in Israel.[156]
- Documentation and reporting of the pregnant woman's *name* is required in the United Kingdom, Poland, India, Zambia, South Africa (until 1996), Turkey and also in the People's Republic of China. The requirement of subsequent notification in Romania and in Switzerland (until 2002), too, apparently must include the name of the affected party.[157]

3.6.3 *Analysis*

The extent to which goals pursued by documentation and reporting requirements are actually attained is difficult to judge. As far as the *analysis* of the material collected through reporting requirements is concerned, some countries such as Italy and the former ČSSR expressly require a regular discussion and analysis of causes. The basis for such discussions will often be quite shaky, however, since the dark figure in the area of reporting requirements – as in the area of terminations themselves – is probably quite high (as expressly admitted in the Federal Republic of Germany and Poland). In spite of such inadequacies, reporting requirements remain an incentive for factor analyses, such as those already presented in some countries (i.e., the Federal Republic of Germany, France, the United Kingdom, Italy, the Netherlands, Sweden, Hungary, Israel, Japan, South Africa and the USA). However, it seems that more effective use could be made of such instruments of evaluation.

3.7 The legal nature of exemptions of terminations from punishment

As mentioned in the preliminary remarks to this chapter,[158] it can be problem-

---

[156] In Israel, notification must be made to the competent official at the ministry of health within five days if the termination is not performed on the grounds of regular indications but rather on the basis of (enumerated) extraordinary circumstances.

[157] In contrast, the situation with regard to anonymity is unclear in Yugoslavia, Japan and Taiwan.

[158] *Supra* II.3.

atic to refer to terminations as 'permissible', since across-the-board use of this term for all terminations that ultimately are not punished could be misunderstood to mean that these terminations are all justified or even that a woman has a legal claim to such a termination. Although this term has nevertheless been chosen instead of other terms – misleading, perhaps, in different ways – to describe terminations that are not (for one reason or another) punishable, this chapter will not come to a close without some clarifying light being shone on the shadow cast by this pragmatic generalization. Admittedly (to anticipate the result), expectations for this illumination should not be too high. For regardless of the highly disparate levels of discussion, even where only a crude distinction is made between terminations considered 'not punishable' (3.7.3) (or something equally undifferentiated) and those considered 'justifiable' (or something comparable), the dividing line is never completely clear.

3.7.1   Disparate levels of discussion: from disputes regarding constitutionality to indifference

A. In Germany, it has been well known for decades that the question of what it actually means when a termination is not 'forbidden' from the very outset or is not punishable despite a fundamental ban is one of the 'hot topics' of the reform discussion. A first milestone in this debate was reached as early as 11 March 1927 with a decision of the Reichsgericht in which for cases involving a 'medical indication' a jurisprudential 'suprastatutory necessity' in the sense of a ground for justification was recognized.[159]

One explanation for the vehemence and duration of this debate certainly lies in the comparatively speaking highly developed criminal law doctrine in Germany: if in a 'tripartite system' it has become customary to differentiate, on the one hand, between non-punishability due to the failure to satisfy the elements of a crime, exemptions due to justification and those due to excuse and, on the other hand, other (objective or subjective) grounds for the exemption from punishment, and if, in addition, the solution of ensuing questions (such as mistake or participation or issues regarding the reimbursement of expenses) is dependent upon this differentiation,[160] even an ideologically value-neutral 'dogmatist' cannot avoid categorizing the cases of 'non-punishable' termination according to the tripartite system – an undertaking which, to be sure, cannot be

---

[159] RGSt 61, 242.

[160] On the various implications discussed in Germany of the legal nature of the exemption from punishment, see also A. ESER, Schwangerschaftsabbruch: Auf dem verfassungsgerichtlichen Prüfstand (Baden-Baden, Nomos 1994) pp. 88 ff. with additional references.

done without grappling with the legal nature of such exemptions.[161] But perhaps even more weighty than this explanation based on criminal law dogma is the deeper conflict concerning the effect that the 'moral message', which is conveyed by categorizing an exemption from punishment as 'justifying', as merely 'excusing' or as in some other way nullifying the fulfillment of elements of crime or leading to exemption from punishment, has on the public's attitude towards the termination of pregnancy and as a result on the public's conduct. Whereas in its first termination decision (BVerfGE 39, 1) the Bundesverfassungsgericht was reticent with regard to this 'values issue' (one that is affected to no small degree by ideology), in its second termination decision (BVerfGE 88, 203) the Bundesverfassungsgericht declared the legal nature of exemptions from punishment for termination and thus also their categorization in the tripartite system to be a question of constitutional import, whereby the Court listed certain minimal prerequisites that must be fulfilled in order for a justifying effect to be recognized on constitutional grounds.[162]

B. Compared to the German elevation of the question of the legal nature of exemptions from punishment for terminations of pregnancy to a constitutional level, the rest of the world does not seem to devote much energy to this classification problem, if indeed the problem is discussed at all.

The lack of relevant discussion in countries with a 'prohibition model', such as Ireland, Egypt and the United Arab Emirates,[163] is not surprising for if there are no express exemptions from punishment there is no need for a dogmatic discussion regarding classification. There is, however, a similar lack of discussion in numerous countries in which statutes provide for exemptions from punishment for terminations – either on the basis of time limits and/or on the basis of indications. These 'blind spots' are found primarily in Arab-Africa, Asia and America. But in a number of European country reports as well, such as those from Great Britain, Italy, Luxembourg, the Scandinavian countries as well as the former socialist countries of Yugoslavia, Poland, Romania, Hungary and the Soviet Union, the question of the legal nature of exemptions from punishment is not articulated in any depth. The authors of the country reports apparently felt that their statements concerning the exemption of terminations of pregnancy from punishment when the prescribed prerequisites are fulfilled – regardless of

---

[161] For details, see W. GROPP, *Der straflose Schwangerschaftsabbruch* (Tübingen, Mohr 1981).

[162] Such as, for example, clearly defined prerequisites for indications as well as formal procedures for determining their existence (*BVerfGE* 88, 204 ff., 274 ff.).

[163] See *supra* II.2.4.2.A and Diagram II/1 (p. 63).

how the statute is formulated – were sufficient, despite the lack of explication concerning the legal character of these exemptions.

C. Although by no means comparable to Germany, there are a number of countries throughout the world where, it is reported, the statutes are clear with regard to the legal nature of exemptions from punishment for terminations or at least there is a discussion concerning the legal nature of exemptions. These countries are, in Europe: France, Greece, the Netherlands, Portugal, Switzerland and Spain,[164] the former socialist ČSSR and the GDR as well as – especially intensively – Austria;[165] in Latin America: Brazil, Costa Rica, Mexico and Uruguay; in Africa and Asia: Ghana, Iraq, Israel, India and Japan as well as in South Africa until 1996.

D. In light of this largely underdeveloped awareness of the problem and the correspondingly weak level of discussion, it comes as no surprise that there are numerous statutory formulations of exemptions from punishment whose legal nature can only rarely be determined conclusively. This is especially true for countries where, as in the aforementioned cases, due to a lack of relevant information in the country report our only recourse is to the statutory language itself. In essence the following general scenario can be drawn:

3.7.2 *Express declarations of permissibility*

There are, after all, a not insignificant number of countries where the legislature has stated more or less clearly that the termination of pregnancy is not only exempted from punishment or excused if the foreseen prerequisites are fulfilled but rather is 'lawful'. Regardless of one's ethical response to this approach, it serves clearly to assure those involved in a termination that they are acting in accordance with the legal system and that, as a result, their actions are at least

---

[164] In the meantime, monographs on the subject have been published in Spain: see, e.g., J.L. DIÉZ RIPOLLÉS, 'Fundamento y naturaleza del articulo 417bis 4 y su relación con las eximentes genericas', in J.L. DE LA CUESTA et al. (eds.), *Criminologia y Derecho Penal al servicio de la persona* (San Sebastian, Instituto Vasco de Criminlogía 1989) pp. 707-718 and LAURENZO COPELLO, El Aborto no Punible (Barcelona, Bosch – S.P.I.C.U.M. 1990). For commentary on the new Swiss Law, see CH. SCHWARZENEGGER and S. HEIMGARTNER in M.A. NIGGLI and H. WIPRÄCHTIGER (eds.), Basler Kommentar, Strafgesetzbuch II (Basel, Helbing & Lichtenhahn 2003) Art. 119 margin No. 2.

[165] For a more recent perspective, see also on Poland E. WEIGEND and E. ZIELIŃSKA, 'Das neue polnische Recht des Schwangerschaftsabbruchs: politischer Kompromiß und juristisches Rätselspiel', 106 *ZStW* (1994) pp. 213-226 at pp. 215 ff.

'not unlawful'. To be sure, this statement is formulated in different ways and to varying degrees, whereby essentially three approaches are distinguishable:

A. From a dogmatic criminal law perspective, the clearest legal position is in countries where under certain circumstances the termination of pregnancy is expressly deemed by law to be '*lawful*', as in the Northern Territory of Australia (or where one norm refers to another norm where lawfulness is expressly stated, a solution recently introduced in Spain[166]), or where termination is at least declared to be '*not unlawful*', as in the reformed law of Western Australia, or the law refers to an '*exclusion from unlawfulness*', as is the case in Greece and Portugal.[167]

B. Much more numerous are the countries where, when the legal prerequisites are satisfied, terminations are referred to as '*allowed*' (as in Italy and the Netherlands as well as in Kuwait and – in the health code – in Peru[168]) or as '*permissible*' (as in Algeria, Jordan and in the former socialist regulations of the Soviet Union and Yugoslavia[169]) or where terminations '*can*' (as in the former ČSSR) or '*may*' be performed (as in Finland and the former socialist regulations of the GDR and Yugoslavia as well as in Lebanon, Libya, India and South Africa[170]). Furthermore, nothing different could be meant where, according to the law, a termination '*shall* be undertaken' if the legal prerequisites are fulfilled (as in Turkey[171]). This manner of speech, which is quite unspecific from a dogmatic criminal law perspective, can perhaps be explained by the fact that this approach is less an appeal to the criminal justice organs and more a matter of clarifying for physicians and healthcare institutions that they are acting 'lawfully' within the framework of the legal system if they terminate a pregnancy

---

[166] This is the case, for example, when new Art. 145 para. 1 CP refers to the indications characterized in Art.417 bis as 'no punible' as 'casos permitidos'.

[167] This assessment with regard to Portugal remains basically unchanged: although the heading of Art. 142 (in the version of the total revision of 15 March 1995), which contains the three indications, refers only to 'not punishable termination of pregnancy', the unchanged Art. 3 of the Law No. 6/84 continues to refer to the 'existence of a circumstance precluding unlawfulness'.

[168] On the basis of general legal rules of necessity, the prohibition model in Iraq may also recognize terminations as permissible and allowed.

[169] Indeed, occasionally the terms 'permissible' and 'authorization' are used in Yugoslavia.

[170] In this regard, the law in South Africa was not changed by the CTPA of 1996 (sect. 2).

[171] The terminology in the former regulation in the ČSSR also alternated, in a similar fashion, between 'shall' and 'can' be undertaken: E/K I pp. 1709, 1731.

when the legal prerequisites are satisfied. This intention becomes especially clear where *'competence'* or *'authorization'* to perform a termination is conferred when the legal prerequisites are satisfied, as in Japan and Tunisia.

C. Addressed primarily to the pregnant woman herself are those regulations that provide her with a *'right'* to terminate her pregnancy, even if only within the framework of an authorization procedure, as in Israel and the former socialist regulations in Yugoslavia, Romania, Hungary and the GDR as well as in Denmark, Norway and Sweden.

3.7.3 *Regulations that differentiate*

Should the preceding remarks give rise to the impression that a clear-cut either-or situation exists, because in the countries mentioned the non-punishability of termination is always either a ground for justification or merely a ground for exemption from punishment (unlawfulness of termination maintained), this assumption would not always be correct. In fact, numerous different approaches have been employed:

- This is true, on the one hand, for all countries where – before indications exempting terminations from punishment or justifying them become relevant – measures that prevent implantation *fail to fulfill the statutory elements* of a prohibited abortion [*Tatbestandsausschluß*]. One example of this is the former West German regulation of 1976, according to which 'procedures whose effect takes place before completion of the implantation of the fertilized egg in the uterus shall not be deemed terminations of pregnancy within the meaning of this Code'.[172]
- Failure to fulfill the statutory elements of the offense – thus distinct from other possible indications – can result from the *fundamental denial of criminal intent* in cases of medically-related terminations; this approach is taken in Belgium.
- Finally, there are occasional time- or indication-based differences within the 'successive time limit indication model'.[173] For if a *'right'* to a termination within a specified time-limit is conferred but thereafter *authorization* on the basis of an indication is required, this situation is hard to explain unless the respective grounds for exemption from punishment are assigned a different legal character. In addition to the Scandinavian regu-

---

[172] § 219d StGB (currently § 218 para. 1 sent. 2). On the subject as a whole, see also *supra* II.2.5.3.

[173] For more on this model, see *supra* II.2.4.2.C.

lations mentioned above,[174] the French regulation is also noteworthy in this context: in France, a pregnant woman in a *'situation de détresse'* can 'demand' termination in the sense of a right until the tenth week of pregnancy, while the performance of a later termination on the basis of a medical or eugenic indication is merely allowed ('can be performed').[175]

- Doubtless the most extensive efforts to differentiate were taken in the Federal Republic of Germany, where the legislature at first held back but at the next opportunity legalized to a great extent the classifications developed in the areas of legal scholarship and practice. In accordance with requirements established by the Bundesverfassungsgericht, the 1995 Act to Amend Aid to Pregnant Women and Families recognizes essentially four different kinds of 'unpunishable' terminations: in addition to the three instances largely taken over from the law of 1976 – namely, preimplantation procedures *conceptually seen as incapable of fulfilling the elements of the termination offense* (§ 218 para. 1 sent. 2), the expressly *not unlawful* medical and criminological indications (§ 218a para. 2 and 3) and the *personal ground for exemption from punishment* for the pregnant woman in the case of a termination performed by a physician following counseling within the first 22 weeks of pregnancy (§ 218a para. 4) – also *the non-fulfillment of the elements of the termination offense* when a termination is performed by a physician, after counseling, within the first 12 weeks of pregnancy (§ 218a para. 1).[176]

3.7.4 *Prohibition and permission in the sense of rule and exception*

Except for extreme cases such as Bahrain and the People's Republic of China where the termination of pregnancy is, by law, largely unpunishable,[177] a basic

---

[174] See *supra* II.3.7.2.C.

[175] Art. L. 162-1 and 162-12 para. 1 *Code de la Santé publique* (E/K I 568), whereby the earlier Art. 317 para. 6 CP was even more unspecific, stating that in the case of a medically or embryopathically indicated termination (L. 162-12 of the aforementioned law) the provisions of the Penal Code were 'not applicable'. In the last analysis, the reformed law of 1992 in Art. 223-11 NCP (E/K III pp. 705 f.) leads to the same result in that it introduces by means of a negative formulation conditions that, when fulfilled, provide for exemption from punishment.

[176] Strictly speaking, the differentiation and classification from a dogmatic criminal law perspective is more complicated. Moreover, it is problematic – primarily in light of the failure of a termination performed by the 'counseling' physician within 12 weeks (§ 218a para. 1) to fulfil the criminal offense § 218 – with regard to its moral message, in that in this stage unborn life is not accorded legal protections. For more on the subject as a whole, see ESER, loc. cit. n. 28, at § 218a margin No. 12 ff.

[177] On this point, see *supra* II.2.4.3.B. and Diagram II/5 (p. 67).

ban on abortion is inherent to most legal orders. Admittedly, considering the numerous exceptions to this ban, it is unmistakable that – with respect to the total number of terminations performed – in a number of countries the ban has become the exception and unpunishability, ostensibly the exception, has become the rule. However, in order to evaluate reliably the relationship, in practice, between the ban on abortion and the permissible termination of pregnancy, more empirical evidence would be necessary than is currently available (this information is presented in the empirical section, *infra* III.). Despite the uncertainties regarding the frequency of termination and the rate of prosecution, an attempt was undertaken (on the basis of the types of prerequisites established for permissibility as well as on statements in the country reports, where available, regarding how these prerequisites are actually dealt with) to make a – concededly rough – assessment. In so doing, three major groups were identified:

- First, countries where a permissible termination is an *exception both de jure and de facto*: European countries belonging to this group include (previously) Belgium as well as the former socialist Romania; additional countries outside of Europe include Brazil, Costa Rica and Egypt.
- The legal termination of pregnancy has become *de jure* the exception but *de facto* the rule in the Federal Republic of Germany, Austria, Switzerland and Japan.
- In the Netherlands, Sweden and the former Soviet Union, the permissible termination of pregnancy appears to be the rule both *de jure* as well as *de facto*.

3.8 Legal claims of the pregnant woman

In situations where terminations are unpunishable or are even expressly permitted, the question arises as to whether the pregnant woman in fact has a legal claim to have her desire to terminate realized. Of central importance is the extent to which women who wish to terminate must be provided access – in the sense of a legal claim – to an unpunishable termination (3.8.1). Additionally, questions concerning the costs of termination as well as the possibility of such costs being absorbed by the public treasury (including social health insurance) must be addressed (3.8.2).

3.8.1 *Claim to the performance of a permissible termination*

Simply because the termination of pregnancy is unpunishable when certain prerequisites are fulfilled and, under certain conditions, public funding may even be drawn upon for its performance, this does not automatically mean that affected women have a legal claim to the actual performance of the procedure. Certainly the right of physicians and/or medical personnel to refuse to participate in a termination, a right that is recognized in many countries in one form or another, makes clear that there is, at least, no claim to a termination performed by a particular physician. But regardless of how this individual component is handled, various approaches in other areas are possible.

In many countries, the issue of a pregnant woman's claim is apparently not considered further. In some countries – as in Ireland – this may have something to do with the extremely limited scope of permissible terminations; it is, however, also the case in numerous legal systems that subscribe to the traditional indication model (e.g., in Belgium (repealed law), Egypt, Ghana as well as the Latin American countries studied here) as well as in a number of countries where the scope of permissibility is broader – such as Great Britain, Taiwan, the People's Republic of China and Japan.

A. Claims when a medical indication is present

In cases involving 'classical' medical indications, it clearly makes sense – regardless of whether additional areas of permissibility can be considered – to affirm the legal claim of a pregnant woman to performance when the relevant statutory prerequisites are fulfilled. For within the framework of this indication, the health interest of the woman trumps that of the embryo; insofar the permitted termination corresponds to therapeutic medical treatment. The parallel to therapeutic treatment is expressly mentioned, e.g., in France, Great Britain, Poland, Ghana and Turkey. Thus, 'permissible' at the same time also means that the physician is obliged to perform the termination. In this sense, the pregnant woman's claim is recognized in Austria, Brazil, (limited to cases involving vital indications) and Iraq; in Mexico and other Latin American countries as well as in South Africa (with the interesting twist that the required permit is issued not to the pregnant woman but to her physician) the question is at least raised by the country reporters.

In countries where a formal procedure for determining the existence of an indication must first take place (conducted, for example, by a commission of physicians),[178] compliance with the procedure and an affirmative finding are seen as prerequisites for a woman's legal claim; this is, for example, the case in Iraq.

---

[178] On this point, see *supra* II.3.4.2.

*B.   Area of application of more broadly defined indications as well as of
      time-bound exemptions from punishment*

Insofar as the scope of permissibility is more broadly defined – as it is in numerous countries,[179] the answer to the question of the legal claims of the pregnant woman also appears to be more open. In this regard essentially two contrasting positions are represented:

a) On the one hand, in some countries an *individual claim to performance of termination is recognized* (apparently emphasizing the right of self-determination of the pregnant woman) in cases beyond those in which the procedure is necessary to eliminate a pressing danger to the life or health of the pregnant woman, if the locally applicable statutory prerequisites (including the absence of a 'contra-indication'[180]) are fulfilled. This was the case, for example, in the former socialist countries; it continues to be the case in Denmark, Italy, Norway, Sweden, Turkey and – at least in practice – in Japan and Tunisia and is currently the case in Switzerland and South Africa as well. Most of these countries provide certain legal precautions in order to *insure, in practice, the availability of termination.*[181]

Recognition of a pregnant woman's legal claims may be linked with a requirement for a formal proceeding to *determine whether the prerequisites for permissibility are fulfilled* as well as with restrictions regarding which institutions may perform the procedure or which institutions are required to do so.

b) In contrast, in numerous countries where the scope of permissibility goes beyond the narrow medical indication, termination is viewed primarily as an exemption from criminal responsibility, and a pregnant woman's *legal claim* to performance of the procedure – be it a general claim or be it a claim against the physician of her choice – is *not recognized.* However, if this group of countries is examined more closely, it becomes clear that further distinctions must be made between countries that limit themselves to an – admittedly far-reaching – exemption from punishment and those that, by means of pertinent legal precautions, approximate – at least in practice – the category of countries that recognizes claims. The former group includes Austria, Israel and, seemingly, the United States,[182] whereas earlier laws of the Federal Republic of Germany as well as

---

[179] On this point, see *supra* the Diagram II/7 (p. 73).

[180] On this point, see *supra* II.3.2.8.

[181] See, for example, Art. 9 para. 4 of the Italian Law No. 194/1978 regarding the legal responsibility of the various regions to verify and insure that termination services are in fact available at hospitals and accredited healthcare facilities; Art. 119 sect. 4 of the Swiss Penal Code (since 2002) is similar.

[182] In the US, to be sure, there is a far-reaching constitutional guarantee that the State not interfere with the decision of the pregnant woman.

Great Britain and Luxembourg accommodate pregnant women in a significant practical way by at least relieving them to some extent of the costs of termination. Furthermore, the new Federal German law as well as the laws in Finland, France, the Netherlands, Portugal, Spain, Australia, and Canada as well as in Switzerland (since 2002) contain rules on accessibility that indicate – to a greater or lesser extent – a step towards convergence with countries that recognize claims.

The issue of *de facto access to termination services* in the United States became quite dramatic in the late 1980s. Across the country, militant abortion opponents began blocking access to clinics providing termination services and began massively intimidating clinic employees.[183] In light of the escalation in this kind of violence, the US Congress responded in 1994 by passing the federal Freedom of Access to Clinic Entrances Act – (FACE), which guarantees access to clinics that provide termination services. FACE provides for criminal and civil penalties if violence is used to obstruct or interfere with clinic access.[184] Meanwhile, the US Supreme Court has addressed a number of cases involving the continuing conflict between the rights of those who wish to abort, on the one hand, and the right of abortion opponents to freedom of expression, on the other: specifically, the issue of the constitutionality of a variety of judicially ordered 'buffer zones' has been considered.[185]

C. Other narrowly defined indications

The question of whether pregnant women have a legal claim to performance in cases involving other, narrowly defined indications – particularly criminological or embryopathic (eugenic) indications – is seldom dealt with explicitly in the country reports.

- As far as *narrow indication models* are concerned, implicit findings in Austria, Brazil and Mexico indicate that the legal claim to performance recognized for (strict) medical indications does not extend to cases involving other indications recognized in the respective countries. In contrast, in Iraq the right to performance of the procedure is recognized for all cases in which a competent commission has found termination to be permissible; thus, the right extends to cases involving the eugenic indication, which is recognized in Iraq by customary law.

---

[183] On the early stages of this development, see WALTHER, loc. cit. n. 38, at p. 55.
[184] Pub.L. 103-259, 108 Stat. 694; codified at 18 USC § 248.
[185] See *Madsen v. Women's Health Center*, 512 *U.S.* 753 (1994); *Schenk v. Pro-Choice Network*, 519 *U.S.* 357 (1997).

- Finally, a number of *special regulations* that provide the pregnant woman with a claim to performance in specific cases are noteworthy. In India, for example, a pregnant woman who seeks to terminate has a legal claim to performance only in cases involving criminological indications – viewed in India as a subcategory of the medical indication – but not in cases involving other kinds of indications; however, the applicable law in cases involving a strict medical indication is not mentioned explicitly in the country report. Furthermore, the requirement in Taiwan that physicians making prenatal diagnoses recommend a eugenically indicated termination to patients in pertinent cases only makes sense if the pregnant woman has a legal claim at least in this type of case to performance of the procedure.

D.   Limitations applying to foreign women
The countries studied here treat differently the question of whether foreign women should have access to permissible terminations.

a) In legal systems that limit permissibility to a *narrow medical indication*, special regulations concerning the 'question of foreigners' are not in evidence; in this regard, apparently, no need for such special regulations is seen. Similarly, legal systems that recognize *criminological* and/or *embryopathic* indications in addition to narrow medical indications also do not appear to see the need for special precautions against foreign women taking advantage of the legal situation.

b) However, if the *scope of permissibility – de jure* or *de facto* – is significantly *broader*, this may be an incentive for women from more restrictive legal systems to make use of these legal options and to terminate their pregnancies in more 'liberal' countries. These so-called liberal countries can be distinguished as follows:

- The most 'foreigner-friendly' countries are those with regulations that confer on pregnant women a legal claim to performance and explicitly include foreign women as potential claimants (like the new Bulgarian law) or at least do not explicitly exclude them (as in Italy, Poland, Turkey and Tunisia). In fact, previous Bulgarian law was significantly more liberal to foreign women with regard to substantive prerequisites for permissibility than it was to its own nationals.
- A similar situation is found in countries where no restrictions are placed on foreign women and where legal claims to performance are not recognized but where the situation has developed in such a way that – *de jure* or *de facto* – no appreciable obstacles are put in the way of women who wish

to terminate. Among these countries are the Federal Republic of Germany, the former Yugoslavia, the Netherlands, Switzerland, Australia, Israel, the United States and, apparently, Canada. Whether and to what extent a particular country in these two groups is actually confronted with the problem of 'abortion tourism' will likely depend, on the one hand, on its geographical location and, on the other hand, on the relationship between its own historical development and that of other legal systems.

• In contrast, numerous legal systems contain various legal restrictions designed to counter 'termination tourism' from taking place domestically. Generally, these restrictions do not focus simply on the nationality but rather on the customary residence of foreign pregnant women in order not to exclude foreign nationals whose permanent residence is domestic. These restrictions typically do not affect (strict) medical indications but rather apply primarily to the expanded scope of permissibility associated with the early stages of pregnancy.

3.8.2 *Compensation for the costs of termination*

The question of whether public funds should be used to cover the costs of termination[186] must be addressed in light of the social welfare system in place in the country under study. From the German perspective, it makes sense to view the problem under the auspices of the existing social and private[187] health insurance systems. From an international perspective, however, it is by no means self-evident that the issue should be viewed solely as a problem faced by insurance industries financed by premiums paid by potential beneficiaries. Another common alternative is to pay for health care with public funds; this approach, which is often combined with systems that rely primarily on individually financed insurance, is used to cover medical costs incurred by the indigent.

A. *Survey*
No legal system that generally and comprehensively withholds public benefits from permissible terminations of pregnancy was discovered in the course of

---

[186] According to the German social health insurance law, the insured has a claim against the (national) health insurance fund for provision of medical treatment (principle of benefits in kind); this can be contrasted with systems in which the insured has a claim to subsequent reimbursement of the costs of medical care (as in Germany's system providing aid to civil servants and its laws governing private health insurance). For the sake of simplicity, attention will not be drawn to these differences in the following.

[187] The following remarks focus on the problems associated with the provision of public benefits, issues central to the country reports.

this project. However, a gap between the prerequisites for permissibility and those for financial subvention is often encountered, primarily in 'liberal' countries.

a)   Medical indication as the sole ground for permissible termination
If medically indicated terminations are seen, in a narrow sense, as therapeutic procedures, it is logical for them to be entitled to the same medical services provided according to the general rules governing *medical treatment*; however, this approach – understandably in light of the 'broad spectrum' of the medical indication[188] – is apparently not taken everywhere. In Costa Rica, for example, sickness benefits may be withheld from women who have terminated their pregnancies (although other health care services are provided).

b)   Models with a more broadly defined scope of permissibility
In countries where the scope of permissibility extends beyond the medical indication, however it is interpreted, the uniform models and the differentiated models treat the 'cost question' differently. Furthermore, within these two models significant differences are found:

aa) Some countries with a *'uniform model'* provide public (insurance) benefits for all terminations allowed by (criminal) law; others do not. Examples of countries that provide public benefits include – in addition to the Federal Republic of Germany until 1993 – the former German Democratic Republic, France, Greece, Great Britain, Portugal, Romania, Sweden, Switzerland, Canada, Taiwan and Uganda. Additional countries that belong to this group but that place some (administrative) restrictions on public benefits include Brazil (where benefits are limited to procedures undertaken in public hospitals) and the People's Republic of China (where benefits are limited to married women).[189] An example of a country that largely avoids providing public financing for terminations, despite far-reaching permissibility, is the United States.[190]

---

[188]   Countries where a broader interpretation of the medical indication has taken root but where for purposes of compensation of costs terminations are equated with medical treatment include Great Britain, Switzerland, Australia.

[189]   Art. 19 II of the new Chinese health protection law no longer contains this restriction.

[190]   This is aptly characterized by the country reporter as a 'double strategy'. The constitutional debate surrounding the cost issue in the US is only partially comparable to the situation in Germany because, for one, regularly at issue in the US is the question of whether the State is not only *entitled* but whether it is in fact *obliged* to provide public funds for the performance of terminations. – On additional political developments, see also WALTHER, loc. cit. n. 38, at p. 51 f.

In countries where public benefits are provided, these benefits are occasionally somewhat different from those provided for therapeutic treatment. Benefits were limited, for example, in a number of former socialist countries where the patient herself was expected to make a co-payment. In contrast, benefits were already expanded, for example, by previous German law to cover the costs incurred by pregnant women prior to termination – particularly those associated with required counseling.[191] In some countries, such as Sweden and Canada, voluntary counseling of a general type – regarding questions of family planning, for example – is seen as a preventive measure and provided free of charge.

bb) In contrast, *differentiated models* regulate the issue of compensation differently, depending on the ground for termination.

- As far as *indications* are concerned, it is standard for the system – regardless of the regulatory model in place – to absorb the costs of terminations that are medically indicated. In Israel, however, the costs of a termination based on any other indication must be borne by the woman herself, and women must also cover the costs of a termination undertaken in accordance with the time-limit model in Austria, Turkey and the United States. Furthermore, in the former Yugoslavia women did not have to pay for terminations undertaken in accordance with the time-limit model if the pregnancy was the result of a failure of an intrauterine device ('indicated' terminations – medical and otherwise – were also provided at no charge to the patient).
- Another form of the differentiation model does not distinguish between terminations that are publicly financed and those whose costs must be carried entirely by the pregnant woman but rather takes a *stairstep approach* to the amount of the co-payment the woman is expected to pay. For example, in the former Soviet Union medically-indicated terminations were performed at no charge to the pregnant woman, whereas a co-payment based on family income was charged for terminations performed on other grounds. As a result of the way that health care is organized in Great Britain and India, only those costs that are incurred in institutions that are part of the health care system can be compensated; thus, terminations per-

---

[191] See also § 4 SchKG on the new German law and the significant public subsidization of counseling centers. Where physicians are recognized as 'counseling centers' and actively engage in counseling, the application of the principle of 'gratis counseling' for women becomes somewhat problematic, in practice, as the fees a physician is allowed to recover from the health care system for counseling are so low that physicians have little incentive to provide the service.

formed in other facilities must be financed entirely by the pregnant woman.

- In some countries, *low-income women* may receive benefits from public funds for unpunishable terminations that are not medically indicated even if they have no health insurance and the healthcare system is based on the principle of insurance. For example, in the Federal Republic of Germany according to the new law on termination of pregnancy, women (regardless of their health insurance status) whose income is below a certain level have a claim to the performance of a termination, with all costs covered by social health insurance. In contrast, higher income women must themselves cover the costs directly incurred through performance of the procedure; if they have health insurance, they have a claim only for performance of services indirectly related to the termination procedure.[192] On the other hand, in the United States public funding has been cut back more and more for 'non-indicated' terminations.[193]

B. *Comparative observations*

An argument for the assumption by the healthcare system of the costs associated with non-medically indicated terminations as well as those that are medically indicated is made in a number of countries; such an approach, it is claimed, would guarantee professional standards of medical care and treatment. There is apparently no direct correlation between the basic regulatory model type and the nature of the rules governing the assumption of costs, even though, from a criminal law perspective, the more the rules governing permissibility restrict the pregnant woman in her autonomy – on a substantive or formal level – the more it makes sense to expect services to be provided by the public treasury: If you have to pay yourself, you want to be able to make your decisions freely.[194]

In light of the bitter debate carried out in Germany over how widely available services provided by social health insurance for non-medically indicated terminations should be, it seems odd that comparable debates in other countries are few and far between. Most importantly, hardly any other country appears to consider this a problem of constitutional import; rather, the issue tends to be viewed solely as a question of legal and healthcare policy.

With regard to the – potential – expectation that restrictive cost regulations might contribute to a reduction in the number of terminations performed, stud-

---

[192] On this point, see § 24b SGB V as well as §§ 1 ff. of the Law Providing Aid to Women with respect to Terminations of Pregnancy in Special Cases [*Gesetz zur Hilfe für Frauen bei Schwangerschaftsabbrüchen in besonderen Fällen*].

[193] For more recent developments, see also WALTHER, loc. cit. n. 73, at p. 51 f.

[194] On this point, see KOCH, loc. cit. n. 38, at p. 1068.

ies from the United States appear to shed light on the question of the extent to which 'cost policies' in force in that country – some of which are quite restrictive – have affected, in the last analysis, the *decision-making behavior of pregnant women*: If, even in this country, which is extremely 'hostile to benefits', an 'avoidance effect' of only around 2% – in relation to the total number of terminations – can be measured, doubts concerning the likelihood of bringing about a measurable decrease in terminations via the pocket book of the pregnant woman are all the more appropriate in countries with less rigid strategies. Since it is clearly evident that the costs of child-rearing in the case of a pregnancy carried to term are incomparably higher than the cost of termination, there is little reason to believe that a pregnant woman who is evaluating her options in economic terms will be decisively influenced one way or the other simply because she herself must pay for the procedure (there is equally little reason to believe that she can be influenced by a discussion of the – intangible – value of the unborn life). However, difficulties in coming up with the necessary funds in a timely fashion may indeed lead to situations where the procedure must be postponed, where the pregnant woman may be forced to accept 'less professional standards' (with regard to the US), or where 'evasive strategies' will be undertaken that undermine compliance with protective procedural rules (as reported for France).

3.9 The right of medical personnel to refuse to participate in the termination procedure

The extent to which physicians and others who, depending upon the responsibilities associated with their jobs, may be called upon to participate to some degree or another in the performance of unpunishable terminations have the right to refuse to take part in the procedure depends on a number of factors. In some countries, there may even be a *prohibition on taking part*; this is the case, for example, for persons working in the area of midwifery/obstetrics in Mexico, where a strict division between midwifery/obstetrics and termination has apparently been adopted. Due to the nature of the discussion, the issue of a true right of refusal can only arise in countries where the scope of permissibility extends beyond narrow medical indications. The following remarks, which concentrate on countries with broader scopes of permissibility, address the question of whether, in fact, such a right is recognized at all and, if it is, examine the kinds of prerequisites that have been established (3.9.1) as well as the various approaches taken with regard to the kinds of 'persons' who may refuse to participate in unpunishable terminations (3.9.2). Finally, various procedural rules that regulate the exercise of the right to refuse are examined (3.9.3).

3.9.1 *Concrete scope*

A. In the majority of countries, a *basic right to refuse* is recognized. Relevant rules and/or case law can be found in numerous (western) European countries as well as in North America, Africa, Israel and Australia. In some countries, however (such as the Federal Republic of Germany, England/Wales, Italy, Austria, Canada and Zambia), it is explicitly stated that the right to refuse does not apply to cases involving (strict) medical indications.

B. In contrast, in a not insignificant number of countries, there is *no statutory right to refuse*. One reason for this is that in some places, i.e., Taiwan, India and Japan, only licensed physicians may perform terminations, and it is assumed that only physicians without personal objections will seek to become licensed. Other countries (e.g., the former Yugoslavia, Finland, Sweden and Switzerland as well as Costa Rica, Canada and Mexico) apparently consider informal solutions in hospitals organized on the basis of the division of labor to be sufficient. In contrast, in some legal systems – particularly former socialist systems – the lack of a right to refuse can be seen as a failure to recognize such conscientious objections as worthy of protection; this approach does not, however, necessarily preclude informal consideration of ideological objections in individual cases. Finally, in countries such as Greece, Turkey, Egypt and Costa Rica, the issue of the right to refuse has apparently not yet been recognized as a concrete problem in need of regulation.

C. In Taiwan and in the People's Republic of China, physicians engaging in prenatal diagnostics are required to recommend that the pregnant woman terminate her pregnancy if a eugenic indication is determined (in the People's Republic this is also true if a medical indication is determined). Thus, to this extent there is a special *positive requirement to participate* that takes precedent over any existing rights to refuse.

3.9.2 *Scope of applicability with regard to 'persons'*

With regard to the *scope of applicability of the right to refuse as far as 'persons' are concerned*, divisions of labor that are part and parcel of organized medical care and that affect the performance of terminations of pregnancy give rise to a number of pertinent issues:

- First, it must be determined whether the right to refuse is available only to natural persons or whether it can also be claimed by institutions, in particular by the governing bodies of hospitals. The latter portion of this question appears to have been answered positively as far as church-run and privately-funded hospitals are concerned. The situation is somewhat different for public hospitals that have traditionally been responsible for providing 'basic' medical care. At any rate, the United States can be pointed to as an example of the explicit granting of the right to refuse to public hospitals and ambulatory surgical centers.

• Of no little significance from a practical perspective is the question of the extent to which the right to refuse is considered to be a personal right of those directly involved in the proceedings, particularly the right of the physician performing the procedure, or, vice versa, the extent to which ranking physicians are afforded the right – deriving from their superior responsibility – to enforce their own objections, even if they themselves are not directly involved in the termination procedure. For example, since the end of 1979 France no longer permits its chief physicians to forbid their assistants to perform terminations.[195] In contrast, the Italian legislature found it necessary to pass a law establishing that the exercise of the right to refuse by medical staff is not subject to the control of superiors.

• The issue of the right of *support staff* to refuse is subject to various explicit regulations; in some places (e.g., Australia, Canada) it is recognized by customary law. If, as in France, England/Wales and Italy, a right to refuse is accorded 'support staff' or if, as in Belgium since 1990, the Netherlands, Poland and some Scandinavian countries, the right is accorded 'medical personnel,' these formulations achieve only a somewhat more precise description of the range of persons affected than has been achieved in the Federal Republic of Germany ('no one') or the USA (no physician, hospital, ambulatory surgical center, nor employee thereof). In France, only those persons directly involved in a particular procedure are accorded the right to refuse.

• Other regulatory differences can be seen with regard to whether the person refusing must refer explicitly to *objections of conscience*. Whereas Federal German law, for example, does not require that specific grounds for refusal be communicated to the pregnant woman,[196] this issue is subject to very different regulations in the various States of the USA. In some States, the refuser must refer specifically to objections of conscience and must even justify – to some extent – the refusal. On the other hand, some States

---

[195] To be sure, under certain circumstances private hospitals in France can issue a blanket refusal to perform terminations. On this point, see also *supra* A.

[196] However, persons who at the beginning of their employment by a particular employer are willing to participate in terminations must justify their actions if later on in their employment by the same employer they seek to make use of the right to refuse.

apply special civil or criminal sanctions if such conscientious objections are not respected.

• Finally, on some occasions the person performing the termination is in need of protection from discrimination. Although it does not support its declaration with a threat of punishment, Austria has declared that no one may be discriminated against in any way whatsoever for performing an unpunishable termination or taking part in its performance or for refusing to perform or take part in its performance.

3.9.3   *Procedural rules governing the exercise of the right to refuse*

One result of a physician's reliance on the right to refuse to participate may be to hinder a woman in her pursuit of a – per se permissible – termination. If the pregnant woman is given the impression, over an extended period of time, that her physician is prepared to perform the termination, the physician's ultimate refusal may lead to the exceeding of statutory time limits and, thus, to the inadmissibility of the procedure. In some countries (such as France, Italy, the Netherlands, Portugal) procedural rules governing the exercise of the right to refuse have been established in order to insure that women are informed in a timely fashion of the attitude of their physicians or that they do not seek medical care from unwilling physicians in the first place.

II.4   IMPERMISSIBLE TERMINATION OF PREGNANCY

Preliminary remarks

This chapter deals with the question of how the countries studied here react – in particular their criminal law response – to the termination of pregnancy in cases where it is considered impermissible. As became clear in the preceding chapters, virtually no country was found, on the one hand, in which the termination of pregnancy was permissible in every respect until birth or in which termination was exempt from any and all regulation or punishment.[197] On the other hand, the differences in the types and the scope of permissibility and/or of punishment of the termination of pregnancy are not insignificant.[198]

With this is mind, four different aspects of impermissible termination will be subject, in the following, to comparative legal analysis:
– how the criminal offense is structured (4.1),
– what modes and instruments of commission are encompassed,
– what the legal consequences are (4.3) as well as,
– how terminations obtained abroad are treated at home (4.4).

4.1   The structure of the criminal offense: from the uniform model to the tripartite model and beyond

With regard to the basic *structural models* that are available to the legislature for dealing with terminations performed by pregnant women on themselves and those performed by others – the latter with or without the consent of the pregnant woman – as well as for dealing with other aggravating or mitigating circumstances, the traditional *uniform model* in the form of a single offense encompassing both self-termination as well as terminations performed by others is found in only a few countries; indeed, it is striking that this model is employed primarily by common law countries (see Diagram II/9, p. 149, Group I/1). It must be kept in mind that many things can be hidden behind this broad sweep of punishability. Whereas in Ireland, for example, the uniform model is deployed in the service of a comparatively comprehensive punishability of terminations, in England/Wales – on account of broader authorizations for termination – it harbors only a bare-bones punishability.

---

[197] See *supra* II.2.4.
[198] See *supra* II.3; see also the overview in Diagram II/6 (*supra* p. 68).

In contrast to this traditional uniform model, recent developments are unmistakably characterized by more or less far-reaching efforts at *differentiation*. For as a superficial glance at Diagram II/9 (p. 149/150) will show, the vast majority of countries attempts to distinguish between various kinds of termination either already on the statutory level or at least at the sentencing level. Indeed, this is true not only for countries where self-termination is fundamentally punishable (Diagram II/9, Group II) but also countries where the pregnant woman is for all intents and purposes not subject to punishment (Diagram II/9, Group III).

Where distinctions are in evidence, they are seen primarily in the form of a subdivision into either two or three categories. It is striking that the classical *dichotomy* between punishable *self-termination* and punishable *third-party termination* – which used to be in force in France and which apparently served as a role model for the countries of the Maghreb (Diagram (II/9, Group 2) – has increasingly been replaced by a *division into three categories*, with particular attention paid to the autonomy of the pregnant woman: *self-termination, termination by third-party with consent* and *termination by third-party without consent of the pregnant woman* (Diagram II/9, Groups 6 and 7). In comparison to this trend toward trisection, which is found in most of the reformed abortion laws in Europe as well as in Latin America and in Arab countries, the Federal Republic of Germany has taken a kind of in-between position: although it continues to subscribe to the fundamental dichotomy between self-termination and termination by third parties, it treats third-party termination without the consent of the pregnant woman as an aggravating factor at the sentencing stage (Diagram II/9, Group 4).

Even among countries where the pregnant woman is basically not subject to punishment (Diagram II/9, Group III), there are a few countries (such as Sweden and Denmark) that employ the dichotomous approach with (unpunishable) *self-termination* and (punishable) *third-party termination* (Diagram II/9, Group 9); but here, too, the three-part division between (unpunishable) *self-termination*, (punishable) *termination by third party with consent* and (punishable) *third-party termination without consent* is apparently taking over, even if this basic model is masked somewhat by additional variations (Diagram II/9, Groups 10-12).

Admittedly, if, in addition to the three-part division at the offense level, the sanction is also considered, it appears that, with the *equal treatment of self-termination and third-party termination with consent*, a return to a new kind of dichotomy is in the offing, namely, the distinction between self-termination and third-party termination with consent, on the one hand, and third-party termination without consent, on the other.

Yet another grouping emerges when the focus is on the *physician*: this grouping is found both in the form of a three-part division between (unpunishable) self-termination, (punishable) third-party termination by a physician and (punishable) third-party termination by a non-physician – an approach that has clearly been adopted in Scandinavia and the Netherlands (Diagram II/9, Group 13) – as well as in the form of the equal treatment as far as sanctions are concerned of punishable self-termination and third-party termination by a physician, on the one hand, and aggravated third-party termination by a non-physician, on the other – as in Austria (Diagram II/9, Group 8).

Naturally, where a legal policy issue involving as much controversy as that surrounding the termination of pregnancy is concerned, *special structural forms* of the criminal offense that cannot be integrated into any of the aforementioned categories may emerge (Diagram II/9, Group IV/14); nonetheless, depending on the basic legal policy approach taken, it is by all means possible for these special forms to attract a more or less significant following.

4.2 Modes of commission: from an all-encompassing approach to special preparatory, participatory and other related offenses

In this section, we will take a closer look at the structure of the individual criminal offenses. Again, this will be undertaken from various perspectives: first, in light of the modes of commission and the subjective side of the offense (4.2.1), then in light of the punishability of attempt (4.2.2), thereafter from the perspective of the type and scope of punishable participation in the offense (4.2.3.), and finally with a view towards possible supplementary crimes of preparation, participation and other related offenses (4.2.4).

4.2.1 *Modes of commission and instruments used to commit the offense*

In countries where the termination of pregnancy is fundamentally punishable, basically *every kind of intervention* is covered that leads to a miscarriage or, as required almost everywhere, to the killing of the embryo; for even in countries where specific instruments were traditionally required (primarily drugs, poison or other harmful substances), today practically all means capable of leading to a termination will suffice.

Discussion of issues such as whether the *killing of a pregnant woman* can be treated as a termination of pregnancy or whether the crime of omission can be based on the *failure to hinder a termination* is found almost nowhere in the world but in the German criminal law dogma.

As far as the *mental element* of the offense is concerned, intent is a prerequisite for the punishability of abortion almost everywhere, as in Germany, although the question of whether *dolus directus* is required as, for example, in Romania and the Soviet Union or whether *dolus eventualis* is sufficient – as conceded by countries with criminal law dogma similar to Germany's – is seldom clarified: in addition to Germany, this is (or was) the case in the GDR, in Switzerland and to some extent in Poland as well. In contrast, if *specific intent* is required, this seems to be understood as a rejection of *dolus eventualis*: this is the case in Belgium, England and (until 1995) in Spain as well as in Australia and Canada. There is, however, a not insignificant minority of countries that punishes even the *negligent* termination of pregnancy: be it in general (as in Italy and Costa Rica)[199] or in the form of negligent causation of a miscarriage as a result of the use of force against or the bodily injury of the pregnant woman (as in Luxembourg[200] and Spain[201] as well as in Brazil and Iraq). In Latin American countries, primarily, *'praeterintentional' abortion* (the result, as a rule, of violence against an obviously pregnant woman) is punished separately. Even the otherwise rather narrowly constrained criminal law in the Netherlands accepts a reduction in the intent requirement by allowing to suffice for the punishability of an act committed against a woman that the offender 'knows or in good faith must suspect that in so doing a pregnancy could be terminated'.

4.2.2   *Attempted termination of pregnancy*

The treatment of attempt has proven to be both extremely diverse as well as highly complex. And this is not only because differences ensue already from the fact that in some countries the pregnant woman is not punishable and this non-punishability obtains all the more in the context of mere attempt, but rather because comparisons can also be made more difficult by the fact that in some countries the *definition of termination of pregnancy*[202] is phrased in such a way that

– regardless of whether a death results, an intervention early in the course of the pregnancy is already seen as an abortion: as can be expected, this is the case primarily in common law countries such as England, Ireland, Austra-

---

[199] The same result may, in practice, come to pass in Mexico, where although intent is required its presence is presumed by law if the physical elements of the offense are fulfilled.

[200] The incorporation of negligence as foreseen by the previous Portuguese CP was lost during the overall revision of 1995, when miscarriage was removed from the catalogue of consequences leading to enhanced punishment for bodily injury.

[201] Although limited in the new regulation of 1995 to gross negligence; note that by definition the pregnant woman herself is exempt from punishment under this provision (Art. 146 CP new version).

[202] For more on this point, see *supra* II.2.5.

lia, Canada, Nigeria and Zambia that focus on the procurement of miscarriage as well as, apparently, the Netherlands, or that

– an attempt is expressly equated with a completed offense: in addition to various European countries (such as Yugoslavia and Luxembourg), this is the case in Arab-African countries in the area of French influence such as Algeria, Morocco and Tunisia, Lebanon and Syria as well as Senegal.

If these technical legal differences are ignored and the focus is instead solely on the respective scope of punishability for attempted terminations, the following picture, as shown in Diagram II/10 (p. 151), emerges:

The attempted commission of the offense is punishable in a large number of countries, in Europe and abroad, *both for the pregnant woman and for third parties*; this is the case even in countries with otherwise largely liberalized regulations such as France (until 1992) and Austria. In contrast, if one considers the countries in which attempt is unpunishable (as in the GDR) or is *unpunishable at least for the pregnant woman* (as in the Federal Republic of Germany) or in which attempt is punished only in certain limited cases (not including, above all, attempts impossible of fulfillment), a clear majority for a restrictive trend with regard to the punishablity of attempt is unmistakable.

4.2.3 *Parties to the termination of pregnancy*

In order for a comparative overview of the criminal liability of all parties participating in the termination of a pregnancy to present a completely accurate and reliable picture, it would be necessary to consider – in addition to the relevant abortion provisions – the respective approaches taken by the various countries to accomplice liability, including whether and how they distinguish between authorship of crime [*Täterschaft*] and participation in crime [*Teilnahme*]. While the country reports do not provide sufficient information for an exhaustive investigation of this issue, an attempt will nevertheless be made (A) to present at least an approximation of the occasionally widely disparate punishability of parties to the crime under conditions where self-termination is fundamentally unpunishable as well as (B) to present differences with regard to the 'accessory' relationship between self- and third-party termination. Due to their *uniform offender principle*, countries such as Italy and Brazil cannot be considered here.

A. Even where *self-termination is fundamentally unpunishable*,[203] the question as to the effect of this approach on possible third-party involvement arises.

---

[203] On this point, see *supra* II.4.1.

Only in Bulgaria and in the former Soviet Union is such involvement considered unpunishable. Other relevant countries (such as Denmark and Israel) apparently treat the involvement of third-parties as punishable, and some countries even have separate offenses penalizing both incitement and abetting of self-abortion (such as the former GDR and ČSSR as well as recently France) or at least punish abetting – but, strangely enough, not incitement – separately (such as Poland and the former Yugoslavia).[204]

B. In countries where *self-termination and third-party termination are punishable* and are sanctioned according to separate criminal offenses and/or are subject to different penalties, the question arises in the context of terminations involving both the pregnant woman as well as a third party (or parties) as to the specific offense and/or penalty to which the parties involved are subject. To the extent that distinctions can be determined at all in other countries with regard to the issue referred to in the Federal Republic of Germany as the 'accessory problem,' the following are the essential findings:

- As far as the *pregnant woman* is concerned, a majority of countries sees her role in the offense as one of authorship [*Täterschaft*] not only when she undertakes the termination herself but also when she merely acquiesces in a third-party termination; as a result, these countries treat both scenarios as self-termination. In addition to the Federal Republic of Germany, countries in this group include Belgium, Greece, Luxembourg, Romania, Switzerland (since 2002) and Hungary as well as a number of Latin American countries (such as Argentina, Chile, Ecuador, Mexico, Peru and Uruguay), Egypt and (until now) Turkey. There are also, however, countries that see the role of the pregnant woman who acquiesces in a third-party termination as merely one of participation [*Teilnahme*] in the third-party offense but nevertheless punish her according to the offense of self-termination. This is the case in Turkey (beginning in 2005) and in Switzerland (until 2002) and, if incitement is present, in Ireland.
- As far as the involvement of *third parties* is concerned, essentially three different approaches can be identified:

– On the one hand, an *accessorial* (or dependent) approach in the sense that the person who incites the pregnant woman to self-termination or the person who assists her in self-termination is subject to punishment according

---

[204] This distinction is apparently derived from a Swiss model without understanding the differences in initial positions.

to the range of penalties prescribed by the offense of self-termination and thus profits from possibilities of mitigation available to the pregnant woman: this seems to be the case in Romania, Peru (since 1991) and Japan; it is also the case in Spain if the third party is neither an incitor nor a principal abettor.

–   The *non-accessorial* (or independent) treatment of involved parties depending upon their position is, however, much more frequent. Countries taking this approach punish third-parties, even mere participants [*Teilnehmer*] in a self-termination, according to the penalties prescribed for third-party perpetration. In addition to the Federal Republic of Germany, this group includes Austria, Belgium, Luxembourg, Portugal, Switzerland (since 2002) and Spain as well as Egypt, Iraq, Tunisia, Turkey, Australia, Japan, Taiwan, Costa Rica and Canada.

–   Still other countries seek to solve the 'accessory problem' by criminalizing *separately* third-party abetting of termination. This approach has been adopted by Switzerland (until 2002), Peru (until 1991), Uruguay and, recently, by France.

4.2.4   *Supplementary crimes of preparation, participation and other related offenses*

Unlike other types of offenses where an extension of criminal liability beyond the completion of an offense by its author is usually possible only in accordance with the general rules of attempt and participation, it appears to be characteristic of the termination of pregnancy that many countries seek to deal with the offense by means of various additional protective and preventive offenses. Such 'preliminary and related offenses' range from independent preparatory acts (A) and participatory offenses (B) to subsequent reporting requirements (C) and various other kinds of protective provisions (D), including provisions that benefit the pregnant woman (E). The following overview is meant to convey only a cursory impression of the diverse attempts made by various legislatures to address peripheral areas that may be of significance for regulating as well as for avoiding terminations of pregnancy.

A. As far as *independently criminalized preliminary and preparatory acts* are concerned, please see Part II.6.1.1 below.

B. *Independently criminalized participatory offenses* are relatively rare: provocation of a termination in France; the attempt by providing an effective abortifacient to incite a pregnant woman to self-terminate after the tenth week of pregnancy in Turkey (until 2004); and participation in a self-termination in Switzerland (until 2002). Finally, in Ireland, a woman can be guilty of procuring an abortion on herself and guilty also of conspiracy for the same purpose.

C. In contrast, various *reporting requirements* that attach when the termination of a pregnancy becomes known or after one has been performed are quite a bit more frequent. These requirements may have different purposes and may be addressed to different target groups:

- In countries where there is a duty of disclosure when an *illegal termination is suspected*, be it applicable to everyone (as in Australia) or to members of medical professions (as in Italy, Mexico and Turkey), the state's interest in prosecution would appear to be dominant. More on this issue can be found at Part II.7.1 below.
- On the other hand, in countries requiring more or less detailed reporting from physicians regarding the *type and number of terminations performed* (as in the Federal Republic of Germany, France, the Netherlands, Poland, Switzerland (since 2002) and South Africa),[205] the purpose of criminal law provisions designed to insure that such requirements are fulfilled appears to be to obtain valid empirical evidence – in part in order to achieve better control of and a reduction in the number of terminations performed.
- In contrast, the purpose of the requirement to *retain documents concerning counseling and indications*, which is encountered in some countries (such as France, the Netherlands and Poland), appears to be more to serve the individual needs of the pregnant woman than to serve possible interests in control.

D. In addition to the aforementioned 'classical' precautions, a number of unusual criminal offenses are worthy of note, for example:

- the independent criminalization of the making of *false statements in application proceedings* in Finland and Norway and of the issuance of a *false certificate* concerning the reason for a termination by a physician, as in Germany and South Africa,
- the criminalization of the *concealment of the birth of a child who dies during the birth process* in Great Britain and India,
- and, last but not least, the special criminalization of the *coercion of a*

---

[205] See also *supra* II.3.6.1 and II.3.6.3.

pregnant woman to (self)-termination in the former GDR, a number of Soviet republics and now also in the Federal Republic of Germany.[206]

E. Finally, a number of requirements *solely in the interest of the needs of the pregnant woman* must be mentioned:

* The obligation of a physician to inform the pregnant woman in a timely fashion of his or her *willingness to participate in the requested termination* in the Netherlands and – although not coupled with a penalty – in Spain.
* Additionally, the failure to comply with the demands of *expedited proceedings* in Poland and Sweden.[207]
* Furthermore, some countries, such as Finland and Norway as well as Hungary, Italy and Portugal[208] used to believe the *medical confidentiality requirement* needed separate re-enforcement.
* Finally, a number of countries seek to guarantee the pregnant woman's *freedom of choice* by making the hindering of a legal termination into a criminal act: this is the case, of late, in France as well as in South Africa.

4.3 Legal consequences of a punishable termination of pregnancy: from fines to life imprisonment

The picture that emerges from a study of legal consequences is also one of extreme diversity. Admittedly, this picture cannot be presented here in great detail, as this would require an assessment of the range of punishment prescribed by an individual country for a punishable termination of pregnancy in terms of that country's sanctioning system as a whole. It is also not possible to consider here either the sanctioning practice in general or the sanctioning practice as it applies specifically to the termination of pregnancy. Despite these shortcomings, a comparison of legal consequences has been undertaken from which one can expect to draw at least an impression of the attitude of a particular legal system towards the termination of pregnancy by looking, first, at the

---

[206] See § 240 para. 4 No. 2 StGB in the version of the 6th StrRG; on this point, see also U. SCHITTENHELM, 'Zweifelhafter Schutz durch das Strafrecht – Einige kritische Bemerkungen zu dem neuen § 170b II StGB', 17 *Neue Zeitschrift für Strafrecht* (1997) pp. 169-172. On the reverse situation, i.e., protection from hinderance of a legal termination, see *infra* E.

[207] A comparable referral duty in Denmark was revoked by the Law of 1989.

[208] On the relationship between the duty of confidentiality and counseling according to the German SchKG, see § 203 para. 1 No. 4a StGB.

severity of the prescribed sanctions (4.3.1) and, second, at how the system responds to potential mitigating or aggravating factors (4.3.2). For a discussion of special consequences, namely, mitigation or aggravation of the sentence when a pregnancy is terminated by a member of a medical profession, see Part II.5.4 below.

4.3.1   General categories

If one does not wish to impute arbitrariness to legislatures in the setting of criminal penalties but rather wishes to give them credit for at least attempting in their establishment of the type and severity of threatened sanctions to give expression – while at the same time possibly considering other factors as well – to a value judgment regarding the legal interest protected by the particular criminal offense,[209] then the penalty established for the termination of pregnancy cannot, naturally, be without meaning for the legal assessment of unborn life and the maintenance or creation of a corresponding consciousness in the general public. If the attempt is made from this perspective to compare legal consequences in various countries, special care must be taken, particularly in the case of termination of pregnancy, not to jump to conclusions: This is for the very general reason that one and the same level of punishment may, on account of the diversity of systems as a whole, seem comparatively high in one country and, in contrast, comparatively low in another, and thus normative distortions can enter into a purely quantitative comparison. Furthermore, restraint is also necessary because, especially where the termination of pregnancy is concerned, one country may accommodate mitigating factors to a greater extent than another, without in so doing wishing to denigrate the fundamental claim of unborn life to protection. As a result, it is certainly possible that a penalty laid down by law that seems rather mild can be a sign, in a positive sense, that the legislature has already attempted to undertake an appropriate balancing test between the interests of an unborn life in protection and the countervailing motives and stresses of a pregnant woman and those who come to help her, instead of simply laying down a symbolically severe penalty that in the day-to-day practice of the criminal justice system may never actually be imposed. As long as these caveats are kept in mind, a comparison of legal consequences should allow for the identification of at least certain basic categories of punishment.

---

[209] For a fundamental explication of the function of punishments laid down by law and the ranges of punishment, see W. HASSEMER, 'Die rechtstheoretische Bedeutung des gesetzlichen Strafrahmens', in A. KAUFMANN (ed.), Gedächtnisschrift für Gustav Radbruch (Göttingen, Vandenhoeck & Ruprecht 1968) pp. 281-291.

As explained above, the cut-off points introduced in order to establish categories must, to a certain extent, be arbitrary. If one decides to categorize the sentencing systems of the various countries on the basis of the highest penalties established for the normal case and in so doing introduces cut-off points at 5 and 10 year prison terms (Diagram II/11, p. 152), countries in which the highest penalty for self- and/or third-party termination does not exceed 5 years in prison (even in aggravated cases) can be brought together in the *lower category*. Using these cut-off points, the group with the mildest threatened punishment includes Austria, Denmark and Sweden (which are relatively liberal) as well as the Federal Republic of Germany. It also included South Africa, which was quite strict with regard to fundamental penalization, at least until the reform of 1996 (Diagram II/11, A). The number of countries that can be assigned to the *middle category*, where the punishment range for normal cases is more than 5 but less than 10 years imprisonment, is smaller still; for even Spain (which belonged to this category until 1995) recognized mitigating grounds that reduced the punishment of pregnant women to much less than 5 years (Diagram II/11, B). The *upper category*, where the threatened punishment for normal cases begins at more than 10 years and in some cases can be as much as life imprisonment, is made up of a comparatively small number of common-law countries (Diagram II/11, C). The overwhelming majority of countries spans the *lower and middle categories* (Diagram II/11, D) or (even more frequently) reaches all the way from the *lower to the upper category*; this latter group, with its broad range, includes recently reformed countries such as Belgium, Greece, Luxembourg and the Netherlands (Diagram II/11, E).

In addition to these basic categories, it is important to note that, under certain circumstances, some countries make due solely with *financial penalties* (such as Luxembourg in cases of self-termination), and some countries allow either imprisonment or a financial penalty, even for third-party terminations (such as the Federal Republic of Germany, Sweden, Spain since 1995, Israel, Tunisia and the otherwise strict South Africa). Going to the other extreme, the range of normal punishments in some countries, which can be up to life imprisonment, is surprising, and doubts as to the constitutionality of such broad ranges of punishment may be justified; for even if no extreme penalties are actually imposed in practice, the lack of determinacy regarding the severity of punishment is readily apparent. Striking leaps in sanctioning – from regular punishments in the lower category to aggravated punishments in the middle and even upper categories – can be found primarily in Latin America as well as in countries heavily influenced by Islam.

4.3.2 *Special grounds for reducing and enhancing punishment*

In comparison to the diverse ranges of punishment prescribed by the various abortion regulations for normal offenses, the picture that emerges with regard to potential special factors that can lead to the reduction or enhancement of punishment is considerably more uniform.

- Except for a not insignificant group (composed mostly of countries influenced by the common law), the majority of countries under study makes use of the possibility of *reducing or enhancing* the normal penalty range by recognizing grounds for mitigation or aggravation
- The most frequently stated ground for *reduction in punishment* requires that the motivation behind the termination be to *save face*; this motive, apparently a specifically Romanist or (possibly Romanist-influenced) Arab phenomenon, can encompass not only the pregnant woman herself but her relatives as well and may even encompass third parties. Occasionally, however, criminological and embryopathic indications are treated merely as grounds for mitigation rather than as grounds for exemption from punishment (as in Peru since 1991). In addition, mitigation of the offense may be provided for third parties if the termination is *consensual*; this is the case in countries where the penalty for third-party termination with consent is less severe than the penalty for self-termination (as in Chile, Mexico and Bahrain – note that in Bahrain third-party termination with consent is unpunishable[210]).
- As far as *aggravating circumstances* are concerned, a pregnant woman's *lack of consent* as well the aggravation of the offense based on a *particular result*, i.e., her death or (usually) serious injury, play an extremely important role; both of these factors are accorded special weight in German criminal law by statutory provisions that allow for sentencing enhancements for enumerated crime typologies [*Regelbeispiele*]. Additional (isolated) grounds for penalty enhancement include the *habitual* performance of abortion (as in France, Spain until 1995, the former USSR as well as Algeria, Morocco and Senegal), its performance on a *commercial basis* (as in Austria, Hungary Switzerland (until 2002) and in the former Yugoslavia) and its performance *for profit* (as in Finland, Romania and Taiwan). These criteria are occasionally found in combination with one another: *ha-*

---

[210] The results from the fact that in Bahrain, one the one hand, the pregnant woman is criminally liable only if she self-terminates with no advice from a physician and without a physician's knowledge (Art. 321), and, on the other hand, a third party is criminally liable only if he or she terminates a pregnancy without the consent of the pregnant woman (Art. 322).

bitualness and profit motive in Norway, Portugal and Sweden; *commercial nature and profit motive* in the GDR. Finally, the penalty can be enhanced if the termination takes place in the *later stages of pregnancy* (as in Costa Rica, India, Zambia, Turkey the United Arab Emirates, the new regulation in Sudan, as well as in a number of States in the United States).

4.4   Termination of pregnancy and international criminal law

4.4.1   *Reasons why women go abroad to terminate their pregnancies*

The final aspect of the termination of pregnancy to be discussed here, one that can be observed taking place between certain countries, is 'abortion tourism', so-called by some to minimize, by others to polemicize the phenomenon. Depending upon the predominating goals and motives involved, two quite different kinds of border traffic can be distinguished. On the one hand, there is 'emigrative' abortion tourism, in which pregnant women from one country travel to various other countries where the (actual or perceived) risk of criminal prosecution is less: for many years women went from Germany to England, Austria and, most frequently, to the Netherlands; they went from Spain to France and to England;[211] and they went from Latin America to the United States. On the other hand, there is 'immigrative' abortion tourism, where certain countries attract pregnant woman from other countries: Australia, apparently, attracts pregnant New Zealanders and the former Yugoslavia apparently attracted pregnant woman from a number of neighboring countries.[212]

Like the goals of pregnant women, the reactions of the countries involved can vary:

- If a particular country becomes a haven for foreign pregnant woman, it can counter this unwanted 'import' by making terminations contingent on a longer stay in the country or on special requirements for official permission.[213]
- In contrast, if pregnant women try to get around the law of their own country by going abroad to terminate, their country can counter this ploy – in 'catch-up' fashion – by expanding the application of its own law to terminations performed abroad. Similarly, it can try to exercise control over abortion activities undertaken abroad by domestic physicians. The follow-

---

[211] See S. Mir Puig, ‚Entwicklung der strafrechtlichen Behandlung des Schwangerschaftsabbruchs in Spanien', 47 *Juristenzeitung* (1992) pp. 985-990, at pp. 986 f.

[212] See also *supra* I.5.1.

[213] On this point, see II.3.8.1.D.

ing remarks are concerned solely with this – international criminal law – aspect of terminations of pregnancy obtained abroad.

Oddly enough, of the countries studied here only the Federal Republic of Germany, apparently, has a special regulation devoted solely to terminations performed abroad; elsewhere, terminations of pregnancy are simply subject to the general rules of international criminal law. The following picture, in essence, results:

4.4.2   Principles of jurisdiction: from (limited) territorial application to an (extended) extraterritorial approach

Regarding the principles used to determine the geographical area of application of their criminal law, the relevant countries can be divided into three groups:

A. First, countries that abide by the *territorial* principle and whose criminal law thus encompasses only those terminations performed within the country. Major representatives of this group – following a long common law tradition – include Great Britain, Ireland, the United States, Australia and Canada, in addition South Africa, Southern Nigeria and Tunisia as well as Chile and, apparently, Ecuador.

B. Second, a number of countries (such as the Netherlands) appear to proceed on the basis of the *active personality* principle and others (such as Israel) on the basis of this principle in combination with the *passive personality* principle, so that in the former case a country's own citizens can be punished for terminations obtained abroad and in the latter case a pregnant woman can be protected against a termination against her will even when she is out of the country.

C. Instead of relying on one or the other of the nexus principles, however, most countries rely on a combination of the *territorial principle with one or with a number of other principles* so that the punishability of termination can apply to both domestic as well as to foreign terminations. Five variations of this kind of combination of various principles have been identified:

• A relatively frequent constellation is the combination of the *territorial principle with the active personality principle*. This arrangement is found within Europe in Austria, Romania, the former Soviet Union and occasionally – according to the case law – in Spain[214] as well as, above all, in a

---

[214]   See MIR PUIG, loc. cit. n. 211, at p. 987.

number of African and Asian countries (as in Egypt, India, Iraq, Japan, Senegal, Turkey and Zambia).

- The combination of the *territoriality principle with the passive personality principle*, as in Belgium, is apparently quite seldom.
- The combination of the *territoriality principle with the active and passive personality principles* is found more frequently. It is, in fact, quite popular in Europe (Greece, Luxembourg, Portugal, Spain and Switzerland) but is also found in Latin America (Costa Rico, Mexico, Peru, Uruguay and, apparently, Brazil) and in Taiwan.
- Occasionally the *territorial principle* is combined with the *active personality* and *representational principles*. This was the case in the GDR and in Hungary.
- The broadest application of criminal jurisdiction abroad is achieved where the *territorial principle* is combined with the *active and passive personality principles* as well as with the *representational principle*. This is the case in Germany, Italy, Yugoslavia and, until the 1992 reform, France.[215]

D. With regard to the application by groups B and C of domestic criminal law to offenses committed abroad, however, this kind of extended jurisdiction is generally possible only when termination is also criminalized by the country of commission,[216] whereby it is true that the requirements concerning the existence of an *identical norm* in the country of commission vary significantly.[217]

4.4.3 *Discrepancies between the punishability of termination at home and abroad*

Depending upon which nexus principle is employed, domestic law can either be limited to the prosecution of terminations occurring at home or it can be used to prosecute both foreign and domestic terminations. Bearing in mind the fallibility of the information provided in the country reports, as far as the treatment of domestic and foreign offenses is concerned, three major groups – some with subgroups – can be distinguished:

---

[215] For current law, see Art. 113-6 through 113-12 NCP.

[216] In this regard, the only exceptions appear to be Romania and the Soviet Union as well as Costa Rica, India, Japan and Zambia.

[217] Compare, for example, Belgium, on the one hand, where the only requirement is that a termination offense exists in the country of commission but whether or not this offense is prosecuted is unimportant (a constellation that was especially important for the coverage of the 'abortion tourism' that took place in the Netherlands at one time, with Switzerland, on the other hand, where criminal liability under Swiss law is barred if the termination of pregnancy is permissible according to the provisions of the country of commission.

A. The first group comprises those countries in which, on the basis of the territoriality principle, termination of pregnancy is punishable from the outset only if committed *at home*. Countries that belong to this group are listed above at 4.4.2.A.

B. In the second group, terminations undertaken by *nationals abroad* are subject to domestic criminal law; however, certain differences with regard to the persons involved can be observed:

- In this group, generally, *all nationals party to the offense are punishable without distinction*: this is the case in Romania, Argentina, Egypt, India, Zambia and Iraq.[218]
- In contrast, if the *pregnant woman is not criminally liable at home*, she is, as one would expect, also not liable for offenses committed abroad: this is the case in the Netherlands, the Soviet Union and Turkey.
- Liability is even more limited according to Japanese law, under which only the terminating *physician* can be held liable for terminations undertaken abroad

C. In another group of countries, domestic criminal law is applicable, as a rule, to terminations occurring both *at home and abroad* as well as to terminations undertaken by both *nationals and foreigners*; here, again, a number of differences must be taken into account:

- Quite often, *all parties to the offense* will be criminally liable if the termination is *undertaken on a national*. Countries taking this approach include, in Europe, Austria, the Federal Republic of Germany, France, Switzerland and, apparently, Greece and, in Latin America, Brazil, Peru and Uruguay.
- The same is true – with the *exception of pregnant women* (who are not criminally liable for terminations performed abroad) – in Portugal, Spain and Israel.
- In contrast, Italy, Yugoslavia and Hungary go a step further in that, under the conditions mentioned above, they also subject terminations undertaken *on foreign women* to domestic criminal liability.

---

[218] Whereby in the latter case the commission abroad is of no practical significance anyway because Iraqi women only rarely leave their country.

4.4.4 *Limiting rules and procedural requirements*

The quite far-reaching extensions of the domestic criminal law of some countries to terminations performed abroad can, however, be qualified in a number of ways:

A. First, on the substantive legal level, an *identical norm* in the country of commission may be required.[219] Other possible substantive qualifications include the disqualification of a domestic penalty that is less favorable to the defendant than the penalty according to the law of the country of commission (this is the case in Austria and Israel) and even the requirement that the milder foreign law be applied, as in Portugal and Switzerland.

B. Second, the domestic prosecution of terminations undertaken abroad depends on procedural devices including certain kinds of complaints or approvals as well as by domestic laws limiting extradition. In Europe, such domestic interests are found primarily in France, Italy and Spain.[220]

C. Furthermore, the principle of *ne bis in idem* can prevent a domestic procedure from taking place if a criminal prosecution has already been conducted abroad. This is the case in Austria, Portugal, Yugoslavia, Egypt and Brazil.

4.4.5 *Summary*

Compared to the special attention paid by the special German regulation § 5 No. 9 StGB to terminations of pregnancy undertaken abroad, interest in the rest of the world in criminal prosecution beyond domestic borders seems to be rather small or at least no bigger for terminations than for other criminal offenses. While there are countries other than Germany that recognize an extension of their criminal law to extraterritorial offenses, none of them has special rules applying only to the termination of pregnancy. In this regard, the especially broad extraterritorial application claimed by German criminal law is exceptional.

Thus, it is not surprising that in regard to a potential nexus to the passive personality principle, the question of whether the fetus can be considered a domestic national – an issue which has also been addressed in France, Portugal,

---

[219] *Supra* II.4.4.2.D.

[220] See also Yugoslavia, Luxembourg, Austria and Switzerland as well as Turkey, Israel, Brazil and Mexico.

Costa Rica and Israel – has been answered in the affirmative only by the Federal Republic of Germany and – with certain reservations – Spain.

The practical significance of criminal prosecution of terminations of pregnancy undertaken abroad also appears to be minimal; in any case, relevant decisions are reported only in exceptional cases – e.g., in France and Spain.

DIAGRAM II.9–1   149

Diagram II/9–1

Overview of the Structure of Punishable Terminations of Pregnancy

ST	=	self termination	W	=	pregnant woman	wC	=	with W s consent
3PT	=	3rd-party termination	3P	=	3rd-party	w/oC	=	without W s consent
p	=	physician	np	=	non-physician			

I. Single Offense Encompassing both ST and 3PT

1

England/Wales
Ireland
Ghana
India
South Africa

II. Differentiation in the Case of General Punishability Including the Pregnant Woman

Dichotomy	Tripartite division
ST ↔ 3PT	**ST ↔ 3PTwC ↔ 3PTw/oC**

2	3	6	7
with mitig. for W	*with mitig. for 3PTwC*	*with mitig. for W and aggrav. for 3PTw/oC*	*equal treatment for for ST and. 3PTwC*
France (old)	USA (some states)	Finland	Belgium (new)
		Greece	Portugal
Australia		Hungary	Spain (old)
Canada		Italy	Romania
	4	Luxembourg	Costa Rica
Algeria	*with aggrav.*	Switzerland (old)	
Morocco	*for 3PTw/oC*	Switzerland (new) from 11 W	Iraq
Kuwait		Spain (new)	Yemen (new)
Tunisia	FRG		Libya
Zambia		Argentina	Qatar
Senegal		Brazil	Sudan
South Nigeria		Chile	United Arab Emirates
		Ecuador	
		Mexico	
		Peru	
		Uruguay	
		Jordan	
		Lebanon	
		Oman	
		Syria	
		Japan	
		Taiwan	

5	8
same threatened punishment for ST and 3PT	*same threatened basic offense punishment for ST and p3PT*
Egypt	Austria

Diagram II/9–2

III. Differentiation in the Case of Exemption of the Pregnant Woman from Punishability	
Dichotomy	**Tripartite division**
9 *(exempt) ST ↔ 3PT*	**10** *(exempt) ST ↔ 3PTwC ↔ 3PTw/oC*
Denmark Sweden USSR Israel Pennsylvania	*with 3P participant in W s ST not punishable* Bulgaria Norway
	11 *with independent basis for criminal liability of 3P participant in W s ST* ČSSR GDR France (new) Poland Yugoslavia
	12 *with W subject to criminal liability for incitement to 3PT* France (new) (?) Netherlands
	13 *with emphasis on the mitig. of the p3PT (exempt) ST ↔ p3PT ↔ np3PT* Denmark Sweden Switzerland (new): till 10 W (Netherlands) Bulgaria Poland USSR Yugoslavia

IV. Special Forms
14 Turkey Bahrain PR China North Yemen Saudi Arabia South Yemen (old)

DIAGRAM II.10 151

Diagram II/10

Criminal Law Response to Attempt

A	B	C		D
attempt completely *unpunishable*	attempted ST* *unpunishable* 3PT** *punishable*	attempted ST and 3PT *punishable*, but with *restrictions*		attempt completely *punishable*
		in general	*only for W****	
GDR	Belgium	Italy	England/Wales	Austria
	FRG/Germany	Portugal (old)	Ireland	Finland
	France (new)	Scotland	Switzerland (new)	France (old)
Egypt	Luxembourg			Greece
Bahrain	Netherlands	Brazil	Algeria	Hungary
	Poland	Costa Rica	Morocco	Spain
	Portugal (new)	Mexico	Tunisia	Switzerland (old)
	(3PT partly)		Zambia	
	Romania	Senegal		Chile
	Sweden		Turkey	Ecuador
	USSR			Peru
	Yugoslavia			Uruguay
	Argentina			Iraq
				Libya
	Israel			Kuwait
	Jordan			Qatar
				Sudan
	Lebanon			Un. Arab Emir.
	Oman			
	Syria			India
	Japan			Ghana
	Taiwan			South Africa
				Canada
				USA (partly)
				Australia (partly)

- Self Termination
- ** 3rd-Party Termination
- *** Pregnant Woman

DIAGRAM II/11

Overview of Consequences

A *Lower category*	B *Middle category*	C *Upper category*	D *Lower and middle categories*	E *Entire range*
Highest punishment for ST and/or TPT not more than 5 years	Range of punishment for normal case more than 5 but less than 10 years	Range of punishment 10 years and more	Range of punishment up to 5 years Enhanced penalty not more than 10 years	Range of punishment up to 5 years Enhanced penalty in the upper range
Austria Denmark Germany Sweden Costa Rica Peru (since 1991) Israel Ghana Sudan Tunisia South Africa (old)			GDR Bulgaria Finland France Hungary Italy Poland Portugal Switzerland (new) USSR Chile Mexico Uruguay	Belgium ČSSR Greece Yugoslavia Luxembourg Netherlands Norway Romania Switzerland (old) Argentina Brazil Ecuador Peru (till 1991)
	Spain South Africa (new) *with reservations* Bahrain Kuwait Zambia South Nigeria Australia/ Queensland		Kuwait Libya United Arab Emirates Senegal India Japan Taiwan	Egypt Algeria Iraq Jordan Lebanon Morocco Oman Qatar Syria Turkey USA
		England/Wales Ireland Canada New York South Australia		

II.5   SPECIAL ROLE OF THE PHYSICIAN

As far as the performance of terminations of pregnancy that are exempt from punishment is concerned, the role of the medical profession is a prominent one. Virtually no other aspect of the regulation of the termination of pregnancy enjoys such far-reaching international consensus: apart from a few exceptions, the termination procedure itself must be performed by a physician (II.5.1). Of course, the fine points of national regulations differ considerably with respect to the rules that doctors who perform terminations must follow (II.5.3). But even in the 'preliminary proceedings' of determining whether the prerequisites are fulfilled in a particular case, physicians frequently assume a special role (II.5.2). Finally, the unique role of physicians in the protection of (unborn) life as well as in the performance of legal terminations is often consistent with special responsibilities conferred by the criminal law (II.5.4). As the physician's involvement is as extensive as it is diverse, a comparative analysis from the perspective of this important role – to supplement the discussion at II.3.4-3.6 above – would appear to be advisable.

5.1   Requirement that terminations of pregnancy be performed by physicians

The need to integrate physicians at the 'implementation stage' is obvious. This applies, to start with, in minimizing the risk to the health of the pregnant woman associated with the performance of the procedure: according to modern standards, no other profession is equipped with comparable qualifying *expertise*. Quite a few legal systems have adopted even more far-reaching restrictions, requiring that only those specialists who, on the basis of their training, appear to be especially qualified – particularly gynecologists but also surgeons – actually perform the procedure.[221] In countries where terminations are permitted only if the prerequisites of a narrow medical indication are fulfilled, the 'therapeutic' basis ensures that the procedure, once it has been approved, is performed in a setting such as that established for medical treatment or comparable gynecological procedures.

In countries where the scope of permissibility is defined somewhat more broadly, the conviction that the pregnant woman should be deterred from going to quacks, back-street abortionists or similar 'professionals' of doubtful qualifi-

---

[221] For more, see *infra* II.5.3.

cations evidently takes on some weight. However, if the requirement that the procedure be performed by a physician or the equivalent is made a prerequisite for the exemption from punishment of the pregnant woman herself, and the threat of punishment is not – as in Sweden and Denmark – limited exclusively to the (medically) insufficiently qualified 'third-party abortionist', this preventive measure becomes a 'good deed' that is imposed and not merely offered. The public interest in minimizing the negative consequences of lay abortions – such as health insurance costs or the evidently considerable utilization in some countries of medical resources for treating the consequences of 'quack abortions' – can also be a motivating factor for the lawmaker as for example in Brazil, Costa Rica, Egypt, Ghana and Mexico.

But the lawmaker also frequently takes advantage of a second characteristic feature of the medical profession as far as terminations are concerned: As a professional group that traditionally feels obligated, on the basis of its self-image, to protect unborn life, its members appear called upon to become a kind of *attorney for the unborn*. Thus, the lawmaker is justified, to some extent, in expecting that physicians will not function simply as the pregnant woman's 'flunky' in deciding whether to perform a termination, but rather that they will also inquire into and consider the evidence that speaks for the continuation of the pregnancy.

5.2   Functions of physicians in preliminary proceedings

Such role conflicts between helping the pregnant woman as a patient and protecting unborn life can be avoided to some extent if the roles of participating physicians are divided: The physician involved in the preliminary examination could support the interests of the unborn child, while the physician who will later perform the termination would be primarily responsible for ensuring that for the woman the termination proceeds 'without incident'. In fact, it appears that such a *division of labor* is widespread; however, in some legal systems the 'representation of the interests' of the unborn during the 'preliminary procedure', at least in some cases, is not seen as the physician's duty (5.2.1); in other legal systems – such as in Germany – in spite of a preliminary examination conducted by a third party, the ultimate responsibility for the termination lies with the physician performing the procedure (5.2.2).

5.2.1   *Functions of the physician in preliminary proceedings*

Insofar as another level of medical authority, in addition to the physician performing the termination, is provided for at all, it can – as described above – have a determinative role in deciding whether to permit the termination (A)

and/or its role can be one of counseling (B). Finally, several of the more peripheral duties of the physician are examined (C).

A. *Decision-making instances* are necessary to clarify the existence of indications within the framework of pure indication models or successive time-limit
indication models. Insofar as this task cannot – as in Austria and India, formerly
in Poland and (probably) in Yemen)[222] – be accomplished by the physician
performing the termination, a multitude of different approaches have been taken.
A discussion of these approaches appears in Part II.3.4.2 above.

B. The *counseling function* of the doctor primarily includes informing the woman
interested in terminating her pregnancy about the medical aspects and risks of
termination. For details, see Part II.3.4 (especially 3.4.3) above. However, there
are also regulations that prevent physicians from disclosing certain information: for example, physicians are prohibited from disclosing the gender of the
fetus throughout the pregnancy in the People's Republic of China and in India
and up until the 12th week in Bavaria,[223] except when the disclosure is medically justified.

C. In some countries, *additional duties* of the physician prior to the termination
of a pregnancy are expressly regulated. Some of these regulations are related to
procedural steps characteristic of the regulatory model in force such as (in the
Netherlands) the decision and explanation of the physician as to whether he or
she is willing to provide the requested service, (in Italy) the confirmation of the
(relative) urgency of the procedure in order to avoiding waiting periods, (in
Germany as well as in Tunisia) the determination of the length of the gestation
period, the preparation of an expert medical opinion regarding the lack of fetal
viability,[224] and even – as in Morocco – the procedure of reporting to the head
of the competent health authority as a substitute for the consent of the husband.
Other such regulations cover actions that, it would seem, should be taken even
in the absence of express legal regulation, such as the verification of possible

---

[222] Additionally, the physician performing the termination occasionally has limited authority to make a determination concerning permissibility as, for example, in Belgium (new
law) and Luxembourg in cases involving indicated terminations up to the 12th week of pregnancy or under previous Finnish law in cases where termination was indicated due to the age
of the pregnant woman or to her already large family.

[223] Art. 18 *Heilberufe-Kammergesetz* [Health Professions Law] in the version of the
Bayerisches Schwangerenhilfeergänzungsgesetz [Bavarian Law of Supplementary Help for
Pregnant Women] of 9 August 1996, see also *BVerfGE* 88, 203 ff., 291.

[224] Such as was the case before being declared unconstitutional in the American state of
Pennsylvania, see WALTHER, loc. cit. n. 38, at pp. 50 f.

contraindications.[225] Italian law is peculiar in that, under certain conditions, it confers special duties on the physician (or other responsible institutions) in cases where a minor is seeking to terminate her pregnancy. Finally, special requirements regarding documentation must also be noted.[226]

5.2.2 *Division of responsibility between the preliminary and the performing stages*

Important differences have been found regarding the legal significance of ascertaining an indication: one the one hand, ascertainment may be granted *legally operative character* so that its legal significance is comparable to that of an official approval;[227] on the other hand, it may be treated simply as an *expert opinion* that leaves the 'ultimate responsibility', at least formally, to the terminating physician.[228] From the statistical information available,[229] however, it must be inferred that in actual practice, the judiciary virtually never engages in 'indication correction' if the rules governing preliminary procedure were paid more than lip-service.[230]

5.3 **Rules covering performance of terminations of pregnancy**

For obvious reasons, regulations concerning the performance of terminations of pregnancy are significant, not only for the woman seeking a termination but

---

[225] In any case, to the extent that such contraindications are based on the medical condition of the pregnant woman (such as seems to be the case in Sweden, Hungary and Turkey and not on the fact that the pregnancy has advanced beyond a certain period of gestation or that the interval between two pregnancies was too short. On contraindications as a hindrance to termination, see generally *supra* II.3.2.8.

[226] As in Great Britain, Italy, Poland and the former Soviet Union as well as in Australia, Brazil, India, South Africa and Turkey.

[227] In this sense, for example, probably in Turkey as well as in legal systems in which the ascertainment of permissibility is the responsibility of a specially appointed commission, such as in Hungary (old law).

[228] Such as, e.g., in the Federal Republic of Germany, in France and in Brazil. Unclear in Luxembourg and Portugal.

[229] See *infra* III.3.

[230] On this set of issues, see also *BGHSt* 38, 144 ff. = BGH *NJW* 1992 pp. 753 ff. (*Theissen* case, see A. Eser, "Ärztliche Erkenntnis' und richterliche Überprüfung bei Indikation zum Schwangerschaftsabbruch nach § 218a StGB', 46 *Juristenzeitung* (1991) pp. 1003-1014 = in Eser and Koch, op. cit. n. 67, pp. 13-47 at pp. 33 ff.; H.-G. Koch, 'Über Schwierigkeiten von Ärzten und Gerichten im Umgang mit § 218 StGB', in Eser and Koch, op. cit. n. 67, pp. 69-84 at pp. 80 ff.) with the attempt of judicial self-restraint in the sense of a 'justifiability control'. However, in most of the adjudicated cases, there was no ascertainment of an indication from a second physician.

also and to a great extent for the medical profession. Rules specifying the medical facilities where terminations of pregnancy may be performed are widespread and may serve both the purpose of protecting the health of the pregnant woman as well as of preventing the number of terminations performed from expanding beyond control. Likewise, regulations concerning the qualifications of the terminating physician are not uncommon. On the other hand, specific rules concerning how the procedure is to be performed – apart from the requirement that the termination take place in a hospital – are quite rare. For further details, see the discussion above at Part II.3.5.

5.4   Special criminal provisions and sanctions pertaining to physicians

As mentioned at the beginning of this section, physicians who participate in a termination of pregnancy find themselves in an ambivalent situation as they are called upon to protect various competing interests that in the case of termination cannot be reconciled. Should a physician fail to meet a legal prerequisite required to exempt a termination of pregnancy from punishment, the question arises as to which of the following is more important: the failure to meet the expectations of his or her role as protector of the embryo, or the fact that the medical interests of the woman were served by means of a professional, medically irreproachable termination procedure.[231] An additional question concerns the extent to which the integration of physicians into the *procedure* leading up to a legal termination needs to be supported by the criminal law.

Most of the statutory methods – elaborated upon previously in Part II.4.1 – that are employed to punish criminal terminations have special provisions aimed especially at physicians and, to some extent, also at members of other health professions. While these provisions were examined above with regard to their position in the overall system criminalizing termination, the focus here is primarily on special regulations targeting health professionals, especially those specifically aimed at physicians. In this respect, additional criminal offenses for the various stages of medical treatment (5.4.1-5.4.3) must be distinguished from special regulations that are classified under the respective disciplinary or professional codes of conduct (5.4.4).

5.4.1   *Sanctions related to the performance of terminations*

Insofar as there are no special criminal statutes that apply specifically to physi-

---

[231] An example can be seen in the controversy in Mexico (in which the above-mentioned arguments are employed) with regard to the ban on the practice of medicine that is foreseen for physicians who are criminally liable for illegal terminations.

cians who perform terminations,[232] and thus general provisions regulating 'third-party terminations' must be relied upon,[233] it is clear from the outset that in making criminal law legislatures have not taken a side with regard to the initially posed question. Hence, the task of determining which aspect of the physician's role is the most important is generally a matter decided during the sentencing process on a case-by-case basis. However, there are legal systems which underscore the physician's role as a healthcare professional by granting physicians certain privileges or, conversely, by threatening non-physicians with heavier punishment; other legal systems stress the responsibility of the physician to the embryo by threatening physicians with heavier punishments than those imposed for 'run of the mill' third-party terminations.

A. Countries that go the furthest in the first direction, such as Sweden, subject only non-physicians to criminal liability for impermissible terminations and threaten physicians with sanctions only for violating procedural regulations (in the sense of Part II.5.4.2, below).[234]

B. The second approach, in the form of heavier sentences for physicians and members of other healthcare professions, can be found, for instance, in quite a few Arab and Latin American countries as well as in Belgium prior to 1990.

C. In aggravated circumstances, the imposition of a *ban on the practice of a particular profession* is, in addition to an increase in the threatened criminal punishment, a possibility. Whereas such a prohibition is optional in numerous countries in cases involving a conviction for impermissible termination, in Mexico it is compulsory.[235] Provisions of this type apply practically only to physicians and members of other healthcare professions. Some countries even provide for a special prohibition against practicing in birthing facilities (Mo-

---

[232] This is the legal position in the Federal Republic of Germany, the former GDR, France, Greece, Great Britain, Ireland, the former Yugoslavia/Croatia, Luxembourg, the Netherlands, Norway, Poland, Portugal, Rumania, Switzerland and Turkey as well as in Hungary and the former ČSSR; likewise in quite a few non-European countries, e.g., in Canada.

[233] For more, see *supra* II.4.1 and II.4.2. Violations against procedural rules inevitably target physicians and are discussed separately *infra* at II.5.4.2.

[234] To this extent, the distinction of being a physician can be seen as a personal feature exempting one from punishment. The new rules of the Russian Federation (1993) and of South Africa may also be classified to this group.

[235] This is also true in Rumania for serious cases (actions by the physician without the consent of the woman or the causing of serious bodily injury to or the death of the pregnant woman).

rocco and Algeria) and some go so far as to prohibit practicing in any clinic that simply admits pregnant women (France).

D. In addition, threats of criminal punishment that are not connected with the 'whether' but with *the way* in which a termination is performed are also noteworthy. At this point, we need not discuss whether the elements of the offense of illegal termination are designed to ensure that terminations are performed in a professional manner or whether cases involving malpractice are to be dealt with by means of the crimes of homicide and bodily harm. In this context, we are looking specifically at regulations of the 'location' (such as a hospital or licensed facility) in which the procedure is performed. The failure to comply with such regulations is often addressed in special provisions as in the Federal Republic of Germany; it is almost always categorized as a regulatory offense and threatened with minor punishment. In a few countries, however (France, Portugal, Rumania), *failure to comply with the 'hospital requirement'* leads to punishment for an impermissible termination, even if the actual substantive prerequisites of permission were fulfilled.

5.4.2 *Criminal sanctions with respect to 'preliminary procedure'*

In numerous countries, a 'safeguarding of procedures' is effected by means of supplementary criminal provisions. Such regulations – tailored, of course, to the regulatory model in force locally – target, by definition, persons involved in the 'preliminary procedures,' i.e., to a great extent, if not exclusively, physicians. Furthermore, they can be directed at those physicians who are generally entitled to carry out terminations and who, in undertaking the procedure, are required to ascertain that the prerequisites have been fulfilled.

A. In cases of exemptions from punishment based on some sort of indication

As far as the utilization of indications or similar exemptions from punishment is concerned (be it within the framework of a pure indication model or of a successive time limit indication approach), criminal provisions can target both the procedure as such engaged in to determine the presence of an indication as well as the physician who goes ahead and performs a termination even though he or she was aware, or should have been aware, that the indication-determination process was in some way deficient.

The former West German law offers illustrative material for both aforementioned approaches: on the one hand, it threatened with punishment physicians who, contrary to better judgment, made a defective determination of an indication, regardless of whether the termination was actually performed; and, on the other hand, it threatened with (a milder misdemeanor) punishment those physicians who performed a termination without a written document confirming the existence of an indication, even if the actual, substantive existence of an indication was confirmed *ex post facto*.[236] With similar results, both the Norwegian and Finnish termination laws contain a special criminal provision that targets procedural violations in cases involving terminations that are determined to be legal *ex post facto*. Conversely, under former South African law, for example, the issuance of an untruthful indication attest as well as the approval of a termination on the basis of a criminological indication despite the absence of the necessary certification from the district judge were threatened with the same punishment as that foreseen for a termination performed in the absence of an indication.

In quite a few legal systems, however, namely those lacking special criminal provisions (such as numerous formerly socialist countries), procedural violations that ensue within the scope of the indication model can only be addressed by means of the general criminal provisions on illegal terminations. Whether this should be done is a matter of contention: in some countries – Luxembourg for instance – it appears that the question was never consciously posed; in other countries – such as France – the issue gave rise to a highly controversial discussion that was not clarified until the issuance of the new Code Pénal.

B.   In cases of exemptions from punishment based on time limits

Similarly, criminal provisions can also help ensure compliance with special procedural regulations within the framework of exemptions from punishment for terminations performed within certain time limits. Noteworthy are violations of legally established waiting periods between preliminary procedures and the termination itself (the Netherlands), or, conversely, the failure to comply with provisions designed to ensure that the process proceeds at a rapid pace (the Netherlands, Sweden).

As far as terminations performed in accordance with the counseling model are concerned (i.e., a model for which indications as such are irrelevant), the new law in the Federal Republic of Germany has deliberately upgraded the *counseling requirement* to a substantive prerequisite for the exemption from punishment.[237] Under the previous law, failure to comply with the counseling requirement could only be punished as a lesser (misdemeanor) offense, and the

---

[236] In the absence of an indication, sanctions are usually imposed for aiding and abetting an illegal termination.

[237] The legal position is similar, for instance, in Austria with respect to the requirement for consultation with a physician.

pregnant woman herself could not be punished if an indication was ascertained *ex post facto*.

In contrast, the failure under the German indication model to obtain an attest from a second physician regarding the presence of an indication leads today, as it did previously, only to punishment for violating the corresponding special procedural rule when it is established *ex post facto* that the termination was justified on account of an indication (again, the pregnant woman remains exempt). Thus, it is currently possible for a termination performed in violation of the counseling requirement (e.g., failure to comply with the required waiting period) to be treated as a less serious offense (merely a violation of § 218b para. 1 sent. 1 StGB) – and the pregnant woman herself may be entirely exempt from punishment – if an indication is ascertained *ex post*.

Some procedural violations are apparently viewed as rather marginal and, insofar as they are sanctioned at all, are classified as lesser or as regulatory offenses. This is the case, for instance, in Sweden with regard to the failure to comply with provisions designed to accelerate the process or with those designed to prevent procedural delays, and in Switzerland (since 2002), with regard to specified procedural requirements.

C.   Criminal provisions applicable to more than one model

Criminal provisions applicable to more than one model include provisions that concretely relate to specific violations relevant to both time-limit based and indication-based exemptions from punishment as well as those provisions that criminalize in a generalized way procedural violations that occur within the framework of the successive time limit/indication model. For example:

- Primarily in eastern European countries (e.g., the former GDR, Poland), the relevant criminal norms are configured as *'Blankettvorschriften,'* i.e., norms codified in one place (here the criminal code) that refer to norms codified elsewhere. This means, first of all, that no distinction is drawn between 'substantive' and procedural violations. Insofar as successive[238] or combined[239] time limit/indications models are concerned, this also means, however, that procedural violations are all lumped together: violations of

---

[238] What is meant by this term is that the presence of an indication attains legal significance only after the legal time limit for an 'early' termination has been exceeded, as apparently is the case in Denmark, see also *supra* II.2.4.2.C.

[239] This refers to regulatory models in which – as in the new federal German law – indications can have legal significance parallel to exemptions from punishment based on time limits.

provisions concerning the ascertainment of indications – e.g., of the requirement to obtain a prompt decision from the responsible level of authority – are thrown into the same criminal basket as infringements of procedural rules that are of special significance for the exemption of punishment based on time limits. In addition, this regulatory technique, taken literally, tends to sweep up even rather marginal procedural violations[240] – as regulation at the procedural level is often quite elaborate. Nevertheless, rule infringements that are considered 'tolerable' can, according to the general criminal law instrument regarding minimal or non-existent threats to society, be exempted from prosecution. This possibility is specifically mentioned, for instance, in the country report for Poland.

- A *'summary' solution* for (supplementary) criminal punishment for mere procedural violations is found, for example, in Norway. There, however, terminations that are not legitimized through the ascertainment of an indication or through an official authorization incur stricter (primary) criminal sanctions.

- Certain *special procedural requirements* for the performance of terminations can be significant regardless of whether the exemption from punishment is based on a time limit or an indication model, as shown, for example, by the hospital requirement. Failure to comply with this requirement is treated in the Federal Republic of Germany and in Italy as a regulatory offense, in Denmark as a misdemeanor. In the new Romanian law, the performance of the procedure outside approved facilities is even incorporated into the basic elements of the crime for illegal termination.

- To what extent *deficits in medical advice and/or disclosure* can affect the validity of the pregnant woman's *consent* and in this way become relevant from a criminal law perspective remains for the most part unclear. Although violations of the consent requirement frequently present an aggravating circumstance, they are still regularly treated as intentional crimes.[241] In some countries – as, apparently, in Brazil – knowingly acting against the will of the pregnant woman may be considered justified in cases of strict (vital) medical indications; as a rule, however, termination

---

[240] An extreme example: performance of the procedure without the woman being presented with a receipt for the portion of the expenses she paid or the number of the receipt being recorded in the medical history (as required by the law of the former Soviet Union). At any rate, however, impermissible 'post-offense conduct' – such as a violation of a duty to report that serves statistical purposes – is not covered by this type of regulation; see also *infra* II.5.4.3.

[241] For further details, see *supra* II.4.3.2.

against the will of the pregnant woman is subject to heightened punishment.

• Bans on the performance of a termination if the woman has not been given the *opportunity to state her reasons* or if the *duration of the pregnancy* has not been established appear to be unique to Germany.

5.4.3 *Other criminal sanctions*

Information on the infringement of subsequent duties to disclose and report can be found at II.4.2.4, II.7.1; with regard to the so-called preliminary offenses, the reader is referred to II.6.1.1. As far as preliminary offenses are concerned, it should be noted that in various countries physicians as well as certain healthcare institutions are expressly exempted from particular rules, such as those prohibiting the dissemination (see II.6.1.1) of instruments used for termination, so as to avoid indirectly making the performance of permissible terminations, in practice, impossible.[242]

5.4.4 *Disciplinary and professional sanctions applicable to the termination of pregnancy*

In addition to instruments of the criminal law, numerous countries – this is true of Iraq, South Africa, USA, and especially of Bavaria – also have professional or disciplinary rules that can be utilized to discipline physicians for deficiencies in the decision-making process or in the performance of a termination. In some countries these rules carry only comparably minor sanctions; in other countries, however, they may even lead to temporary bans on the practice of medicine or even to revocations of the license to practice.[243] Whether the decision to get involved is left to the discretion of the professional association or whether such events are a matter for state disciplinary organs remains open, for the most part, in the country reports, as do – with respect to the principle of 'ne bis in idem'– the thoroughly problematic relationship between the various types of procedures and the frequency with which disciplinary measures are actually imposed in practice.[244]

---

[242] For further details, see *infra* II.6.1.1 and II.6.1.2.

[243] Federal Republic of Germany (especially detailed: Bavaria), France, Greece, Great Britain, the Netherlands, Austria, Poland, Portugal, Sweden and Switzerland as well as Australia, Brazil, Costa Rica, Ghana, Iraq, Israel, Mexico, South Africa and the USA.

[244] The statistical data on prosecution are mostly limited to the number of prosecuted or convicted and do not indicate the extent to which the numbers physicians are involved. As far as data are provided on the legal sanctions imposed, professional bans, etc., are not mentioned specifically.

II.6   PREVENTIVE MEASURES

In the attempt to avoid terminations of pregnancy, both repressive as well as supportive preventive methods are possible. As far as the former are concerned, in the following (beyond the provisions – discussed above – that are directly connected to the prohibited performance itself),[245] diverse offences connected with the pre-termination phase as well as other related offenses are addressed (II.6.1). The latter seek – beyond regimentation in the sense of a 'preliminary procedure' leading up to a permissible termination[246] – through guiding or supportive measures to prevent the occurrence of 'endangered' pregnancies or to encourage their acceptance, after the fact, by the parents and especially by the pregnant woman herself (II.6.2). While some countries – in particular those where the scope of permissibility is rather limited – more or less unequivocally prefer repressive methods, others – primarily those with a broader scope of permissibility – rely more on the principle of 'motivation through help', whereby in addition to examining the general measures available for the support of families[247] particular attention must be paid to the extent to which the prevention of termination is aspired to as well as to the types of instruments employed. As expected, numerous countries make use of both approaches, with highly divergent emphases, while in some places it appears that not much hope is held out for either method of prevention.

6.1   Additional criminal offenses

Of the related offenses introduced in Part II.4.2.4, independent preparatory and preliminary acts must be considered under the rubric of preventive criminal norms (II.6.1.1); provisions designed (primarily) to preserve a certain 'public profile' of termination of pregnancy must also be considered (II.6.1.2).

6.1.1   *Independent preparatory and preliminary offenses*

Access to the instruments or drugs used to perform or induce a termination of pregnancy may be made subject to punishment in various ways. In so doing, some countries stress the aspect of *dissemination* (the 'supply side'), whereas

---

[245] See *supra* II.4.
[246] See *supra* II.3.
[247] See *supra* I.2 as well as – more detailed – E/K III pp. 15 ff.

others stress *acquisition* (the 'demand side'): the French regulation, which punishes persons who 'present, offer, make possible the offering, sell, put on sale, make possible the sale, distribute and make possible the distribution of all types of medication and items ... suited for causing or furthering an abortion', provides an especially detailed example of the efforts to cover the *'supply side'* in a manner that is as airtight as possible (similar details can be found in the Belgian statute). Lawmakers are for the most part satisfied with more general definitions of the elements of the offense – if, that is, they pay any attention at all to this area. So, for instance, Iraq criminalizes the 'delivery', Mexico the 'dissemination', and Morocco the 'sale' or 'marketing in another manner', while Kuwait, Oman and Senegal subject the 'distribution' of abortifacients to punishment and Portugal, Australia (Queensland), Canada, Turkey and Zambia as well as southern Nigeria punish 'delivery' or 'procurement'.

While in the Federal Republic of Germany, which subscribes to the view that the pregnant woman should remain unpunished as far as possible, it is made clear by means of a personal ground of exemption from punishment that the pregnant woman herself as 'someone who was supplied' cannot be held responsible for having participated in the offense, the issue of the *punishability of the pregnant woman* is not addressed in most of the other country reports.

6.1.2 *Prohibitions against advertising and dissemination of information*

Among the countries that limit public advertising and information about termination of pregnancy by means of criminal proscription, legal systems that strive generally to avoid all (public) advertisement in this area should be distinguished from those systems that try specifically to prevent the dissemination of information on illegal terminations. Some statutes (Brazil) treat announcements, sales pitches or advertising directed at an unspecified public as acts constituting the crime. Other statutes use formulations that foresee a narrower relationship to concrete audiences, such as 'offering' (Greece, Canada), 'referrals' (Egypt)[248] or 'counseling' (Spain until 1995). Especially widely formulated proscriptions, those that subject to punishment all promotional information – even regarding legal opportunities to abort and drugs or methods that do not work, can be found in countries such as France, Algeria and Morocco.

On the other hand, in some countries prohibitions on the advertisement of termination are derived only indirectly from *more general provisions*. This is the case, for example, in parts of Switzerland, where cantonal provisions prohibit the distribution of 'pulp fiction'. Other options include the general of-

---

[248] Here there is a complicity provision that requires that the principle act, the performance of a termination, actually be carried out, see Art. 261 Egyptian Penal Code.

fenses of public exhortation to commit a crime and public endorsement of an already committed crime (Portugal, Argentina, Ecuador, Uruguay and Peru).

Offering a contrast to the multitude of legal systems with more or less far-reaching prohibitions against advertising is the *'permissive counterpart'*, composed of three countries: the People's Republic of China and India, where advertising for terminations is not only not prohibited, but even appears to be carried out by the government, and Tunisia, where in the absence of a prohibition against advertising, public family planning centers offer counseling on the termination of pregnancy.

As in the case of the availability of items used to perform terminations, it is also necessary to make sure from a technical legal perspective that, in the broader area of advertisement, *healthcare practitioners* are allowed to receive necessary information and that they are allowed to further disseminate such information. Where the wording of the statute criminalizes even the dissemination of information on legal methods and means of performing terminations, special provisions providing for exceptions are needed. Some countries have enacted provisions that expressly allow information specifically directed at physicians and other healthcare practitioners;[249] occasionally, more general provisions are utilized, as in Canada, according to which information that demonstrably serves the public interest is permissible.

6.2   Government services

The country reports present a variety of material concerning efforts to counteract terminations through the use of government services in support of the family and in the area of family planning/birth control. It was suggested to the authors of the country reports that with regard to this point they concentrate on those measures specifically aimed at reducing terminations. Of course, goals are not always easy to ascertain, particularly if measures obviously falling within the rubric of general family policy have been changed due to the reformation of the prerequisites for a permissible termination.

6.2.1   *Legislative intent*

Support of the family – regardless of how it is concretely expressed – is seen primarily as a general social responsibility or even as the realization of social rights. The avoidance of termination is seen more as a positive side effect than

---

[249] As in the Federal Republic of Germany (including counseling locations), France (physicians and pharmacists), Greece (with express authorization for instruction through family planning centers).

as a specific goal. However, there are a whole string of countries (e.g., the Federal Republic of Germany, Austria) in which a liberalization of the law of termination was consciously 'flanked' by a broadly designed program of family policy. The primary goal is, along with the financial well-being of the family, to promote the compatibility of family and career, e.g., through the provision of sufficient resources for child care outside the home.[250] Apart from isolated measures specifically designed to reduce the demand for terminations, legislative activities must be seen primarily in light of the fact that the debate concerning the reform of the law of termination also offered occasion for stocktaking and reassessment of family policy from the perspective of social justice. On the whole, in most countries the regulation of termination has proven itself to be much less of an indicator of a specific policy toward families than has the local system of social services.

6.2.2 *Individual measures*

As far as *special services* aimed at preventing terminations are concerned, a distinction must be drawn between (a) those that are aimed at avoiding unwanted – and therefore endangered – pregnancies and (b) those that serve to promote acceptance of such pregnancies after the fact. Finally, some measures have a double function in that they are based on a combination of prevention and acceptance (c).

a) Measures that make *access and use of contraceptives* easier are designed to help prevent unwanted pregnancies. In this vein, the decline of traditional advertising, information and marketing prohibitions must be mentioned.[251] Nevertheless, only a few countries – the former GDR, Italy (with delivery in family counseling centers), the Netherlands, the former ČSSR (since 1987), Spain (only with a prescription in official counseling centers) and Tunisia – provide dependable contraceptives such as the 'pill' and contraceptive coils to women at no cost. A string of additional countries – such as the Federal Republic of Germany, Luxembourg, and Turkey – provide the 'pill' free to needy and/or to young women, and in Sweden the cost of contraception is subsidized by the state with the express goal of reducing the number of terminations.

---

[250] On the right to a place in preschool for children starting at the age of three under the new German law, see § 24 SGB VIII (Aid for Children and Youth) in the version of the *Schwangeren- und Familienhilfegesetz* [Act to Aid Pregnant Women and Families] of 27 February 1992 (*BGBl.* 1992 I pp. 1398 ff., 1400).

[251] See E/K III p. 40.

- A larger number of countries (such as Hungary, South Africa, the People's Republic of China, India) have taken steps to improve the population's *knowledge of family planning issues*. In some countries, such as in the former GDR, this complex of information is seen as one aspect of the counseling provided to pregnant women seeking termination; elsewhere, as in Turkey, it is seen as a *general concern*, where through its title – 'Demographic Planning Statute' – the relevant law clearly expresses its priorities (this law even contains a criminal provision intended to counteract the distribution and use of ineffective contraceptives). Such general counseling regulations are found also – and probably not completely coincidentally – in countries such as Sweden, Austria (promotion of counseling in matters of family planning, economic and social concerns of expectant mothers, sexual concerns and issues in partner relationships), Japan (counseling centers for eugenic protection) and Canada, in which the scope of permissible terminations is rather broad and there is no previous counseling requirement.
- Some countries attach special significance to *sex education* in school (Luxembourg, Poland) and for youth (Federal Republic of Germany and Sweden[252]) or to premarital counseling (Hungary) and thereby give *particular target groups* special attention. A regionally as well as temporally limited pilot project carried out in Sweden in the 1970s shows that such efforts can indeed influence the frequency of termination.

b) Government services that promote the *acceptance of existing but initially unwanted pregnancies* and in so doing are supposed to prevent terminations are naturally those of a primarily financial sort. The form taken on by these services must always be seen in the context of general family policy measures because they grant additional necessary aid where the general measures are insufficient.

- *Targeted aid measures* such as those available in the Federal Republic of Germany since 1984 from the foundation 'Mother and Child – Protection of Unborn Life',[253] are mentioned in only a few country reports. The country report on Switzerland, for instance, alludes to public and private aid, although in a non-specified form, that apparently goes beyond the general

---

[252] Here, women older than 30 are seen as a special counseling target-group, and opportunities for family-planning counseling are incorporated into the regular gynecological examinations.

[253] The following are among the services offered: housing aid, household help during pregnancy and after birth, aid in purchasing linens, clothing and household items as well as financial support for child care if the mother must be absent for her career or education.

catalogue of services.[254] The basic problem with such measures with respect to their suitability to prevent terminations appears (as in the Federal Republic of Germany) in light of the time pressure caused by the already existing pregnancy, to lie in finding – with a justifiable amount of bureaucratic effort – solutions that offer pregnant women long-term perspectives for themselves and their children.

- *Counseling concerning the generally available services for families* is also regarded in some countries as a preventive measure. The German legislature has devoted particular attention to this aspect of counseling[255] and in addition has urged counselors to support pregnant women in the assertion of claims, in the search for housing and (day)care and in the continuation of their education.[256]

c) With some measures, it must be assumed that they are not only designed to prevent unwanted pregnancies but are also supposed to promote the acceptance of such pregnancies after the fact.

- Primary examples of this so-called *double function* are efforts intended to *raise the public consciousness* of the value of unborn life. Such efforts are foreseen by the new Hungarian law and urgently recommended in the country report for Austria; they can also be seen as an integral part of sex education.
- A pragmatic approach to the aforementioned double function is to require – be it with regard to pregnant women or be it in a broader scope – disclosure and counseling sessions to address the physical and psychological *consequences of termination* and the associated risks. Both the Federal Republic of Germany and Luxembourg have adopted this approach, which is based on the hope that knowledge might motivate people to use dependable contraceptives and might also play a role in the decision-making process in individual cases.

A few country reports contain informative comments with regard to the extent to which *adoption* is a possible means of preventing terminations.[257] On the

---

[254] See also Art. 120 para. 1 lit. b) No. 2 Swiss Penal Code in the version of 2002.

[255] See § 2 SchKG 1995 and § 2 of the *Gesetz über Aufklärung, Verhütung, Familienplanung und Beratung* [Law on Education, Contraception, Family Planning and Counseling] of 1992.

[256] § 2 para. 2 p. 2 SchKG.

[257] The possibilities of placing a child in an institution or with a 'substitute family' or foster parents (see § 33 f. SGB VIII for the Federal Republic of Germany) outside of the

one hand, they follow the *basic notion* that a pregnant woman cannot be forced to carry a child to term simply because adoption is a possibility. This corresponds to the fact that a legally binding decision to give up a child for adoption cannot be made until after birth. On the other hand, it is clear for a variety of reasons (as in the USA) that adoption is often considered a socially desirable alternative to termination, even though its estimated numerical significance is rather low.[258]

The concrete *treatment of the 'adoption issue' within the scope of the decision-making process* diverges considerably: in some countries the advising physician has absolutely no duty to mention this possibility (this used to be the case in Poland). Other countries, such as Luxembourg and Israel, have enacted provisions according to which the possibility of releasing the child to adoption must be raised during counseling, especially to single women. The new legal position in Germany, according to which the right to counseling under § 2 SchKG (i.e., *not* the special counseling required for conflicted pregnancies) also includes the right to information concerning 'the legal and psychological aspects associated with an adoption', appears to be more or less comparable to the position in these countries.[259] Only rarely – in Switzerland (since 2002) and in some regions of Italy, for instance – has information concerning adoption been made an obligatory part of the counseling process in anticipation of a permissible termination.

---

formal adoption procedure is only occasionally addressed in the country reports (Poland, Iraq); thus, these issues cannot be examined further within the scope of this comparative analysis.

[258] If on the other hand it is mentioned in the country report on Iraq that giving up for adoption is not seen as an alternative to termination, this must be viewed in light of the very restricted permissibility in Iraq of this procedure (only medical and embryopathic indications).

[259] § 2 para. 2 No. 8 SchKG 1995, likewise § 2 para. 2 No. 8 of the Law on Education, Contraception, Family Planning and Counseling of 1992. Corresponding information services are planned in Poland under the Family Planning Law of 1993.

II.7 ROLE OF TERMINATION OF PREGNANCY IN THE PROSECUTORIAL ARENA

In conclusion, special regulations concerning the prosecution of the crime of impermissible termination will be considered, including the duty to report planned offenses to the police or comparable authorities (II.7.2), the duty to report offenses that have already been committed (II.7.1), special rules regarding the statute of limitations (II.7.3) and special rules having to do with the actual criminal prosecution of this offense (II.7.4). The reader is referred to III.2 below for statistical data regarding prosecutorial practice.

7.1 Duty to report terminations of pregnancy already committed

As far as cases involving terminations performed with the consent of the pregnant woman are concerned, there is generally no direct victim to report the crime to the police or otherwise to initiate prosecution.[260] This makes all the more significant the question of whether third parties who become aware of a suspected illegal termination are authorized or even obligated to report their suspicions to criminal justice authorities. Particular attention should be focused on physicians and other medical professionals because in the course of their professional lives they are particularly likely to run across relevant information. Thus, they are the most obvious group to be considered in the context of a duty or right to disclose; on the other hand, medical professionals are traditionally subject to special duties of confidentiality.

To be sure, duties to report that are especially addressed to physicians and that *expressly concern illegal terminations* are rare.[261] Noteworthy are, for example, some cantonal regulations in Switzerland that address freelance midwives as well as physicians and encompass attempts as well as completed acts, and a Spanish decree from the year 1902 that concerns 'evidence of an unnatural birth process'. Most interesting, however, are the exceptionally comprehensive former Bulgarian regulations. They regulated down to the last detail the

---

[260] Even the father of the aborted child can usually be ruled out, be it that had no knowledge of the pregnancy or be it that he also agreed to the termination. On this point, see also *infra* III.2.2.

[261] Reporting duties with regard to the performance of permissible terminations, commonly based on statistical and epidemiological grounds, are not the concern here. See *supra* II.3.6 as well as *infra* III.1.1.

physician's duties of examination, treatment, documentation and reporting related to the care of a woman following a presumed criminal termination and threatened medical personnel who did not comply in a timely fashion with the duty to report ('in writing') with criminal prosecution for obstruction of justice.

Regulations aimed at physicians concerning duties or rights to report illegal terminations that have already taken place illustrate the *conflicting goals of prosecutorial and healthcare interests:* From a criminological perspective there is hardly a better possible informant than the physician treating a woman for complications such as those that are apparently common following a termination performed by a layperson; on the other hand, it stands to reason that women will hesitate to seek medical attention, even if they know that failure to seek treatment may prove fatal, if they must fear that in seeking treatment they are in fact giving themselves up to criminal justice authorities. In light of this, there are numerous regulations that restrict the physician's duties or rights to report out of consideration for the patient's interests. Hence, in Italy, Brazil, Costa Rica and Turkey, for instance, a physician's[262] duty to report, non-compliance with which is subject to criminal sanctions, applies only insofar as reporting does not expose patients to the danger of prosecution. In cases where the woman could be prosecuted for illegal termination, the physician providing follow-up treatment must observe the duty of confidentiality; thus, the duty to report is especially relevant in cases where a termination has been performed without the consent of the woman.[263] France takes a 'middle of the road' approach by making it optional for physicians and other healthcare professionals to report illegal procedures that they have discovered. In practice, this corresponds more or less to the legal situation in Germany, where the authority of physicians to breach the duty of confidentiality in order to protect higher interests (here for instance the health interests of other women as potential victims of 'back street abortionists') can be derived from general rules.[264]

7.2 Duty to report planned illegal terminations

This project did not uncover any special criminal provisions that expressly threaten sanctions for the failure to report impending illegal terminations. Now

---

[262] In Turkey, nurses, midwives and other medical personnel are put in the same category as physicians.

[263] In Turkey, also for procedures undertaken with the consent of the pregnant woman within the first 10 weeks of gestation and performed by an unauthorized person.

[264] See TH. LENCKNER, 'Verschwiegenheitspflicht und Zeugnisverweigerungsrecht des Beraters', in A. ESER and H.A. HIRSCH (eds.), *Sterilisation und Schwangerschaftsabbruch* (Stuttgart, Enke 1980) pp. 227 ff. at pp. 236 ff.

and then, however, more broadly formulated duties to report may apply: The statutes in Ghana and Israel, where general crime prevention provisions also cover illegal terminations, go the furthest. On the other hand, punishment under the law of the former Yugoslavia was possible for impending terminations only in certain aggravated cases.

7.3   Special rules on the statute of limitations

Normally the general rules on limitations apply to illegal terminations. This issue was not, however, discussed in detail in the country reports and is not the subject of comparative analysis here. Special regulations on abortion offenses are reported in only two countries, and in both cases the otherwise applicable period of limitation is curtailed: According to the criminal law of the former GDR, prosecution of solicitation as well as of aiding and abetting a criminal termination was barred by the statute of limitations in three instead of the regular eight years; and under Swiss law, the period of limitation for self-abortion and for third-party abortions with the consent of the woman considering the special evidentiary problems amounts to only three (until 2002: two) (instead of the regular five to ten) years.

7.4   Special rules for prosecuting cases of illegal termination

7.4.1   *Prosecutorial discretion*

In conclusion, as far as the issue of special procedural regulations with regard to the offense of illegal termination is concerned, only a few of the country reports contribute relevant material. Guidelines are occasionally found in countries where prosecution is governed by the principle of discretionary prosecution. Examples include a detailed Dutch directive that defines the general thrust of the approach to be taken by criminal justice authorities as well as an Israeli order – in the meantime repealed without any apparent practical consequences – according to which charges for illegal terminations should only be brought in special cases. In other countries, criminal justice authorities appear informally to impose certain restrictions on themselves. Especially noteworthy is the practice in England – inspired by health policy considerations – not to prosecute women for self-induced abortions; the posture of Irish criminal justice authorities, which tolerate the distribution and use of drugs preventing implantation of the fertilized egg despite the fact that the legality of these activities is subject to question, is also worthy of mention.

7.4.2   *Features peculiar to the criminal process*

With respect to prosecutions for illegal termination, various types of special procedural regulations arise. Noteworthy examples include:

- From a German perspective, the special *prohibition of use of evidence* according to § 108 para. 2 StPO is the most important. Accordingly, items found at a physician's office in the course of an unrelated search that are connected to a termination are not admissible in a prosecution against the patient for a crime pursuant to § 218 StGB.
- As a result of a regulation in Uruguay, *the examining magistrate* is obliged to suspend the procedure in abortion cases if the adjudicating judge could refrain from imposing a punishment. Since the action taken by the examining magistrate is final and cannot be appealed, the discretion of the adjudicating judge is circumvented.

Part III

STATISTICAL INFORMATION

Introduction   177

III.1   Termination Statistics   178

III.2   Crime Statistics   185

III.3   Judicial Statistics and Trends in Prosecution   187

INTRODUCTION

Any comparative description and analysis of the statistical data gather in this study faces a fundamental difficulty; namely, the differences in the state and quality of the available data are considerable, if not extreme. Hence, an evaluation can be made only with great caution.

III.1   TERMINATION STATISTICS

1.1   State of the data

If one asks how prevalent the termination of pregnancy actually is in a particular country, the following issues must be clarified right from the beginning: does one mean (only) the number of procedures deemed permissible, for which the people involved have actually, or at least purportedly, fulfilled the substantive and procedural legal prerequisites? Or does one want information – especially if an attempt is to be made to evaluate the scope of unreported cases – regarding the prevalence of illegal terminations? The fact that data concerning unreported cases are encumbered from the start with greater or lesser uncertainties cannot be cause for surprise. In the meanwhile, in some cases, even when dealing with statistical data derived from a state-imposed duty to report,[1] one must allow for considerable deficits (i.e., under reporting), be it that the affected institutions or physicians are not sufficiently complying with their duty to report, be it that along with the procedures that are reported as legal, an investigation into the true number of actually occurring terminations might need to take other areas, such as illegal terminations or those that are carried out abroad, into account.[2]

Evidently, the countries that were the subjects of this study are by no means equally interested in the empirical clarification of the actual prevalence of terminations. Even efforts being made statistically to record the number of procedures that comply with legal requirements are too diverse. In places where the scope of permissibility is restricted to a narrowly defined medical indication, a centralized reporting system is a rarity. Conversely, the more permissive countries are more likely – exceptions prove the rule – to have an interest in recording the true numbers.

Nevertheless, extensive data that can be considered reliable are available for many countries over a longer period of time (see Table III/1, *infra* pp. 190/191). Insofar as data are to be had, the most interesting information is, of course, the number of terminations performed annually (expressed, for better comparison,

---

[1]   See *supra* II.3.6.

[2]   See C. TIETZE and S.K. HENSHAW, *Induced Abortion: A World Review*, 6th (and final) edn. (New York, Alan Guttmacher Institute 1986 with 1990 supplement); S.K. HENSHAW, 'Induced Abortion: A World Review, 1990', 16 *International Family Planning Perspectives* (1990) pp. 59-65, 76.

in terms of the number of terminations per 1,000 or 100 live births,[3] per 1,000 or 100 known pregnancies,[4] per 1,000 or 100 women of childbearing age[5] or per 1,000 inhabitants[6]) and their distribution among the various prerequisites for a permissible termination.[7]

1.2 Comparative prevalence of terminations of pregnancy

In light of the lack of uniform data, any comparison must be confined to countries and parameters for which there is more than only sporadic information (1.2.1). In making such comparisons, the prevalence of terminations of pregnancy in relationship to the respective models of regulation as well as to special procedural prerequisites, like counseling or authorization, is most interesting (1.2.2). Additionally, the developments in the various countries should, if possible, be compared over longer time periods (1.2.3).

1.2.1 *Frequency of the termination of pregnancy in various countries*

'Epidemiological' data on the prevalence of non-criminal terminations have been presented for England, France, Germany, Italy, the Netherlands, Switzerland and Yugoslavia, as well as for those Scandinavian counties included in this project and a few eastern European states. For non-European countries, usable data can be found in the country reports on Canada, the People's Republic of China (with proviso), Israel, Japan, South Africa, Tunisia and the USA. In order to be able to present for comparative purposes information from some other countries, we decided, after some hesitation, to include in the overview presented here (see Table III/1, *infra* pp. 190/191) countries like Austria, Greece,

---

[3] Federal Republic of Germany, former GDR, Italy, Yugoslavia, Poland, Rumania, Sweden, Switzerland, Australia, Israel, Canada and Tunisia.

[4] Netherlands, Rumania, Sweden, Hungary, Bulgaria and former ČSSR, Israel, Tunisia and USA.

[5] Federal Republic of Germany, former GDR, the Netherlands, Poland, Rumania, Sweden and the other Nordic countries, Switzerland, Hungary, Bulgaria and former ČSSR as well as – outside of Europe – Australia, Israel, Japan, Canada, Tunisia and USA. Some of the discrepancies in these data may be due to the fact that the standards of comparison are not uniformly defined: In some countries, the data encompass women between 15 and 44 years of age (e.g., Federal Republic of Germany, Canada) whereas elsewhere the age range extends to 49 years (e.g., Poland, Japan).

[6] Rumania, Israel.

[7] Federal Republic of Germany, France, Great Britain (England/Wales and Scotland), Croatia as part of former Yugoslavia, Poland, Finland, Hungary, Israel, Japan and South Africa.

India, Ireland, Mexico, Spain and Taiwan, even though the only data available are fragmentary or estimative.[8] We are restricting ourselves, however, as far as that goes, to presenting the reported numbers of terminations (presumed to be) performed annually, and we will either refrain from making comparisons based on calculations that would normally be necessary in order to compare countries with different populations, or we will put other people's calculations that are based on estimates in parentheses in order to indicate the special difficulties associated with them. This approach provides at very least an insight into what, according to expert opinion, the order of magnitude of the number of terminations in a particular country might be. Whereas the fact must be taken into account that officially reported data tend to underreport to a greater or lesser extent, the estimates reported here may deviate in either direction, both up or down, from the (unknown) actual number.

Even a quick glance is sufficient to reveal the enormous spread in the data summarized in Table III/1 (pp. 190/191). Unless otherwise noted, the average respective values calculated for the years 1980-1982 are always given. On the one hand, this allows parallel time periods to be compared – something that appeared to be more important than the attempt to present the most up-to-date information available. On the other hand, this method allows certain fluctuations to be eliminated.

1.2.2 Comparison in the relationship to the respective regulatory model and counseling system

Even a cursory comparison of numbers indicates that countries with – and despite – similar models of regulation show an enormous spread in the frequency of termination. A grouping according to the type of regulatory model (see Table III/2, p. 192) confirms this. It should be borne in mind that the conspicuously low rate for *South Africa* (with its narrowly defined 'indication' model) is based solely on those procedures legally carried out within the country borders. According to estimates of unreported terminations, these statistics do not reflect even 1% of the total number of actually occurring terminations.

It is an eye-catching fact that permissive regulations can be associated with both above average (e.g., USA, eastern European countries) as well as with remarkably low rates of frequency (e.g., the Netherlands, Tunisia). Already from this observation alone, one must conclude that the establishment by the (criminal) law of the prerequisites for permitting termination is not necessarily of compelling significance for the prevalence of terminations. This also holds true

---

[8] See India, where approximately 500,000 terminations are officially reported annually, but where estimates are ten times higher.

at the procedural level, especially for the regulation of counseling (see Table III/3, p. 193). The available figures do not support the logical assumption that more hurdles lead inescapably to fewer terminations.

1.2.3   *Developments in the number of terminations over time*

It stands to reason that an attempt should be made to interpret the available data on the frequency of terminations over time. To this end, we have relied on material from various international surveys[9] in addition to the material in the country reports. Thus, the maximum amount of information was taken into consideration, even though it does not all refer to the same time period.

The numerical developments – always in reference to 1,000 women of reproductive age – are summarized in diagrams Part III/1 – III/4 (*infra* pp. 194-198).[10] In order to facilitate the identification of any possible effects of legal changes, these changes are noted in the diagrams (□ = 'liberalization,' ○ = toughening of the legal prerequisites for termination).

The data reaching back the furthest in time come from eastern European nations, but also from England/Wales, Scotland and the Scandinavian countries as well as Japan and Tunisia.[11] According to these figures, an increase for the second half of the 1960s is typical. Bulgaria and Rumania are the only exceptions, possibly due to restrictive changes in the law. The increase, however, did not continue steadily. Rather, it came to a complete standstill after several years; frequently the tide even turned in the other direction. But for some countries, like England/Wales, Norway and Sweden, a renewed, although less pronounced increase is noted for the second half of the 1980s.[12] Nevertheless, one may generalize without reservation the observation made specifically of the USA, namely, that even the decriminalization of the termination of pregnancy does not lead to an inexorable escalation in its frequency.

This leads to the question of the *effects of changes in the law* on the officially reported frequency of the termination of pregnancy. From the existing data it is apparent that in response to their own ('liberalizing') reforms some countries experienced a considerable increase, one which is difficult to explain solely in terms of the gradual establishment of a functional reporting procedure. This is

---

[9] TIETZE and HENSHAW, op. cit. n. 2; HENSHAW, loc. cit. n. 2; United Nations, Department for Economic and Social Information and Policy Analysis, *Abortion Policies: A Global Review,* Volume I-III (New York, United Nations 1992-1995).

[10] The division into several diagrams was necessary for purposes of clarity.

[11] For Sweden and Japan with divergent standards of comparison (and therefore not shown in the diagrams) even since 1951 or 1949.

[12] Regarding the temporary increase in Sweden around 1980, see *infra* III.1.3.

true for England/Wales and Scotland, but also for Tunisia and the USA. In other countries, however, the legislature apparently passed reform legislation only after increases in the frequency of termination had already taken place, be it – as, for example, in Italy – that statistical information is only available for the post-reform period and the statistics are quite stable from the beginning, or be it – as in Norway and Sweden as well as, to some extent, in Denmark – that the existing data for the pre-reform period show a comparable increase in frequency. If one includes for the Federal Republic of Germany procedures performed in the Netherlands and England during the early 1970s on women who were German residents, then this country must also be included in the latter group of northern countries.

1.3 Considerations regarding possible variables

In the final analysis, the country reports provide no clear causal proof with regard to the variables that ultimately influence most significantly the frequency with which pregnancies are terminated; instead, the reports can at most provide some food for thought.

- In cultures strongly shaped by religious beliefs, the *moral condemnation of abortion* emanating from religion may, on occasion, lead to low rates;[13] on the other hand, it may also be (co-)responsible for a sizable 'black market'.[14] Societies that are less morally resolute regarding the termination of pregnancy can nevertheless establish policies that are pragmatically designed to deter terminations, and these policies can shape a corresponding public consciousness and give rise to effective 'preventative behavior'. This is true namely for the Netherlands and, with some reservations, also for countries such as Yugoslavia/Slovenia and Japan. On the other hand, this kind of (relative) moral indifference might indeed make it easier for temporary disturbances – like, for example, Swedish media reports that stir up anxiety about the health risks of the 'pill' – to affect the willingness to deal with unwanted offspring by means of termination and to consider the termination of pregnancy the 'comparatively-speaking lesser evil'. In some countries, a high rate of termination accompanies *poor accessibility of oral contraceptives and/or restrictive regulations concerning voluntary sterilization* sought for purposes of family planning, which is why the presumption of a causal connection between the two phenomena is not unrea-

---

[13] E.g., regarding former Yugoslavia (with reference to Kosovo) E/K I p. 939.
[14] See, e.g., Brazil and other Latin American countries, E/K II 142 f. and 1272 ff.

sonable.[15] This would also mean that it is realistic to hope for widespread acceptance of the proposition that it is better to engage in contraception than it is to abort.

- With respect to *social services* (particularly *financial assistance for families and mothers*),[16] which differ widely from country to country, their effects in the area of prevention cannot be proven simply by looking at the numbers but rather only through conjecture in the qualitative sense. Because these social services are generally not specifically aimed at deterring the termination of pregnancy, but rather more generally at alleviating the burdens associated with child care, this is not unduly surprising. Something similar holds true for the integration into and upbringing of a child in an extended family or clan – a possibility that in industrial lands can apparently be fallen back upon only in exceptional cases.

Altogether, it is certainly true that some things that argue in favor of the proposition that legal measures to regulate the termination of pregnancy can influence to a certain degree the prevalence of the procedure in a particular country. However, this influence often appears to be only temporary. Hence, one would also do well not to transfer rashly observations from totalitarian countries and eras to democratic societies that function under completely different conditions. But above all, the demonstrated influences of legislative measures must be tempered by the observation that comparable legal conditions with regard to the termination of pregnancy may be accompanied by extreme differences in the frequency of officially reported terminations. In light of this, it is noteworthy when comparatively low levels of frequency persist despite a permissive legal stance over a longer period of time (such as in the Netherlands, Canada and Tunisia), or when elsewhere, also in countries without restrictive legislative measures, a clear, long-term trend towards decreasing numbers of officially reported terminations can be seen (as in the former GDR, Finland and Norway since 1975, Denmark since 1980 and perhaps also Japan since 1985).

Even when this result falls short of some expectations connected with this project,[17] the finding can still be viewed as significant that the practical implications of the concept of (criminal) legal regulation as an isolated factor in the prevalence of the termination of pregnancy should not be overestimated. This

---

[15] See HENSHAW, loc. cit. n. 2, at pp. 62 f.

[16] For an in-depth discussion, see E/K III pp. 15 ff.

[17] The introductory remarks to the project as a whole already expressed, however, a certain reservation in the face of impossibly high expectations, see E/K I p. 8. See also B. PAETOW, 'Bericht über das Kolloquium 'Recht und Praxis des Schwangerschaftsabbruchs im internationalen Vergleich'', 97 *ZStW* (1985) pp. 1074-1086.

might also be valid with respect to a possible indirect, 'normappellative' effect, about which one can hardly do more than speculate. Thus, one must caution against exaggerated expectations that the (written) word has any power to influence behavior: insofar as rigid prohibitions accompany serious estimates of a considerable number of illegal procedures, this also means that the various offenders act according to their own private value systems more than they follow any (demanding) normative appeal. Apparently it cannot for a moment be taken for granted that a society will muster the political power – and allocate the necessary recourses – to make pragmatically effective inroads in the fight against the termination of pregnancy.

The dimensions in which the problem must be viewed become clear when estimates are considered of how many women in a country in the course of their lives feel constrained to, and actually do, undergo a termination. *Henshaw*[18] has undertaken to provide estimates for numerous countries represented in this project, according to which approximately – statistically seen – every Hungarian, Czech, or Slavic woman has undergone a termination at least once in her lifetime. Among the Italians, Danes, Norwegians, Swedes, Australians and Japanese, it is every other woman, but among the Dutch not even one in every six women has terminated a pregnancy. While – again statistically seen – eight out of ten American women experience a termination, only three out of ten Canadian and four out of ten French women do. For the Federal Republic of Germany (in former West Germany), *Henshaw* quotes a rate of about 20% on the basis of statistically recorded terminations; if one takes as a basis the estimated figures presented in Table III/1 *infra* pp. 190/191), then the result is somewhat more than twice as high, corresponding approximately to the rate for France. Finally, the data on Ireland are extremely impressive: if one takes the number of Irish women alone who terminate their pregnancies in England and there truthfully report that they come from the Emerald Isle, then it would mean that every eighth Irish woman terminates a pregnancy in the course of her life without subjecting herself to criminal liability. That is – in light of the rigid legal position on the termination of pregnancy within the Irish borders – a more than clear indication of the relativeness of the power of the law to control behavior.

---

[18] On the following, see HENSHAW, loc. cit. n. 2, pp. 62 f.

III.2   CRIME STATISTICS

There are also considerable differences with respect to police crime statistics and judicial reporting of impermissible terminations among the countries participating in this project.

2.1   State of the data

Criminal statistical data (cases charged or registered by the police) are reported only for a minority of the participating countries. These data refer in part to longer time periods (Federal Republic of Germany, Great Britain, Japan, Peru), thus permitting the recognition of certain trends; occasionally, however, they are available only for isolated years (France, Italy, Costa Rica, Canada, Ivory Coast), which considerably restricts their value for research purposes. There are no such figures in most of the country reports because, apparently, most countries do not keep statistics in this area, or, if they do, the information is not accessible to the public.

The available data usually do not differentiate between the various forms of criminal abortion ('self-inflicted' or 'third-party'); occasionally (Poland, Canada), one finds the observation – presumably also true for other countries – that it is primarily people without the prerequisite medical qualifications who are prosecuted for performing third-party terminations. Related offenses (such as criminal violations of the duty to obtain counseling or of reporting requirements) are hardly ever shown separately. For instance, they are included in the German judicial statistics but not in the criminal statistics kept by the police. In addition, neither the judiciary nor the public prosecutor appears to be particularly concerned with abortions occurring without the consent of the pregnant woman or those performed against her will. In Switzerland, for example, the country report mentions that between 1950 and 1980 only a few relevant convictions were registered.

2.2   Comparison and evaluation

Thus, a detailed comparison of crime statistics in this context would appear to be unproductive. At any rate, it can be said, from an overall perspective that the significance of prosecution of criminal termination offenses, in practice, is negligible. Insofar as information is provided over longer time periods, the trend towards declining numbers of reported cases and suspected offenders is clear. For a few countries, the long-term data include periods both before and after a far-reaching 'liberalization'. In these countries, it is characteristic that the decline – from a higher starting level – had already begun long before the reform and that the decline continued thereafter – now from a much lower level – to the point where prosecution, for all intents and purposes, has become insignificant.

Several country reports expressly emphasize a restraint on the part of prosecutors in pressing charges for illegal terminations that cannot always – as for example in Belgium or the Netherlands – be explained by the principle of discretionary prosecution and that occasionally even leads to a kind of 'truce' between law enforcement agents and physician-run facilities for the performance of terminations.

Explanations for the low levels of prosecution are varied. Problems with regard to the clearing up of criminal cases as well as evidentiary difficulties are cited in the reports on the Federal Republic of Germany, Belgium, Portugal and Switzerland as well as Taiwan, Canada and Mexico. These problems are especially apparent when, from a medical standpoint, the procedure was correctly performed, since in such cases there are no complications that could be used as evidence of an offense, and in the specific constellations that arise in cases involving collaborating offenders, all of whom have an interest in secrecy. Additionally, abortion is an offense for which there is little chance that the victim, generally the person most likely to report a crime, will come forward. As examples from the former Yugoslavia, Japan, Mexico and Black Africa indicate, primary triggers of prosecutorial activity apparently include malpractice committed by either physicians or lay practitioners, cases that have become medically complicated as well as police notification prompted by 'conflicts in more intimate social relationships' and those prompted by the 'questionable motives of third parties' (as reported in the Federal Republic of Germany, Belgium and Brazil) – also, charges are sometimes brought by husbands who are offended by the termination. The physician who can practice without complications appears in hardly any country to face even a nominal risk of prosecution.[19] Spectacular charges against individual physicians, such as those reported in Belgium and Canada,[20] as well as – with certain parallels – in the Federal Republic of Germany and France have made themselves felt more as an impulse strengthening the trend towards decriminalization than as a persuasive demonstration of the protection of life by means of criminal law.

---

[19] This seems also to be the case in Austria. Even though almost 20% of Austria's convictions are based on § 96 Abs. 1 StGB, it must not be forgotten that this offense subjects not only physicians who perform terminations but also other participants (other than the pregnant women) to criminal liability. It is not known how the convictions reported under § 96 Abs. 1 Austrian StGB are distributed between physicians as principal offenders and non-physician participants.

[20] See also H.-G. KOCH, 'Über Schwierigkeiten von Ärzten und Gerichten im Umgang mit § 218 StGB', in A. ESER and H.-G. KOCH, *Schwangerschaftsabbruch: Auf dem Weg zu einer Neuregelung* (Baden-Baden, Nomos 1992) pp. 69-84, with additional references to relevant legal proceedings in the Federal Republic of Germany.

III.3   JUDICIAL STATISTICS AND TRENDS IN PROSECUTION

3.1   State of the data

The statistics kept of relevant *trials and convictions* are somewhat better than crime statistics kept by the police. Most European countries keep and publish at least those statistics based on convictions involving the principal termination offenses; on account of the fragmentary condition of police statistics, we will concentrate our comparative analysis on trials and convictions. In contrast, only a minority of the reports from non-European countries (Costa Rica, Japan, Canada, South Africa, Argentina, Chile, Ivory Coast) cite material on point. Israel presents a special case since no charges for illegal termination have been pressed there since 1963, hence rendering discussion of its law enforcement statistics moot.

Because the reported figures on convictions frequently do not differentiate between the various 'roles' of the parties involved (self-inflicted or third-party, medical or lay practitioner), a comprehensive comparison can only follow on the basis of summary information regarding convictions in practice. The following analysis must also restrict itself to the principal termination offenses: statistics regarding convictions for violations of supplementary criminal provisions, such as violations of procedural rules requiring counseling and/or ascertainment of indications and advertising prohibitions, are contained in too few country reports to enable us to make comparisons. Even where such information is given (as for the Federal Republic of Germany), it testifies to the marginal forensic significance of these offenses.

In conclusion, we note that only a few country reports contain detailed information about sentencing. Whereas this information may prove to be of interest in and of itself, for instance regarding the frequency of specific sanctions, it is not possible to make comparisons on such a narrow basis.

3.2   Comparison and evaluation

In the tenor of a temporal snapshot, the situation as it existed at the beginning of the 1980s is portrayed first (see Table III/4, *infra* p. 199). In this Table, the assignment of countries to particular regulatory models follows the classification already undertaken in Diagram II/6 above (p. 68).[21] Aside from a few exceptions, the pertinent regulatory model had, in this time period, already been established for a few years, so that phenomena due to a transition from one model to another can be discounted.

The data, once calculated, result in a range between 0 (Luxembourg, the Netherlands, Israel) and almost 200 (Argentina) annual convictions. Argentina accounts for almost 41% of all the convictions reported here. The average number of annual convictions calculated for all the countries is 23. If one considers the different populations of the respective nations, the following picture emerges (see Table III/5, *infra* p. 200): Chile has almost caught up with Argentina (7.0 convictions per 1 million inhabitants) in the top position. Above the average of 1.2 are Austria and South Africa (each 1.8), Spain (1.6), Costa Rica (1.5) as well as Yugoslavia/Croatia (1.3), while the Federal Republic of Germany clearly lies below the mean.

For some countries, *developments in the number of convictions over a longer time period* are presented. In isolated cases (France, the Netherlands, Japan), the data goes back to the beginning of the twentieth century; for most countries, however, the reporting begins for the most part some time after the end of World War II. The particular starting point cannot always be conclusively determined; regardless, for most countries a drastic decline in the number of convictions – starting from initial levels of different heights – may be observed. Where the changes turn out to be smaller – as in Greece, Yugoslavia/Croatia and the Netherlands – the initial figures are usually (with South Africa as an exception) already at low levels. In Table III/6 (*infra* p. 201), this development covers the time periods from the respective beginning of reporting (for the Netherlands: effective date of Article 251 bis nlStGB) to a fundamental reform in the law on the termination of pregnancy or (where such never occurred) the entire period of reporting; the initial level for each country is set at 100%. Where available, 'post-reform' developments are provided for purposes of comparison.

Insofar as the country reports contain information about the severity of punishment, prison sentences that are not suspended for release on probation seem to be rather uncommon exceptions. While it appears that fines are the most common punishment in the Federal Republic of Germany, conditional prison sentences or suspended prison sentences with release on probation apparently dominate in Belgium, France (after 1975), Austria and Costa Rica; in Austria, however, after the reform of 1975, a proportional increase of sentences imposing fines is apparent. The occasional leniency seen to have been granted to women who aborted (above all in the Federal Republic of Germany and in

---

[21] For countries that appear there but do not appear in the following overview, we are unable to make any corresponding statistical statement.

Belgium) appears to be reflected less in the severity of the imposed sanctions as in the greater selectivity in prosecution, i.e., in the greater chances of acquittal or dismissal of charges.

If an *evaluation* of the data conveyed here is attempted, it is noteworthy that even in Argentina and Chile (the countries with the highest numbers of criminal cases), where illegal terminations are presumed to be prevalent, the author of the Latin America report has stated that 'the number of criminal prosecutions measured against that of abortions is irrelevant', and 'a practical decriminalization has been brought about, against which, as far as can be seen, there is no serious resistance'.

As the example of the Netherlands shows, even a virtually complete de-criminalization can be accompanied by very low rates of legal termination. In view of the common assumption that there is enormous disparity between the magnitude of criminal prosecution and the number of unreported cases of illegal termination,[22] this can hardly be surprising – even if some of the estimates regarding the extent of unreported cases are highly inflated. It is very obvious that even in countries where abortion is viewed as a criminal act directed against unborn life, in practice, efforts to investigate and prosecute terminations are not anywhere near comparable to efforts made with regard to crimes against 'born life'. Two questions that will not be addressed here concern, first, the general – police-enforced health – conditions that would be required in order for unborn life to enjoy effectively the same category of protection under criminal law as born life, and, second, the kind of society that would be prepared to pay this price. The moral conception of equality between born and unborn life is, at least as far as the practice of law enforcement is concerned, a long way – one might even be tempted to say worlds – away.

---

[22] See *supra* III.2.

TABLE III/1–1

Prevalence of the Termination of Pregnancy

country	registered (r) or estimated (e) number of terminations	per 1.000 women between the ages of 15 and 44	per 1.000 live births
Germany	110.900 r	8,5	180
Bulgaria	136.000 r	74,9	1.100
ČSSR	103.800 r	32,1	440
Denmark	22.500 r	20,5	430
GDR	89.800 r	24,7	380
England/Wales	129.000 r	12,5	200
Finland	14.300 r	13,1	220
France	178.200 r 280.700 e	15,7	220 (350)
Greece (1983)	100.000-300.000 e	(50-100)	(750-2.240)
Hungary	79.300 r	35,7	580
Ireland[1]	3.225 r	?	?
Italy	226.500 r/e[2]	19,0	370
Yugoslavia(1984)	358.300	70,5	950
Netherlands	21.000 r	6,5	120
Norway	13.600	16,2	270
Austria (~ 1980)	90.000 e	?	(1.000)
Poland	136.600 r	16,8	190
Romania (1977-1979)	392.000 r	85,2	950
Scotland	9.500 r	8,7	140
Sweden	33.600 r	19,8	360
Switzerland (1981)	13.400[3] r	9,5	180
Spain (1987)	64.000	(8)	?

1   Terminations performed in England.
2   Extrapolation from incomplete data, see E/K I 862.
3   Based on a private survey, see E/K I 1526.

TABLE III.1   191

TABLE III/1–2

Prevalence of the Termination of Pregnancy (cont.)

country	registered (r) or estimated (e) number of terminations	per 1.000 women between the ages of 15 and 44	per 1.000 live births
USSR (1982)	11.000.000[4] r	(181)	(2.080)
Israel	15.300 r	18,4	160
Japan	595.000 r	22,5	390
Canada (1982)	77.500 r	13,0	210
Mexico	500.000-2.000.000 e	?	?
South Africa (1981-1982)	950 r	0,2	10
Taiwan (1979)	120.000-150.000 e	?	?
Tunisia	207.000 r	14,9	90
Turkey (1987)	530.000 e	46,0	?
USA	1.570.000 r	29,0	430
PR China	10.205.000 r	46,4	500

4   Including cases involving complications following spontaneous births and illegal terminations.

TABLE III/2

Prevalence of the Termination of Pregnancy According to Type of Legal Regulatory Model*

	Indication-based exceptions from the prohibition on termination			
	more "narrow" regulation		*more "broad" regulation*	
with ↓ *proce-dural require-ments* ↑	**A** South Africa 10	**C** Romania 950	**A** Finland 220 Italy 370 Poland 190	**C** Germany 180 England 200 Scotland 140 France 220 (-350) Switzerland 180 Hungary 580 Israel 160 Australia 230 Canada 210
without	**B**	**D**	**B**	**D** Japan 390

	Exemption from punishment for a set time period combined with indication-based exceptions to punishment			
	more "narrow" regulation		*more "narrow" regulation*	
with ↓ *proce-dural require-ments* ↑	**A** Tunisia 90	**B** Bulgaria 1100 ČSSR 440 Greece (750-2240) USSR (2080)	**C** Denmark 430 GDR 380 Yugoslavia 950 Norway 270 USA 430	**D** Sweden 360
without				**E** Austria (1000)

	Exemption from punishment for a set time period with no indication-based restrictions		
	A Netherlands 120		**B** PR China 500

* Per 1,000 live births; same time period as in Table III.1.
   For interpretation of the data, see III.1.2.2 (p. 195 f.).

TABLE III.3   193

TABLE III/3

Prevalence of the Termination of Pregnancy According to (Minimum) Procedural Prerequisites for Early Intervention*

Regulatory model	Voluntary counseling	Obligatory counseling	Review or authorization	Voluntary counseling + review/ authorization	Obligatory counseling + review/ authorization
Non-Graduated Indication Model			Switzerland 180 Canada 210 South Africa 10	Israel 160	Poland 190
Graduated Indication Model	England/Wales 200 Scotland 140 Australia 230	France 220 (-350) Italy 370 Hungary 580	Romania 950	Finland 220	Germany 180 (-270)
Combined (successive) Time Limit-Indication Model	Denmark 430 Greece (750) Yugoslavia 950 Sweden 360 Tunisia 90 USA 430	Bulgaria 1100 ČSSR 440 GDR 380 Norway 270 USSR (2080)			
Pure Time-Limit Model		Netherlands 120			

*   Per 1,000 live births: same time period as in Table III.1. Not taken into consideration here are requirements as to who may perform a termination (such as, in particular, the requirement that the termination be performed by a physician).

Diagrams III/1–III/4

Developments in the number of officially reported terminations per 1,000 women between the ages of 15 and 44*

The source of the data on the following countries and years is: United Nations, *Abortion Policies, A Global Review*, 3 Volumes (New York, 1992–1995):

ČSSR:	1988	Netherlands:	1987–1990
GDR:	1985–1990	Norway:	1988
India:	1985–1989	Poland:	1988–1991
Ireland:	1988–1990	Rumania:	1980, 1985–1991
Israel:	1988–1990	Sweden:	1988
Japan:	1988–1990	Tunisia:	1989–1991
Yugoslavia:	1983–1989	USA:	1986–1991

The source of the data on the following countries and years is: *Yearbook of Nordic Statistics* (Stockholm 1992 ff.):

Denmark:	1987–1994	Norway:	1989–1994
Finland:	1987–1994	Sweden:	1989–1994

Miscellaneous Annotations:
(1)   West Germany, including terminations performed in the Netherlands and Great Britain.
(2)   West Germany, excluding terminations performed in the Netherlands and Great Britain.
(3)   Including terminations in England.
(4)   Excluding terminations in physicians' offices.
(5)   Until 1979 including in-patient treatment for complications due to spontaneous or illegal abortions.
(6)   Excluding terminations in the USA.
(7)   Incomplete data.
(8)   Until 1979 including in-patient treatment for complications due to spontaneous or illegal abortions.
(9)   Data for 1988-1994 are taken from the annual report of the Italian Minister of Justice on the implementation of the law (Art. 16 of Law No. 194, enacted May 22, 1978) on the protection of motherhood and with regard to the termination of pregnancy.
(10) Data for 1987 (Yugoslavia) and 1988 (Bulgaria) from H.P. DAVID, 'Abortion in Europe, 1920-1991: A Public Health Perspective', 23 *Studies in Family Planning* (1992), pp. 1-22, 2.
(11) Data since 1988 from the Office for National Statistics, *Abortion Statistics* (London 1989 ff.)
(12) Data are taken from Ministerio de Sanidad y Consumo, Dirección General de Salud Pública, *Interrupción Voluntaria del Embarazo* (Madrid 1988 ff.)
(13) De facto decriminalization since the beginning of the 1970s, see E/K I p. 1011.

---

* The data are taken from the various country reports in E/K I or E/K II unless otherwise indicated.

DIAGRAM III.1   195

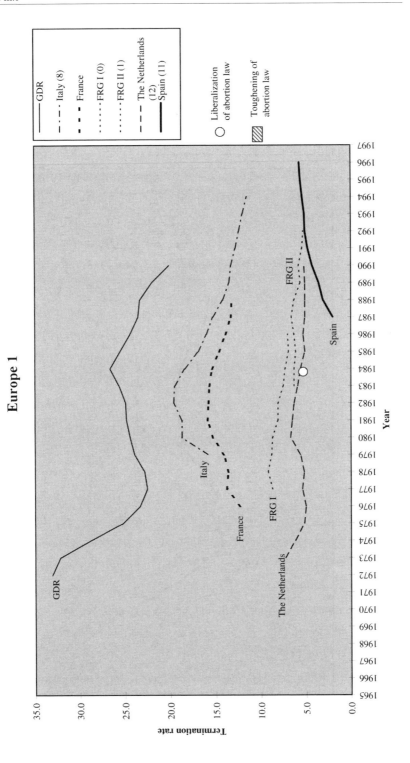

DIAGRAM III/1

Europe 1

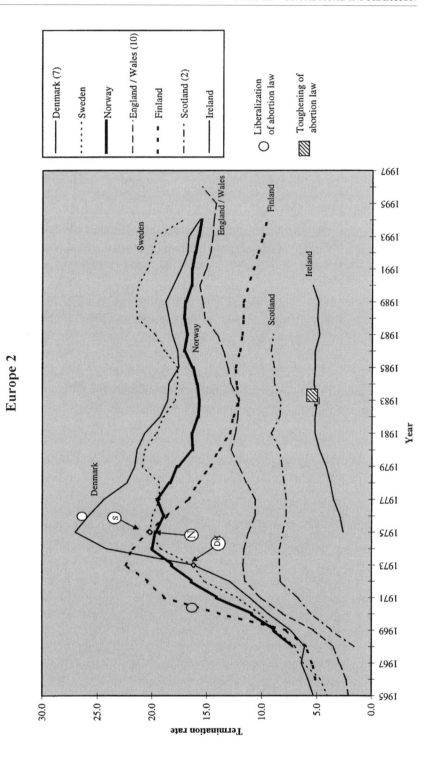

DIAGRAM III/2

Europe 2

DIAGRAM III.3197

DIAGRAM III/3

Eastern Europe

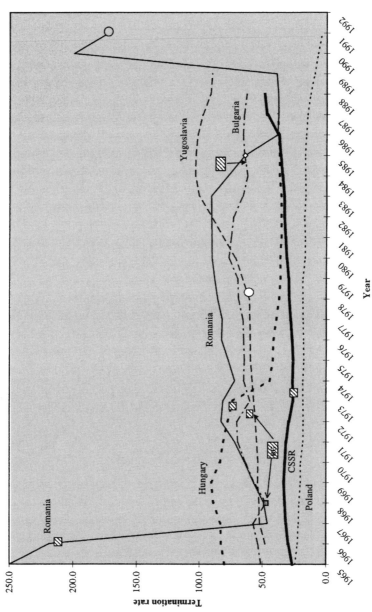

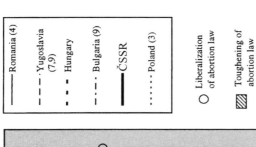

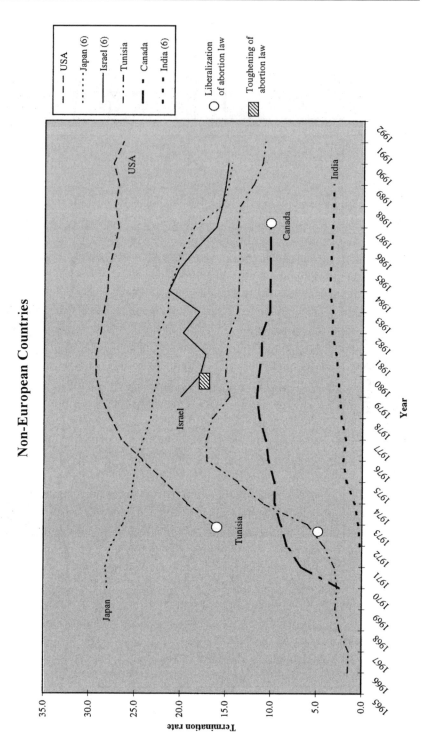

DIAGRAM III/4

Non-European Countries

TABLE III.4   199

TABLE III/4

Number of Annual Convictions for the Termination of Pregnancy[1]

	Indication-based exceptions from the prohibition on termination			
	more narrow regulation		*more broad regulation*	
with ↓ *proce- dural require ments-* ↑ *with out*	**A** South Africa 45 Chile 79.6	**C** Luxembourg 0 Portugal[2] 3 Spain[3] 61	**A** Italy[4] 4 Poland[5] 6.5	**C** Germany (old) 33.2 England/ Wales 2.4 France[6] 11.0 Switzerland[7] 6.0 Hungary 1.4 Israel 0
	B	**D** Belgium[8] 3 Argentina[9] 197.5	**B** Costa Rica[9] 3.75	**D** Japan 0.2
	Exemption from punishment for a set time period combined with indication-based exceptions from punishment			
	more narrow regulation		*more broad regulation*	
with ↓ *proce- dural require- ments* ↑ *with out*	**A**	**B** Greece[10] 5.6	**C** Yugoslavia/ Croatia[8] 6	**D**
				E Austria 13.75
	Exemption from punishment for a set time period with no indication-based restrictions			
	A Netherlands 0		**B**	

1 If not otherwise indicated: ł 1978-1982.
2 ł for the years 1978, 1980 and 1981.
3 ł 1977-1978.
4 ł 1980-1981.
5 ł 1978-1981.
6 For the year 1978.
7 ł for the years 1978, 1980 and 1982.
8 ł 1977-1980.
9 ł 1979-1982.
10 ł 1977-1981.

TABLE III/5

Annual Number of Convictions for the Termination of Pregnancy
per 1 Million Inhabitants*

	Indication-based exceptions from the prohibition on termination			
	more narrow regulation		*more broad regulation*	
with ↓ proce-dural require-ments ↑ with out	**A** South Africa 1.8 Chile 6.6	**C** Luxembourg 0 Spain 1.6	**A** Italy 0.1 Poland 0.2	**C** Germany(old) 0.6 England/Wales 0.05 France 0.2 Hungary 0.1 Israel 0
	B	**D** Belgium 0.3 Portugal 0.3 Argentina 7.0	**B** Costa Rica 1.5	**D** Japan 0.002
	Exemption from punishment for a set time period combined with indication-based exceptions from punishment			
	more narrow regulation		*more broad regulation*	
with ↓ proce-dural require-ments ↑ with out	**A**	**B** Greece 0.6	**C** Yugoslavia/ Croatia 1.3	**D**
				E Austria 1.8
	Exemption from punishment for a set time period with no indication-based restrictions			
	A Netherlands 0		**B**	

*   See notes to Table III.2.

TABLE III.6   201

TABLE III/6

**Developments in the Number of Convictions for
Impermissible Termination of Pregnancy over Longer Time Periods**

Country	Time period	Number of convictions
Germany	1960 1974	1809 94 (5.2 %)
	1976* *1985*	*90* *10 (11.1 %)*
Belgium	1963 1980	121 1 (0.8 %)
England/Wales*	*1969* *1983*	*52* *3 (5.8 %)*
France	1919 1974	131 10 (7.6 %)
Greece	1965 1977	10 5 (50 %)
Yugoslavia/Croatia*	*1972* *1980*	*13* *8 (61.5 %)*
Netherlands	1912 1966**	24 29 (121 %)
	1967* *1978*	*33* *0*
Austria	1955 1974	710 56 (7.9 %)
Poland	*1970* *1981*	*10* *3 (30 %)*
Portugal	1954 1981	37 1 (2.7 %)
Japan	1908 1948	293 68 (23.2 %)
	1949* *1986*	*69* *0*
South Africa	1968/69 1981/82	43 31 (69.8 %)

*   *italics* = post-reform time period.
**   effective beginning of decriminalization, see E/K I 1009.

Part IV

CONCLUDING REFLECTIONS
FROM A LEGAL POLICY PERSPECTIVE

Preliminary remarks   205

IV.1 Review: Findings – Insights – Trends   207

IV.2 Outlook: Starting Points – Guidelines   244

IV.3 A Proposed Regulation   295

Preliminary Remarks

'Concluding reflections from a legal policy perspective', the title given to this, the last section of our study, requires explication; indeed, each and every aspect of the title must be addressed.

First: whereas this work, up until now, has concentrated primarily on the depiction of general social conditions and historical developments, the presentation of legal rules and comparative analyses, and the assessment of empirical data, at this point we have adopted a *political* perspective. In so doing, we have moved from description to evaluation. To be sure, the inclusion in the preceding chapters of an occasional value judgment was unavoidable; indeed, the choice of issues and the amount of attention paid to each issue may, in and of themselves, be seen as political statements. Similarly, a value judgment may be discerned in the very words used to express an idea. But whereas the writing of the foregoing sections was characterized by efforts to achieve the greatest possible objectivity and the expression of subjective judgments – to the extent not explicitly identified – unintentional, this concluding section deals with political considerations that, as such, cannot be free of value judgments. This does not mean that subjectivity has replaced objectivity for, as politics based on scholarship, this policy section cannot ignore the determination and analysis of facts and norms as reported in previous sections. However, policy statements may be influenced, more or less consciously, by preconceptions and value judgments that – even with the best of intentions – cannot always be acknowledged completely. To this extent, policy is not free of subjectivity.

Second: as it appears here, the terms 'politics' and 'policy' are not used in the sense of general party politics but rather in the sense of *legal* policy. Correctly understood, the goal of legal policy cannot be to adopt a certain position simply because it reflects the platform of a particular party. Rather, in the attempt to solve socially significant problems, scholarly legal policy, if it is to be legitimate, must, in the drafting of regulatory options, consider existing knowledge as impartially as possible.

Third: To be sure, it is extremely difficult to attain this high standard, particularly when the problem at hand is as complex as the issue of the termination of pregnancy. Although in connection with this research project the Max Planck Institute alone has produced nearly 5,000 pages of text, this contribution represents only a tiny fraction of that which has been written and postulated all over the world in the course of human history with regard to the question of the appropriate way of dealing with unwanted pregnancies and their termination. All of this would have to be considered if one wanted one's conclusions to be universally binding. Since this simply cannot be achieved here, we have consciously chosen not to speak of conclusions but rather of legal policy *reflections*. By choosing this term, we wish to indicate that our deliberations are not intended to be seen as compulsory or as universally applicable. Rather, they are just one point of view, a view whose plausibility, we hope, is augmented by many years of study of the abortion issue, both at home and abroad.

Fourth: Although we have referred to *concluding* reflections, this should not be taken to mean that the 'last word' has been spoken in this area. Last words are out of the question with regard to an 'eternal problem' such as abortion. But like all studies, this one, too, must come to an end. This need not mean, however, the end to all discussion. On the contrary, nothing would be more desirable than for the conclusion of this study to serve as a springboard for future endeavors.

In this vein, the object of the following is threefold:

- By means of a kind of retrospective and review of the multifaceted material presented in the country reports (E/K I and II), the various empirical studies, and the foregoing comparative legal cross-section (I to III), the first step will highlight essential findings and point out insights that cannot be ignored if things are taken as they are and not as one wishes they might be (IV.1).
- However, since we do not wish to engage merely in a description of the status quo, we begin in a second step to look for ways to solve this problem in the future. Here, fundamental starting points and authoritative guidelines are established (IV.2).
- Finally, in the concluding step we propose a regulation; this proposal is not, however, meant to be seen as the only possible solution to the truly complex issues surrounding the termination of pregnancy (IV.3).

IV.1   REVIEW: FINDINGS – INSIGHTS – TRENDS

1.1   Ideological prejudices

If in this day and age there is still such a thing as a 'war of convictions', the turmoil surrounding the termination of pregnancy provides a large field on which to fight the battle. To be sure, this battle is not being fought everywhere – think, for example, of Austria and Norway, where the termination of pregnancy, despite far-reaching reforms, has apparently faded away from the political stage. The number of countries is considerably larger, however, in which one aspect of termination or the other, indeed sometimes whether or not it should be tolerated at all, continues to provide fuel for the political discourse. This alone would not be problematic – it might even indicate a positive development as far as the valuing of unborn life is concerned – if not for the fact that the debate is often carried out with methods that demonstrate a lack of respect for the convictions of the opponent and that in so doing make unbiased, reform-oriented dialogue impossible. These methods are not limited to spectacular organized boycotts, the destruction of clinics, or even fatal attacks, as have actually occurred in the United States. Rather, they also include campaigns to discredit opponents using language as a weapon, be it on the one hand the use of terms such as 'self-appointed protector of life', which suggests narrow-minded zealotry or, on the other hand, the unceremonious designation of supporters of permissive contraceptive and termination regulations as 'abortion enthusiasts'.[1] The speed and suddenness with which this technique can co-opt previously harmless terms is illustrated by the expressions 'germinating', 'nascent', and 'unborn' life: Whereas the first two of these expressions were used regularly until the 1970s in communications of the Catholic Church,[2] an institution that can hardly be suspected of

---

[1] For criticism of this – by now even more acrimonious – style of debate regarding the termination of pregnancy, see A. ESER, 'Aspekte eines Strafrechtlers zur Abtreibungsreform', in: D. HOFMANN (ed.), *Schwangerschaftsunterbrechung. Aktuelle Überlegungen zur Reform des § 218* (Frankfurt/Main, Suhrkamp 1974) pp. 117-177, 320-329 at pp. 19 ff.).

[2] See, e.g., the address of Pope Pius XII on 'Vernichtung keimenden Lebens', 29 October 1951, the 'Stellungnahme der Deutschen Bischofskonferenz zur Strafrechtsreform', 25 September 1970, the 'Erklärung der Beschofskonferenz der DDR', 3 January 1972, all of which are reproduced in: K. PANZER (ed.), *Schwangerschaftsabbruch § 218 StGB, Eine Dokumentation* (Köln, Bachem 1972) pp. 14 f., 18 ff. and 25 ff.

a lack of respect for unborn life, one can be accused of disrespect in this area if one uses either of these two expressions today.[3]

Although the effect of verbal sparring of this nature may seem to extend merely from the unpleasant to the tiresome, terminological labeling must be taken seriously if it adversely affects the substance of a discussion or attempts to force opposing opinions into a particular ideological corner. The most brazen of the various notorious simplifications is perhaps the designation of a regulation as a 'time-limit model' ['*Fristenlösung*'] because a regulation based on time limits may not only be unconstitutional in the eyes of some but also may imply hostility to unborn life. On the other hand, it is also possible that one who does not wish to see termination of pregnancy completely free of criminal liability but rather wishes to see it coupled with certain prerequisites can be termed a supporter of an 'indication solution', with the accompanying implication that one has failed to respect a woman's right to self-determination and has at the same time revealed antagonism to emancipation. The situation is similarly oversimplified and prejudicial in the Anglo-American sphere, where one is categorized either as 'pro life' or as 'pro choice' – and the interpretation of the term in question as praise or insult is left to the discretion of the observer. These kinds of characterizations leave no room for nuances.

The finding that substance-distorting simplifications have long ceased to do justice to the facts and norms composing the debate surrounding the termination of pregnancy must be emphasized yet again as one of the most important findings of this study. At this juncture, it is necessary only to point out the existence of such terminological sniping, for unless it is suppressed, serious dialogue with an eye to reform is impossible. Who would deny that the debate surrounding the termination of pregnancy involves ideological preconceptions and fundamental convictions that, for many, are inviolable? Reason for concern arises, however, only when such prejudices are held out to be the sole and absolute truth and when legitimate arguments are displaced by a misleading or even discrediting war of words.

---

[3] To avoid such suspicions and to ward off accusations that I have failed to stick to a 'politically correct' regime in the following remarks, allow me to point out at this juncture that I have tried to concentrate more on the subject at hand and less on words and phrases. The latter only become important if particular expressions become associated with certain legal consequences. These kinds of positive and negative insinuations should not be read into the following, where, depending on the situation, terms such as embryo and fetus, emerging, germinating, and unborn life, and child, are used more or less interchangeably. Of course, where the context calls for more specificity, the appropriate term has been selected. For a discussion of terminological and conceptual considerations, see *infra* IV.1.3.1, text at n. 6 f., IV.2.2.2, text at n. 31, and G. JEROUSCHEK, 'Werdendes Leben versus ungeborenes Leben', 156 *Goltdammer's Archiv für Strafrecht* (1988) pp. 483-492 at pp. 484 ff.

In order to respond to these kinds of prejudices, various aspects of our study are reproduced in the following. Although some readers may view these findings as self-evident and others approach them more skeptically, in any case they appear weighty enough to be beyond dispute in future policy debates and thus in a position to contribute to the return of dispassionate, balanced, and reasoned debate.

1.2   The reality of the termination of pregnancy

1.2.1   *Termination of pregnancy: an ancient and worldwide phenomenon*

Whatever one's personal convictions on the subject, legal history and comparative law leave no room for doubt that unwanted pregnancies have been terminated all over the world – by one means another – since time immemorial. Even though homicide has not been uncommon throughout the history of humankind, it is important not to overlook a fundamental reality: namely, whereas life after birth has always been surrounded by a virtually seamless protective wall and safeguarded by the severest criminal penalties, the taking of life before birth has not been subject to the same taboo nor has it been punished with equal severity.

This statement of fact is not made in order to minimize the gravity of termination but rather to debunk the false premise that termination is a phenomenon of our time, the result of a modern-day deterioration in morals, and that a simple return to 'old values' and 'stricter morals' would serve to reestablish the same protection for unborn life as exists for life after birth. Without repeating too much of what has already been said on this subject in our comparison of legal history[4] and which has been proven in other studies as well,[5] the fact cannot be ignored that – in one way or another – the regulations for the protection of unborn life lag behind those for the protection of life after birth. This may be

---

[4] See *supra* I.5 and in more detail – E/K III 61 ff.

[5] With regard to western tradition, see, e.g., G. JEROUSCHEK, Lebensschutz und Lebensbeginn. Kulturgeschichte des Abtreibungsverbots (Stuttgart, Enke 1988) pp. 12 ff.; S. DEMEL, Abtreibung zwischen Straffreiheit und Exkommunikation. Weltliches und kirchliches Strafrecht auf dem Prüfstand (Stuttgart, Kohlhammer 1995) pp. 66 ff. With regard to Africa, Indonesia, and Islam, see R. SCHOTT, 'Die Verfügung über Leben und Tod in traditionellen afrikanischen Gesellschaften', in B. MENSEN (ed.), Recht auf Leben – Recht auf Töten. Ein Kulturvergleich (Nettetal, Steyler 1994) pp. 9-58 at p. 21; W. STÖHR, 'Leben und Töten in der Vorstellung altindonesischer Völker', ibidem pp. 59-78 at pp. 60 ff. and A.TH. KHOURY, 'Recht auf Leben – Recht auf Töten aus der Sicht des Islams', ibidem pp. 79-94 at. p. 88. On the 'morality of abortion', see R. DWORKIN, Life's Dominion (New York, Knopf 1993) pp. 30 ff.

because to some extent, as in earlier 'animation' theories, the protections deemed appropriate for life in general were not extended to the early phase of pregnancy, or because exemptions from criminal liability have been created in response to the needs of pregnant women, or because threatened criminal penalties have been reduced, or because pregnant women have been granted certain privileges.

At the same time, it would be incorrect to assume on the basis of less extensive sanctioning that termination enjoys social acceptance. For no matter whether prosecuted or ignored, it seems that nowhere and never has the termination of pregnancy been viewed as a completely 'normal' method of birth control. Apparently it has been seen as an intervention that – be it out of respect for the value of the new life as such or be it only due to the complexity of the method or the risk for the pregnant woman – is not accepted as a 'norm' but merely tolerated as a 'last resort'.

Thus, the socio-legal approach to the termination of pregnancy moves from the categorical to the incremental: It is no longer a matter of sanctioning the taking of a life before and the taking of a life after birth equally or even of appearing to do so; rather it is only a matter of the mode or the degree with which the sanctioning of the termination of a pregnancy can deviate from the sanctioning of the killing of a person after birth. It is only on this incremental level, upon which the social practice of termination has apparently always been based – more or less consciously – all over the world, that various deviations from the sanctioning practice in cases of the killing of 'born' life have been adopted. In this way, as will be shown in the following section on the various legal methods of regulating the termination of pregnancy (1.3), these differences even on a normative level have been significant in various countries and epochs – in some cases, as in the Federal Republic of Germany after the reform of 1975, the law went so far as to make permissible termination the rule rather than the exception.[6] But even in countries where the response to the killing of born and unborn life differs solely in the severity of the threatened penalties, the termination of a pregnancy is evidently viewed differently than the killing of an individual after birth.

1.2.2 *Frequency of termination and prosecutorial practice*

A characteristic of the aforementioned divergence in attitude appears to be that the discrepancy between the frequency of termination and the frequency of prosecution for termination is far more drastic than in the case of murder or manslaughter.

---

[6] See E/K I 111.

To be sure, this schism can be attributed in part to the 'dark area' effect, which obscures, to varying degrees, our knowledge concerning the incidence of termination. Even though in some countries efforts have been made to determine the number of illegal as well as legal terminations,[7] these isolated areas of transparency are hard-pressed to reverse the overall impression that no one really wants to know exactly how many pregnancies are being terminated. Whether or not the motivating factor is to escape reality, to cover up a socially embarrassing phenomenon, or to demonstrate tolerance in a pragmatic way, a comparable lack of interest in the clearing up of homicide offences is unthinkable. Thus, it comes as no surprise that special reporting requirements are less common where the charging and prosecution of illegal abortion is at issue[8] and more common where information regarding the frequency, modus, and motivation of termination is sought.[9] The latter is the case, however, primarily in countries whose reformed laws do not place the termination of pregnancy and homicide on the same level.

To the extent that the data provide insight into the incidence of termination,[10] the criminological significance of this phenomenon can hardly be more forcefully illustrated than by means of a comparison to the frequency of homicide. Whereas the pre-unification territory of the Federal Republic of Germany registered approximately 1,470 homicides in 1993,[11] the corresponding number for terminations of pregnancy is 110,900. This number is still comparatively low if viewed in relation to the number of live births that took place in the same time period. Indeed, for every 1,000 live births in the Federal Republic of Germany, there were 180 terminations, a figure that places the Federal Republic, in an international perspective, somewhere in the middle. In Bulgaria, for example, the comparable figure was 1,100, meaning that at that time, at least, more pregnancies were terminated than were carried to term.[12]

These highly astonishing termination rates are even more remarkable when they are seen in relation to the frequency of prosecution. Even if the lack of good data means that any conclusions drawn from them must be taken with a grain of salt,[13] the average annual number of convictions – in the Federal Re-

---

[7] For more, see *supra* III.1.

[8] See *supra* II.7.1, 7.2. Even though reporting requirements regarding completed and planned terminations most certainly do exist, it is by no means true that these provide a full picture of what is going on.

[9] For details, see *supra* II.3.6.

[10] See *supra* III.1.2.

[11] G. KAISER, Kriminologie. Ein Lehrbuch, 3rd edn. (Heidelberg, C.F. Müller 1996) p. 712.

[12] See *supra* III.1.2.1 and Table III/1 (pp. 190/191).

[13] See *supra* III.3.1.

public of Germany between 1978 and 1982 this number was 33, a figure that, although small, was somewhat above the international average[14] – can hardly be taken seriously in light of the aforementioned annual termination figure of over 100,000. This impression is not much improved if one considers the fact that in previous years police registrations and judicial convictions tended to be higher and that, in addition, abortions that would at one time have been illegal have since been rendered inactionable by reform-related legalization. In any case, the conviction statistics display such a low order of magnitude that even in an era of decreased criminalization they can hardly be characterized as socially significant.

This picture of a great discrepancy between normative pathos and prosecutorial apathy becomes even gloomier if one considers the grounds commonly given as reasons for prosecution: in fact, abortion prosecutions are less likely the result of direct police investigations and are more likely the by-product of investigations initiated for other (often tax-related) reasons or of conflicts in intimate relationships or are a result of the unsavory motives of third parties.[15]

Although no assessment of this finding is intended, the sobering impression drawn from empirical evidence remains that the termination of pregnancy occurs frequently all over the world yet meets with only a negligible amount of prosecutorial resistance.

1.2.3 *Attitudes towards contraception and termination*

The reasons underlying the far-reaching *de facto* tolerance – or at least the lack of serious, comprehensive prosecution – of the termination of pregnancy can hardly be found elsewhere than in certain fundamental attitudes. Certainly, current attitudes to termination cannot simply be assumed, without more, to apply as well to earlier generations of humankind, just as central European experiences cannot be assumed definitive for other continents and cultures. But even if one recognizes that attitudes towards termination differ both throughout history (vertically) and geographically (horizontally) and accepts that the trend

---

[14] See *supra* Table III/6 (p. 201), whereby a continuing decreasing trend was observed in the 1990s. For more recent information, see Statistisches Bundesamt, *Rechtspflege – Strafverfolgung 2002* (Wiesbaden, Statistisches Bundesamt 2004) pp. 28/29: 5 persons tried/ 2 persons convicted.

[15] See *supra* III.2.2. For a study on the Federal Republic of Germany that was conducted in connection with this project, see K. LIEBL, *Ermittlungsverfahren, Strafverfolgungs- und Sanktionspraxis beim Schwangerschaftsabbruch* (Freiburg, Max-Planck-Institut für ausländisches und internationales Strafrecht 1990) pp. 82 ff. See also ALBRECHT, loc. cit. n. 20, at pp. 204 ff., 222.

towards permissiveness has been continuous, it is still difficult to ignore the fact that the prevention or termination of unwanted pregnancy – even if achieved by means of the destruction of a developing human being – is judged differently than is the killing of an individual after birth. To be sure, the number of those who consider the fruit of the womb equal in every regard to an individual outside the womb and consequently see abortion as murder may have been greater in the past and in other places than here and now, where such groups are known to the public less because of the numbers of its supporters and more through the spectacular nature of its actions. But even if one assumes that the relationship between tolerance and rejection in the past is the reverse of what it is today, there are sufficient indications that even in those days the termination of a pregnancy was neither seen as completely insignificant nor as tantamount to murder by either the parties involved or by the public at large.[16]

This finding is even more valid today, in the wake of the fundamental change in attitude towards family planning that has been observed virtually everywhere in the world,[17] a not insignificant result of which was its influence on the movements favoring the reform of termination laws.[18] The existence of this connection does not mean, however, that proponents of better family planning are necessarily uncritical supporters of abortion; after all, subsequent to the propagation of better contraception the termination of unwanted pregnancies should be superfluous. At the same time, it is unmistakable that termination is seen if not as a preventive then at least as a corrective method of 'birth control' and as a 'prenatal' intervention is judged differently than is a 'postnatal' killing. Whether the 'birth' moment is in fact – from legal and ethical perspectives – of sufficient import as to justify such fundamental differences in treatment, including the occasional push for complete decriminalization of termination, is not the issue here.[19] Rather, in this context we are concerned solely with the empirical finding that 'prenatal' termination of pregnancy and 'postnatal' killing apparently have always been viewed differently and that, in any case, there is a growing trend in this direction.

The studies of attitudes in the 1980s in pre-unification West Germany, carried out in connection with this project, support these findings.[20] Even if that

---

[16] See literature cited at *supra* n. 5.

[17] See *supra* I.4.2.

[18] See *supra* I.4.4 and *infra* IV.1.2.4.

[19] But see *infra* IV.2.2.2.

[20] Studies were conducted from three perspectives: first, from the perspective of pregnant women, see B. HOLZHAUER, Schwangerschaft und Schwangerschaftsabbruch, Die Rolle des reformierten § 218 StGB bei der Entscheidungsfindung betroffener Frauen, 2nd edn. (Freiburg, Max-Planck-Institut für ausländisches und internationales Strafrecht 1991); sec-

study focused on the implementation of the reform law of 1975, general conclusions regarding attitudes towards the termination of pregnancy can be drawn from the data it gathered:

It is noteworthy with regard to the attitudes in this context of *pregnant women* that the women, who for purposes of the study were divided into three different groups – namely, those who terminated and whose decision to terminate was clear from the start (group 1), those for whom the pregnancy was fraught with conflict (group 2), and those for whom there was no question that they would continue their pregnancies (group 3)[21] – for the most part adhered to the same criteria despite their different attitudes towards the distinction between termination and killing:

Whereas 81.9% of the first group thought that termination in the first three months of pregnancy should be at the discretion of the woman (as compared to 54.9% of the second group and 31.1% of the third group), only 20.8% of the pregnant women in group 3, who apparently never considered not carrying their pregnancies to term, thought that termination should be equated with indefensible killing (as compared to 3.0% and 3.9% in the first two groups). This indicates that even in the group least inclined to terminate almost 80% saw a moral difference between termination and homicide.[22]

The findings regarding the fundamental attitude of *physicians* were comparable. Although in this profession, the influence of religious attitudes plays a not insignificant role, and although a considerable portion of probands – almost 30% – were Catholic and Catholics tend to be stricter in their judgments, all in all only 33.5% thought that termination should be equated with indefensible

---

ond, from the perspective of physicians, see M. HÄUSSLER-SCZEPAN, Arzt und Schwangerschaftsabbruch, Eine empirische Untersuchung zur Implementation des reformierten § 218 StGB (Freiburg, Max-Planck-Institut für ausländisches und internationales Strafrecht 1989); and third, the from law enforcement perspective, see LIEBL, op. cit. n. 15. See also M. HÄUSSLER and B. HOLZHAUER, 'Die Implementation der reformierten §§ 218 f. StGB, Empirische Untersuchungen zu Einstellung und Verhalten von Ärzten und schwangeren Frauen', 100 ZStW (1988) pp. 817-854, and H.-J. ALBRECHT, 'Schwangerschaftsabbruch – empirische Untersuchungen zur Implementation der strafrechtlichen Regulierung des Schwangerschaftsabbruchs', in: A. ESER et al. (eds.), Zweites deutsch-polnisches Kolloquium über Strafrecht und Kriminologie (Baden-Baden, Nomos 1986) pp. 195-223; G. KAISER,'Was wissen wir über den Schwangerschaftsabbruch? Ergebnisse eines empirischen Forschungsprojekts', Aus Politik und Zeitgeschichte – Beilage zur Wochenzeitung Das Parlament, B14/ 90 (30 March 1990) pp. 21-31 at pp. 24 ff.

[21] For more on this assignment, see HOLZHAUER, op. cit. n. 20, at pp. 163 ff.; HÄUSSLER and HOLZHAUER, loc. cit. n. 20, at pp. 820 ff.

[22] See HOLZHAUER, op. cit. n. 20, at pp. 198 ff.; on the attitude of women from an empirical, comparative legal perspective, see ALBRECHT, loc. cit. n. 20, at pp. 212 ff.

killing; and of those who equated termination with killing, almost 60% expressed understanding for her decision if the woman could square the termination with her conscience.[23]

A much stricter attitude can be found among participating *judges and pros-ecutors*; this is not surprising, to be sure, in view of the fact that their duties, as law enforcement agents, include prosecution. However, insofar as almost one third of this professional group disagrees with the mandate of the Federal Constitutional Court that termination be criminalized and almost one half finds that a more liberal regulation than that of 1975 would be sensible,[24] it is apparent that here, too, a considerable number of probands distinguish between murder and homicide.[25]

Although they are considerably more difficult to measure, comparable attitudes towards termination can also be found in the *general population*: this is the case, for instance, in Mexico, where the lackadaisical attitude towards prosecution – prevalent all over the world – is combined with the 'silent toleration, even acceptance of termination by the society' and in Taiwan, where 'sympathy with and compassion for the woman' is reported.[26]

Leaving open the question of which policy consequences, if any, are to be drawn from this, it must in any event be noted as a starting point that distinctions between termination and killing after birth are made by a significant segment of the population.

1.2.4 *Reform-inducing factors*

Even if – as previously determined – distinctions between prenatal termination of pregnancy and postnatal killing have long been made the world over, it is necessary to draw attention to the time frame within which this circumstance came to pass. Whereas for an extended period of time this kind of distinction was made but the differences on a normative level remained relatively small, a precipitous expansion in the normative chasm between termination and postnatal killing has been discernable virtually worldwide at the latest since the advent of the twentieth century. In the process, termination, has occasionally been de-

---

[23] See HÄUSSLER-SCZEPAN, op. cit. n. 20), at pp. 122 ff., 132 ff.

[24] See LIEBL, op. cit. n. 15, at pp. 125 ff.

[25] For additional discussion of attitudes towards various regulatory schemes, see *infra* IV.1.4.2.

[26] For details, see E/K III p. 503 text accompanying nn. 25 ff. No less noteworthy is the empirical, comparative legal observation that in some places termination, although criminal, is considered less serious than property offenses and on the same level as homosexuality and prostitution offenses. See ALBRECHT, op. cit. n. 20, at p. 203.

criminalized to such an extent that in relation to homicide the deviation is no longer quantitative but rather more like a qualitative leap.[27]

As for the causes of this relatively recent development, it seems that three factors are primarily responsible for precipitating, setting the direction, and determining the extent of the reform movements in the twentieth century.

The first factor, very generally speaking, is the modification of the traditional abortion law in response to far-reaching *societal changes*. In any case, this was the motive that was mentioned most frequently by law makers – to the extent that intentions and motivations were expressed at all in connection with the reform of the laws regulating the termination of pregnancy.[28]

To be sure, these societal changes did not come from out of the blue but rather had a more profound origin in the more farsighted goals of *family planning*: having children was no longer a question of an uncontrollable 'fate'; instead, a child was the result of a 'responsible' decision. In this regard, the triumph of family planning by means of contraception proved, ultimately, to be a driving force for fundamental reforms in the laws regulating the termination of pregnancy.[29] Even if the avoidance of unwanted pregnancies was particularly important, this does not mean that termination was to serve as an unproblematic outlet by which to put an end to pregnancies resulting from forgotten or unsuccessful contraception. Rather, decriminalization of the termination of pregnancy was in part geared to finding better ways to curb the incidence of termination.[30]

No less important was a different '*self-image of women*'. The new self-image was not only concerned with emancipation and efforts to achieve equal rights in general but was also concerned with the position of women in the family in particular: The less a woman's role in society is seen as limited to that of mother and housewife, the more meaning is attached to the structure of the rest of her life, which is in no small degree dependent on the timing and number of childbirths.[31]

Finally, certain additional socio-political factors cannot be ignored that have in fact always been associated with the abortion phenomenon but that were not taken seriously until recently. One of these is the concern for the *health of the pregnant woman*, who faces more risks when the only way she can terminate her pregnancy is by undergoing an illegal procedure: one tries to respond to this in accordance with the maxim 'if terminations are going to be performed then

---

[27] For an overview of reforms throughout history, see E/K I pp. 61 ff. with diagram I/1 (p. 64).

[28] See *supra* II.2.1.

[29] See *supra* I.4.4.

[30] See *supra* II.2.1. See also *infra* IV.1.3.1, 1.4.3.

[31] With regard to these factors, see *supra* I.3, II.2.1.

let them at least be terminations without complications'.[32] Another factor is the *elimination of discrimination* as seen in the aforementioned arbitrariness in the prosecution of the termination of pregnancy.[33]

1.2.5 *Effects of the (West) German reform of 1975*

After these rather global statements, let us now turn to a specific abortion re-form law and examine the extent to which the legislative goals pursued by the reform were actually achieved. The (West) German reform of 1975 presents us with a suitable example.[34] Even if we concentrate on the previously mentioned need to eliminate discrimination, thereby putting off consideration of the goal of providing greater protection for life, which by means of 'help instead of punishment' was meant to curb the incidence of termination,[35] we are con-fronted with a mixed picture. The goal of achieving more justice through more equality in the criminal protection of life from the very beginning – in the pro-cess dispelling the suspicion of a 'coincidental' criminal law[36] – was achieved to the extent that the reform of 1975 appears to have led to the virtual disappear-ance of dangerous illegal terminations and even to the reduction of 'dark area' figures.[37] To the extent that success can be seen in this, however, it may be seen as having been achieved at the cost of a *'de facto'* decriminalization of the termination of pregnancy.[38]

Even on this reduced basis, however, the charge that criminal law is arbitrary with regard to the termination of pregnancy and that equal treatment is lacking in practice does not appear to have been eliminated. The primary reasons for this must certainly be sought on the practical level; for, as the studies of inves-

---

[32] See *supra* II.2.1. See in addition *supra* I.4.4.

[33] See *supra* IV.1.2.2. See also *supra* II.2.1, III.2, 3.

[34] For its goals, see generally A. ESER, in A. SCHÖNKE and H. SCHRÖDER (eds.), *Strafgesetzbuch: Kommentar*, 19th edn. (Munich, C.H. Beck 1978) introductory remark 2 to § 218, with additional references.

[35] On this point, see *infra* IV.2.3.1/2.

[36] This was how the goal of the legislature was described in KAISER, loc. cit. n. 20, at p. 23; see also HÄUSSLER and HOLZHAUER, loc. cit. n. 20, at p. 817; LIEBL, op. cit. n. 15, at p. IV.

[37] This statement is supported by the findings of HÄUSSLER and HOLZHAUER, loc. cit. n. 20, p. 854, whereby a similar trend was already apparent prior to the reform of 1975 (see E/K I 237); see also the reservations expressed by F.C. SCHROEDER and C. ROXIN, reported from H. ARNOLD and I. GEISSLER, 'Bericht über das Kolloquium 'Die Implementation des reformierten § 218 StGB – Empirische Untersuchungen zu Einstellung und Verhalten von Schwangeren und Ärzten'', 100 *ZStW* (1998) pp. 855-870 at pp. 853 f. resp. 866).

[38] See KAISER, loc. cit. n. 20, at p. 28.

tigations, prosecution and sentencing in practice have shown, the intensity and selectivity of criminal prosecution depends both on the varying attitudes of law enforcement as well as on the social class to which the woman in question belongs. For whatever reason, it appears to be as follows: be it because of frequent unwanted pregnancies, be it because of insufficient knowledge of legal ways of terminating, or be it because of the danger of attracting the attention of law enforcement agencies as a 'side-effect' of another social conflict pregnant women who are prosecuted are chiefly from the lower social classes.[39]

Nevertheless, one would make it too simple if one were to ascribe the coincidental nature of prosecution solely to particular social factors or varying attitudes of the law enforcement agencies. Rather, weak links leading to unequal, even arbitrary application of law may also be found on the normative level. A classic example of this can be seen in the indications that entitle a woman to a terminate: in the interpretation of these indications, differences arise not only among physicians but also between physicians and jurists with relevant experience and even among jurists.[40] Therefore, it is worthwhile to look carefully at the experiences associated with various regulatory modes.

1.3   On the ways of regulating the termination of pregnancy

1.3.1   *Variety of regulatory approaches*

One of the most remarkable findings gained from the comparative legal study of the termination of pregnancy is that there may well be no two abortion regulations in the world that are substantively identical. To be sure, the various national regulations of murder and manslaughter are not carbon copies of one another either.[41] But when comparing criminal laws in various countries, even if one considers the effects on sanctions due to various motives and methods of carrying out the crime, the differences in degree among crimes against born life appear minimal in comparison with the qualitative differences that can be seen in the treatment of illegal abortion and permissible termination of pregnancy all over the world.

---

[39] For details, see LIEBL, op. cit. n. 15, at pp. 82 ff., 107 ff., 177 ff.; see also KAISER, loc. cit. n. 20, at p. 24 f.

[40] On a study conducted of physicians and legal experts concerning their knowledge and interpretation of norms, see HÄUSSLER-SCZEPAN, op. cit. n. 20, at pp. 181 ff. as well as HÄUSSLER and HOLZHAUER, loc. cit. n. 20, at pp. 832 ff.; see also IV.2.3.1, *infra*.

[41] For more on this point, see, from a reform-political and comparative legal perspective, the structural analysis by A. ESER and H.-G. KOCH, 'Die vorsätzlichen Tötungstatbestände', 92 *ZStW* (1980) pp. 491-560.

Of the wealth of variations discussed elsewhere,[42] only three variables will be mentioned again here. Although these variables may appear to be of a more formal or peripheral nature, they can still be useful in bringing attention to value differences and even, in some cases, in revealing moral uncertainties in the collective understanding.

This is the case with regard to fluctuations in *terminology*. Whereas in crimes against born life, terms such as 'kill', 'cause death', and comparable expressions are used, in crimes against unborn life, a wide and variable range of words is employed – and not only in Germany.[43] Also, it would be wrong to suspect that formulations that appear to downplay the seriousness of the procedure, such as 'termination of pregnancy' ['*Schwangerschaftsabbruch*'] in contemporary German usage – or the even more dismissive 'interruption of pregnancy' ['*Schwangerschaftsunterbrechung*'] as in the regulation in the former GDR – a term whose parallel, by the way, is common in languages (both Anglo and Romance) with derivations from the Latin 'interruptio' – , are a result of a modern decay in morals. For the expression 'causing miscarriage of a woman', which dates back to a much earlier era, could hardly be more dismissive. Also to be considered is the fact that the term '*Abtreibung*', generally translated as abortion, dates back to the early 16th century and is completely devoid of all reference to killing. Furthermore, not even the word '*töten*' [kill] is immune to devaluation: This can be seen in the replacement of the original version of the Criminal Code of the German Reich of 1871, which refers to '*Abtreibung*' [abortion] of the 'fruit of the womb' or '*Tötung*' [killing] in the mother's womb (§§ 218-220), by the Decree for the Protection of Marriage, Family, and Motherhood of 1943, which refers to the '*Abtötung*' [destruction] of the fruit of the womb.[44] Whereas from a subjective point of view, the term '*Abtöten*' may even seem worse because of its contemptuous aftertaste, its introduction by the national socialist legislature apparently was meant to disparage the object of the abortion procedure, namely, the fruit of the womb.[45]

Comparable ambivalence is apparent in the expressions 'germinating' and 'nascent' life. Even if it appears wise, from the perspective of political correctness, to refer to 'unborn' life in order to avoid arousing the suspicion of a lack of regard,[46] high regard can certainly be attributed to both 'germinating' and 'nascent', in that they refer to 'life' in terms of a human and not to a developmental

---

[42] For details, see *supra* II.1, II.2.

[43] For details, see *supra* II.2.5.1.

[44] *RGBl.* (*Law Gazette of the German Reich*) 1943/I, 140 at § 5 p. 140 with the implementing order of 1943, *RGBl.* 1943/I, 169-171 at § 2 p. 170.

[45] See DEMEL, op. cit. n. 5, p. 115 f.

[46] See *supra* IV.1.1 text accompanying nn. 1 f.

phase prior to the onset of 'humanness'. This, too, can be an important political statement in light of contemporary schools of thought that do not recognize the need to protect human life until after birth.[47]

Even more variety can be found in the *location in the code* where the termination of pregnancy is regulated; indeed, the question of location may be even more illuminating with regard to value judgments than language and is a second variable of criminal-political importance. The political message can change, depending upon where in the spectrum of regulations from criminal law to social welfare law the laws regulating the termination of pregnancy are located.[48] If abortion is understood as a problem of a purely criminal nature and accordingly regulated solely in the criminal code, as in the 'classical' tradition, this is – perhaps not conclusive but certainly credible – evidence that the primary goal of the statute is to protect unborn life. On the other hand, the greater the distance that has opened up between regulations governing the termination of pregnancy and the criminal law and the closer the ties have become to health and social welfare law (as can be seen most clearly in Scandinavian countries, but in Italy and in some of the states in the US as well), the more the scales shift in favor of the pregnant woman. Remarkably, however, the majority of countries, including those that have already come up with a law reform, take a position somewhere in the middle, in which – although the technical aspects of the regulations may be quite varied – the basic norm prohibiting abortion remains anchored in the criminal law; in addition to this norm, however, there are regulations outside the criminal code that exist in part to protect the interests of the pregnant woman (for example by the covering of costs or the provision of other supportive social measures), in part for the purpose of better protecting unborn life (of these, the most noteworthy is the counseling requirement). This middle-of-the-road group, to which in fact the German regulation belongs, may provide one of the most important political statements; namely, that the phenomenon of termi-

---

[47] Discussions in this area – even those that took place as late as the early part of the 20th century – used to be much less inhibited. This is apparent from the fact that the use of the term 'Leibesfrucht' [fruit of the womb] in the original §§ 218-220 *RStGB* went unchallenged. Although these sections were consolidated into a single section, § 218, by the law of 18 May 1926, the only change in terminology was from 'Leibesfrucht' [fruit of the womb] to 'Frucht im Mutterleib' [fetus in the mother's womb]. In addition, it was determined – oblivious to possible conflict with regard to 'Frucht' as the object of the procedure – that the fetus, or fruit, 'could not yet be a 'Mensch' [man or woman] in a legal sense'. See, e.g., the highly respected commentary by R. FRANK, *Das Strafgesetzbuch für das Deutsche Reich*, 18th edn. (Tübingen, Mohr 1931) § 218 note 1. On the inadequacy of all efforts in this area with regard to terminology, see also F.C. SCHROEDER, 'Unaufrichtigkeit des Gesetzes', 25 *ZRP* (1992) pp. 409-410 at p. 409.

[48] For more on the five models, see the categorization *supra* in II.1.1.

nation cannot be dealt with solely by means of the criminal law but rather in the pursuit of a better protection of life – and not only, as one might perhaps think, as a unilateral concession to the interests of the woman – non-criminal law instruments must also be employed. Only those who put ideology over reality will be able to close their minds completely to the new reform movement that calls for 'help instead of punishment'.

An additional variable in the systematics of law that can be illuminating with regard to the status conferred upon the protection of life is *the location of the abortion regulation within the criminal code*. Despite the logical assumption that the prohibition of abortion, serving as it does the protection of life, has traditionally been handled together with crimes against life, this location is in fact – as can be seen from comparative studies[49] – a rather infrequent exception. Remarkably, abortion is treated together with crimes against life primarily in the as yet unreformed regulations of Latin American and African-Arabic countries so that the reformed regulations of Greece and the Federal Republic of Germany, in which this location has also been chosen, stand out all the more. In contrast, in the vast majority of countries studied, the termination of pregnancy is not – or at least not exclusively – dealt with in close proximity to the homicide offenses; rather, the spectrum ranges from treatment proximate to offenses concerning the protection of life and limb or offenses concerning the person in general to offenses that typically aim to protect general interests like family order and public morality, whereby the latter interest can still be found in the new regulations of Luxembourg and Belgium. Although the separate regulation of the termination of pregnancy and homicide offenses may, in and of itself, be enough to accuse a country of insufficient interest in the protection of unborn life, it at least indicates that born and unborn life are valued differently. For even if the systematic arrangement of crimes in a criminal code is not necessarily patterned on a particular hierarchy of the objects of legal protection [*Rechtsgüter*], practically the only explanation for the decision to regulate the termination of pregnancy separately from the offenses that protect born life is that unborn life is in some way distinguishable from born life, or indeed, that it is less worthy of protection.

Finally, the regulatory diversity is even greater if one considers a third variable, namely the numerous *combinations of substantive norms*, both prohibitive and permissive, *procedural requirements*, and possible *supportive measures*. We will return to this plethora of variations – which has developed in the context of the termination of pregnancy to an extent unthinkable in the context of the killing of born life – when we discuss the various regulatory models.[50]

---

[49] See *supra* II.1.2 with additional references.
[50] See *infra* IV.1.3.3.

1.3.2   *The interdependence of regulatory diversity and social mores*

Although at first the legal landscape with which the comparativist studying the termination of pregnancy is confronted seems astonishingly diverse, the variety should not, in fact, be unexpected, given the high degree of interdependence between the regulation of termination and social mores. To be sure, the treatment of general homicide offenses is not completely free of various national prejudices, either; this is apparent, for example, in the existence of more or less extensive grounds for the exemption from punishment in cases such as self-defense and necessity and in the different ways in which assorted aggravating or mitigating factors affect punishment. These differences are minimal, however, whereas the differences in the regulation of terminations can go so far as to be of a qualitative nature.

In the search for an explanation for the varying moral attitudes towards the protection of born and unborn life, differing constitutional standards should be considered first. As shown by our constitutional overview,[51] not even human beings *after* they are born are guaranteed protection of life by all constitutions, and the position of the unborn, constitutionally speaking, often proves to be even weaker, in part because the general guarantees of protection of life are not extended to the unborn, in part because the equality of born and unborn life before the constitution is denied.

The extent to which this kind of constitutional hierarchization of values affects the prevailing moral attitude or whether the creators of the constitutions simply reflect the general mores is certainly an interesting practical- legal as well as normative-doctrinal question. The answer, to be sure, does not change the fact that, for whatever reason, when compared to the claim of born life to protection, the claim of unborn life is assessed differently from country to country, particularly with regard to the extent and the severity of criminal sanctions.

There is no other way to explain the fact that discussions concerning the legal value [*Rechtsgut*] affected by the termination of pregnancy are conducted from country to country with varying intensity, if at all, other than by pointing out that different countries display a wide range of moral attitudes and the level of acknowledgment of the significance of this issue varies around the world: in fact, the degree of vehemence found in the Federal Republic of Germany is virtually unparalleled.[52] This finding is even truer in light of the legal nature of exemption from punishment when a pregnancy has been terminated: whereas, for example, in the Federal Republic, the statutorily mandated 'non-illegality' of a termination performed by a physician after counseling was raised to the

---

[51] See *supra* II.2.3.
[52] For details, see *supra* II.2.2.

level of a constitutional question (and, as is well known, was responsible for the partial nullification of the reform law of 1992), in many other countries – even those whose criminal law doctrine is highly developed – comparable discussion simply does not take place, and the significance of the issue is perhaps unrecognized.[53] Granted, it would be interesting to know how much or how little the general mores are influenced by the significance which is accorded the issue by the legal profession or, vice versa, the degree to which general disinterest in such questions discourages legal professionals from engaging in serious doctrinal discussions. At this point, however, all that can be said is that there are country-specific value differences not only on the normative level but in the ability of the legal profession to recognize the significance of the issue and in the outlook of the general public as well.

These kinds of value differences appear to make themselves felt in two primary areas: first, with regard to the assumed relativity of the protection of unborn life, which becomes more significant the more other, competing interests must be taken into account;[54] and second, with regard to temporal factors that affect the protection of unborn life, i.e., when, in a growing number of countries, the point at which protection begins has been pushed back from conception to implantation and when as a result of additional time-bound cut-off points more or less far-reaching options to terminate are created.[55]

Finally, dependence on value judgments may arise from certain fundamental legislative convictions. This can perhaps be seen most clearly in the comparison of symbolism and realism: the more the legislature relies on the demonstrative proclamation of protection of life, the less it wants the symbolic strength of simple and clear prohibitions to be riddled by countless exceptions, even if, in reality, criminal prosecution is insufficient and lags far behind the high normative expectations. On the other hand, the more regard the legislature has for regulations that reflect reality, the more likely it will accept a more differentiated approach.[56] Although more or less far-reaching, recent trends in reform are clearly in the direction of reality.

1.3.3 *Model-building criteria*

In light of the dependence of the legal regulation of the termination of pregnancy on certain legal and ethical presuppositions and policy goals, factors that differ from country to country, it can come as no surprise that no two regula-

---

[53] For details, see *supra* II.3.7.
[54] On this point, see also *infra* IV.2.2.1.
[55] On this point, see *supra* II.2.5, II.3.1.
[56] See also *supra* IV.2.1.2.

tions the world over are completely identical. Nevertheless, despite the great variety in appearance, regulatory patterns can be identified that are traceable to certain fundamental models. As has already been demonstrated in the structuring and the cross-sectional presentation of these fundamental regulatory models,[57] the building of the models depends to a great degree on the criteria that are viewed as essential, whereby the determination of essentiality is, of course, itself dependent on presuppositions and value judgments.

If in this preliminary decision one at first allows oneself to be led entirely by the parameter representing the ideological 'sticking point', as it were, in the current legal policy discussion – at least in Germany – , that parameter would be the reviewable *indication* for the termination of a pregnancy, the necessity or dispensability of which is accorded model-building character. In comparison to the categorical role played by the various indication criteria, as seen in the so-called 'indication model' ['*Indikationsmodell*'], the role of the time-limit criterion of the eponymous 'time-limit model' ['*Fristenmodell*'] is a subordinate one; for even if the borderline between permitted termination and prohibited abortion is lastly drawn by means of time limits, strictly speaking this is presupposed by the question of whether and to what extent, if at all, the (timely) exemption from punishment must also be rationalized in one way or another on the basis of certain grounds for termination – and, indeed, what is an 'indication' if not such a rationalization? In this respect, the decisive front line in fact passes between models that require indications and models that do not – whereby the latter, instead of relying on the indication, rely on other criteria, like, for example, time-based limitations or counseling.

The antithetical nature of the contrast between models that rely on indications and models that do not is blurred by the fact that the requirements for proving the existence of an indication are extremely varied. This may be seen in the breadth or narrowness of the various categories of indications – indeed the diversity of indications around the world is practically overwhelming[58] – and in the more or less strict procedural requirements for determining the presence of an indication, i.e., in one country a third opinion as well as judicial review may be required whereas another country may make do without the one or the other, so that in the final analysis the finding of an indication is based solely on the self-assessment of the pregnant woman.[59] If, in addition to the various prerequisites for proving an indication, possibly different legal consequences are also taken into consideration, for example, complete justification on the one

---

[57] *Supra* II.2.4.

[58] For more details, see *supra* II.3.2, and Diagram II/8 (p. 89).

[59] For more on these various forms, see *supra* II.3.4.2.

hand or mere exemption from punishment on the other,[60] the overall picture becomes even more complex and clear divisions between models more difficult.

In light of this finding, what are we to think, from a legal policy perspective, of the – oft-polemic – confrontation of the 'indication solution' and the 'time-limit solution?' The answer depends primarily upon the purposes and preferences associated with each model:

In so far as the free, unrestricted choice of the pregnant woman regarding continuation or termination of her pregnancy should yield to the protection of unborn life, the indication model may appear to be the more suitable but by no means the only method. Certainly, it is appropriate insofar as the requirement of an indication gives expression to the conviction that a pregnancy should not be terminated at the whim of the pregnant woman but rather that a termination should take place only if the existence of certain grounds can be proven. However, not even a time-limit model must necessarily afford the woman complete freedom of choice; for, apart from the fact that by means of a cut-off point based on the duration of the pregnancy the time-limit solution itself places a restriction on the termination of pregnancy and in so doing restricts the self-determination of the pregnant woman, additional restrictions, such as a requirement to obtain counseling, may apply. Thus, neither the characterization as a 'time-limit' solution – implying dependence solely upon a particular moment in time – nor the cursory equation of time-limit solutions with the free and unbridled self-determination of the pregnant woman is correct. As a result, the 'demonization' of all kinds of time-limit solutions appears to be consistent only with the perspective of someone for whom even the tiniest contribution from the woman to the decision-making process is an untenable evil. But whether in fact those who see a time-limit solution in each judicially unreviewable indication solution and who believe that all time-limit solutions are nothing more than a cover for the free and unbridled self-determination of the pregnant woman really want to go this far will remain unclear, so long as they are not aware of the shortsightedness of their argumentation.

To be sure, to the extent that the goal really is a process of determining the existence of an indication in which the pregnant woman herself plays absolutely no part and for which, as a result, both third party as well as judicial review are essential, the characterization as an indication solution is certainly appropriate. However, if this characterization is to apply only to regulations like those described above – namely those requiring the existence of an objective indication, identified by a third party and judicially reviewable – the only

---

[60] For more on these kinds of – socio-ethically significant – distinctions and their consequences, see *supra* II.3.7.

country that could today boast a 'true' indication model would be the Federal Republic of Germany.[61] For as soon as an indication required by law need not be formally identified by a third party and/or is not judicially reviewable, we are no longer dealing with a true indication model. This is, however, the case practically everywhere in the world – with the exception of Germany. This terminological exclusion may not, in fact, awaken much interest in the affected countries since the classifications used in Germany are not in use everywhere. In contrast, the finding of the Federal Constitutional Court that 'indispensable principles of a *Rechtsstaat*' require that the determination of the existence of an indication be state-controlled might well meet with less indifference.[62] Even though this statement was made specifically in the context of the prerequisites for a legally 'justified' termination, this limitation allows only those countries to avoid the verdict of an insufficient rule of law in which the mere fulfillment of the prerequisites for a punishment-free termination does not bear on the question of the termination's legal justification. Given that meaningful discussions concerning the legal nature of a termination conducted in accordance with the law rarely takes place outside of Germany, this is, however, the case in only a negligible number of countries.[63] With all due respect, one can only hope that when the Federal Constitutional Court, in its unconditional proclamation of 'essential principles of a *Rechtsstaat*', implicitly attributed to many countries with highly developed legal cultures a lack of compliance of their termination regulations with the rule of law, it did so because of its ignorance of foreign law rather than in the spirit of know-it-all arrogance.[64]

However, increasingly few countries appear to be convinced by the rigorism of this extreme fixation on indications. For, to the extent that reforms have been

---

[61] See *supra* II.3.4.2, especially F.

[62] *BVerfGE* 88, 274.

[63] See *supra* II.3.7.

[64] Perhaps I might be allowed to introduce on this point a personal experience: coincidentally, on 28 May, 1993, the day of the announcement of the Federal Constitutional Court decision, I arrived in Sweden to begin a lecture tour. At that time, there was a discussion in Sweden concerning the desirability of introducing a constitutional court with jurisdictional powers patterned on the German constitutional court. These efforts, in light of the perceived presumption of a self-righteous court placing itself above a clear majority of the parliament and, in addition, imposing upon the parliament detailed instructions of what to do, met with a persistently muted response. Incidentally, my position regarding the BVerfG decision was influenced to no small degree by these impressions: A. Eser, 'Aufbruch zu neuem Weg, Halt auf halber Strecke', 76 *Kritische Vierteljahresschrift für Gesetzgebung und Rechtswissenschaft* (1993), Sonderheft 1/1993, pp. 132-139. See also IV.2.1.1, *infra*, text accompanying n. 130.

undertaken recently,[65] even countries that require particular grounds for the termination often do without judicial review or – as in the majority of countries in this category – the determination of an indication is put into the hands of physicians, or even, – as, for example, in France and Norway in the case of the *general emergency indication* – left up to the judgment of the pregnant woman altogether.[66]

Nevertheless, it would be wrong to view these regulations as pure 'self-determination models' or, if any time-related limitations whatsoever are made, simply to dismiss them as 'time-limit models'. For as long as the exemption from punishment is conditioned on the existence of certain crisis situations, the pregnant woman, if she abides by the law – and, indeed, why should her loyalty to the law be questioned? –, cannot treat the termination of a pregnancy purely as a matter of self-determination. This is all the more true if she is urged or even required to obtain *counseling*. For even if counseling is not designed to determine the existence of specific, indication-like emergency situations, the very fact that a counseling session can be expected implies that the termination of a pregnancy is not something to be left up to the unfettered decision-making of the pregnant woman. In order to give expression to the deference due this independent object of legal protection, whose interests are not completely identical to those of the pregnant woman herself, it is difficult to deny the model-building character of the theory behind counseling. This is all the more true in light of the fact that, increasingly, countries are relying less on punishment and more on assistance and counseling.[67] Therefore, it is also misguided to describe counseling models as 'time-limit models' simply because they permit termination within a particular period of time following counseling.

Finally, how little the phrase 'time-limit solution' actually means becomes apparent when the decision to terminate a pregnancy within a defined time period is a choice left entirely up to pregnant woman herself. For, although the woman may terminate the pregnancy within this time period without having to answer to anyone and without even having to get counseling, the dominant thought behind the exemption from punishment is not the time factor but rather that of the *self-determination* conceded to the pregnant woman. Thus, the English expression 'pro choice' is actually a much better description of the situation; the failure to focus on self-determination also helps to explain the difficulties encountered in translating the term *'Fristenlösung'* [time-limit solution] into

---

[65] For more details, see *supra* I.5 as well as – more detailed – E/K III pp. 625 ff.
[66] For details, see *supra* II.2.4.3.
[67] See *infra* IV.2.2.4, text accompanying n. 226, IV.2.3.2.

English.[68] Accordingly, these kinds of regulations should instead be called 'self-determination models', a term that by now is no longer uncommon,[69] in order to give expression to the essential character of the regulation. Reference to a time factor in this context appears to be feasible only to the extent that self-determined terminations are subject to a temporal limitation.

Although the fundamental significance of these criteria was not fully appreciated at first, they played an intuitive model-building role in the comparative legal cross-section: In the discussion of the traditional confrontation between the 'indication solution' and 'time-limit solution', we sought to bring attention to the finding that a growing number of countries neither leave the termination of pregnancy completely up to the pregnant woman, nor do they subject it completely to the control of a third party; instead, they require a reason for the termination, the determination of which is to a great extent entrusted to the woman's sense of responsibility, and even if time limits apply, they are not the true basis for the regulation but rather function solely as a limiting factor. As a result, the regulations providing exemption from punishment can be divided into three subcategories: the *indication model on the basis of third party evaluation*, on the one hand; the *time-based exemption on the basis of self-determination*, on the other; and in between the *conflict-oriented discourse model*, which, in accordance with current terminology, can also be referred to as a 'counseling model'.[70] It would indeed be a great achievement if, in response to the aforementioned substantive arguments, this division into three subcategories would help overcome the superficial polemic between the indication and the time-limit solution.

While on the subject of model-building criteria, at least two additional phenomena should be mentioned: the first is the *general exemption from punishment of the pregnant woman*, which is becoming more and more commonplace;[71] the second is the increasing importance of *procedural factors*. The following remarks are devoted to the latter.

1.3.4   'Medicalization' – 'proceduralization' 'socialization'

Without wishing to minimize the fundamental significance attributed in the preceding comments to the occasionally contradictory criteria of the indication

---

[68] It makes no difference if the German term appears in English language translations as 'periodic model', as 'time-limit option', as some similar term that relies on the time factor, or if it is simply left untranslated, the fact of the matter is that the term 'Fristenregelung' leaves people stymied.

[69] See *supra* II.2.4.3.D.

[70] For more on these three subcategories, see *supra* II.2.4.3 C-E, and Diagram II/6 (p. 68).

[71] For more, see *supra* II.4.1, but see also *infra* IV.2.2.4.

requirement, to the role of self-determination or co-determination on the part of the pregnant woman, and to the contribution of counseling, we turn our attention at this point to several additional issues characteristic of the current developments in the laws regulating the termination of pregnancy.

The first of these can perhaps be referred to as a *medicalization* trend, in which the role of the physician is becoming steadily more important. This was dealt with in more detail – although in slightly different form – in the comparative legal cross-section[72] and can be seen in a variety of developments. It is most obvious in the reallocation of punishability between the pregnant woman and the physician: whereas in the past and, indeed, up to and including the present time, the pregnant woman herself carried primary criminal responsibility for the abortion (and at most was treated less harshly than a lay participant in the procedure), in a growing number of countries, the pregnant woman today is completely exempt from punishment.[73] As a result, in light of the *de facto* disappearance of quacks and other lay abortionists,[74] the physician has become the major addressee of threatened criminal sanctions. It is quite understandable – despite the infrequency of prosecution[75] – that physicians may begin to feel 'instrumentalized' and may see themselves as scapegoats, sent in place of the pregnant women, who are the true offenders, into the desert of criminality. Two possible explanations for the approach taken by lawmakers are, first, that physicians are not in the same existential conflict situation as the pregnant woman or, second, that physicians, as professionals, are expected to exhibit more loyalty to the law.[76]

But even where the lever of preventive criminal law is not applied solely to physicians but rather – as still is the case in most countries – the pregnant woman herself remains criminally responsible, the physician plays a pivotal role since only those terminations that are performed by physicians are unpunishable. The effect of this 'without the physician, nothing doing' phenomenon is to increase the burden on physicians, as their decisions and behavior determine both their own criminal liability as well as that of pregnant women. The possibility that legislatures are not reallocating this kind of decision-making responsibility consciously does not apply, at any rate, to the Federal German Parliament, which, in introducing § 218c Criminal Code in 1995, increased the obligations of the

---

[72] See the general overview *supra* II.5. See also *infra* IV.2.2.4, text accompanying nn. 218 ff.

[73] See *supra* II.2.4.1.D, II.4.1.

[74] See E/K I p. 237 on the developments in the Federal Republic of Germany.

[75] See *supra* III.1.

[76] See also *infra* IV.1.4.2, text accompanying n. 111, as well as *supra* II.5.1.

physician.[77] Furthermore, the obligations imposed on the physician in § 218c Criminal Code are not limited to the performance of the termination as such but rather attach already to the determination of an indication or can play a role in the counseling process. In this context, the Federal German rule offers, comparatively speaking, a wealth of interesting material.

An unavoidable result of the aforementioned development is an increasing *proceduralization* of the law of termination. As already discussed in detail in the comparative legal cross-section, this can be observed in three different phases and forms: first, the requirement that certain conditions be fulfilled (e.g., the determination of an indication and/or counseling); second, the requirement that the termination itself be performed in a certain way (e.g., by a physician and/or in the hospital); and third, the requirement that subsequent to the termination certain formalities be observed (e.g., the documentation of the termination or the requirement that it be reported to particular authorities).[78] The goals of such procedures are both short- and long-term. The short-term goal involves the individual pregnancy and its concrete continuation or termination, the primarily issue in the determination of an indication, for counseling and with regard to the requirements of the termination procedure itself; the long-term goal focuses on termination as a social phenomenon and how it can better be addressed in the future after its causes, as revealed by the reporting requirement, become known. In this context, it must not be forgotten that a fundamental change in perspective has taken place: earlier, society sought to fight abortion with repressive criminal law; today, society places more value on prevention. Currently, it is felt that the best method is to prevent unwanted pregnancy through use of education and birth control and, if such a pregnancy does occur, to discourage its termination by means of assistance and counseling.

Finally, there are some trends in the same vein that can be depicted as the *socialization* of the handling of the termination of pregnancy. This development might seem somewhat surprising, given that the increasing consideration for the needs and the choice of the pregnant woman appear indicative of a trend towards individualism. But this is a superficial way of looking at things that overlooks the wider social context of the conflicted pregnancy. This social dimension finds expression in those indications for termination that have always been viewed as 'social' or – as is the case for most of the medical indications – in those indications in which social components play a role.[79] Here, again, the

---

[77] For more details, see A. ESER, in A. SCHÖNKE and H. SCHRÖDER (eds.), *Strafgesetzbuch: Kommentar*, 26th edn. (Munich, C.H. Beck 2001) § 218c margin No. 1 with further references.

[78] See *supra* II.3.4-6.

[79] For details, see *supra* II.3.2.3.B.

importance of the physician becomes apparent, as the extent to which social factors are seen as burdens depends upon the physician's 'power to define' the relevant norm and situation [*Definitionsmacht*].[80] In this way, physicians in fact take on the role – even beyond that ascribed them under the key word 'medicalization' – of a 'social controlleur'.[81]

Although these kinds of socialization trends appear at first glance to provide some relief to the pregnant woman who wishes to terminate, they may in fact have just the opposite result. If the people around her are asked to become involved, and, for example, her partner or one or more of their parents in fact declare themselves ready and willing to contribute financially and to help look after the child, the pregnant woman's conflict situation and with it the grounds for terminating her pregnancy may disappear.[82] Additionally, the pregnant woman's social contacts may also find themselves facing certain obligations, like, for example, parents' or partner's duty to assist in overcoming the emergency situation, and the criminal law may come into play to protect the pregnant woman from undue pressure from third parties. In this activation of social contacts, an area that, strangely enough, has so far been greatly neglected, only a few countries have made as much headway as the Federal Republic of Germany.[83]

1.4   On the role of criminal law – other leading factors

1.4.1   *Irrelevance of criminal law?*

With regard to the efficacy of criminal law in the context of the termination of pregnancy, the dissonance between expectations and disappointments could hardly be greater. Whereas some favor the primary if not exclusive use of criminal law in the fight against abortion, others allege its complete ineffectiveness. Whereas some see the punishment of abortion as a necessary consequence of the rule of law, others see in it nothing more than a symbolic gesture, completely out of touch with reality. In short: whereas some – hoping against hope – defend the legitimacy of applying criminal law, others – although perhaps conceding its deterrent effect – deny any justification for its existence whatsoever. To what extent these hopes and fears are brought on by moral rigorism or moral laxity, loyalty to principles or willingness to make concessions, loss of contact with reality or recognition of the true state of affairs, differing assess-

---

[80] See E/K III 69, text accompanying n. 19.
[81] For a comparison to France, see E/K II p. 507.
[82] See *supra* II.3.3.4.C.
[83] For details, see *supra* II.2.2, II.3.3.4.

ments regarding the interest of the child in life and the needs of the pregnant woman, greater or lesser willingness to dismantle social discrimination, or other affirmative or resignative attitudes is perhaps a provoking question but one that is, in the last analysis, unanswerable. For the bundle of factors that plays a role in the replacement of criminal law is as complex as the conflict surrounding the termination issue itself. And even if ideologies such as conservatism and faith in the state, on the one hand, and liberalism and individualism, on the other, imply different political camps, any attempt to impose a political straight-jacket would be futile; for just as a basically conservative outlook can be distrustful of a criminal law with merely symbolic effects and thus expect more efficiency from practical assistance programs so can liberalism, on the side of the right to free development of personality and its prerequisite, the existence of unborn life, be supportive of pertinent state legal protections, including criminal law. Thus, instead of speculating, perhaps wrongly, about ideological prejudices, the truly important question in this context appears to be whether the role of criminal law in the termination context is really filled as badly as some claim it to be and others refuse to acknowledge.

Without engaging in an exhaustive analysis, the criminal law skeptics appear – at least at first glance – to be more in touch with reality, both on a factual, criminological level as well as from a normative, comparative legal perspective.

On an empirical level, it is impossible to ignore the large numbers, absolute as well as relative, of abortions. Regardless of how one looks at the numbers, how one juggles and interprets them, and what reservations one makes based on the various methods of data-keeping and the dark figures,[84] the termination of pregnancy has proven itself to be a worldwide phenomenon;[85] moreover, this fact cannot be downplayed by using the criminal law to distinguish between illegal and legal terminations. For regardless of whether criminal law has withdrawn of its own accord and tacitly accepted the 'legality' of certain terminations or whether it has continued to hold its own and in so doing has had to put up with more and more frequent violations, the criminal law sees itself as a 'failure': No matter which of these paths it chooses, the numbers of illegal abortions or legal terminations, astonishingly high in comparison to the killing of born life, are an undeniable indicium that criminal law alone cannot be expected to have a decisive preventive effect. The skepticism in the criminal law awakened by comparatively high termination rates all over the world is consid-

---

[84] See *supra* III, III.1.1.

[85] For details, see the comparative legal overview of the frequency of the termination of pregnancy, *supra* III.1.2.

erably strengthened if prosecution statistics are considered:[86] Even disregarding the more or less extensive punishment-free zones created by the criminal law itself, the number of attempted and successful prosecutions for criminal abortion lags so far behind the termination rate that prosecution cannot be taken seriously, even in countries with a strongly prohibitive model.[87] And, indeed, the concern is justified that the gaping discrepancy between *de jure* criminal liability and *de facto* prosecution will increasingly undermine public confidence in criminal law the more it trumpets its exclusivity in the termination context, the more prominent its refusal to compromise, and the less willing it is to take on a subsidiary role.

Even the qualified hope that particular features of the various legal regulatory concepts, at least, will have a preventive effect should not be overestimated, prima facie. For given the great variety among regulations governing the termination of pregnancy[88] and given the fact that corresponding differences in abortion and prosecution rates cannot be substantiated,[89] the assumption of direct causality between the legal regulatory modus and severity of sanctions, on the one hand, and actual behavior in the abortion context, on the other, is simply not warranted. But this is not all; rather, the criminal political theory that one need only tighten the criminal law screw to bring about a decrease in the number of terminations is turned on its head when forced to acknowledge that emphatically permissive regulations are often associated with remarkably low frequencies, as in the Netherlands and Tunisia.[90] No less sobering in light of the question addressed here, namely, the relevance of criminal law, is the finding that neither extensive exemptions from punishment – as in the USA – nor the complete suspension of the law of abortion – the result, in Canada, of a Supreme Court decision – necessarily leads to an inexorable increase in the frequency of abortion.[91] Finally, the easy manipulability of the criminal law, as seen most clearly in the context of indication models when, for example, the absence of a social indication is compensated for by a corresponding expansion of the medical indication,[92] seems to prove the irrelevance of legal regulations.

These as well as other phenomena that expose the weaknesses of criminal law seem in fact to lend support to the criminal law skeptics. At the same time,

---

[86] For details, see the comparative legal overview of criminality, *supra* III.3, and Tables III/4-III/6 (pp. 199-201).

[87] See *supra* IV.1.2.2.

[88] See *supra* IV.1.3.1.

[89] See *supra* III.1.2.1, III.1.2.2 and III.3.

[90] See *supra* III.1.2.2.

[91] See E/K II 1091 and 615 ff. as well as *supra* II.2.3.1 n. 40 ff., III.1.3.

[92] See *supra* II.3.2.3.B as well as *infra* IV.2.3.1.

the field should not be conceded to them too quickly. For even if one does not look directly to normative principles for rescue – like a human rights requirement to protect life or the use of criminal law as a last but at the same time indispensable resort (more on this later),[93] it is by no means certain, even considering empirical evidence, that criminal law has in fact absolutely no relevance in the termination context. Essentially, all that appears to be proven is the following: on the one hand, termination cannot be combatted efficiently or appropriately by criminal prohibition alone; on the other hand, as unlikely as it is for the decision to continue or terminate a pregnancy to be taken solely on the basis of the existence or absence of a criminal prohibition (monocausal), it is equally unlikely that a given legal regulation will lead only to decisions either to continue or to terminate pregnancy (monofinal). If, in light of this, criminal law cannot be credited with a sure and inevitable effect, this does not necessarily mean that it exerts no influence whatsoever. In the following, several of the project's findings on this point will be addressed.

At the outset, it is necessary to bring attention to two general issues. First, the problem posed by all kinds of multifaceted decisions, namely, that it is difficult enough to ascertain which motives are contributory and which dominant for one single decision and that this difficulty is compounded if one tries to identify and quantify the motives of a large number or group of people. But since the only question here is whether criminal law – despite the fact that, alone, it cannot be expected to exercise a preventive effect – has at least an inhibiting influence on the termination rate, the measurability of this influence is at most of quantitative, and not of principal, concern. Additional support for this perspective is the ambivalent fact that, on the one hand, the ineffectiveness of criminal law can be measured by means of actually completed terminations (although the exact extent of this 'negative' side, even, is masked by dark figures) but that, on the other hand, this 'gray-shrouded failure' may be countered by an as yet unstudied 'dark area of success';[94] namely, by women who chose to continue their pregnancies and carry them to term and whose choice was influenced to no small degree by existing criminal regulations. For even if counseling, and not prohibition, is the decisive factor in the decision to continue a pregnancy – as, indeed, was shown by our study of the attitudes of pregnant women –,[95] since counseling is a part of the criminal system of regulation, these are decisions that, in the last analysis, are attributable to the criminal law.

From this perspective, the previously described *effects of statutory amendments* deserve a short recapitulation.[96] We are confronted in this context with

---

[93] See *infra* IV.2.2.
[94] See ESER, loc. cit. n. 1, at pp. 160 ff.
[95] See HOLZHAUER, op. cit. n. 20, at pp. 278 f., 286 f.
[96] For details, see *supra* III.1.3.

the rather strange finding that, although the termination rate increases following liberalizing reforms, there is no corresponding measurable decrease following the enhancement of criminal penalties. This is not, however, proof that criminal law is irrelevant; on the contrary, if the easing of the criminal law is followed by an increase in the termination rate, then the law must have had an inhibiting effect prior to the change. It is, of course, a separate question altogether if a criminal law whose repressive role is merely to slow things down is by itself sufficient or if termination should also be affirmatively discouraged by constructive prevention (as by means of counseling). But even if the latter approach is preferable from a legal policy standpoint, as shown in one of the following sections (2.3.2), this does not change the fact that, viewed pragmatically, the termination rate apparently does reflect the existence and severity of criminal regulations.

This finding cannot be discredited simply because the various parties involved in the termination process may respond to criminal law in different ways and to different degrees. Even if it inhibits pregnant woman less effectively than it does physicians, as our attitudinal study has shown,[97] and even if the depth of its effect on physicians depends upon whether the pregnancy is to be terminated on the basis of medical or merely on the basis of social grounds,[98] these differences do not rob criminal law entirely of its relevance; this is truer still, the more a woman wishing to terminate must depend upon the cooperation of a physician who is wary of the risk of criminal liability. Naturally, we must also consider the legal policy question of whether pregnant women should be made to depend upon the willingness of physicians to take risks. It would, perhaps, be better if we could find a solution that spares the pregnant woman from feeling like a humiliated supplicant and the physician from feeling like a means to an end and that, to the extent possible in the termination context, allows the woman and her physician to deal with each other 'in good conscience' as equals. But so long as this is not the case and the criminal law prevails, its role as one of a host of influences affecting the decision for or against termination cannot be completely disregarded.

Even the previously discussed *manipulability of grounds underlying indications*, identified as yet another weakness of criminal law,[99] has a positive side. For if the existence of indications were in fact irrelevant to the justification of a termination, we would no longer need to concern ourselves with the ins and

---

[97] For details, see HOLZHAUER, op. cit. n. 20, at pp. 332 ff.; HÄUSSLER-SCZEPAN, op. cit. n. 20, at pp. 209 ff., 234 ff.; HÄUSSLER and HOLZHAUER, loc. cit. n. 20, at pp. 817 f., 851 f.

[98] On such differences in attitude, see HÄUSSLER-SCZEPAN, op. cit. n. 20, at pp. 147 ff., 181 ff., 228 ff.

[99] See *supra* n. 92 and accompanying text.

outs of their boundaries. On the other hand, it is also possible that these kinds of manipulations could have a detrimental effect on the general level of acceptance of the law in society and would thus be intolerable from a legal policy standpoint.[100] However, from a practical standpoint, even regulations that are legally and ethically corrupt may have an inhibitory effect on termination insofar as they require adaptations or detours that would otherwise be unnecessary.

Finally, let us consider *abortion tourism*, a widespread phenomenon[101] that can also be interpreted in more than one way. On the one hand, criminal law is powerless to react if a termination that cannot be obtained in its own jurisdiction or can only be obtained there with great difficulty can be obtained simply by traveling to another jurisdiction.[102] Also, the standing of a country's criminal abortion law cannot be the best if people make use of such escape routes. In a kind of 'election by foot', such actions show, in a way that could hardly be clearer, how pregnant women and physicians, people who otherwise tend to be law-abiding citizens, feel themselves misunderstood in this regard from their own legal system and thus disregard the call of the law. But even in this failure the practical relevance of criminal law is evident in that it would not be necessary to take such steps to bypass the law were it in fact completely powerless.

Even if these are not the only factors that speak for or against the relevance of criminal law, the essentials should by now be clear: whereas it would be unrealistic to claim that criminal law is of no practical significance whatsoever, it is equally unrealistic to expect that criminal law alone can lead to the decision not to terminate. What is left is the possibility of co-influencing the decision whether or not to terminate, whereby the extent of such an effect is immeasurable both in individual cases and in general. Thus, it is all the more important to identify other factors that can be expected to play a leading role in influencing decisions in the termination context.

---

[100] See IV.2.1.3, *infra*.

[101] Abortion tourism need not be between countries, like, for example, from Germany to neighboring Holland (see E/K I 76, pp. 110, 234 f.), but can also be within a country, for instance between Baden-Württemberg and Hessen (see HÄUSSLER and HOLZHAUER, loc. cit. n. 20, at pp. 837, 842, 844, 853, 866 f.; HOLZHAUER, op. cit. n. 20, at pp. 296 ff., 309 ff.; ALBRECHT, loc. cit. n. 20, at p. 209); for more recent information, see the report in the Süddeutsche Zeitung, 7 August 1997. On similar occurrences in other countries, such as Yugoslavia, Ireland, the Netherlands, Poland, Australia, Costa Rica, Canada and Mexico, see E/K I pp. 773; 918; 1010; 1408 f.; II 95; 301; 638, 694. In addition, see, *supra*, I.5.1, II.4.4.1, and C. FORDER, 'Abortion: A Constitutional Problem in European Perspective', 1 *Maastricht Journal of European and Comparative Criminal Law* (1994) pp. 56-100 at pp. 77, 80.

[102] In this context, individual cases of successful 'border controls' between Holland and Germany, as reported in LIEBL, op. cit. n. 15, at p. 82, are no more than coincidental exceptions from the less successful rule.

1.4.2   *Prevalence of psychosocial and socioethical factors?*

While it is difficult to quantify the extent of this phenomenon as well, the astonishing fact remains that, despite widespread termination of a quite significant number of unwanted pregnancies, not all of these pregnancies end in termination. Although in some cases this may be due to changes in the emotional attitude of the pregnant woman herself, in which she gradually comes to tolerate or perhaps even accept an unwanted pregnancy,[103] a more or less large proportion of such unwanted pregnancies are continued. As this phenomenon cannot be attributed solely to criminal prohibition (this would, as seen before, be too much to hope for), there must be additional factors located somewhere in the motivational spectrum between the affirmative desire to have a child, on the one hand, and the repressive threat of punishment, on the other, that cause a pregnant woman to carry an in fact unwanted pregnancy to term. Additional factors must also be at work in the case of a physician who is not deterred by the criminal risk alone but who nevertheless resists a woman's wish to terminate.

It is difficult to cover these kinds of factors in their entirety; we can at most bring attention to them by type. If the findings of our attitudinal study can be generalized, there are remarkable differences between pregnant women and physicians with regard to the factors that influence them decisively.

For *women* who are confronted with unwanted pregnancies, criminal law plays a subordinate or at most an indirect role, if it plays a role at all. Instead, fundamental moral attitudes and/or the psychosocial circumstances of her life exercise a decisive influence on her behavior. The former are presumably most influential among the women of group 3 (described in IV.1.2.3, *supra*), whose decision to continue an unexpected pregnancy is made without notable conflict. Although this may appear to be the 'obvious' course of conduct, because unborn life should be respected and its destruction, therefore, rejected, the source of this moral conviction, naturally, can also receive sustenance from legal regulations, and criminal sanctions can prove to be both a guiding principle and an amplifier. In this context, the indirect, value-building role of criminal law increases as the lack of an original ethical basis increases, and the resulting vacuum is filled by the symbolic power of criminal law. Although in this case it may seem appropriate, in the last analysis, to credit criminal law with the primary role in the decision to continue the pregnancy, we must avoid jumping to the wrong conclusion; for as long as it is less the fear of criminal punishment and more the positive attitude toward unborn life that motivates a woman to carry her pregnancy to term, it is this fundamental moral attitude – however it is

---

[103] For more on positive as well as negative changes in attitude during pregnancy, see HOLZHAUER, op. cit. n. 20, at pp. 213 ff.

formed and fostered – that is the primary factor. If this is true even for only a fraction of women with unwanted pregnancies, serious efforts must be made to strengthen fundamental moral attitudes; and if criminal law plays a role in this process, its potential to threaten is less important than the clarification and communication of its moral message. We will return to this point later on.[104]

Admittedly, the proportion of women with unwanted pregnancies whose positive fundamental attitude motivates them, as previously discussed, to continue the pregnancy, should not be overestimated. Given that a not insignificant portion of the women who participated in our attitudinal study, namely, 45.75%, were found to belong to group 3, i.e., 'pregnant women with no conflict',[105] for which the positive fundamental attitude appears to be determinative, and assuming that the results of this spot check can be generalized beyond the concrete limits of the study, we are still confronted by the fact that something over half of all women with unwanted pregnancies are not swayed by a positive fundamental attitude to unborn life: be it that they in fact terminate their pregnancies – like the 41.5% in group 1 – and in so doing show themselves to be unaffected by a positive fundamental attitude,[106] or be it that they – like the 12.75% in group 2, i.e., the 'women in conflict' – are less influenced by general legal-ethical principles and more by the concrete circumstances of their own lives.[107] This kind of outweighing of normative considerations by existing or anticipated psychosocial conflict cannot, by the way, be ruled out completely, even among the women of group 3, who, in the absence of conflict, continue their pregnancies: the loaded question remains whether they would continue to be true to their fundamental moral convictions if they found themselves in less favorable life circumstances or if the future looked less rosy.

Last but not least, in a discussion of the psychosocial factors that influence a woman's decision for or against the continuation of her pregnancy, the role of her *partner* as well as other members of her social network must be considered. Aside from the anticipated deterioration in her situation, the acceptance of the pregnancy on an emotional level by the partner or other people close to her is apparently of great significance.[108] In this way, it might even be possible for the influence of fundamental socioethical values to increase, since members of the

---

[104] See *infra* IV.2.1.2.

[105] See HOLZHAUER, op. cit. n. 20, at pp. 163 f.

[106] In response to questions, this group displayed extraordinarily strong support for a woman's right to self-determination. See HOLZHAUER, op. cit. n. 20, at pp. 200 f.

[107] See HOLZHAUER, op. cit. n. 20, at pp. 332 ff.; HÄUSSLER and HOLZHAUER, op. cit. n. 20, at pp. 818, 851 f.

[108] For details, see HOLZHAUER, op. cit. n. 20, at pp. 219 ff., 252 ff.; HÄUSSLER and HOLZHAUER, loc. cit. n. 20, at pp. 818, 839 ff.

pregnant woman's social network are not subject to the same kind of pressure as is the woman herself and thus are in a situation in which it may be easier for morality to retain the upper hand. As attractive as it may be to use the influence of her social contacts as a stabilizing moral force, as it were, it is advisable to use caution to avoid turning the encouragement to take responsibility for her own actions into a display of manipulative paternalism, a transformation that is all the more likely if the admonition is given from a pedestal where the absence of pressure makes it easy for the speaker to advocate a more exacting moral stance. Most of the time, however, it is less likely that the woman will be forced by a strict moral partner to continue a pregnancy against her will and more likely that she will feel abandoned by her social network in general and by the father of the child in particular.[109] Thus, it is impossible to overestimate the importance of efforts, begun comparatively recently, to remind the father of his own obligation to the child and to make him live up to his responsibility.[110]

The decision-making process of *physicians* differs significantly from that of pregnant women. This is not to be taken lightly because the medical profession, on account of the aforementioned 'medicalization trend',[111] plays a key role in the obtaining of unpunishable terminations, and the exercise of the physician's 'power to define' the relevant norm and situation is in no small measure dependent upon the physician's own attitude towards termination. In comparison to its effect on the pregnant woman herself, it is not surprising that the woman's concrete living situation does not play a significant role in physicians' decision-making processes, at least not to the extent that, during the decision-making process itself, the concrete psychosocial conflict experienced by the pregnant woman outweighs the physician's fundamental value system. This is because physicians are not themselves, personally, sufficiently affected.[112] Instead, normative factors appear to be more important to physicians.

However, a certain amount of fine-tuning of this general statement is necessary. First, with regard to the type and rank of norms that influence physicians' decisions concerning the willingness or refusal to perform a termination, the medical profession itself has postulated that criminal regulations are less determinative than the profession's deontological self-image, which in addition to

---

[109] See HOLZHAUER, op. cit. n. 20, at pp. 221 ff.

[110] When speaking out in legal policy discussions in favor of holding fathers responsible for their actions, I was repeatedly confronted by the pervasive failure to recognize their co-responsibility. See *infra* IV.2.2.4, text accompanying nn. 228 ff.

[111] See *supra* II.5, IV.1.3.4.

[112] For more on these results and the results referred to in the following text, see our attitudinal study of physicians, HÄUSSLER-SCZEPAN, op. cit. n. 20, at pp. 132 ff.; HÄUSSLER and HOLZHAUER, loc. cit. n. 20, at pp. 822 ff.

being influenced by professional values may also be influenced by religious convictions.[113] To be sure, the general emergency indication has taken on a special role: whereas there are apparently no particular acceptance problems associated with the other kinds of indications, the majority of physicians interviewed stated that they felt the conflict between the professional duties to protect life and to help pregnant women facing this indication to be especially fraught.[114]

Refinement concerning the relevance of possible criminal liability is also necessary. Whereas physicians in general tend not to be impressed by formal threats of punishment and are more likely to take seriously the informal censure of professional colleagues, here, again, the emergency indication has a special status. For in contrast to the widely held assumption that legal regulations are only meaningful on a symbolic level, our attitudinal study of the emergency indication revealed both a norm-building as well as a deterrent effect on physicians.[115]

This finding with regard to the acceptance of norms and the decision-making process of physicians can be interpreted in two different ways. On the one hand, it may be disturbing from a moral standpoint that physicians must be threatened with criminal penalties before they refrain from performing terminations. Also along these 'amoral' lines, as it were, is the current call by the medical profession for the reinstatement in the criminal code of a time-based limitation on the use of the embryopathic indication[116] – as though physicians would not, if left to their own devices, think twice before performing 'late-term abortions' based on genetic factors. On the other hand, a positive interpretation, from a legal standpoint, is that the law as such, even if it does not affect the fundamental attitude to termination in principle, plays at least a norm-building role in the establishment of some limits. At the same time, this strength also reveals a weakness, for if physicians are only influenced by criminal law to the extent that they are uncertain of their own moral position – as in the case of an emergency indication –, then their 'lack of scruples' with regard to terminations performed on the basis of other indications shows that criminal law has very little effect when it does not conform with generally accepted values.

---

[113] HÄUSSLER-SCZEPAN, op. cit. n. 20, at pp. 209 ff., 217 ff.

[114] HÄUSSLER-SCZEPAN, op. cit. n. 20, at pp. 234 f.

[115] HÄUSSLER-SCZEPAN, op. cit. n. 20, at pp. 239 f.

[116] For the perspective of the Federal Medical Association [*Bundesärztekammer*], see the 'Erklärung zum Schwangerschaftsabbruch nach Pränataldiagnostik', 95 *Deutsches Ärzteblatt* (1998) pp. A-3013-A-3015 and the 'Richtlinien zur pränatalen Diagnostik von Krankheiten und Krankheitsdispositionen', 95 *Deutsches Ärzteblatt* (1998) pp. A-3236-A-3242. On the underlying problem of so-called 'late abortions', see *infra* IV.2.2.2 nn. 198 f. and accompanying text.

1.4.3   *Determining conduct by means of proceedings?*

If, as could perhaps be concluded from the preceding remarks, the realities of life threaten to outweigh pregnant women's moral convictions and – as in the case of physicians – legal requirements should facilitate norm-building and norm-obedience, it makes sense to try to influence the decision-making process in the termination context by means of appropriate procedural measures. In fact, these kinds of proceduralization were found to be characteristic of reform developments in this area.[117] If these measures are to influence the decision to continue or terminate a pregnancy, they must be implemented while the decision-making process is still ongoing. Therefore, the requirement of an indication and/or of counseling is of the utmost importance in this context. To be sure, this does not mean that procedural requirements accompanying or even following the actual performance of a termination have no influence on behavior: take, for example, the requirement that terminations be performed in hospitals, which limits accessibility, and post-termination reporting requirements, which may deter over-eager physicians. Furthermore, even if the review takes place ex post, merely subjecting the finding of an indication to review and, consequently, the physician to possible legal action can serve as a deterrent with regard to future unwanted pregnancies. However, to the extent that the goal is to influence decisions concerning the continuation or termination of an existing pregnancy, the following remarks will concentrate on the aforementioned precautionary measures that take effect prior to a still impending termination.

From this perspective, let us first take a closer look at the *requirement of an indication*, the older[118] of these two precautionary measures. Certainly, the greatest inhibitory effects can be expected from narrowly-formulated indications whose application is strictly controlled. But even if its rigorousness can be justified,[119] it is doubtful that this kind of approach is realizable since strict uniformity of application would require a control apparatus greater even than that achieved by the expert commissions established by the Nazis and can hardly be expected from today's physicians who, working independently and without special qualifications, are authorized virtually everywhere to determine whether or not a termination is indicated.[120] However, perhaps it is a mistake to view pro-

---

[117] See *supra* II.3.4, IV.1.3.4 and *infra* IV.2.3.3.

[118] Even without assuming that the goals in those days were the same as those of current indication requirements, it is noteworthy that efforts to formulate a statutory exemption from punishment date back to a Portuguese draft of 1786 (see E/K I p. 1270).

[119] Concerns in this regard are addressed *infra* at IV.2.3.1.

[120] For more details, see *supra* II.3.4, II.5.2. Although in some countries the identification of indications is undertaken by commissions or specially selected physicians, this does

ceedings by which conduct may be determined in terms of their coercive potential instead of relying on the moral authority of a call to take responsibility for
one's own actions. If divested of its repressive character and strengthened in its
appeal to the conscience, perhaps more could be expected from the indication
requirement than it currently achieves.

Oddly enough, grounds for optimism can be found, of all places, in the ambiguous atmosphere in which indications have been dealt with traditionally.
Again, if our empirical attitudinal studies of pregnant women and physicians[121]
can be considered representative, one certainly cannot ignore the fact that the
indication requirement, as long as it is seen merely as an obstacle on the road to
termination, can always be surmounted by a woman who is determined to terminate – if necessary through consultation with several physicians.[122] In such
cases, the indication requirement is experienced by both pregnant woman and
physician as a negative 'shackle' and not as a factor offering positive guidance.
However, indications, as shown by the attitudinal studies, can be just that, particularly for women who have not yet made a firm decision one way or the other
and for whom, therefore, the conversation with the physician regarding the existence of an indication can be decisive.[123] For these women, the indication
requirement can in fact serve the purpose for which it is actually intended: first,
the substantive indication functions as a guiding principle with regard to the
factors to be considered in the termination context, and second, the formal process of identifying an indication provides a forum conducive to discourse between the physician and the pregnant woman.

Realistically, one should not pin exaggerated hopes on any kind of procedure
in which one person sits quasi in judgment over another. Whereas the instance
responsible for determining the existence of an indication – even if in the form
of a single physician – must insist upon an exhaustive process of clarification
prior to recognizing an indication, the main concern of the pregnant woman
herself, understandably, is to reveal as little as possible. Needless to say, the
trust necessary for open and honest discourse is not promoted by this atmosphere: all the more important, therefore, the praiseworthy efforts of a growing
number of countries to use *counseling* to influence pregnant women's deci-

---

not guarantee uniformity. Furthermore, uniformity can also not be achieved by means of
judicial review ex post unless all cases are decided by the same body, a completely unrealistic expectation.

[121] See *supra* IV.1.2.3.

[122] See HOLZHAUER, op. cit. n. 20, at pp. 293 ff., 307, 324 ff., 382.

[123] See HOLZHAUER, op. cit. n. 20, at pp. 288 f., 298 f., 325; HÄUSSLER and HOLZHAUER,
loc. cit. n. 20, at pp. 830 ff.

sions. Fortunately, the Federal Republic is one of the forerunners of this reform movement.[124]

By means of this approach, which is oriented more to advising than to judging, the chance of discourse increases as the woman feels that she is being taken more seriously and viewed as an equal partner; this in turn requires that there be no foregone conclusions regarding her ultimate decision.

Given that this approach, determining conduct by means of proceedings, may leave something to be desired[125] – not surprising in light of its newness –, and given the unlikelihood of finding a better concept even if the survey were extended, we must look to the future, not the past, for answers.

---

[124] For details, see the overview *supra* II.3.4 and *infra* IV.2.3.2.

[125] See *supra* III.1.2.2, see also HÄUSSLER-SCZEPAN, op. cit. n. 20, at pp. 167 ff.; HOLZHAUER, op. cit. n. 20, at pp. 262 ff.; HÄUSSLER and HOLZHAUER, loc. cit. n. 20, at pp. 824 ff., 853; on the subject as a whole, see also *infra* IV.2.3.2.

IV.2   OUTLOOK: STARTING POINTS – GUIDELINES

2.1   Regulatory maxims

In the attempt to draw legal policy conclusions from the preceding findings and insights, it is important to keep two things in mind:

First, it must not be forgotten that legal policy deliberations are inevitably influenced by subjective fundamental convictions, ideological pre-judgments and subjective assessments and, therefore, cannot claim to be purely objective.[126] Despite sincere efforts at objectivity, we are dealing here with value judgments that, in the final analysis, are personal and thus do not necessarily reflect the opinions of others who participated in the project. This is true even for the authors of this volume: while thanks are due to *Hans-Georg Koch* for critical comments and discussion of these concluding legal policy reflections, ultimate responsibility for this section lies with its author, *Albin Eser*.

Second, the mere fact that worldwide virtually no two regulations governing the termination of pregnancy are alike[127] leads to the conclusion that there is no single true or 'right' solution; as a result, the most we can do is to try and identify the more or less feasible among them. In so doing, it is extremely important to establish which regulatory maxims serve as guiding principles. Three aspects of these maxims must be examined more closely: their ultimate protective aim (2.1.1); their societal acceptance and efficiency (2.1.2); and their efforts at communicating a transparent and consistent message (2.1.3).

2.1.1   *Clarity with regard to the regulatory goal and normative preconditions*

Although it is a truism that the assessment of a regulation depends on what is expected from it, more than a few diverging opinions with regard to the wisdom or failure of a termination regulation are due to the simple fact that – consciously or unconsciously – they are based on different goals and correspondingly different expectations. Without having to address in detail at this point the interests to be protected and the resulting clashes in the termination context,[128] the formation and, later, the assessment of a regulation turn out differently depend-

---

[126] See the Introduction to the project as a whole in E/K I p. 8 as well as *supra* IV and *infra* IV.3.

[127] See *supra* IV.1.3.1.

[128] For more on these issues, see *infra* IV.2.2.

ing upon which aims are pursued, singly or in connection with others, and at what price.

If the goal is exclusively and absolutely the protection of unborn life, there is, logically, no room for compromise in favor of the pregnant woman: if this approach is taken, every terminated pregnancy is essentially a failure of the abortion prohibition. On the other hand, if a termination regulation pursues primarily population-related policy goals, compromises in the form of an exception from the abortion ban would be possible if, for example, it is suspected that the fetus is carrying genetic defects that would result in a demographically 'inferior' life; to be consistent in this rubric, however, not only termination – with the exception of eugenic-embryopathic grounds – but also sterilization and, indeed, every method of contraception would have to be forbidden.

The situation is fundamentally different if from the very beginning an approach is adopted in which the achievement of one single goal takes a back seat to the pursuit of a plurality of interests. The most important example of this approach is when, in addition to the protection of unborn life, the possibly competing interests of the pregnant woman are to be taken into account as well: As a weighing of interests in such cases is inevitable, it would be intellectually dishonest to speak here in terms of an absolute protection of life. We will return to this point later.[129]

Yet another situation arises if the prevention of unwanted pregnancies is the motivating force and termination is merely to be avoided in favor of less intrusive methods of birth control: the regulatory goal of such a scheme is less the preservation of unborn life for its own sake and more an attempt to check – and at the same time to limit the risks of – a flow that, for all intents and purposes, is unstoppable. To be sure, even from this standpoint, the more unborn life that can be saved the better; however, the true regulatory goal, that of protecting unborn life, remains secondary since from the very beginning this approach does not strive for the preservation of each and every fetus. Instead, as terminations cannot all be prevented anyhow, the goal here is at least to keep them under control. Clearly, the more the regulatory goal is cut back in this way, the less laws governing the termination of pregnancy can be seen as substantive norms protecting life and the more they become procedural control norms designed to prevent misuse.

Obviously, in addition to these various regulatory goals other emphases are possible. But the sole point of this discussion should by now be clear: the legislature must clarify for itself as well as for the recipients of its message which regulatory goal it has adopted with regard to the termination of pregnancy. For

---

[129] See *infra* IV.2.2.2.

depending upon the protective aim of a regulation and its range, it may be necessary to engage in a weighing of interests. If so, this weighing of interests should not be seen as something foreign and contradictory but rather as a process that is an inherent part of the system. Thus, the compromise as such is not offensive; rather, this label is at most applicable to the prioritization that led to the compromise. The individual goods and preferences to be protected will be addressed in some detail in the following. At this point two general conditions must be mentioned as they are of fundamental concern.

Of primary importance are *constitutional requirements* and the corresponding framework within which statutory regulations on the termination of pregnancy must fit. For what good is a model, no matter how sensible from a legal policy perspective, if it is likely to be rejected by the constitutional court? The fear of rejection, however, can have a paralyzing effect on the legislature as we have seen in the Federal Republic of Germany, where some of the actions taken to have statutes declared unconstitutional have been successful.[130] In any case, though this country is one of comparatively few in which there are any relevant constitutional norms at all, the Constitutional Court has taken yet another – virtually prescriptive – step to restrict even further the freedom of the legislature. This becomes even more fatal – not least from the perspective of the theory of the state – the more the legislature sees itself as the mere executor of orders from the constitutional court: for in these circumstances the legislature no longer seeks the optimal solution, from a legal policy perspective, but rather a solution that will 'pass muster' when challenged before the constitutional court. The following, however, is just as true for organs of state as it is generally: bowing is not conducive to a clear view of the path ahead. This should not be interpreted as a call to ignore statute-like decisions of constitutional courts and not at all as a call for disobedience to an organ of state that is so essential for the rule of law and that has contributed so much to legal developments as has the German Constitutional Court; nevertheless, the legislature should be encouraged to pursue its own views of legal policy and, in the pursuit of an independent implementation of the constitution, not to see legislative freedom limited – by means of incidental judicial remarks, for example – to an extent greater than required by binding determinations of the judiciary.[131]

It is well known that additional normative requirements are drawn from fundamental tenets of *social ethics*. In this regard the Catholic Church is at the fore, with its demand that unborn life be protected by the criminal law and its unwill-

---

[130] For more on this point as well as on the following, see *supra* II.2.3.1.

[131] See already A. ESER, 'Schwangerschaftsabbruch: Reformversuche in Umsetzung des BVerfG-Urteils', 49 *Juristenzeitung* (1994) pp. 503-510. See also *supra* IV.1.3.3 n. 64 and accompanying text.

ingness to make concessions, even in cases involving medical indications truly vital to the pregnant woman.[132] As difficult as the separation of morality and law may appear in the context of the termination of pregnancy and regardless of the resulting feeling that one must simply inject one's own moral rejection of the killing of unborn life into the assessment of termination from a legal policy perspective, here, too, the basic religious neutrality of the secular state cannot be disregarded.[133] This does not necessarily mean that the churches should not take part in the discussion but rather that their demands can be binding on the state legislature only to the extent that they have been enshrined in the constitution. The ensuing role need not be a small one, being that the interpretation of the constitution does not take place in an intellectual vacuum but rather under the influence of historical and sociological determinants in whose development churches and other ideological communities have made not insignificant contributions throughout the years.[134]

2.1.2   Norm-consciousness and social acceptance

The role of social ethics – and with it the role of the literally standard-setting ideological forces – would certainly be significantly reduced were it exhausted in the aforementioned influence on legislation. For if the finding is correct that the continuation or termination of an unwanted pregnancy depends less on criminal prohibitions and more on fundamental socioethical convictions and/or psychosocial aspects of the woman's life,[135] then we must strive for the greatest possible accord between legal structures and socioethical norm- consciousness. This need not mean that the criminal law should be sacrificed in favor of a possibly lax abortion morality nor that criminal law should accede to the demands of a high morality; for in both cases the law would be in danger of losing its intrinsic evaluating and determining function. Indeed, however, the pursuit of accord could lead to two positive developments: on the one hand, the absence of an 'appealing function' of the law could be made up for by society's ethical value-consciousness and, on the other hand, legal norms might be ca-

---

[132] On this point as well as with regard to the positions of other religions and ideologies, see *supra* I.4.5.

[133] For the basics, see *A. Hollerbach*, Grundlagen des Staatskirchenrechts, in J. ISENSEE and P. KIRCHHOF (eds.), *Handbuch des Staatsrechts*, Vol. VI (Heidelberg, C.F. Müller 1989 pp. 471-555, esp. at pp. 533 f.

[134] See P. MIKAT, 'Staat, Kirchen und Religionsgemeinschaften', in E. BENDA et al. (eds.), *Handbuch des Verfassungsrechts der Bundesrepublik Deutschland* (Berlin, de Gruyter 1983) pp. 1059-1092, esp. at pp. 1061 ff.

[135] See *supra* IV.1.4.2.

pable of demonstrating and stabilizing the binding force of values that have suffered under the general decline in morality.

The dismissal of this as mere 'symbolism' such as has no place in modern criminal law[136] would be justified only if the issue involved in the use of criminal law to oppose termination were solely a matter of sanctioning a purely ideological 'sham' value that has lost its original legitimacy as well as any basis in contemporary reality. However, this is not the case, as should be clear solely on the basis of the claims of unborn life.[137] For no matter how large the exceptions to the termination prohibition may be, the fundamental value of unborn life and its claim to protection are not subject to dispute. Not even the concession that the existing variety in regulatory models reveals their irrelevance changes this; for even if the similarity or difference of regulations in fact has no visible effect on abortion and prosecution rates,[138] the relative unimportance of modality does not necessarily mean that any and all criminal sanctions are absolutely superfluous. This conclusion could be drawn only if, despite a complete renunciation of the use of criminal law, the necessary norm-consciousness can be established equally clearly and forcefully by means of other norms.

The fact that the Federal Constitutional Court has taken on this fundamental challenge is in itself praiseworthy, other grounds for criticism notwithstanding; at any rate, criticism does not appear to be justified with regard to the Court's finding that the use of criminal law– in any case here and now – is not entirely superfluous.[139] For whatever else speaks for and against the educational and supportive role of criminal law with regard to norm-consciousness, the following three aspects cannot be ignored. First of all, on a fundamental level, the basic assumption – less a matter of criminal law and more a matter of the general legal functions of the state – is that one of the inherent tasks of the state and the law is to declare certain interests worthy of protection and to help stabilize socioethical rules of conduct that support these interests or, if such rules do not exist, to create them. Second, even if, on an instrumental level, this goal could be realized by means of regulations in various other areas of law, like, for example, by expressing disapproval of the termination of pregnancy through the withholding of social services (as was considered by the Federal Constitutional

---

[136] For both general and detailed information on this phenomenon from an author who does not take this position, see M. Voss, *Symbolische Gesetzgebung, Fragen zur Rationalität von Gesetzgebungsakten* (Ebelsbach, Gremer 1989).

[137] On the question of what is deserving of protection, see *infra* IV.2.2.1.

[138] See *supra* IV.1.4.1 nn. 87 ff. and accompanying text.

[139] For details, see *BVerfGE* 39, 45 ff.; 88, 257 f.

Court),[140] this approach – a kind of negative social control – would seem to be both dysfunctional and misbegotten if, in the final analysis, it in fact pursues punitive goals: since punitive goals are foreign to branches of the law not designed for them, their presence there may lead to distortions. Finally, there is in fact no occasion to pay this price for other perversions as long as a norm system like the criminal law exists whose specific function is to identify those values and rights that are especially deserving of protection and to safeguard them by means of appropriate sanctions. Thus, so long as unborn life is viewed as an independent good worthy of protection and so long as social ethics alone cannot be expected to provide this protection, legal underpinnings cannot be abandoned, and the use of sanctions as a last resort cannot be relinquished completely. This does not mean, however – and this possible misunderstanding must be countered immediately –, that the termination of pregnancy can only be regulated by means of criminal law but rather that minimal regulations for safeguarding and sanctioning purposes are indispensable and must remain available.

Were this kind of value-clarification to be denounced as 'symbolism', the denunciation should not only be taken calmly but should even be affirmed in a positive sense. Even if one takes exception to the perhaps old-fashioned concept of the 'moral-building power of criminal law', the rectitude of the idea intrinsic therein has not diminished over time: first, if it is, in fact, desirable that well-informed people be less influenced by threatening criminal provisions than by socioethical convictions and, second, if it can be assumed that a legal community tends to express 'moral-building' convictions by means of legal rules governing behavior and that these rules are, in the last analysis, safeguarded by criminal provisions, the legitimacy of the symbolification of values by criminal law cannot be contested.

To be sure, sympathy for 'symbolic criminal law' has limits that must be taken seriously. It becomes questionable, for example, if declining acceptance has caused the symbolic value in need of protection to lose its social fundament or if criminal law, as the traditional defense mechanism, has in effect lost its functional power. If things are as they seem, it is at this level that the problems of the traditional criminal abortion law have their roots. The problems begin when, in the context of a termination, unborn life is no longer the one and only relevant protected good but instead other rights and interests – i.e., those of the pregnant woman – must also be taken into consideration.[141] These problems are compounded by the impression that – regardless of the sincerity of the proc-

---

[140] See *BVerfGE* 88, 250, 258 as well as the expert opinion prepared for the *BVerfG* by R. STÜRNER, *Der strafrechtliche Schwangerschaftsabbruch in der Gesamtrechtsordnung* (Tübingen, Mohr 1994) pp. 27, 79 ff.

[141] For the same approach, see *BVerfGE* 88, 253 f.; see also *infra* IV.2.2.1.

lamation itself – the oft-proclaimed equality of born and unborn life is not taken seriously, as can be seen both in the nature of existing laws as well as in their practical implementation.[142] These doubts intensify when the question is put whether, over the years, the 'fruit of the womb', as it has traditionally been called, has in fact been afforded the same claim to protection that has been afforded independent, born life as is sometimes presumed in a perhaps undeserved glorification of history.[143] Finally, the claim of great esteem for unborn life loses its fundament almost entirely when the fetus is denied protection on the basis of its status as human life until it becomes a 'person' – at some point after birth.[144]

But even if positions like the former are rejected as – literally – spiritual aberrations (because based on actual spirituality rather than on human potency)[145] and the fundamental claim of unborn life to protection continues to be controlling,[146] it must be admitted that criminal law as a protective instrument is precarious and has lost social credibility. It is possible that criminal law has always been shaky in this regard, but, unlike today, the shakiness was perhaps not always so obvious that it could not be overlooked. This is especially and – because only grudgingly admitted – painfully evident in legal systems that have implemented a total criminal prohibition model: If these systems experience a high number of abortions but as good as no prosecutions,[147] the criminal sanction cannot be meant seriously, neither from the perspective of the state nor in the eyes of its citizens. If this is the case, the threat of punishment as the only protective instrument for unborn life is, in fact, nothing more than contrafactual symbolism and, not only that, it is hypocritical because the alleged sanctity of unborn life, backed up by the severity of a prohibition, is, in fact, only a pretense if the only possible sanction is criminal punishment, an option that is, however, practically never used.

---

[142] For more on this point, see *infra* IV.2.2.2.

[143] For more on this point, see G. JEROUSCHEK, op. cit. n. 5.

[144] See, e.g., N. HOERSTER, 'Forum: Ein Lebensrecht für die menschliche Leibesfrucht?', 29 *Juristische Schulung* (1989) pp. 172-178; N. HOERSTER, *Abtreibung im säkularen Staat, Argumente gegen § 218*, 2nd edn. (Frankfurt/Main, Suhrkamp 1995) pp. 69 ff., 79 ff.

[145] For a more detailed explication of this position, see A. ESER, Neuartige Bedrohungen ungeborenen Lebens. Embryoforschung und 'Fetozid' in rechtsvergleichender Perspektive (Karlsruhe, C.F. Müller 1990) pp. 39 ff.

[146] On this point, see A. ESER, loc. cit. n. 1, at pp. 147 ff.; A. ESER, 'Schwangerschafsabbruch zwischen Grundwertorientierung und Strafrecht', in A. ESER and H.-G. KOCH, *Schwangerschaftsabbruch: Auf dem Weg zu einer Neuregelung* (Baden-Baden, Nomos 1992) pp. 85-107, at pp. 89 ff.

[147] See *supra* III.2.2, III.3.2.

Thus, those regulatory models that rely neither solely nor primarily on punishment but rather on help and counseling to prevent the termination of pregnancy are, at least in this regard, both more honest and more true to reality. Even if, in the last analysis, these efforts are not always successful, as is admittedly often the case, these kinds of regulatory models cannot be reproached for being merely symbolic. This is because the simple fact that the state has not contented itself with a mere prohibition and the threat of punishment but rather has established a counseling requirement and provided the necessary counseling services (services that are used to a much greater extent than is criminal prosecution in legal systems with a total prohibition model) means that the will of the state to protect unborn life is not only proclaimed in the law but is also implemented in practice. Finally, one more significant social aspect must be mentioned in this context: whereas these days criminal law alone is rarely considered a viable means of preventing terminations of pregnancy, the counseling approach – even if it is only an additional means of preserving unborn life – is enjoying an increasingly positive reception.[148] Nevertheless, rejection of a counseling requirement is less likely to come from the more conservative wing and more likely to come from circles that give priority to the (unlimited) self-determination of the pregnant woman or that dispute all claims of the fetus to an independent right to life. But in the confirmation of the value-building function of the counseling requirement, these rejections can hardly be outdone: after all, for what reason other than that unborn life has a genuine claim to protection could the state legitimately subject the pregnant woman to a counseling requirement?

Even if more could be said on this point, two final conclusions with regard to the regulatory maxims at issue here can now be drawn:

On the one hand, it is a legitimate if not required task of the state to build the value-system necessary for the protection of unborn life. As long as no other promising instrument is available, criminal law remains, in the last analysis, indispensable as a basis for the appropriate rules of conduct.

On the other hand, criminal law can be neither the foremost nor the only means of combating the termination of unwanted pregnancies. Rather, in the interest of the greatest possible social acceptance, among other things, the following two factors appear to be of significant import for the effectiveness of a legal regulation: first, an appropriate consideration of all the rights and interests affected by a termination and second, the positive support provided by a value system through preventive counseling instead of repressive punishment, although on this level the importance of the professional qualifications and ethical empa-

---

[148] See *supra* IV.1.4.3 n. 124 and accompanying text; *infra* IV.2.3.2.

thy of the institutions and people involved in the termination process cannot be underestimated.

2.1.3 *Transparence and consistence of the conduct-determining message*

Still premature at this point is a discussion of the actual content of the conduct rules from which the individual – namely, the pregnant woman and the physician – should receive guidance in the decision regarding the continuation or the termination of a pregnancy; instead, the issue concerning the demands that can be made more formally on the statutory rules of conduct must first be raised. Thus, the main focus of attention here is less on the content of the conduct-determining messages directed to the individual addressee and more on the character and form of the conduct regulations to be made by the legislature. As a result, the various prohibitions and permitted activities as well as other prerequisites of criminal liability or exemptions from punishment that appear as examples in the following were chosen only in part in order to discuss their objective correctness or to evaluate them from a legal policy perspective; for regardless of how important these issues are for the conduct of an individual (for which reason they will be dealt with more extensively in subsequent sections), this section, dedicated to regulatory maxims, will address from a more formal standpoint the degree of transparence and consistence that the legislature with its regulations must achieve in order reasonably to expect obedience from basically law-abiding citizens.

As far as the *clarity and transparence* of the essential conduct rules are concerned, it is hard to imagine a regulation of the termination of pregnancy that is more unfathomable to the ordinary citizen than the German regulation. Even if, on the one hand the attempt to do justice in a discriminating way to different time frames, different kinds of conflicts, and different degrees of disapproval must be appreciated, the attempt has nonetheless led to a statutory labyrinth that is hardly to be outdone in complexity.[149] Not even jurists understand it right off the bat, and for lay people, comprehension of the core conduct rules is significantly more difficult. Thus, it should come as no surprise that misinterpretations of the applicable law are common even among physicians who deal professionally with the termination of pregnancy. Some of these misinterpreta-

---

[149] This finding, which applied already to the 1974 regulation (A. ESER, 'Schwangerschaftsabbruch: der rechtliche Rahmen', in A. ESER and H.A. HIRSCH (eds.), *Sterilisation und Schwangerschaftsabbruch* (Stuttgart, Enke 1980) pp. 105-126 at pp. 106 ff.), is even more justified in regard to the exemption from the statutory prohibition as per § 218a par. 1 StGB, introduced in 1995 (see ESER, loc. cit. n. 77, introductory remark 8 to § 218 as well as margin No. 1 ff., 13 ff. to § 218a).

tions, those that – as revealed by our attitudinal study of physicians – consist simply of incorrect classification of indications,[150] can perhaps be explained as misunderstandings that arise when physicians, whose perspective is, of course, medical, are required to interpret legal language. However, to the extent that the ultimate responsibility of the terminating physician and the function of the identification of indications are not recognized as mere 'help in the decision-making process',[151] the basic underlying legal concept has proven itself to be difficult to understand. Similarly, it is less conducive to illumination and more to obfuscation if, as is currently the case in German law, the physician must, from the interplay of various norms, infer the requirements applicable to the different roles in which he can participate in the termination of a pregnancy.[152]

These criticisms are not meant to advocate either an unsophisticated or a simplistic, black-and-white approach to the prohibition or non-prohibition of the termination of pregnancy since the comprehensibility of conduct rules can suffer if essential questions are left unregulated. Material illustrative of this may be found primarily in those regulations that fail to clarify the time frame in which the abortion prohibition applies as well as the circumstances in which an exemption from punishment may be possible and that leave up in the air the consequences of procedural shortcomings.[153]

In order to remedy these kinds of conceptual problems, the conduct rules to be obeyed in the termination of a pregnancy must be composed in such a way that the people affected are able clearly to determine the breadth of the prohibition well as the substantive and procedural conditions under which termination may be permitted.

No less important than the transparence of individual conduct rules is the internal *consistence and coherence* of the conduct-determining message in its entirety. In this regard, too, the German law provides a classic example of normative contradictoriness. This does not mean – to prevent any possibility of an additional misunderstanding – that every substantive compromise should be designated an unacceptable inconsistence, for, as implied above and as will be inspected more closely in the following, in the context of a termination of pregnancy, a weighing-up is an unavoidable necessity if one wishes to accord neither the unborn life nor the pregnant woman absolute priority.[154] But this need of 'practical concordance' is not the issue here. Rather, in this context the issue is the inconsistence of the conduct-determining message if, on the one hand, a

---

[150] For details, see M. HÄUSSLER-SCZEPAN, op. cit. n. 20, at pp. 171 ff.

[151] See E/K I pp. 171 ff. and *supra* II.3.4.2, text accompanying n. 136.

[152] For details, see ESER, loc. cit. n. 77, introductory remarks 1, 14 ff. to § 218.

[153] For illustrative material, see *supra* II.2.5.3, II.3.4.2.F, II.3.4.3.G, II.3.5.3, II.5.4.2-4.

[154] See *supra* IV.2.1.1, and *infra* IV.2.2.2-3.

(merely) 'counseled' (but not indicated) termination is considered unlawful despite the fact that it does not amount to an offense but, on the other hand, defense of the fetus against imminent danger is not allowed, and a physician-patient contract for the performance of an termination, an unlawful procedure, retains its validity.[155] The declaration that one and the same termination is simultaneously both unlawful *and* legally incontestable as well as entitled to legal protection in its implementation is internally inconsistent and therefore a mixed normative message unsuited to clear behavioral direction. Put another way, it basically robs the declaration of conduct as 'unlawful' of its legal function of disapproval.

Hardly less questionable is the morally corruptive effect of a regulation that requires for its exemption from punishment that a termination be performed by a physician but declines to designate this action as lawful and in so doing knowingly leads an entire professional group, from which law-abiding conduct is otherwise expected, down the path of wrongdoing. The state itself is not above engaging in the systematic instrumentalization of unlawful conduct in order to achieve a socially tolerated (if not even a desired) goal if it tasks its institutions and agencies with assuring a sufficient array of out-patient and in-patient facilities for the performance of (merely) 'counseled' (but not indicated) and therefore unlawful terminations.[156]

Leaving aside at this point the issue of the substantive correctness of one or another of these contradictory positions, the normative two-facedness that they express cannot be characterized as anything other than disastrous for the credibility of the conduct-determining message. The fact that this contradictory finding failed to spark the expected outcry in both the organized medical and legal associations as well as in the public at large[157] – excepting representatives of the church and other circles that reject any exemption from punishment whatsoever for non-indicated abortions – is probably due to a mixture of 'reform fatigue' and result-oriented pragmatism: With the help of counseling, pregnant women are presented with an easy route to exemption from punishment; a pos-

---

[155] For more on this and other inconsistencies in the current regulations (§§ 218a ff. *StGB*) that can be traced to requirements established by the Federal Constitutional Court, see A. ESER, 'Verhaltensregeln und Behandlungsnormen', in A. ESER et al. (eds.), *Festschrift für Theodor Lenckner* (Munich, C.H. Beck 1998) pp. 25-54 at pp. 26 ff. See also the criticism of STÜRNER, loc. cit. n. 140, at pp. 20 ff.

[156] In accordance with § 13 par. 2 Schwangerschaftskonfliktgesetz, as revised by the SFHÄndG.

[157] The lukewarm reaction of physicians' associations to an inquiry conducted by the Juristen-Vereinigung Lebensrecht [*Jurist Association Right to Life*] (see their publication Schriftenreihe No. 13, Cologne 1996) can be viewed as symptomatic even if one wanted to claim that the jurist association is biased.

sibly bad conscience can be soothed by the declaration that the merely 'counseled' termination is 'unlawful;' and at the same time the – in the eyes of quite a few offensive – reimbursement of costs for non-indicated terminations is avoided.[158] If one is unwilling to tolerate this kind of double standard, the following are basically the only possible alternatives:

Either the legislature retains the *unlawfulness* of certain terminations – such as those that are merely 'counseled' but not indicated (as in the current regulation) – but, to be consistent: does not preclude actions geared to defending the fetus from imminent danger; does not consider valid a physician-patient contract for the performance of the termination; does not require the *Länder* to provide the necessary facilities; does not countenance professional standards regarding the carrying out of such terminations; and does not tolerate in any other form the performance of such terminations, let alone promote them.

Or the legislature designs the substantive and procedural requirements for the termination of pregnancy in such a way that terminations can be viewed as permissible and, accordingly, treated as *lawful* actions. As a result, the legal consequences barred by the preceding alternative remain, in principle, possible, although not imperative. The latter is especially true for the indeed troubling issue of reimbursement of costs for the termination of pregnancy. Because even if the termination is lawful, this does not necessarily mean that every case automatically presents a cognizable claim for reimbursement. After all, not all medical procedures are reimbursable simply because they are lawful.[159] At this point it is not too soon to note the preferability of this regulatory alternative.

2.2   Protected values and conflicting interests

Without seeking to devalue in retrospect the foregoing regulatory maxims, their more instrumental-methodological character must nevertheless be kept in mind. Thus, one does not in fact get to the heart of the matter until one examines the interests that must be protected and the associated potential conflicts. It is not

---

[158] Whether the possibly far-reaching preclusion of reimbursement was in fact one of the main motivations behind the decision to retain the wrongfulness of the (merely) 'counseled' termination is open to speculation. This speculation is fueled by the statement in the minority opinion of Constitutional Court Justice E.-W. BÖCKENFÖRDE that: 'the main thing appears to be that in any case payment will not be made' (*BVerfGE* 88, 364). On the subject as a whole, see also ESER, loc. cit. n. 77, introductory remark 8 to § 218, § 218a margin nos. 12 ff., 18.

[159] On this point, see A. ESER, Schwangerschaftsabbruch: Auf dem verfassungsgerichtlichen Prüfstand, Rechtsgutachten im Normenkontrollverfahren zum Schwangeren- und Familienhilfegesetz von 1992 (Baden-Baden, Nomos 1994) pp. 95 ff.; for largely similar treatment in this regard, see STÜRNER, op. cit. n. 140, at pp. 20 ff.

until this point that the decisive, legal policy die is cast. Essentially, the following questions must be addressed: First, the rights and interests to be considered in the context of the termination of pregnancy (2.2.1), then the relative nature of the protection of life as seen from the perspective of a balancing of interests (2.2.2), the autonomy of the pregnant woman (2.2.3) and, finally, potential status-related responsibilities (2.2.4).

2.2.1 *Plurality of rights and interests*

If one thinks of the protection of life in categorical terms, it can be irritating that when the question of the rights and interests affected by a termination of pregnancy is raised, the talk, without further reflection, is of plurality, as though, from the very beginning, the unborn life is not considered an independent, *singular* value to be protected. While to some this might seem to represent a break with sacrosanct traditions, they must be prepared to learn that, in fact, the belief in the 'sanctity' of unborn life – in contrast to long-cherished expectations that I, too, shared – was not, in the past, as deeply held as one might like to think.[160] In any case, in our day and age in the countries that we studied, unborn life as a 'singular', independent value to be protected was found only in a since-rescinded abortion prohibition in South Africa.[161] With the 'Choice on Termination of Pregnancy Act' of 1996, however, this country went so far as to give up its 'singular' position and to defect, so to speak, to the opposite camp.[162] Thus, the era of regulations serving exclusively to protect unborn life appears to be over, at least in the secular world. In this alone one need not necessarily see an undesirable trend in need of correction because, as even the German Federal Constitutional Court has found (and one can hardly accuse this court of a lack of respect for unborn life), the protection of life cannot be seen as an absolute; rather, other legal values may compete with the right of the unborn to life.[163]

---

[160] For more on the evolution of the role of the criminal law in the protection of life, see A. ESER, 'Zwischen 'Heiligkeit' and 'Quality des Lebens'', in J. GERNHUBER (ed.), *Tradition und Fortschritt im Recht, Festschrift zum 500jährigen Bestehen der Tübinger Juristenfakultät* (Tübingen, Mohr 1977) pp. 377-414, 383 ff. On the variety of gradations and limitations imposed on the protection of life by current law, see H.-G. KOCH, 'Das Grundrecht auf Leben und differenzierter strafrechtlicher Lebensschutz', 88 *Zeitschrift für ärztliche Fortbildung* (1994) pp. 211-219.

[161] See *supra* II.2.2, whereby the prohibition model subsequently introduced in Chile under Pinochet (1989) can be considered a new addition (see E/K III p. 845).

[162] See, e.g., *supra* II.2.2; E/K III p. 873 ff.

[163] According to the Federal Constitutional Court, 'Legal values affected by the right to life of the unborn – assuming the claim of the pregnant woman to protection of and respect for *her* human dignity (Art. 1 par. 1 of the Basic Law) – include above all her right to life and

Thus, in a first step the *plurality* of objects of protection to be considered in regulating the termination of pregnancy must be recognized.

Even if unborn life cannot claim a 'singular' right to protection, this does not mean that it cannot at least be accorded a position of *primacy*. Nonetheless, as shown by our comparative legal overview of existing protected interests, this is by no means a given, being that the worldwide spectrum of protection reaches from the protection of individual life to general population policy to the preservation of certain sexual mores;[164] moreover, in recent years the health interests of pregnant women[165] and their right to choose freely[166] are recognized more and more frequently as primary legal values. It is perhaps more appropriate to describe this as an undesirable trend because, regardless of whether unborn life must repeatedly take a back seat to the interests of the pregnant woman, on a practical, weighing-up level,[167] the degradation of unborn life is qualitatively different if its primacy has already been denied on the general, or theoretical, level where legal values are identified. The German Federal Constitutional Court also appears to take this differentiation between two levels of values into consideration when it allows unborn life, in certain exceptional circumstances and despite its fundamental priority, to yield to the competing rights of the pregnant woman.[168] Furthermore, even in the Netherlands – where exemptions from punishment are extensive – the preamble to the reformed termination of pregnancy law mentions the 'legal protection of unborn human life' first.[169]

Close behind are the interests of the *pregnant woman*. This has not always been the case: in the Roman Empire, for example, the goal of the abortion prohibition, which was not introduced until relatively late, was primarily to serve the interests of free males in legitimate offspring.[170] In addition, this approach – which may occasionally be observed up to our own time – was geared more to population-oriented policy goals than to the individual concerns of pregnant

---

physical integrity (Art. 2 par. 2 of the *Basic Law*) as well as her right to self-fulfillment (Art. 2 par. 1 of the Basic Law)' *BVerfGE* 88, 253 f. (emphasis in original).

[164] For details, see *supra* II.2.2.

[165] This trend is clearest in former socialist countries. See *supra* II.2.2, text accompanying n. 7.

[166] This trend can be observed in Sweden and the United States (see *supra* II.2.2, text accompanying n. 8) and recently in South Africa as well (see *supra* n. 161 and accompanying text).

[167] On this point, see also *infra* IV.2.2.2-3.

[168] See *BVerfGE* 88, 255 f. For a similar approach, see D. LORENZ, 'Recht auf Leben und körperliche Unversehrtheit', in J. ISENSEE and P. KIRCHHOF (eds.), op. cit. n. 133, at p. 7.

[169] See E/K I p. 1068.

[170] See ESER, loc. cit. n. 160, at p. 384.

women.[171] Today, however, in addition to the right of the unborn to life, the rights of the pregnant woman herself have received such fundamental and extensive recognition that there is hardly any room to consider additional individual or public interests.[172] The diversity of the legal values of the pregnant woman that may affect the right of the unborn to life, including human dignity, the right to life and physical integrity, as well as the right to self-fulfillment, has already been addressed by the Constitutional Court in a relatively sophisticated manner;[173] in contrast, on an international level, only the interest in health and the freedom to make decisions have received significant attention.[174] The extent to which these various concerns of the pregnant woman, ultimately, can be summed up in terms of autonomy and the extent to which they challenge the right to life of the unborn will be taken up later in the section devoted to the balancing of interests.[175]

Even if the natural 'duality in unity'[176] of mother and child is dominant when the interests affected by the termination of pregnancy are assessed, it is not the only perspective to be considered. Namely, one must not forget the *man*, whose role as *father* of the child and/or *partner* of the pregnant woman does not yet appear to have been accorded appropriate consideration. This can perhaps be explained in terms of the conflicting roles in which he finds himself: on the one hand obliged to the child and on the other hand pursuing his own interests. While traditionally he gladly repressed his obligation to the child if – as most likely in the case of an unwed father – he wanted to ignore both the child and his co-responsibility arising from his role as procreator, his positive interest in hoped-for offspring, if confronted by the opposite interest of the pregnant woman, is less and less likely to prevail as the legal order accords her interest more and more recognition. The comparative findings with regard to the interests of the man and how these interests are treated in the context of a termination are equally conflicted: whereas at most only occasional traces of the original primacy of the Roman husband can be found[177] (in other words, a man who would like to

---

[171] On this point, see *infra* nn. 180 f. and accompanying text.

[172] But see *infra* nn. 180 f. and accompanying text.

[173] *BVerfGE* 88, 254 (see *supra* n. 163).

[174] For details, see the overview *supra* at II.2.2.

[175] See *infra* IV.2.2.3. On the basic issue, see generally A. ESER, 'Auf der Suche nach dem mittleren Weg, Zwischen Fundamentalismus und Beliebigkeit', in M. LANGER and A. LASCHET (eds.), *Unterwegs mit Visionen, Festschrift für Rita Süssmuth* (Freiburg, Herder 2002) pp. 117-139.

[176] As almost proverbially formulated in *BVerfGE* 88, 253, 276, although without drawing all necessary consequences – as criticized in the dissenting opinion of E.G. MAHRENHOLZ and B. SOMMER (*BVerfGE* 88, 341 f.). See also *infra* IV.2.2.3/4.

[177] See *supra* text accompanying n. 170.

become a father can no longer force the woman to continue the pregnancy), the tendency today is to hold him responsible in his procreative role[178] (i.e., a man who does not want a child must support one anyway if the woman chooses to continue the pregnancy). The best way to deal with the resulting conflicts of interest will be addressed separately later on.[179]

The catalogue of interests affected by the regulation of the termination of pregnancy may appear to be incomplete if a variety of public interests that have traditionally influenced the prohibition of abortion or that may or may not still play a role in shaping modern regulations governing the termination of pregnancy are not considered. These include, for example, *population policy*, which, depending upon the established goals, can be pro-birth as well as anti-birth, the safeguarding of the *family unit* or *sexual mores* or, very generally, the provision of certain *minimum socioethical standards*.[180] Without wishing to deny such guiding principles any legislative significant whatsoever, today they no longer appear weighty enough to be afforded independent status as protected interests.[181]

2.2.2 *Relative nature of the protection of life*

In the case of an unwanted pregnancy, as was shown above, the basic conflict is between the mother and the child, a dilemma whose inescapable, symbiotic nature makes it especially tragic and whose solution in favor of the pregnant woman can only be achieved at the expense of the unborn life. This one-sidedness of the sacrifice is more difficult to justify the less vital the interests of the woman that are at issue. Even if by continuing the pregnancy the woman puts her own life at risk, life is pitted against life, a collision of values such as, if both parties to the conflict were already born, the choice of one life over the other would not, according to traditional principles, be justified.[182] Whereas the Federal

---

[178] For details, see the overview *supra* II.2.2, II.3.4.3 as well as *supra* IV.1.3.4 text accompanying nn. 78 f.

[179] See *infra* IV.2.2.4 text accompanying nn. 229 ff., IV.2.3.2, text accompanying n. 266.

[180] For additional details and references to various countries, see *supra* II.2.2.

[181] If one wished, for example, to justify a prohibition of abortion on the basis of a pro-birth approach, it would also be necessary, to be consistent, to prohibit contraception. Or if a young woman were to be denied an abortion of an unwanted pregnancy in order to force her to take the path of sexual abstinence, the child, already conceived and then carried to term, would be instrumentalized as a threatened evil.

[182] For details, see TH. LENCKNER in A. SCHÖNKE and H. SCHRÖDER, op. cit. n.77, § 34 margin No. 23 f., 30. Note that this maxim is neither as old nor as uncontroversial as many would like to think; see, e.g., M. KAYSSER, *Abtreibung und die Grenzen des Strafrechts* (Berlin, Duncker & Humblot 1997) pp. 110 f. with additional references, who argues that

Constitutional Court does not necessarily preclude legal justification, even in cases involving non-vital interests of the pregnant woman,[183] and other legal systems have in some cases gone much further in permitting the termination of pregnancy,[184] this appears to be compatible with the previously mentioned principle – i.e., that the sacrifice of human life is not justifiable – only if it, even in a conflict between two already born lives, is not generally and without exception valid, or if, in a conflict between an already born and an unborn life, the factors decisive for the balancing of interests are not necessarily the same as in a conflict between two already born lives.

In an attempt to address these questions without prejudice and to concentrate on the essential points, it is necessary, above all, to examine critically the widespread assumption that life is entitled to absolute protection and that born and unborn life are equally valued.

With regard to the alleged *absoluteness* of the protection of life, an honest discussion can be impeded by someone who, though invoking it, in fact does not support it and instead uses it, as in the following argument, to pursue the devaluation of unborn life: if the absoluteness of the protection of life prohibited all killing of life and if the termination of pregnancy were nonetheless permitted then the fetus would not yet appear to be human life in terms of deserving the same degree of protection. All the same, such 'false friends' of life before birth have managed to identify a sore point: namely, if 'absolute' is understood in its etymological sense, i.e., as meaning unlimited and unconditional, then, in fact, life must be guaranteed in all circumstances and at any price.

However, this is neither practically nor legally the case. If it were the case in practice – using the avoidable death toll on the highways as an example – speed limits, which are proven to decrease the number of accidents and thereby to enhance the protection of life, would long since have taken priority over the

---

the constellation 'life against life' is not applicable to the pregnancy conflict (p. 125). With regard to conflicts involving already born lives, see also J.-M. PRIESTER, 'Rechtstheoretische Überlegungen zur Reform des Abtreibungsrechts', in W. KÜPER and J. WELP (eds.), *Beiträge zur Rechtswissenschaft, Festschrift für Walter Stree und Johannes Wessels zum 70. Geburtstag* (Heidelberg, C.F. Müller 1993) pp. 869-900 at p. 886.

[183] In that, in addition to the medical indication, criminological and embryopathic indications and even social or psychological conflicts in the sense of the former, general emergency indication according to § 218a par. 2 No. 3 StGB (old version) could also be acknowledged by the constitution as (justifying) exceptions. See (already) *BVerfGE* 39, 150 and *BVerfGE* 88, 257, 272, 325 ff.

[184] In that within time-based exemptions, permissibility of abortion is assumed without proof of a special reason to abort; for details see the comparative legal overview, *supra* II.3.7.

mere self-fulfilling maxim of 'free tempos for free citizens' [Freie Fahrt für freie Bürger]. Moreover, if the absoluteness of the protection of life were truly taken seriously, life-preserving measures would, as a result, be incontestable, and economic interests in cost reduction and corresponding limitations on services would not be feasible.

However, it is not only by means of such practical concessions that the absoluteness of the protection of life is subject, more or less consciously, to question; rather, the unconditional inviolability of human life, without exception, as the claim of 'absolute' protection appears to guarantee, is in fact not provided for by law. As sobering as this may be and as much as one may wish for the contrary, it cannot be denied that even life as a 'highest value within the constitutional order'[185] is subject by law to possible intervention (Art. 2 Par. 2 Sent. 1 Basic Law) and as a result is not absolutely guaranteed.[186] Also, it would be purely wishful thinking to dismiss this deficient protection as an inadequacy that is limited to Germany alone; for even if the aforementioned provision of the Basic Law can be seen, as in the words of former President *Herzog*, as a 'stunningly indifferent formulation',[187] the absoluteness of the protection of life in other legal systems as well is diminished by means of at least three well-known 'classical' exceptions from the prohibition against killing: deadly self-defense (including defense of property), killing in war and, to the extent that it has not been repealed in the meantime, the death penalty. Granted, a common objection at this point is that the prohibition against killing applies only to the killing of 'innocent' life, but even this more limited prohibition is contradicted not only by accepted practice but also by the claim to absoluteness itself: If, for example, deadly self-defense can be employed against attackers who are not criminally responsible (like the mentally ill or children) or completely uninvolved civilians (perhaps even one's own citizens) can be killed in a bombing attack, one can hardly refer to the victims as 'guilty' life. Most importantly, however, the absoluteness of the protection of life cancels itself out if, from the very beginning, it applies only to certain categories of people.[188] As a result, the Federal Constitutional Court, although otherwise tireless in the promotion of life, does not speak of life's 'absolute' protection; rather, the talk is always of a

---

[185] As emphasized programmatically by the *Federal Constitutional Court* in its first time-limit judgment: *BVerfGE* 39, 42.

[186] For more on the limited guarantee of the basic right to life, see LORENZ, loc. cit. n. 168, at pp. 3 ff., 7 ff., 22 ff., as well as ESER, loc. cit. n. 175, at pp. 122 ff.

[187] R. HERZOG, 'Die Menschenwürde als Maßstab der Rechtspolitik', in H. SEESING (ed.), *Technologischer Fortschritt und menschliches Leben* (Munich, Schweitzer 1987) pp. 23-32 at p. 28.

[188] On this subject, see ESER, op. cit. n. 145, at pp. 28 ff., 33 ff., 39 ff.

'principled' protection according to which certain exceptions are permitted.[189] In sum, the most that can be claimed is a *principled* rather than an absolute protection of life.

This limitation has two major repercussions: first, if the protection of life is merely 'principled', then *exceptions* are possible; and second, the conflicting interests must be subject to a *weighing-up*, or a balancing test. As a result, exceptions from the abortion prohibition are, ultimately, a matter of the balancing of conflicting interests.

If people were more aware of the inevitability of a weighing-up, some of the disagreements regarding principles would be exposed as fruitless, terminological superficialities, and attention could be redirected to more fundamental issues. A prominent example is 'Life's Dominion'[190] by the American legal philosopher *Ronald Dworkin*, a book that is currently enjoying a great deal of attention. Certainly, much of what is presented in this volume with regard to the history of humanity, the various religions as well as recent statutes and case law is both interesting and impressive because it illustrates yet again the eternal, ideologically-driven struggle concerning the acceptability of the killing of unborn life. Nor is it surprising that *Dworkin* arrives, ultimately, at the goal, apparently sought from the very beginning, of allowing the termination of pregnancy under limited circumstances. It is surprising, however, that certain fundamental assumptions, initially presented as insurmountable hurdles, are ultimately overcome after having been brought down to more manageable size. This applies to the widely-accepted thesis, uncritically adopted by *Dworkin*, that if the fetus is recognized as a person it is entitled to independent rights and freedoms that exclude a killing in the same way as in the case of an already born person. This (supposed) inevitability is avoided most easily, naturally, if the fetus is denied the character of a person – an attribute that is, in any case, highly controversial and difficult to define. According to *Dworkin*, this does not preclude the recognition of the intrinsic value of unborn life, but may open the door to a balancing of its interests with those of the pregnant woman, primarily as regards her right to 'procreative autonomy'. The irritating part of such constructions is less the substantiation of human (including unborn) life as a value in and of itself – after all, in so doing it creates a basis for protection independent of a possibly non-

---

[189] On this point, see the excerpt from *BVerfGE* 88, 255 f. quoted *supra* at n. 168, as well as LORENZ, loc. cit. n. 168, at p. 7. See also A. ESER, 'Antworten auf Fragen von Abgeordneten', in A. ESER and H.-G. KOCH, *Schwangerschaftsabbruch: Auf dem Weg zu einer Neuregelung* (Baden-Baden, Nomos 1992) pp. 227-239 at pp. 228 ff.

[190] New York, Knopf 1993 (German version: R. DWORKIN, *Die Grenzen des Lebens, Abtreibung, Euthanasie und persönliche Freiheit* (Hamburg, Rowohlt 1994)).

existent constitutional guarantee of life.[191] However, even in the choice of words it is difficult to harmonize the fact that life, 'sanctified' and 'inviolable' as it is on account of its intrinsic value, should nevertheless take a back seat to the right to self-determination of the pregnant woman, thus making possible the killing that is the exact opposite of the ostensibly claimed 'inviolability'. Most surprising of all is the fact that a thinker of *Dworkin's* stature embraced such widespread conceptual-formal superficialities according to which, on the one hand, a certain label (fetus as person) may seem to require 'absolute' compelling consequences, whereas, on the other hand, this result may be avoided if a different conceptual label is chosen. If, in contrast, one is aware of the fact that not even already born life – as explained above – is spared every balancing test, the argument with regard to the appropriate conceptual label decreases in importance and attention can instead be focused on the criteria decisive for the balancing of interests.[192]

Before this can be addressed from the perspective of the pregnant woman, an additional assumption, one that affects the fetus itself, must be scrutinized: namely, the alleged *value-parity of born and unborn life*. Until now I, too, have proceeded from this assumption.[193] But the more time I spend on the subject the harder it is for me to close my mind to the insight that, in this context as well, moral claims and legal assessments take separate paths. Although this cannot be fully developed here, let me point out two aspects that appear essential. The first involves the irrefutable comparative legal phenomenon that traditionally and all over the world the killing of unborn life is sanctioned less severely and the sanctioning is more easily open to exceptions than it is in the case of the killing of already born life.[194] If such concessions are made even where – such

---

[191] For a comparable discussion regarding the claim to protection of embryos created outside the womb, see A. Eser, 'Strafrechtliche Schutzaspekte im Bereich der Humangenetik', in V. Braun et al. (eds.), *Ethische und rechtliche Fragen der Gentechnologie und der Reproduktionsmedizin* (Munich, C.H. Beck 1987) pp. 120-149, at pp. 138 ff.; A. Eser, 'Forschung mit Embryonen in rechtsvergleichender und rechtspolitischer Sicht', in H.-L. Günther and R. Keller (eds.), *Fortpflanzungsmedizin und Humangenetik*, 2nd edn. (Tübingen, Mohr 1991) pp. 263-292, at pp. 277 f., 284 ff.; Eser, op. cit. n. 145, at pp. 28 ff.

[192] For additional criticism of Dworkin, see Kaysser, op. cit. n. 182, at pp. 137 ff., whose perspective I cannot share to the extent that she apparently views the termination of pregnancy as an omission with regard both to carrying the pregnancy to term and giving birth, neither of which are, in her opinion, compulsory.

[193] See most recently A. Eser, in A. Schönke and H. Schröder (eds.), *Strafgesetzbuch: Kommentar*, 25th edn. (Munich, C.H. Beck 1997) preliminary remark 9 to § 218 with an overview of current opinion. For an earlier treatment, see Eser, loc. cit. n. 1, at pp. 150 f. on quantitative value differences.

[194] See *supra* IV.1.2.1, IV.1.2.3, IV.1.3.1-2.

as in German law – unborn life is deemed to have the character of an independent, highly personal legal value independent from the life and protective good will of the mother, they cannot be explained unless unborn life is accorded lesser value than is born life.[195] This legal graduation becomes easy to explain if – second – one pays more attention to the sociopsychological factor than is the case if one views life from an abstract-normative perspective, thereby ignoring completely the concrete individual development. To be sure, this does not change the fact that the human potency, whose existence begins at conception, has a claim to protection;[196] this claim increases, however, the more the unborn life unfolds. The assumption, for example, that a woman who has just learned that she is pregnant will assess the life growing in her in the same way as if she were in the ninth month is highly unlikely, even if the pregnancy is greeted with joy. If in the shaping of the law one does not wish to ignore completely this social reality, it is difficult to deny, even if one sees – as I do – the moment of conception as the foundation of the moral and legal claim of life to protection, that the value of this (unborn) life increases with advancing development.[197]

Only when seen in this light – and this is a not insignificant consequence – is it possible to explain why the permissibility of the termination of a pregnancy *can be different depending on the duration of the pregnancy* and why permissibility decreases as the pregnancy advances. To be sure, this phenomenon is frequently explained in terms of the increasing risks associated with the termination procedure in the later stages of pregnancy; however, the decision as to self-endangerment could certainly be left up to the pregnant woman alone – if, that is, the time-related complications of the termination procedure were not also influenced by the developmental status of the fetus.[198]

An even more important – and until now widely neglected – consequence arising from the phenomenon of increasing value coupled with correspondingly

---

[195] Whereas previously I sought to avoid this conclusion – while maintaining the claim of 'parity', I recognized the smaller 'weight' of the unborn life in the balancing process with an already born person in the form of the pregnant woman (see *supra* n. 193) – this differentiation, regardless of its analytical correctness, now appears to me to be unable to justify the resulting legal consequences if it does not acknowledge a value-oriented difference between born and unborn life.

[196] See *supra* IV.2.1.2, text accompanying n. 145.

[197] This categorical determination appears legitimate to me even if the criteria by which the advancing value and claim to protection of life are measured vary according to time and culture – for which reason here, too, no more than a highly circumstantial 'snapshot' could be expected from an attempt (hardly viable within the framework of this study) to identify these criteria substantively.

[198] For an impressive treatment of this point, see PRIESTER, loc. cit. n. 182, pp. 895 ff.

increasing protection of life is the establishment of a *generally applicable maximum time limit* for the legal termination of pregnancy. Even if developmental biology shows that all the building blocks necessary for life are present if not at conception then at least by the time of implantation (from which point on the development of multiple fetuses is no longer possible) and that all that these building blocks need is an uninterrupted opportunity to unfold, there are two developmental milestones in the relationship between mother and child that are of considerable importance: one of them is birth, at which time the child comes forth from the mother and begins a life as a separate, independent being. The other is viability of the fetus, which is generally reached in the twenty-second week of pregnancy: even if the fetus (in fact) remains within the mother's body beyond this stage in its development and continues to be dependent on her, it could (hypothetically) survive independently, outside the womb. Whereas birth traditionally is associated with a qualitative increase in protection, in that henceforth the stricter homicide offenses apply, the attainment of viability is not – at least not in German law – met with a comparably significant increase in protection. This does not appear to me to be reconcilable with the increased value of the developing life.

A radical correction is necessary to remedy this situation, with the termination of advanced pregnancies limited in two ways: First, terminations, as a rule, must be possible only prior to attainment of *fetal viability*, regardless of other, earlier turning points like, for example, the twelfth week for purposes of indications;[199] in this way, too, embryopathic terminations, currently deemed pos-

---

[199] Whereby this is revolutionary, perhaps, at most in a formal-legal sense but not in a substantive-legal or medical-practical sense; for even if a medically indicated termination appears, for lack of a formal time limit, to be permissible until birth, the concrete weighing-up process in the individual case is determinative, whereby the dangers to life and limb that the pregnant woman must endure increase (thus possibly precluding abortion) the closer the pregnancy comes to the birth phase (see ESER, loc. cit. n. 77, § 218a margin No. 34, 42. In fact, it appears that physicians will perform abortions at a time when the procedure can only be carried out by means of 'feticide' (the deliberate destruction of the fetus in the womb) only in extreme cases. For empirical information, so far quite meager, on 'late term abortions' after attainment of viability of the fetus, see the Government's response to the 'Small Inquiry' from Member of Parliament H. HÜPPE et al.: 'Spätabtreibung ungeborener Kinder', *BT-Drs.* 14/749, 14/1045. – Although the possible misuse of terms like 'viability' must be kept in mind (for an impressive treatment on this point from a legal-historical perspective, see R. PETERS, *Der Schutz des neugeborenen, insbesondere des mißgebildeten Kindes* (Stuttgart, Enke 1988) pp. 33 ff., 110 ff., 248 ff., we are not dealing here with allowing the post-natal death of a (born) infant because of reduced viability in the sense of (as medical professionals like to say) 'incompatibility with the [personal? social?] life', but rather with just the opposite, namely, an increase in protection by moving up the point in time after which abortions can as a general rule no longer be performed to the stage in the pregnancy

sible without regard subject to a deadline, could be prevented at later stages.[200] Second, subsequent to this point in time a termination performed by a physician should, in light of the nearness of the developmental stage to birth, be tolerated only in cases of severe, vital indications, either on the part of the mother or on the part of the child.[201]

With the adoption of this kind of limitation on so-called 'late term abortions', the Federal Republic of Germany would not stand alone; rather, it is, remarkably, precisely in countries such as Norway, Sweden, and the Netherlands – where termination in the early phase of pregnancy is relatively unproblematic – that termination in the late phase of pregnancy is dealt with more restrictively.[202] This may appear inconsistent but only to those who equate

---

at which the child could survive outside the womb. When and under what circumstances this stage, as a rule, is reached (at the 28th week, as was long assumed, or already between the 22nd and 24th week, as is currently believed), is less a normative question and more a question of biological-medical experience that depends to a great extent on developments in medicine.

[200] See *supra* IV.1.4.2, n. 116 and accompanying text, whereby, to be sure, the demand for the fundamental – but not absolute – reorientation of the final abortion deadline to the attainment of viability can be criticized in that, currently, a proper understanding of the weighing-up process to be undertaken would not, absent unusual circumstances, allow for a termination all the way up to the onset of birth. For more on this subject, see ESER, loc. cit. n. 77, § 218a, margin No. 43 with additional references.

[201] See *infra* IV.3.1, n. 298 and accompanying text – whereby the follow-up question as to the legal nature of such an exemption from punishment, i.e., justification, excuse or a merely personal exemption, is not least dependent upon the general principles according to which conflicts between 'life and life' are adjudged. On this point, see *supra* n. 182 and accompanying text.

[202] On this point, see generally *supra* II.2.5.3, II.3.2.3.C. For information specifically on the Netherlands, see E/K I pp. 1019 f., 1073, where the law makes clear that manslaughter according to Art. 287 of the Dutch Penal Code on account of the statutory definition in Art. 82a applies to 'the killing of a fruit [of the womb] from which it can honestly be expected that it is capable of staying alive outside the womb'. After attainment of viability, a 'late term abortion' in the Netherlands can apparently be performed only if the disorder of the fetus is very severe, whereby this must be classified by the physicians as a 'natural death'. For more on this point, see the February, 1998, 'Rapport van de Overleggroep late zwangerschapsafbreking' by an advisory committee of the Ministry of Health on 'Late zwangerschapsafbreking: zorgvuldigheid en toetsing', with a comparative legal overview. Although the legal approach employed in Norway is different, in Norway, too, there is a time-related deadline such that if 'there is reason to believe that the fruit of the womb is viable, permission to terminate the pregnancy will not be given', see E/K I p. 1476 [§ 2 par. 5]. An earlier Swedish regulation was similar (E/K I pp. 1416 f., 1452 ff., 1471 [§ 3 par. 2]); for recent amendments, see E/K III pp. 779 f. – Moreover, it is also noteworthy that in Japan where, despite an indication model, an abortion may be obtained solely on the basis of the pregnant woman's wishes, the procedure is only considered a termination 'so long as the

the reform of the law of termination with the greatest possible decriminalization. However, those who wish to see expression given to the growing claim to protection associated with the advancing development of life will recognize in the time-dependent increase in resistance to the termination of pregnancy a sign of consistence.

2.2.3 The pregnant woman: autonomous yet bound by an obligatory weighing-up process

While the formulation of this heading may seem a bit unusual, it is an attempt to capture in the most concise form possible the tension-filled position of the pregnant woman.

As numerous and diverse as other interpersonal and societal conflicts of interest may be, in one respect they cannot compete with the profoundness of the dilemma that characterizes an unwanted pregnancy: namely, the aforementioned singularity of the physical symbiosis in which fate binds mother and child to one another: a 'duality in unity',[203] whose resolution prior to birth in favor of the one can only take place, tragically, at the cost of the other. Even if additional interests – like, for example, those of the father or husband or those of the state in pursuing its chosen population control policy – should also be taken into account in this charged confrontation, these interests are merely incidental and are secondary in comparison to the fundamental bipolar conflict between mother and child. Therefore, the fundamental precedence of unborn life may at most be forced to yield to the pregnant woman but not to other interests, which may be afforded some weight but which are in no way decisive. Thus, the *pregnant woman* – and no one else – is the only serious party to the charged confrontation at issue here.

In this context, the concept of *autonomy*, which encompasses the various concerns of the pregnant woman, is of essential significance. The term 'autonomy' was chosen over the term 'self-determination' for both conceptual as well as emotive reasons; the result is both inclusive as well as exclusive. On the one hand, the ambit of autonomy can be interpreted broadly enough to encompass all concerns of the pregnant woman that she believes are relevant, by vir-

---

fetus is not viable outside the womb' (§ 2 par. 2 *Maternity Protection Act*): this is currently considered to be the case until the 21st week of pregnancy, see E/K III p. 859. See also K. YAMANAKA, 'Medizinische Eingriffe im japanischen Strafrecht', in A. Eser and H. NISHIHARA (eds.), *Rechtfertigung und Entschuldigung, Ostasiatisch-deutsches Strafrechtskolloquium Tokyo 1993* (Freiburg, Max-Planck-Institut für ausländisches und internationales Strafrecht 1995) pp. 189-212 at p. 198.

[203] See *supra* IV.2.2.1, n. 176 and accompanying text.

tue of her own rights, to her opposition to continuation of the pregnancy, beginning with the prevention of risks to her own life and health and the avoidance of familial and social predicaments and including as well the untrammeled development of her personality and the exercise of her freedom to reproduce. Although the listing of these interests does not mean that they should, without more, enjoy precedence over the unborn life, they at least belong to the area of life that the pregnant woman may normally structure as she pleases. On the other hand, this should not be understood as a free-for-all; for without wishing to depreciate the self as expressed in the term *auto*-nomy, the legality element in auto-*nomy* also merits a certain amount of attention, even if only to the extent that the power to make one's own decisions is coupled with responsibility. To this extent the term 'autonomy' is more immune to the not infrequent misunderstanding connected with the term 'self-determination': namely, that the pregnant woman can, by virtue of her unfettered decision-making freedom, highhandedly ['selbstherrlich'], as it were, determine the fate of the unborn life. For without repeating what has been said elsewhere,[204] it continues to be necessary to counter the short-circuited reasoning by which the concept of autonomy is overemphasized in excessively emancipatory terms and discredited through a perversion to 'self-aggrandizement' ['*Selbstherrlichkeit*'] without accountability. Whereas it is virtually incontrovertible, on the one hand, that in terminating a pregnancy the woman determines not only her own fate but also the fate of another human entity and thus the legalization of the termination of pregnancy cannot be justified simply by the right of the pregnant woman to self-determination, on the other hand, the fundamental conflict cannot be reduced to antagonism between the right of the unborn to life and the right of the pregnant woman to self-determination, with the latter then dismissed on account of its insignificance in comparison with the former. In sum, in recognizing autonomy, a right to behave as desired, without justification, is not conceded nor is self-determination established as a value in and of itself; rather, in recognizing autonomy, the pregnant woman is accorded the right to assert own life, health, welfare, and other personality interests, as long as she does so in a responsible manner.[205]

---

[204] As, principally, in ESER, op. cit. n. 159, at pp. 44 ff.

[205] Similarly, the characterization of abortion as a 'decision of conscience' can be defended against the – frequently polemical – misunderstanding that abortion is justifiable simply as an act of freedom of conscience as guaranteed by Art. 4 of the Basic Law. If a 'responsible and conscientious decision' is expected of the pregnant woman – as is the case in § 219 par. 1 StGB – then freedom of conscience as such does not supply the reason for the abortion; rather, the appeal is to use the conscience as an instrument in order to guarantee with as much certainty as possible a responsible decision. On this point, see ESER, op. cit. n. 159, pp. 50 ff.

Thus, if autonomy understood as responsibility is neither purely self-interested nor arbitrary, the conscientious *weighing-up* of the rights and interests that collide in the termination context, finally, is determinative. The specific factors to be considered depend, for the most part, on the circumstances of the individual case; at any rate, the basic factors were sketched out in the foregoing sections on the plurality of affected legal values and on the relativity of the protection of life, despite life's fundamental priority. Accordingly, if one does not give way to legally unrealistic wishful thinking, one must proceed from the assumption that although human life – including unborn human life – in fact represents a maximum value, it does not enjoy absolute protection nor does it enjoy protection at any price. Also, despite its fundamental priority over other rights and interests, it is not spared a weighing-up process with them, and, lastly, the value of life is not linear and unchanging but rather is dynamic and continually increasing, so that complete parity of born and unborn life from the onset of pregnancy cannot be assumed.

While pre-stabilized rankings, as it were, appear impossible in light of the inherent relativity of legal values, the weighing-up problem proves to be even more complex if one also considers the rules that have been developed for the comparable weighing-up process in cases of justifying necessity.[206] Though in such cases, the abstract hierarchical relationship between the conflicting legal values is, in fact, the first step to be taken, it is by no means the only step nor the determinative one: rather, an all-encompassing weighing-up of all the relevant factors must take place, in which, in addition to the general hierarchy of the directly affected legal values, further factors like, most importantly, the concrete life situation, the kind and degree of the potential dangers as well as other concerns must be taken into consideration. As far as the permissibility of the termination of pregnancy is concerned, this means that the die is not already cast with the confrontation between the (abstract) greater right of the fetus to life and the (abstract) lesser (because not vital) interests of the pregnant woman but rather that an all-encompassing weighing-up must be carried out, in which, in addition to the developmental state of the unfolding life, the concrete life situation of the pregnant woman, including her own defensible concerns, is taken into consideration.[207]

Who, then, is in the best position to undertake this weighing-up process? The pregnant woman herself or a higher authority? Should the criteria be autono-

---

[206] For a thorough discussion of this point, see TH. LENCKNER, *Der rechtfertigende Notstand* (Tübingen, Mohr 1965) pp. 90 ff.; see also LENCKNER, loc. cit. n.77, § 34 margin nos. 2, 22 ff.

[207] See A. ESER, in A. SCHÖNKE and H. SCHRÖDER (eds.), *Strafgesetzbuch: Kommentar*, 24th edn. (Munich, C.H. Beck 1991) § 218a margin No. 5 f.

mous or heteronomous? These questions have both a substantive and a formal side: substantive in so far as the factors to be considered in the weighing-up process can, by means of certain indications, be identified (and those that are not to be considered can be eliminated); formal in so far as the weighing-up process can be left up to the self-assessment of the pregnant woman or can be made subject to the review of a third party. If it is clear that, in conceding the very first indication, the Rubicon is crossed and the real possibility that unborn life will be demoted to second place cannot be undone, the only real issue left is the identification of the concerns of the pregnant woman that may be given priority. But since, in the final analysis, this means nothing more than advising the pregnant woman of the factors which legitimately may be considered more important than the life growing within her, and which may not, it represents a not insignificant restriction of her autonomy. This seems to be completely justi-fied if the fundamental priority of unborn life cannot be brought home any other way; in this regard, the *obligatory nature* (referred to in the heading to this section) of the weighing-up process itself expresses the responsibility, closely connected to autonomy, for making a decision based on the dictates of con-science. Whether and to what extent, however, the responsibility of the preg-nant woman should be reviewed by a third party is a question to be addressed in the context of other procedural issues.[208]

2.2.4   *Status-specific responsibilities*

There are essentially five categories of people who can participate in various ways in the termination of a pregnancy. Traditionally, these are the *pregnant woman* who performs a termination on herself or allows someone else to per-form a termination and a *third party* who performs a termination on the preg-nant woman. As a result of the amendments in abortion law in the twentieth century, a special role has fallen to the *physician,* in that the permissibility of a termination depends on its being performed by a medical doctor.[209] A new addi-tion in some countries is the *counselor,* whose consultation in an attempt to avert a termination may be required by one means or another. Although, natu-rally, he has always been affected (in the past only as an adjunct to the pregnant woman), the woman's *partner* and/or the *father* of the child has recently been awarded more attention.[210] This trend towards differentiation may be appreci-

---

[208] See *infra* IV.2.3.1.

[209] For details, see *supra* II.3.5 and II.5.1.

[210] For individual references regarding these various participants, see the following re-marks. Additional information concerning other participants, both throughout history and around the world, can be found in the comparative legal overview (*supra* II.3.3.4, II.3.4.3.C, D).

ated in that it allows different relationships to the child in question as well as various kinds of motivating factors and functions to be better accounted for. At the same time, however, not all of the recent developments are plausible.

As far as the *pregnant woman*, the person connected via a symbiotic 'duality in unity' with the unborn, is concerned, an almost revolutionary about-face is, to some extent, apparent. Whereas on German soil, for example, the pregnant woman herself was treated as the sole offender well into the twentieth century – as a result of which the performance of an abortion by a third party could at most be seen as the abetting of an abortion performed by the pregnant woman herself[211] – and it was not until 1943 when the Nazis implemented the 'Decree for the Protection of Marriage, Family, and Motherhood' that an abortion performed by a third party was classified as a felony, a more serious crime even than self-abortion (which was a misdemeanor),[212] in a growing number of countries, a termination performed by the pregnant woman herself is not subject to any punishment whatsoever.[213] Up until reunification, the German Democratic Republic took this approach. The Federal Republic of Germany, in contrast, has not yet gone quite this far: it has always adhered to the fundamental punishability of the pregnant woman (§ 218 par. 1, 3 StGB). However, in that the pregnant woman can avoid punishment if she fulfills the counseling requirement and the termination is performed by a physician before the 22nd week (§ 218a par. 4 StGB) and in that the attempt of the pregnant woman to terminate is generally not punishable (§ 218 par. 4 sent. 2 StGB),[214] the trend toward granting privileges to the pregnant woman has been unmistakable in the Federal Republic, as well. Therefore, it may appear to be a very small step to exempt the pregnant woman from any and all criminal liability whatsoever – as has been demanded by several German reform proposals.[215]

---

[211] For an overview of the controversy at that time, see G. RADBRUCH, 'Abtreibung (218-220 RStrGB)', in K. BIRKMEYER et al. (eds.), *Vergleichende Darstellung des deutschen und ausländischen Strafrechts,* Vol. V (Berlin Otto Liebmann 1905) pp. 159-183 at pp. 179 ff.; in contrast, for the very early efforts of the *Reichsgericht* [Supreme Court of the German Reich] to treat the actions of a third party as independent, full-blown perpetration, see already *RGSt* 1 (1880) pp. 350 ff. as well as *RGSt* 61 (1928) pp. 242 ff., 251.

[212] § 218 in the new version of the Decree of 18 March 1943 (*RGBl.* I, p. 169).

[213] For details, see the comparative legal overview, *supra* II.4.1, with diagram II/9 (part III).

[214] For additional exemptions from and mitigation of punishment for the pregnant woman, see the overview in ESER, loc. cit. n. 77, introductory remarks preceding § 218, margin No. 26.

[215] See the SPD-proposal of 21 June 1991 *BT-Drs.* 12/841, Art. 14 § 12 par. 2, according to which only the termination of someone else's pregnancy would be punishable. The proposal presented by parliamentarians from the group Alliance 90/The Greens on 6 June 1991, *BT-Drs.* 12/696, punished the termination of pregnancy only as an offense against the preg-

But even if only a small step, it would be one too many because it would entail not merely a quantitative but rather a qualitative leap. As much as the pregnant woman – the one most directly affected by a conflicted pregnancy – may expect human understanding, as great as the significance awarded her assessment of the conflict situation may be,[216] as far as the effective protection of the unborn life can be accomplished only with her and not against her, and as numerous as the many other reasons that speak for a general exemption from punishment for the pregnant woman may be, the fundamental objection to all of this remains that the complete release of the pregnant woman from her responsibility, on principle, to the life growing within her could be misunderstood. Not only that, in so doing, the exceptional character of the termination of a pregnancy could be lost and the compulsory weighing-up process so important for responsible action hardly be made clear, and not only that the counseling of the pregnant woman – essential for the counseling model – could be enforced only indirectly through a corresponding inquiry by the physician, thus (over)burdening the physician with all the responsibility; rather, if this approach were adopted the bottom would be knocked out from beneath the requirement that all terminations be performed by a physician because, if a pregnant woman were completely free from all criminal liability, she could settle for any form of termination, including terminations performed by lay abortionists.[217] In contrast, in retaining the fundamental criminal liability of the pregnant woman (as well) – even if there are numerous exceptions to liability – expression is given to the claim of the unborn life to protection and to the corresponding responsibility of the pregnant woman.

---

nant woman within the framework of 'serious bodily injury'. In the proposal presented by parliamentarians from the group PDS/Left List on 1 July 1991, *BT-Drs.* 12/898, abortion was completely legalized and was restricted only in cases of regulatory violations (§ 6).

[216] See *infra* IV.2.3.1, nn. 258 ff.

[217] The avoidance of this kind of undesirable development by offering the pregnant woman freedom from punishment only if the abortion is performed by a physician would necessarily increase the 'dependence conflict' as it exists between the pregnant woman and the physician even if her exemption from criminal liability is not exclusively dependent upon the performance of the abortion by a physician but rather is dependent as well on her own previous actions (like prior counseling); for if the pregnant woman's exemption from criminal liability were exclusively to depend upon finding a physician willing to perform the procedure, with the physician's performance a necessary as well as sufficient condition, the pressure on the physician would be so great as to be unbearable: Whereas the pregnant woman – herself free of all criminal liability whatsoever – could afford any and all 'unscrupulousness' so to speak, the physician would have to take on, in addition to the physician's own responsibility for the fate of the unborn, the responsibility of the pregnant woman – a transfer of responsibility that is neither fair nor justifiable in a legal-ethical sense.

Diametrically opposed to the easing of criminal responsibility with regard to the pregnant woman, the responsibility of the *physician* has grown continuously over time. Put informally, today it is practically impossible for a termination to be exempt from punishment if it is not performed by a physician;[218] as a result, reference to a 'medical gatekeeper' is not uncommon.[219] This increase in power is simultaneously both an honor and a burden: it is an honor in that in the key role reserved for it in the termination context, an area that is complex both ethically and in terms of human conflict, a special mark of public trust with regard to the medical profession may be seen; it is a burden in that the role of 'social controlleur' is difficult to reconcile with the traditional profile of a physician's duties, not to mention the contradictory pressures to which physicians may find themselves subject from individual pregnant women[220] or from groups within society in terms of expansive or restrictive views with regard to the performance of terminations altogether.

Physicians can be expected to carry out these kinds of duties only if two factors are satisfied: First, it must be possible for physicians to reach their own, independent decisions concerning the performance of a termination, when legally permissible, in order to avoid degenerating into mere 'instruments' [*Erfüllungsgehilfe*] of pregnant women;[221] this means that physicians must be able to inquire into the reasons that have caused the pregnant woman to choose to terminate. Second, it must be possible for the physician to be sure that his or her actions in following the legal instructions of the pregnant woman are legal; if this is not the case, physicians who take their responsibilities seriously – and such physicians are necessary for the effective protection of unborn life – can

---

[218] For details, see *supra* II.5, IV.1.3.4.

[219] K. PETERSEN, 'Abortion: the Case for Non-intervention', 4 *European Journal of Health Law* (1997) pp. 239-251 at p. 248.

[220] On this point, see *supra* n. 217 and previous text.

[221] Even if it is undeniable that medicine sees itself more and more as a 'service' industry and, correspondingly, physicians believe themselves entitled (if not required) to do anything that they are asked to do, this must be tolerated – even if one balks at the thought of medicine as following the dictates of the market place a la 'the laws of supply and demand' – only so long as the interests of the 'customer' alone are affected. However, as soon as in the case of abortion the rights and interests of the unborn life are also recognized (as constitutionally guaranteed in Germany and, in any event, legally-ethically required), the physician has a responsibility not only to the pregnant woman but to the child as well (on the relationship involving not two but three parties, see ESER, loc. cit. n. 1, at pp. 105 ff.). If an abortion were to be legitimated simply as a 'service' at the will of the pregnant woman, the 'physician' would be demoted to a 'medical technician' acting with no independent self-responsibility. See also *supra* I.4.6.

hardly be expected to agree to perform a termination. Both points will be dealt with again later.[222]

Although not as central as the physician, the *counselor*, too, is taking on a greater preventive role in the period preceding the termination of a pregnancy.[223] The responsibility associated with counseling increases as counseling evolves from the mere presentation of information into a prerequisite to the exemption from punishment, as is the case in the current regulation of the German Criminal Code (§ 218a par. 1 StGB). In Germany, the counseling of the pregnant woman in an emergency and conflict situation according to § 219 StGB is hardly less important than the requirement that the termination be performed by a physician. On the contrary, whereas the requirement that terminations be performed by physicians primarily guarantees the professional nature of the procedure – although it may serve other functions as well[224] – and thus the physician must literally carry out the termination, counseling is geared toward the prevention of termination altogether. Therefore – with a view to the current discussion regarding the propriety of allowing church-sponsored counseling centers to bestow proof-of-counseling certificates – it is simply a mistake to attribute to the counseling and certification process active participation in a subsequent termination that takes place despite efforts to prevent it.[225]

Even if, realistically speaking, counseling is not a panacea for termination, it would appear that, with the well-founded prospect of achieving more by means of assistance and counseling than by means of criminal prohibitions alone, the establishment of the most effective counseling system possible would be well

---

[222] See *infra* IV.2.3.1, text following n. 259; see also *infra* IV.2.3.3.

[223] On the various forms of counseling and the various kinds of counselors and counseling centers that have been considered, see the comparative legal overview *supra* II.3.4.

[224] For even if, historically speaking, the medical professionalism of the abortion procedure enjoyed, with a view to the health interests of the pregnant woman, top priority (see *supra* II.5.1), the bringing in of a physician can also, naturally, take on preventive significance: be it in the form of purposeful persuasion of the pregnant woman (similar to counseling, as discussed below) or be it by means of a refusal to perform the abortion on the basis of the physician's own findings (as discussed above).

[225] The mistaken approach taken by groups advocating the withdrawal of Catholic counseling centers from the counseling system operating in tandem with the criminal law (for more, see E/K III p. 634) appears to me to rely primarily on a persistent and purely causal interpretation of the counseling certificate instead of acknowledging the risk-reduction effect of counseling and the corresponding lack of accountability for the abortion. See also A. ESER, 'Wertebewußtsein schaffen', Ein Gespräch zur Diskussion über die Schwangerschaftsberatung', in 52 *Herder-Korrespondenz* (1998) pp. 178-183 at pp. 180 f. Parts of which also appeared in J. REITER (ed.), *Der Schein des Anstoßes, Schwangerschaftskonfliktberatung nach dem Pabstbrief* (Freiburg Herder 1999) pp. 126-135 at p. 126 f.

worth the effort and the investment.[226] This is especially true with regard to the quality of the counseling as a whole and of the counselors themselves. Since it is extremely difficult for the criminal law to guarantee high quality counseling,[227] the counselors' sense of personal responsibility and a corresponding climate of responsibility at the counseling centers are decisive. These issues, too, will be dealt with later.[228]

As far as the developments with regard to the legal responsibility of the pregnant woman's *social environment* is concerned, they have been varied and, in some cases, even contradictory. Whereas under Roman Law abortion was seen as an act harming the interests of the husband and, as a result, the protection of unborn life was more or less in his hands,[229] today, according to German law, the father may be liable for a crime by omission if he fails to prevent the woman from terminating her pregnancy.[230] And whereas in some countries the permissibility of the termination of pregnancy continues to depend upon the consent of the husband, reforms are increasingly curtailing his right to participate in the decision.[231] On the other hand, the Federal Constitutional Court has tried to counter the effect on women of social contacts who promote abortion by stating that the abandonment of a pregnant woman and the application of pressure to make her obtain a termination should be criminalized;[232] Parliament has responded by passing at least some of the called-for legislation.[233] Last but not least the extent of the influence that the partner's attitude can wield in the pregnant woman's decision for or against a termination has achieved increasing recognition; as a result, a greater degree of partner involvement in counseling sessions is being advocated.[234]

If an attempt is made to draw legal policy conclusions from all of this, the result might well amount to a tight-rope walk between the increasing co-responsibility of the pregnant woman's social contacts and the pregnant woman's autonomy, which must nonetheless be respected. On the one hand, the pregnant woman's partner, the father of the child, is to be included in counseling to a

---

[226] See *supra* IV.1.3.3, IV.1.4.3, IV.2.1.2 at n. 148.

[227] Take, for example, the case of a pregnant woman who was counseled in an illegal manner and who, by means of an invalid counseling certificate, was aided and abetted by a third party in procuring a (consequently) illegal abortion. See also ESER, loc. cit. n. 77, § 218 margin Nos. 52 f., § 219 margin Nos. 22, 25 f.

[228] See *infra* IV.2.3.2, text following n. 275.

[229] See *supra* IV.2.2.1, text accompanying n. 170.

[230] See E/K I pp. 209 f.

[231] See *supra* II.2.2, II.3.3.4, IV.1.3.4.

[232] See *BVerfGE* 88, 204, 296 ff.

[233] It added § 170 par. 2 and § 240 par. 1 sent. 2 StGB.

[234] See *supra* IV.1.4.2, text accompanying nn. 108-110.

greater extent than in the past, both in order to encourage the pregnant woman as well as – and this is not infrequently necessary – to shake him into acknowledging his own personal responsibility for the new life in whose creation he was a co-participant. On the other hand, he must not be allowed to extol his co-responsibility for the child to such an extent that it ends up depriving the pregnant woman of her rights, i.e., that it forces on her his own decision for or against a termination. This is because the effect on him is not comparable to the effect on her: as he does not share in the symbiotic relationship that exists between mother and child, he is affected in a less existential way. Similarly, the rest of the pregnant woman's social contacts should be integrated, primarily in order to bolster her sense of responsibility and – especially in cases involving a minor – to be prevented from pressuring her in one direction or the other.

Finally, *third parties* who play an active role in a termination in disregard of any and all prerequisites to permissibility – e.g., without prior counseling, without an indication and/or without a physician – are engaging in criminal activity. As the range of conduct that is still actually prohibited has, in many countries, become very small,[235] there is, in fact, no particular reason to respond with lenience if, through the failure to comply with expansive regulations designed to exempt a wide range of abortions from punishment, a pregnancy is terminated illegally. On the contrary, if protection of human life is really taken seriously, the normal penalty for termination should, at very least, not be less than the penalty for bodily injury. The fact that in Germany disproportionate penalties still exist, despite a reform of the penalty ranges by the Sixth Act to Reform the Criminal Law [*6. Strafrechtsreformgesetz*] (1998) – the highest penalty for termination is only three years (§ 218 par. 1 StGB) whereas the highest penalty for simple bodily injury is five years (§ 223 par. 1 StGB) –, and the fact that, in some cases, a mere fine rather than incarceration may suffice illustrate yet again the quasi-schizophrenic relationship between the dramatic likening of abortion to murder and the highly discrepant sentencing practice.

2.3 Protection and legitimation through procedure

In order to nip a misunderstanding in the bud, it should be noted that despite the allusion in the heading to *Niklas Luhmann's* book of very similar title[236] his system theory will not be introduced here nor should the impression be awakened that all problems implicated in the protection from or the legitimation of the termination of pregnancy can be solved simply by employing rules of pro-

---

[235] For details, see *supra* II.4.1, with diagram II/9 (part III).
[236] N. LUHMANN, *Legitimation durch Verfahren* (Neuwied, Luchterhand 1969).

cedure. Instead, these few, carefully chosen words are meant to express the conviction that in the problematic area surrounding the termination of pregnancy, a greater influence on behavior can be expected from the deliberate implementation of certain formal procedures to be followed than could be achieved when there were only traditional prohibitions to work with. Of the various kinds of procedural safeguards and control mechanisms that are catching on all over the world, from the requirement that terminations be performed by physicians to the subsequent documentary and reporting requirements,[237] only the two most important procedural prerequisites for the termination of a pregnancy will be evaluated here from a legal policy perspective: first, the process by which indications are ascertained and second, counseling.

2.3.1   *Emergency indication: from third party evaluation to discourse*

In order to avoid raising false hopes, I will begin by restating my starting position. Those who expect absolute protection of unborn life will not, from the very outset, warm to the creation of indications that legally justify the termination of pregnancy. Those who do accept such indications, in principle, but who consider a formal process for ascertaining the existence of indications that merit a legal justification to be indispensable will not gain much from the forthcoming remarks – I fear – except perhaps confirmation of their own prejudices. Appreciation for these comments can only be expected from those who share with me the following premises: first, that – as has already been determined here in accordance with the Federal Constitutional Court – exceptions to the fundamental protection of unborn life may be legally justifiable;[238] second, that the rule-of-law-based principle (considered essential by the Federal Constitutional Court), according to which the existence of an indication must be ascertained by a third party and must be reviewable by the state,[239] is neither immutable for all eternity nor is it beyond improvement; and third, that – as will be explained in closing – legal justification alone, without more, cannot be equated with moral approval.[240]

If we proceed from the premise that, under certain conditions, the termination of pregnancy may be legally justifiable, in the main, two questions concerning the necessary weighing-up of the conflicting interests must be considered: on the more substantive side is the description of legally justifying exceptions

---

[237] For details, see the comparative legal overview, *supra* II.3.4-6. For a preliminary assessment of this proceduralization trend, see *supra* IV.1.3.4.

[238] See *supra* IV.2.2.1 (n. 163), IV.2.2.2/3.

[239] *BVerfGE* 88, 274; on this point, see *supra* IV.1.3.3, text accompanying nn. 62 ff.

[240] See *infra* IV.2.3.3.

in the shape of indications and on the more procedural side are issues of competence and form in the process of ascertaining the existence of these indications, whereby, to be sure, the two questions are to some degree intertwined.[241]

As far as the *conception and definition* of legally justifiable exceptions from the prohibition of the termination of pregnancy, embodied in *indications*, are concerned, the initial choice between a stricter restriction to danger to life and health of the pregnant woman, on the one hand, and the willingness to consider social factors, on the other, is often seen as pivotal. Whereas the latter approach may appear to be boundless, the feeling is that the former can be counted on to create a narrow field of exceptions. In practice, however, this assumption has been widely disproved. In Switzerland, for example, where until 2002 the exemption from punishment for a interruption of pregnancy depended on the existence of 'a danger to life or great danger of long term, serious damage to the health of the pregnant woman that cannot be averted any other way' (Art. 120 par. 1 StGB), the application of this comparatively narrow medical indication was highly disparate from canton to canton: indeed, it has at times been interpreted so expansively as to take on the mantle of a general social indication.[242] This illustrates not only the greater or lesser flexibility of the legal definitions of indications but also the dependence of their interpretation on the fundamental attitudes of those who apply them. As an additional example, the rise and fall in the number of medical indications, depending on whether or not a social indication is recognized or has been abolished, is a behavioral pattern that is not much different.[243] Even if laxity cannot be ruled out in such practices, it would be too easy simply to attribute these kinds of stretching and compensatory mechanisms to the unscrupulous abuse of law. Namely, insofar as medical indications are not simply tied to the existence of certain somatic symptoms, but rather – as in any case is necessary if a weighing-up process is to be taken seriously – depend on the overall health of the pregnant woman, the consideration of psychological strains cannot be avoided. As a result, the individual circumstances of the pregnant woman must be taken into account. Furthermore, a phenomenon of sociopsychological complexity cannot be overlooked on this level: whereas the narrow or broad application of an indication must appear discriminatory to the pregnant woman disadvantaged by it, it has been shown yet again that those responsible for third party review of the indication (e.g., physicians,

---

[241] On this two-layered approach to the problem, see *supra* IV.2.1.3, text following n. 153 and IV.2.2.3, text following n. 207.

[242] For more details, see E/K I pp. 1509 f., 1526 f., 1545 as well as H.-G. KOCH, 'Über Schwierigkeiten von Ärzten und Gerichten im Umgang mit § 218 StGB', in ESER and KOCH, op. cit. n. 189, pp. 69-84.

[243] For more on this point, see *supra* II.3.2.3.B, IV.1.4.1, text accompanying n. 92.

experts or courts) are apparently less motivated by legal requirements than by fundamental socioethical attitudes – with the result that the establishment of an appropriate sense of values is of primary importance.

But even if the definition problem could be solved, for example by limiting termination even in the early phase of pregnancy to a narrow medical indication and tying the indication to specific somatic symptoms, the question of the substantive correctness of such a scheme would remain. No matter how one reacts to it, it cannot be denied that with the creation of (at first) purely medical indications, a dynamic development led to ever greater consideration of psychological and social factors.[244] To be sure, this appears to confirm, on the one hand, that there is no stopping once the floodgates are opened. But one could just as easily put the opposite question: namely, whether it is possible that previous floodgates were closed too tightly and that the resulting overpressure, to the extent that it was unable to dissipate unseen, is only now revealed in its true dimensions. In fact, it is worth remembering that even when there were no recognized exceptions to the prohibition on abortion, various outlets allowed for the non-punishable termination of pregnancy, such as – in a way that avoided the criminal law entirely – simply declaring the termination to be a therapeutic medical procedure and not questioning its medical indication any further.[245] Whereas such dodging practices may seem somewhat dubious from a formal legal perspective and were not, in any case, available to all women, the extreme hardship of those affected is apparent in that pregnant women were willing to take both medical as well as criminal risks to terminate their pregnancies. And for them, even then, it cannot have been solely a matter of averting dangers to their health but rather more one of escaping a no less dreadful social fate. The latter may in fact no longer be a factor, in that unwed mothers and illegitimate children are not plagued with the same social stigma that dogged them in recent generations, a stigma that, by the way, unwed fathers have always been able to evade much more easily.[246] Nevertheless, it would be both insufficient and contradictory to permit a pregnant woman to avert dangers to her health by means of an termination but to pay no attention to her personal life plan, her professional goals, her family situation or to other subsequent social problems. Particularly if human beings are seen as a single entity comprised of body and soul

---

[244] For details on the development of the theory of indications, E/K III pp. 66 ff.

[245] On this as well as other expansive trends, see E/K III pp. 68 ff.

[246] And indeed not only with the biological help of nature ('pater semper incertus'). Rather, supported by the ideological lenience of society, unwed fatherhood was legally ignored up until our own time in that a father and his illegitimate child were considered 'not related' (see K. KROESCHELL, *Rechtsgeschichte Deutschlands im 20. Jahrhundert* (Göttingen, Vandenhoeck & Ruprecht 1997) pp. 49, 212, 222 f.).

and if the appropriate respect for the possible severity of psychosomatic illnesses is not withheld, a scheme limited to the consideration of dangers to physical health must be faulty – basically, in such a conception pregnant woman is not taken seriously as a person.

While, as we have just seen, it is difficult, on a conceptual level, to define indications for the termination of pregnancy both appropriately and sufficiently clearly,[247] the difficulties only become greater when the focus is on the more procedural questions of determining in what *form* and in whose *competence* the ascertainment of an indication should belong and should take place. One should not seek to escape this question even if – as in the case of the 'successive-time-limit-indication models'[248] and, thus, of the new regulations in the Federal Republic of Germany – no proof of indication is required in the first trimester of pregnancy; for to the extent that this approach allows for the exemption from punishment but not for the legal justification of the termination, the question remains of what to require from the pregnant woman in terms of the ascertainment of an indication should she want the termination to be considered legally justified.

If one proceeds on the basis of the fundamental principles laid down by the Federal Constitutional Court and mentioned above, the 'self-indication' of the woman is insufficient; instead, the existence of the indication must be ascertained by a third party and must be reviewable by the state.[249] While the Federal Constitutional Court may hope by means of this sort of quasi state-run, third party control to achieve both a termination-reducing effect as well as the fair treatment of pregnant women, its approach must be greeted with skepticism. If, for example, as shown by our questionnaire of women,[250] almost half the pregnant women requesting the finding of an indication received a positive response from the first physician consulted and the rest, through the consultation of additional physicians, brought the overall success rate up to 91.3%, the filter function of the indication ascertainment requirement, with a rejection rate of less than 10%, is rather low. If, of the women who were rejected, 43.8% still did not give up on a termination, the requirement of a formal indication loses even more of its significance. And finally, if the other half of the women who were unable to secure a positive ascertainment of an indication carried their pregnan-

---

[247] For these two demands, which can be reduced only with difficulty to a single common denominator, see ESER, op. cit. n. 159, pp. 77 ff.

[248] More on this point can be found at *supra* II.2.4.2.C with diagram II/4.

[249] This can be in the form of judicial review or review by 'third parties whom the state may trust on account of the special responsibilities associated with their position [Pflichtenstellung]:' *BVerfGE* 88, 274.

[250] See the references listed in *supra* IV.1.2.3, at n. 21.

cies to term not because of this obstacle but rather for personal reasons, the efficiency of third party control is approaching zero. Although it might be claimed – not without great cynicism – that this shows that the requirement presents no real hindrance, the path to the ascertainment of an indication, strewn as it not infrequently is with obstacles, is in fact experienced by many woman less as a help and more as a burden.[251] Finally, although in part for different reasons, more than three quarters of physicians also experience the ascertainment of an indication – to the extent that they do not dismiss it as a purely formal 'ritual' – as a burden.[252]

Now, it would perhaps be unnecessary to recoil from these kinds of requirements if, in the interest of the protection of life, the system by which indications are ascertained were to be improved so as to do justice to its filter function and at the same time be fair to the pregnant woman. These goals can only be achieved, however, if two conditions are met: first, it must be possible to describe legitimate terminations of pregnancy in an objective way and second, it must be possible to evaluate such situations uniformly and reliably in practice. Persistent doubts remain with regard to the feasibility of both of these conditions.

It is less a matter for concern that any effort whatsoever be made to describe the grounds for termination; for even if the attempt fails to yield absolute clarity and certainty, the formulation of grounds for termination by means of some sort of 'indication' could at least serve as a guide to the orientation of the weighing-up and decision-making processes. However, to the extent that the formulation is also expected to function as the basis of a binding third party judgment, the attempt to objectify the individual emergencies of individual pregnant women in such a way as to enable a third party to comprehend and do justice to them on a case-by-case basis is comparable to trying to square the circle: the more one tries to do justice to the individuality of a particular pregnant woman's conflict, the more it defies objective description. The more one tries to describe conflicts in a general way in order to promote uniform treatment, the greater the danger of missing the unique emergency situation of individual women; for although the external circumstances of conflict pregnancies may appear similar, the individual gravity of the conflict depends not least upon the value system of the particular woman involved. If, however, it is precisely the intolerable inner conflict that ultimately serves as the basis of the permissibility of the termination and that, out of respect for the individual personality of the woman, cannot be

---

[251] For results obtained in our attitudinal studies and for references to additional relevant publications, see HÄUSSLER and HOLZHAUER, loc. cit. n. 20, at pp. 830 ff.; HOLZHAUER, op. cit. n. 20, at pp. 287 ff.

[252] See HÄUSSLER and HOLZHAUER, loc. cit. n. 20, pp. 834 f. and HÄUSSLER-SCZEPAN, op. cit. n. 20, at pp. 147 ff.

evaluated in any other way than by the woman herself, from her own subjective situation and life perspective, then all attempts to define indications objectively and in such a way as to be reviewable by third parties are doomed to failure because a pregnant woman's individual life perspectives and the establishment of her priorities can neither be determined nor assessed let alone decided on her behalf by a third party.[253]

Even if it were possible to define pregnant women's individual conflicts sufficiently generally while at the same time insuring that sufficient attention be paid to the specifics of each and every case, a reliable and uniform ascertainment of indications by a third party would still not be guaranteed. This is not a reference either to the occasional laxity in the recognition of indications or to rigorous harshness that may occur from time to time to the detriment of unborn life or as a quasi-disciplinary measure aimed at supposedly shameless pregnant woman. Rather, it is a the result of issues that confront even conscientious doctors, experts and courts: Such problems may arise already in the fact-gathering process, where a woman's ability to cope with pressure may affect her capacity to articulate and to express herself; additional problems may arise in the decision-making process, where both the interpretation of legal requirements as well as the assessment of individual emergency situations depend upon the fundamental attitudes of the evaluators and where, as a result, similar situations do not always yield similar results.[254] In any event, it was a sobering experience for me to discover in the course of our study of how indications are ascertained, based on the law in force in Germany since 1975, that in the evaluation of similar cases physicians may come down very differently and that even the assessments of expert jurists, asked to evaluate pertinent hypotheticals, differed considerably from one another, with these differences apparent both in the decision as to the type of indication implicated by the fact pattern as well as in the ultimately decisive question regarding the permissibility of the proposed termination.[255]

A serious attempt to redress such discrepancies and the ensuing lack of uniformity in the permissibility or impermissibility of the termination of pregnancy[256] would require not only the deliberate selection and training of the

---

[253] On this complex of issues, see also ESER, op. cit. n. 159, at pp. 78 f., 101 f., and KOCH, loc. cit. n. 242, pp. 69-84.

[254] On these issues, too, see ESER, op. cit. n. 159, at pp. 80 ff.

[255] For details, see HÄUSSLER and HOLZHAUER, loc. cit. n. 20, at pp. 833 ff. and HÄUSSLER-SCZEPAN, op. cit. n. 20, at pp. 201 ff.

[256] Whereby the *Federal Supreme Court* apparently found this to be neither absolutely necessary nor even possible in that it declared itself satisfied with a mere 'reasonableness test' ['Vertretbarkeitsprüfung'] – for which I had previously argued (see A. ESER, "Ärztliche

physicians allowed to participate in the process of ascertaining indications but also provide for the review of their actual decisions in order to insure uniform treatment. The latter requirement would survive even the reintroduction of expert committees if the ascertainment of indications is to proceed uniformly at both the regional as well as the local level. While it is unlikely, in any case, that suitable personnel for this kind of elaborate indication-control apparatus could be found, in view of the not insignificant costs associated with such an undertaking, it might well be a better use of limited funds to offer pregnant women the prospect of support for their children, should they choose to continue their pregnancies. Probably the highest price to be paid for a perfect indication-control system, however, would be the sociopsychological price, for the more a woman sees herself pitted against a quasi state-run authority with the power to grant or refuse her request, the more both the atmosphere of trust as well as the trust-building aspect of the physician-patient relationship suffers, a relationship that is in fact indispensable for a comprehensive approach to the handling of conflict-besetted pregnancies.

It is perhaps the intuitive recognition of the shortcomings and follow-up costs of a perfectionistic indication-control system that has caused such systems to play only a relatively limited role in other countries. This does not mean that other countries do not also have regulations for ascertaining the grounds warranting a termination, comparable to the German process of ascertaining indications and, in some cases, even more detailed.[257] Today, however, as far as the early stages of pregnancy are concerned, judicial review of the ascertainment process is practically nowhere to be found. This means that, should the self-portrayal or self-assessment of the pregnant woman herself not be considered sufficient, at very latest the medical finding will be accepted. Although the latter approach certainly reflects a qualitative leap, it has nonetheless been adopted by various neighboring countries such as France, Italy, and, more recently, Belgium.[258]

Indeed, the decisive issue here is what an indication regulation, ultimately, should be. Even though the foregoing objections might appear to be critical of

---

Erkenntnis' und richterliche Überprüfung bei Indikation zum Schwangerschaftsabbruch nach § 218a StGB', in ESER and KOCH, op. cit. n. 189, pp. 13-47) – both from the civil law (*BGH NJW* 1985, 2753) as well as from the criminal law perspective (*BGHSt* 38, 156); on the subject as a whole, see also ESER, loc. cit. n.77, § 218a margin No. 36 with additional references.

[257] On the extent and variety of these kinds of regulations, see the comparative legal overview, *supra* II.3.4.2.

[258] Other countries that have adopted this approach include Great Britain, Norway, and, with some reservations, Austria: for details, see *supra* II.2.4.1.C, II.3.4.2.C.

the indication idea as such, they are in fact critical only of the claim that it is unthinkable for the legality of a termination to rely on an emergency situation that has not been ascertained by a third party and is not subject to judicial review. Those who are satisfied with formal facades will perhaps not be bothered by the fact that this instrument is practically meaningless. If, however, one adds to this the engendered costs, ranging from lax treatment to sociopsychological counterproductivity to insufficient attention on a case-by-case basis to arbitrary prosecution, the mere appearance of formality can hardly form the basis for an adequate foundation. Compared with this, the more honest and hopefully the more effective alternative, it appears to me, would be to base the legitimation for the termination of a pregnancy on the existence of an emergency situation as assessed by the pregnant woman herself after she has undergone serious counseling and engaged, conscientiously, in a weighing-up process.[259] Accordingly, in connection with the indication-complex the following conditions seem to me to be both necessary and sufficient:

First, it is fundamentally necessary to retain and to clarify in the law that the decision regarding the continuation or termination of a pregnancy is not an act of free and unbridled self-determination but rather depends upon the existence of an emergency or conflict situation that the woman does not believe can be resolved in any way other than by the termination of her pregnancy. In this regard, the description, in the form of indications, of factors that may significantly affect the decision may help provide orientation for the weighing-up process.

Second, the self-assessment of the pregnant woman can suffice for the ascertainment of an emergency or conflict situation if it is certain that the woman, fully aware of her responsibilities, has engaged in the necessary weighing-up process – particularly by means of discourse with her physician (discussed next) and counseling (discussed in the following section).

Third, the physician carrying out the termination procedure must, as an additional major participant, be able to act not merely as the pregnant woman's 'instrument' ['*Erfüllungsgehilfe*'] but rather in the physician's own right. In order to achieve this goal, the physician must ask the pregnant woman to present the reasons for terminating her pregnancy and, if necessary, may discuss them

---

[259] As to this position, which I have held since the beginning of the 1990s (see, e.g., ESER, loc. cit. n. 146, at pp. 87 ff.; ESER, op. cit. n. 159, at pp. 24 f., 82 f., 104 ff.), not even the *Federal Constitutional Court* (in *BVerfGE* 88, 274 f.) has been able to convince me otherwise. Indeed, the characterization 'self-indication' ['Selbstindikation'] of the pregnant woman as used by the *BVerfG*, if not simply to be seen as a polemical exaggeration, gives reason to fear an incomplete understanding of the process, which I deliberately call by the more limited term 'self-assessment' ['Selbsteinschätzung'], where conflicting interests are weighed against one another.

with her. This should not be viewed as a disguised third party-indication-ascertainment requirement, as it were, in which the physician sits quasi 'in judgment' over the woman's application for approval; instead, in such a discourse the point is for both people to arrive at a decision that each finds morally acceptable.[260]

Fourth, it is necessary to acknowledge generally the changed paradigm behind this altered approach: it is less a matter of reviewability by the state and decision-making power vested in a third party, deciding from on high, upon which a pregnant woman believes herself dependent and to which she has difficulty expressing her innermost feelings and more a matter of engaging in an exchange based on trust, of two equals conducting a conversation designed to assist the woman both in arriving at a responsible decision and in winning the participation of the physician. As a result, open discourse becomes all the more important, as does the counseling process, to which we will now turn.

2.3.2   *Prevention through counseling*

As in the previous section in the indication context, a warning against false assumptions is necessary here, too, although this time for just the opposite reason: whereas the indication requirement is a relatively well-established procedure whose adequacy and efficiency have increasingly been called into question, counseling for pregnant women is a relatively new instrument whose probation period is still ahead but whose track record so far gives every reason for optimism.

Although the exact origins of the counseling approach are still unknown and therefore an earlier occurrence cannot be ruled out, it is noteworthy that in the first instance that we found, namely, a 1956 resolution of the Hungarian Ministry, counseling could replace a personal or familial indication if the woman was not swayed from her desire to terminate her pregnancy despite being informed of the effects of a termination and despite all attempts on the part of the commission to convince her otherwise.[261] Equally noteworthy is the fact that in England, subsequent to the introduction of the Abortion Act of 1967, a counseling network established itself, also in the absence of a legislative basis, the importance of which was, as in Hungary, nonetheless recognized almost immediately by state authorities.[262] It was in this context that the Alternative Draft

---

[260] See also ESER, loc. cit. n. 146, at p. 105 and ESER, op. cit. n. 159, at pp. 100 f. It is noteworthy that in Sweden a major aim of the conversation between physician and pregnant woman is to make it easier for the physician to reach his or her own decision (E/K I p. 1416).

[261] E/K I p. 1676 f. For additional historical reminiscences, which do not, however, claim to be comprehensive, see E/K III p. 84, text accompanying nn. 16 ff.

[262] E/K I p. 700.

[*Alternativ-Entwurf*] of 1970 introduced its counseling idea, an approach that was not unknown on the international level but was new on German soil and one that has since become a firmly established part of the reform discussion.[263] The decisive breakthrough was achieved, finally, when the 'counseling concept' underlying the Act to Aid Pregnant Women and Families [*Schwangeren- und Familienhilfegesetz*] of 1992 was recognized, in principle, by the Federal Constitutional Court.[264] Abroad, as well, the counseling approach is playing an ever increasing role in the reform of laws governing the termination of pregnancy, whereby, again, the array of different strategies employed is impressive.[265]

The sudden appearance of counseling on the scene and its rapid spread can probably be explained by the coming together of two developments: a sobering-up following a rejection of ideology and a support-oriented, focusing on reality. As far as the former is concerned, the insight could no longer be repressed that abortion cannot be dealt with by means of a simple prohibition alone and that the controlled letting-off of steam, as it were, by means of a limited number of indications can achieve a formal legalization but can hardly function as an effective check on the number of terminations performed; for even if in the course of the process of ascertaining an indication, the woman herself is given the opportunity to speak personally, she may hesitate before agreeing to an open and comprehensive exchange if it appears to her that the decision is predetermined and if she must fear that any of the statements that she makes in the indication-ascertainment process can be used against her later. Thus, for those who no longer wished to close their eyes to reality, there was nothing else to be done but to call off the specter of punishment and to make way for the helping hand: it became necessary for those doing the (ad)judging from above to get off their high horse, so to speak, and instead to find a way out of the conflict by means of a counseling process in which the parties involved are more or less equals. Since, in addition, it appears that this path can be traversed only in accordance with – and not against – the will of the pregnant woman, the goal of the counseling process should be to assist her in coming to a decision for which she herself carries the responsibility. To be sure, this does not mean simply pointing her in the most comfortable direction, namely, that of termination, for especially if the pregnant woman is in fact to be taken seriously as a moral person and if she wants to be taken seriously, the issue of responsibility with regard to the unborn life may not be left out of the counseling context;

---

[263] See E/K I p. 77 ff. and ESER, loc. cit. n. 1, at pp. 142 f., 173 ff.

[264] *BVerfGE* 88, 204, 264 ff. See also *supra* II.2.3.1, II.2.3.2.

[265] For details on this point as well as for a variety of counseling regulations, see the comparative legal overview, *supra* II.3.4 as well as III.1.2.2 and E/K III pp. 81 ff.

indeed, this issue must be central to the weighing-up process. In addition, counseling opens up a forum in which others who are affected by the unwanted pregnancy – and who may perhaps offer a way out of the conflict, such as the pregnant woman's partner as the father of the child or his or her parents – can be brought into the dialogue and where, finally, with an eye to the future, birth control counseling can take place.[266]

Expectations are one thing, experience another; thus, the question naturally arises as to the effectiveness of the counseling concept in practice. Information on the subject is, to be sure, not easy to come by because with an instrument as new as this one, the observation period is still much too short to have carried out sound studies. Additionally, this new concept still requires both testing and fine-tuning. Nevertheless, existing reports of experience with counseling give reason for optimism. In our attitudinal studies, for example, as yet the most comprehensive available with regard to the social counseling of pregnant woman,[267] 82.5% of the women, a great majority, expressed satisfaction with the counseling process because they felt themselves understood and accepted. This can be seen positively even if the women apparently seek out primarily those counseling services that reflect most closely their own moral approach and frequently (almost two-thirds of the women studied) the woman's goal is to acquire a certificate proving the fulfillment of the counseling requirement. In any event, even in these cases, the door to a conversation is open. This is not meaningless even for the group of pregnant woman who wanted to terminate from the very beginning and who did, in fact, terminate,[268] and who were not swayed by the counseling process from their preconceived idea. While this failure to convince is not surprising, it is even more impressive that, from the group of so-called 'conflicted' pregnancies, approximately one-third of the women who continued their pregnancies following uncertainty at the start credited the counseling process with a significant effect on their decision. The percent of women who wanted help, be it through aid to mothers and children or in the decision-making process, is also impressive: between 30% and 40%.[269]

---

[266] The legal comparative overview cited in the preceding footnote gives information regarding the extent to which these goals and aspirations have taken hold in the various counseling regulations.

[267] These consist of the study of the decision-making process of affected women by HOLZHAUER, op. cit. n. 20, at pp. 262 ff., as well as the preliminary report by HÄUSSLER and HOLZHAUER, loc. cit. n.20, at pp. 824 ff. (with conference report pp. 855 ff.). The following data are taken from these studies.

[268] For more on the three different groups of pregnant women, see *supra* IV.1.2.3, text accompanying n. 22, with additional references.

[269] See also the as a newer report on the time period 1993-1997, '15. Erhebung Beratung in anerkannten katholischen Schwangerschaftskonflikt- und Schwangerschaftsberatungs-

In addition, experiences in other countries that place more emphasis on aid and counseling than on punishment are promising. When in Sweden, for example, where in the first 12 weeks of pregnancy there is no counseling requirement, some 30% of pregnant women voluntarily take advantage of the available counseling service, this proves that there is in any case a need for counseling. Even more remarkable is the observation that, on the one hand, the overall decrease in the number of terminations among women under 20 years of age can be attributed at least in part to the high rate at which women in this age group take advantage of the availability of counseling and that, on the other hand, the increase in the termination rate among women over 30 can be correlated to the fact that members of this age group are especially unlikely to seek counseling.[270] Even if, perhaps, at first glance, the figures still seem low, only a few years after the introduction of the counseling requirement, estimates in France concerning the success rate of counseling ranged between 5% and 10%.[271] The Netherlands must also be mentioned here, where, in light of the unusually far-reaching retreat in the punishability of termination, the astonishingly low termination rate can hardly be attributed to anything other than this country's especially well-structured, obligatory counseling process.[272] Finally, even where the inadequacy of the existing counseling practice is bemoaned, as it is, for example, in Great Britain, Italy and Israel,[273] hope can be seen in the fact that demands have been made to improve the counseling service.

The same response can be given to those in Germany who would like to see greater and more rapid success in the counseling process. Although the effectiveness of the process may still leave something to be desired, this at most raises questions concerning the existing organization of the system, not, however, concerning the counseling concept as such. Thus, deficiencies in the process should not be seen as a reason to give up but rather as a motivation to improve this relatively new instrument (still in need of further refinement), which is designed to avert terminations. As I am not an expert in psychology, I am in no position to give a magic formula guaranteed to decrease the frequency of terminations: instead, I will address at this point three additional fundamental points:

---

stellen', presented by the *Deutscher Caritasverband*, according to which almost 25% of the women counseled chose to bear a child (pp. 55 ff., 145). Even if other counseling centers cannot produce comparable figures, this should be seen less as grounds for criticism and more as a challenge for them to rethink their counseling methods.

[270] See E/K I 1425 pp. 1441 f.

[271] E/K I p. 526.

[272] See E/K I pp. 1000 f., 1023 ff., 1069 ff., as well as *supra* II.3.4.3, III.1.2.2.

[273] See E/K I pp. 700 ff., 845 and II 509 f.

The first point concerns the *target group*, that is, the group upon which the counseling process should focus its attention. Recalling the three aforementioned groups of woman defined on the basis of their attitude to their pregnancy, we must accept the fact that the women of group 1, those who have already decided to terminate their pregnancies, are affected neither by the threat of punishment nor by mandatory counseling; in this respect, this group is, from the very beginning, unsuited for helping to establish the effectiveness of counseling. From the other extreme, it would be equally inappropriate to use women from the third group, those for whom pregnancy presents no conflict whatsoever, to boost the success rate of the counseling process. Thus, it is the women of group 2 to whom the greatest attention should be paid: those who experience conflict with regard to their pregnancies, who vacillate between continuation and termination and who are therefore – apparently like their counterparts in England[274] – especially in need of aid and counseling in arriving at a responsible decision. This does not mean that members of this group should be 'urged' to continue their pregnancies nor that the other two groups should be ignored completely; rather, the group-specific peculiarities must be taken into consideration both in the setting of goals as well as in the organization of the counseling process. Whereas a woman who belongs to group 1 and is thus unshakably resolved to terminate her pregnancy should be counseled primarily with regard to future birth control and whereas in the case of group 3, encouragement and support in carrying the pregnancy to term may suffice, the women of group two, women for whom the pregnancy represents a conflict, must be of primary concern: the counseling process should enable them to make a conscientious, responsible decision in which, in addition to their own concerns, their duty towards the unborn life is taken into consideration in an appropriate fashion. If indeed the effectiveness of the counseling process must be measured, this is the decisive group.

The second point was touched upon already in the previous paragraph when mention was made of the *setting of goals* for the counseling process. In this context, a tightrope must be negotiated between the capability of a woman to make her own, responsible decision and her duty to obtain counseling. On the one hand, the counseling process, although it must be oriented to the goal of continued pregnancies, must in any case remain open to all possible outcomes: were this not the case, women could not be expected to engage without fear in an open and comprehensive exchange. On the other hand, this openness with regard to the final decision does not necessarily preclude the woman's duty to be prepared to receive counseling. Although its opponents seek to discredit

---

[274] See E/K I p. 702.

mandatory counseling by naming it 'forced counseling' incompatible with the very essence of counseling, to my mind this criticism remains unpersuasive – unless, that is, the concept of counseling is diluted to such an extent that all that is left is a mere conversation whose participants are completely free to talk about whatever they want, a conversation that is entirely devoid of any formal requirements whatsoever. On the contrary, as long as the pros and cons of a particular decision as well as the possible confrontation with unpleasantries remain a part of a true counseling process, the counseling character of such an exchange does not disappear merely because the pregnant woman may not refuse to participate. However, if all objections to mandatory counseling were based on the contention that no pregnant woman should be confronted against her will with her responsibility for the unborn life, this would be an interpretation of self-determination so one-sided that it would be unacceptable in light of the fundamental claim of the unborn life to protection.[275] Furthermore, if counseling were to be put entirely at the discretion of the woman, one of the corner-stones of the counseling concept would break away. Thus, if the twin objectives are meant seriously, namely, that the child be accorded appropriate respect in the weighing-up process and that no hasty decisions be made, it should be possible to expect the pregnant woman to agree to engage in counseling. In addition, this expectation – if not contrary to the interests of the pregnant woman – applies as well to the father of the child, just as all those who might be able to contribute to a solution to the conflict should be included in the counseling process.

Furthermore, the third point to remember is that the success of the counseling concept rises and falls with the *quality of the counseling centers*. Issues such as whether the counselors should be physicians or people recruited from other professions and how the counseling center should be organized in other areas are secondary to the main requirement; namely, that pregnant women in their emergency and conflict situation feel understood and accepted and that, at the same time, the counselors' sense of responsibility for unborn life is not neglected.

Within the framework established by these three salient points, there are, of course, additional aspects whose significance for the conception and effectiveness of a counseling system cannot be underestimated. These include, most importantly, the way in which the woman's duty to obtain counseling and the duty of the state to offer counseling are structured, the determination of the subject matter to be discussed during counseling (currently, approaches around the world in this area are quite diverse), the establishment of a waiting period

---

[275] See *supra* IV.2.2.3.

between counseling and termination, and, finally, the possibility of sanctions if conditions of the counseling process are not met.[276] A more detailed explication and analysis of these kinds of points is impossible within the scope of these more fundamental reflections; besides, we are dealing here with variables that, in the last analysis, depend upon which basic concept of counseling has been adopted.[277]

2.3.3 Lawful termination of pregnancy

From a legal-ethical perspective perhaps the most essential difference between the German reform discussion and the discussion in other countries is the bitter wrangling over whether a termination in accordance with the law should be declared 'lawful' or merely 'exempt from punishment but unlawful'. Whereas in Germany this question has been treated as a matter of constitutional proportions,[278] it plays no significant role whatsoever abroad, not even in countries with a dogmatic theory of crime comparable to the German 'Verbrechens-konzept'.[279] Instead, it is almost always simply assumed – even in countries whose statutes do not directly allude to lawfulness – that a termination that is not punishable is 'permissible'.[280]

Although by coming out in support of the proposition that terminations carried out in accordance with the law be declared lawful I face the prospect of erroneous accusations of a lack of respect for unborn life, I do not want to hide my stance on this fundamental question. In so doing, however, I would like immediately to quash possible misunderstandings: This is not a question of lending support to a matter of complete indifference; indeed, in declaring an action 'lawful', a socially relevant conduct rule is established that is tantamount to a grant of permission (a 'you may', if you will) from the legal system.[281] Additionally, this declaration has its price in that the various prerequisites for lawfulness must be structured in such a way that a secular legal system can tolerate the behavior in question.

---

[276] For a taste of the variety in the structure of counseling around the world, see *supra* II.3.4.3 as well as E/K III pp. 83 ff.

[277] For my own position on how counseling should be structured, see ESER, loc. cit. n. 146, p. 104, and the joint comment of A. ESER and H.-G. KOCH, 'Plädoyer für ein 'notla-genorientiertes Diskursmodell'', in ESER and KOCH, op. cit. n. 189, pp. 162-239 at pp. 186 f. Additionally, my own preferences – which are not, however, meant to exclude equally worthy alternatives – can be inferred from the following regulation (*infra* IV.3.2).

[278] See *BVerfGE* 88, 274 ff.

[279] For details, see the comparative legal overview *supra* II.3.7.

[280] On this terminology, see also *supra* II.3.0.

[281] See generally, ESER, loc. cit. n. 155, at pp. 25-54.

As far as the question of structure – which has yet to be put into concrete terms – is concerned, it appears to me not only reasonable but in fact absolutely necessary to create a regulatory mechanism for the termination of pregnancy that enables participants in the process to see themselves as acting in a way that is not merely 'not punishable but unlawful' but rather in a way that is 'lawful'. As comprehensive arguments in favor of this possibility are presented elsewhere,[282] only three especially significant aspects will be addressed here:

First, one must free oneself of the misconception that the characterization of a particular action as 'not unlawful' is the same as according it 'socioethical approval'. Even if sociopsychological perceptions like 'morally worthy of approval' or even 'socially desirable' can be associated with the term 'lawful', these kinds of overtones are by no means inherent in the term. Rather, 'not unlawful' or 'lawful' means no more than that the individual who acts according to legally prescribed conditions acts 'in harmony with the legal order', and, thus, can do so in the unmistaken belief that his or her behavior will not be termed 'a violation of the law' or, even worse, 'criminal'. In other words, the declaration of lawfulness, as an instrument of social control, is simply a matter of demarcating an area of activity in which conduct is legal but not necessarily morally commendable.[283] Thus, a declaration that the termination of pregnancy in conformity with the law is 'lawful' in no way precludes divergent moral assessments as it preserves the option of not making use of a lawful opportunity, namely, by continuing the pregnancy.

Second, everything must be done to provide the emergency-oriented discourse and counseling approach with the legal recognition necessary for obtaining societal acceptance, presently the only approach that appears promising. In order for this to be achieved, terminations performed in conformity with the law must be rescued from the grey zone of disreputability and illegality to which – as (merely) 'counseled' terminations that are 'exempt from punishment but unlawful' – they are currently relegated: If a termination appears to be unavoidable, it must be clear that the path set out by law is the only legally practicable way. However, this characterization is internally inconsistent if the state portrays its own solution as 'unlawful'.[284]

---

[282] See ESER, op. cit. n. 159, at pp. 88 ff. See also ESER, loc. cit. n. 131, at pp. 507 f., 510.

[283] The *Reichsgericht* – unlike the *Federal Constitutional Court* – seems to have been well aware of this distinction in its landmark recognition of the medical indication as a '*supra*-statutory ground of justification:' See *RGSt* 61, pp. 242, 256 as well as KAYSSER, op. cit. n. 182, at pp. 111 ff., 154.

[284] On the necessary transparence and consistence in the behavioral message, see *supra* IV.2.1.3.

At very least, physicians are owed both clarity and freedom from contradiction. Since the interest in the protection of life is best served if terminations of pregnancy remain the responsibility of law-abiding and conscientious physicians and are not allowed to fall into the hands of medical personnel who are willing to do anything as long as they need not face the risk criminal liability, such physicians must be able to rely on their assessment of a termination as lawful if it is performed in accordance with all legal requirements.[285]

Third, the constitutional legitimacy of the regulation proposed here and its feasibility in light of criminal law doctrine must be addressed. In my opinion, constitutional jurisprudence does not present an insurmountable obstacle, as the regulation in the Act to Aid Pregnant Women and Families of 1992 concerning (merely) 'counseled' terminations that was declared unconstitutional admittedly contained only a quite rudimentary requirement for an emergency situation and therefore refinement in fact appeared to be called for.[286] The concept supported here attempts to do justice to exactly this concern in a two-pronged approach: first, by making sure that the requirement of an emergency and conflict situation that appears inescapable to the pregnant woman is expressed with sufficient clarity in the law; and, second, by ensuring a responsible and conscientious weighing-up process furthered by appropriate counseling and ensuring also that the physician be informed of the reasons for termination and thus enabled him or herself to make a responsible decision. Whether or not this concept should be treated as a legal justification, as I have proposed on the basis of a combination of substantive criteria and procedural requirements[287] and which proposal has already attracted a considerable following,[288] may be a subject for

---

[285] For additional untenable inconsistencies in and effects of the current understanding of the 'counseled' termination as 'exempt from punishment but unlawful', see A. ESER, 'Aufbruch zu neuem Weg, Halt auf halber Strecke', 76 *Kritische Vierteljahreszeitschrift für Gesetzgebung und Rechtswissenschaft,* Sonderheft 1/1993, at pp. 132-139 and ESER, loc. cit. n. 155, at pp. 25 ff.

[286] On this point, see ESER, op. cit. n. 159, at pp. 52 ff., 113 f.

[287] See ESER, op. cit. n. 159, at pp. 100 ff., 108 ff. See also ESER, loc. cit. n. 131, p. 408 and loc. cit. n. 77, § 218a margin No. 18.

[288] Namely, W. HASSEMER, Prozedurale Rechtfertigungen, in H. DÄUBLER-GMELIN et al. (eds.), *Gegenrede, Festschrift für Ernst Gottfried Mahrenholz* (Baden-Baden, Nomos 1994) pp. 731-751 at pp. 736 ff.; J. WOLTER, 'Verfassungsrechtliche Strafrechts-, Unrechts- und Schuldausschließungsgründe', 143 *Goltdammer's Archiv für Strafrecht* (1996) pp. 207-232, at pp. 226 ff.; see also W. GROPP, 'Das 2. Urteil des BVerfG zur Reform der §§ 218 ff. – ein Schritt zurück?', 141 *Goltdammer's Archiv für Strafrecht* (1994) pp. 147-163 at pp. 160 ff.; H.-J. RUDOLPHI et al., *Systematischer Kommentar zum Strafgesetzbuch, Besonderer Teil,* loose-leaf edition, 6th edn. (Luchterhand, Neuwied April 2000), § 218a margin No. 2, as well as F. MUÑOZ CONDE, 'Sterilisation of the mentally handicapped', *Law and the Human Genome Review* No. 2, January-June 1995, pp. 175-196 at pp. 190 ff.

additional debate.[289] From a legal policy perspective, at any rate, attention much be focused on viewing the unwanted pregnancy as a conflict in which the pregnant woman is less in need of threats than of help. If by means of discussion and counseling the interests of the unborn life can be served, this counseling approach must be seen as an opportunity in the interest of the pregnant woman as well. In order for her to take advantage of this mutual opportunity, she must, by fulfilling the legal requirements, be able to act in a way that is 'in accordance with the law'.

---

[289] Like, for example, debate with KAYSSER, op. cit. n. 182, at pp. 151, 156 ff., who does not fundamentally reject a procedural legal justification but who apparently finds such a justification not to go far enough since procedural grounds for legal justification – naturally – also have prerequisites and thus imply limitations that conflict with KAYSSER's thesis that there is a 'lack of criminal law competence to regulate the abortion problem' (p. 9): This is indeed not the goal pursued here – as we do not wish entirely to forego the clarification of values brought about by means of the criminal law (see *supra* IV.2.1.2).

IV.3 A PROPOSED REGULATION

Preliminary remarks

The indefinite article in the heading is no accident; indeed, it was chosen deliberately. It is meant to express the fact that there is no single true or 'right' way to regulate the termination of pregnancy[290] but rather that, depending on aspirations and preferences, regulations exhibiting a great variety in form and context are possible. Accordingly, the following proposed regulation can do no more than reflect legal policy goals, some of which are expressed directly while others, although they are in the background, are left unspoken.

While the legal policy reflections presented here could not be entirely free of subjective assessments and convictions,[291] the following proposed regulation is equally unable to claim pure objectivity or complete impartiality. Rather, as is in fact the case for all legal policy decisions as such, it is to some extent an expression of particular value judgments and life experiences. Any attempt to deny this would be either dishonest or out of touch with reality. Thus, it must be made perfectly clear from the start that this proposal is an expression of our personal opinions, opinions that are not necessarily shared by all participants in the project. It is all the more important to us to thank at this point those whose country reports gave us access to a treasure trove of comparative legal material and those whose empirical studies made possible invaluable insights: without the scholarly contributions of these participants, the development of a legal policy opinion would not have been possible. We are especially grateful to those who in the course of the project participated in legal policy discussions and who, in some cases by advocating opposing opinions, contributed to a sharpening and corroboration of our views.

It will come as no surprise that the following proposal is not entirely new; rather, it relies heavily on the discussion drafts for a revised regulation of the termination of pregnancy on the basis of a 'conflict-oriented discourse model' that were submitted for a hearing before the Bundestag's Sonderausschuss *'Schutz des ungeborenen Lebens'* [Special Committee for the Protection of Unborn Life] on 13-15 November 1991.[292]

The positions adopted on the basis of the material presented at that time were confirmed, for the most part, both by the comprehensive comparative legal cross

---

[290] On this point, see *supra* IV.2.1.

[291] See *supra* IV.

[292] ESER and KOCH, loc. cit. n. 277, at pp. 200 ff.

section as well as by post-study reflection. Thus, only a relatively small number of serious modifications were necessary – primarily with regard to the proposed maximum time limit for a termination.

3.1 Maxims and guiding principles

Although the preceding reflections could conceivably be seen as an advance legislative 'motive', the following is a summary of the essential principles and guidelines towards which the proposed regulation is geared.[293]

1. Human life is worthy and in need of legal protection even prior to birth.[294]
2. Beyond the risks and daily stresses naturally associated with pregnancy, the pregnant woman can be negatively affected in ways that are especially fraught with conflict, up to and including existential crises affecting the very fabric of her life. In its uniqueness and inescapability, the conflict resulting from the symbiotic 'duality in unity' of the pregnant woman with the child growing within her cannot be compared to other conflicts of interest.[295]
3. The resolution of the conflict by terminating the pregnancy is not simply a matter of the safeguarding of the pregnant woman's own dignity and rights; rather, it is at the same time the disposition by a third party over the fetus. As it is not purely a matter of the self-determination of the pregnant woman, the termination of a pregnancy requires justification.[296]
4. In weighing-up the conflicting interests in order to determine whether a termination is justified, it must be considered on the side of the unborn

---

[293] In addition to referring to the preceding reflections, references will also be made to the 'motive' in the aforementioned 'conflict-oriented discourse model' (*supra* n. 292), to the extent that the issues in question are treated more extensively there. The same applies to positions of legal political relevance, such as those underlying the '*Rechtsgutachten im Normenkontrollverfahren zum Schwangeren- und Familienhilfegesetz von 1992*' written in collaboration with CH. HÜLSMANN and H.-G. KOCH (ESER, op. cit. n. 159) or which were developed earlier (ESER, loc. cit. n. 146; H.-G. KOCH, 'Grundfragen einer Neuregelung des Schwangerschaftsabbruchs im vereinten Deutschland', in ESER and KOCH, op. cit. n. 146, at pp. 109-118; ESER, loc. cit. n. 189; ESER, loc. cit. n. 131).

[294] See *supra* IV.2.1.2 text accompanying nn. 20 f., IV.2.2.1, ESER, loc. cit. n. 146) pp. 98 ff.; ESER and KOCH, loc. cit. n. 277, at p. 164.

[295] See *supra* IV.2.2.1, IV.2.2.2, ESER, op. cit. n. 159, at pp. 44 ff.; ESER, loc. cit. n. 189, at pp. 227 ff.

[296] See *supra* IV.2.2.3, Eser, loc. cit. n. 146, at pp. 95 ff., ESER, op. cit. n. 159, at pp. 50 ff.; ESER and KOCH, loc. cit. n. 277, at p. 165.

that its value increases with advancing development.[297] Upon the attainment of viability, the point at which the child could also survive outside the mother's womb, a termination of pregnancy, as a rule, is prohibited.[298]

5. Protection of the unborn life to the extent it is due is a complex task that can neither be realized solely by means of criminal prohibitions nor in the absence of all criminal law backing whatsoever.[299] Thus, avoidance of unwanted pregnancy must begin with responsible birth control, and, when a pregnancy has come to pass, prevention through support and counseling must have priority over the application of criminal law.[300]

6. The goal of counseling is to enable the pregnant woman, in awareness of her responsibility, to make a conscientious decision regarding the continuation or termination of her pregnancy and if necessary to support her with appropriate measures.[301] Her social contacts and especially the man jointly responsible for creating the life in question must also be included in appropriate fashion in the counseling process.[302]

7. Not least in order to minimize its effects, the termination must be performed by a physician. On the basis of the corresponsibility that he or she shares, the physician must both counsel the pregnant woman and for purposes of the physician's own decision-making process must also require the disclosure of her grounds for terminating.[303]

8. As conduct rules that should give clear information concerning the scope of permissibility and the requirements to be fulfilled, the legal norms relating to the termination of pregnancy must be internally consistent and

---

[297] See *supra* IV.2.2.2 especially text accompanying nn. 193 ff.

[298] A possible example may be a 'vital' indication either on the part of the pregnant woman – if through the carrying of the child her life would be seriously endangered – or on the part of the child – if due to grave damage or developmental disturbances it could not survive the birth. See *supra* IV.2.2.2 especially text accompanying nn. 199 ff.

[299] Employment of criminal law in general see *supra* IV.1.4.1, ESER and KOCH, loc. cit. n. 277, at pp. 165 f.; ESER, op. cit. n. 159, at pp. 65 ff., as well as, particularly for the criminal liability (also) of the pregnant woman, *supra* IV.2.2.4, ESER and KOCH, loc. cit. n. 277, at pp. 188 f.

[300] See *supra* IV.1.3.4, IV.1.IV.4.3, 2.3.2, ESER and KOCH, loc. cit. n. 277, at pp. 182 ff.; ESER, op. cit. n. 159, at pp. 26 f., 83 ff.

[301] See *supra* IV.2.3.2, ESER, loc. cit. n. 146, at p. 104; ESER, op. cit. n. 159, at pp. 83 ff., as well as ESER, loc. cit. n. 131, at pp. 508 f.

[302] See *supra* IV.1.3.4 text accompanying nn. 79 ff., IV.2.2.4 text accompanying nn. 229 ff., ESER, loc. cit. n. 146, at p. 106.

[303] See *supra* II.5., IV.1.3.4, IV.2.2.4 text accompanying n. 221, ESER, loc. cit. n. 146, at p. 105; ESER, loc. cit. n. 189, at pp. 213, 234. For discussion on the disclosure requirement, see also ESER, op. cit. n. 159, at pp. 100 f. as well as ESER, loc. cit. n. 131, at p. 507.

may not contribute to a situation in which law-abiding individuals who fulfill in good faith all legal requirements nonetheless engage in conduct that is unlawful. Thus, the grounds for a legal termination must be structured in such a way that, when they are fulfilled, the termination is to be considered lawful.[304]

9. Justice can best be done to these various aspirations with a 'conflict-oriented discourse or counseling model'. Whereas on the one hand this model counters the erroneous assessment of a termination as a one-sided, autonomous decision of the pregnant woman (a misjudgment associated with the 'time-limit model based on self-determination') and on the other hand avoids the failure to recognize that the ultimate responsibility for a conscientious decision lies with the pregnant woman (a failure underlying the 'indication model based on third-party evaluation'), the two major achievements of the model favored here are as follows: first, it demands a weighing-up process whose determining criterion is a conflict that the pregnant woman cannot avert in any way other than through termination; and second, the belief that, to the extent medical issues are not involved, the gravity of the conflict and the undueness of the burden in terms of personal costs to the pregnant woman of expecting her to continue the pregnancy ultimately cannot be assessed in a more suitable way than by the pregnant woman herself on the basis of appropriate counseling and in the awareness of her responsibility.[305]

10. Even if a termination as such is lawful, follow-up questions concerning the reimbursement of expenses and the suitability of offering other social and insurance services remain open: the offering of such services is not out of the question as it would have to be in the case of an unlawful termination; on the other hand, neither is it a necessary consequence since in general lawful medical procedures, without more, do not necessarily result in the reimbursement of expenses. Thus, in this regard as well, the

---

[304] See *supra* IV.2.1.1, IV.2.1.3, IV.2.3.3, ESER, op. cit. n. 159, at pp. 88 ff. and ESER, loc. cit. n. 131, at p. 510.

[305] For discussion of the tripartition and the various functions and effects of these regulatory models, see generally *supra* II.2.4.3 C-E, IV.1.3.3, ESER, loc. cit. n. 146, at pp. 92 ff.; KOCH, loc. cit. n. 293, at pp. 112 f.; ESER and KOCH, loc. cit. n. 277, at pp. 167 ff. For discussion concentrating on the weaknesses of the indication model, see *supra* IV.1.4.3, IV.2.3.1, ESER, loc. cit. n. 146, at pp. 97 ff., ESER, op. cit. n. 159, at pp. 74 ff., ESER, loc. cit. n. 189, at pp. 231 ff. For discussion favoring the discourse model, see ESER, loc. cit. n. 146, at pp. 103 ff., ESER, op. cit. n. 159, at pp. 82 f., ESER, loc. cit. n. 131, at pp. 507 f.; ESER and KOCH, loc. cit. n. 277, at pp. 171 ff.

regulatory model recommended here retains a large degree of legislative discretion.[306]

Plainly, the preceding maxims and guiding principles are formulated in such a way as to preserve for lawmakers a great deal of latitude in their legislative endeavors. This approach was taken already in the aforementioned submission to the Parliamentary Committee for the Protection of Unborn Life.[307] The three separate discussion drafts submitted to the committee had in common that, with regard to the termination of pregnancy, all were based on the same basic maxims and guiding principles as appear here. From a technical statutory perspective, however, the three drafts remained true to different degrees to embodiment in the criminal code itself. Moreover, Discussion Draft 1 addressed the protection of embryos outside the womb in addition to the issue of the termination of pregnancy, Discussion Draft 2 made due with a blanket criminal norm, and Discussion Draft 3 could be seen as part of a more far-reaching law regulating broader issues of reproductive medicine.[308] In contrast, the following proposal – commensurate with the goal of this project – is limited to the regulation of the termination of pregnancy. This limitation is not meant, however, as a rejection of a possible inclusion in a more comprehensive law protecting life or a law encompassing the entire spectrum of human sexuality and reproduction. In addition, more than did the previous proposals, this proposal places value on informing citizens by means of direct conduct rules – not merely by means of indirect messages that must be inferred from the definitional elements of a crime – of how they should behave in order for their actions to be in line with the legal order. Nonetheless, it goes without saying that 'may' can not be understood as a recommendation and certainly is not meant as 'must'. In an equally differentiated way, this proposal, like the previous drafts, provides criminal provisions that apply specifically to each of the three roles a person may play in the termination of a pregnancy (pregnant woman, physician or third party).[309]

Although the influence, both substantive and procedural, by the German background and experience on this proposed regulation is undeniable, the proposal may nevertheless provide food for thought to other legal systems as well.

---

[306] See *supra* IV.2.1.3, text accompanying n. 158; ESER, op. cit. n. 159, at pp. 95 ff. – For discussion of additional 'supporting' measures, see KOCH, loc. cit. n. 293, at pp. 116 f.; ESER and KOCH, loc. cit. n. 277, at pp. 190 ff.

[307] See *supra* n. 292.

[308] For details, see ESER and KOCH, loc. cit. n. 277, at pp. 177 ff., 200 ff.

[309] For more on the various demands depending upon the norm addressee, see – in addition to the sources cited in n. 304 to guiding principle 8 – ESER, loc. cit. n. 155.

3.2 Proposal of a law to regulate the termination of pregnancy [310]

§ 1 Area of application

(1) Termination of pregnancy within the meaning of this law is the ending of a pregnancy after the completed implantation of the fertilized egg in the uterus [with the goal and] in such a way that the prenatal life will die in the womb or, as a result of the intervention, will not stay alive outside the womb.
(2) Termination of pregnancy shall not be considered a method of birth control equivalent to the prevention of conception.

§ 2 General prohibition

Termination of a pregnancy is punishable and is permissible only [by way of exception] under the following conditions [listed in § 3].

§ 3 Conditional permissibility of the medical termination of pregnancy

(1) A termination carried out by a physician with the consent of the pregnant woman prior to the end of the twelfth week of pregnancy is permitted [allowed, lawful/not unlawful], if
1. the pregnant woman considers herself to be in an emergency or conflict situation that appears to her [even] after [despite] counseling in accordance with § 4 and a subsequent reflection period of a minimum of three days to be an undue burden that cannot be resolved any other way, and
2. the physician has required disclosure of the request of the pregnant woman and her reasons for the termination [and has discussed them with her].
(2) The same applies until the child has attained viability in the event that
1. according to medical findings, the termination of the pregnancy, bearing in mind the current and future life situation of the pregnant woman [or on account of the expectation of grave damage to or developmental disorder of the child][311] is indicated in order to avert the risk of a serious infringe-

---

[310] In the following, unless otherwise indicated text appearing in brackets is to be seen as an equally acceptable alternative.

[311] The decision to include this alternative in the law depends to a great extent on whether, for sociopsychological reasons, one wishes to avoid any appearance whatsoever of discrimination against disabled life – as was the case in the German reform of 1995, which expunged the embryopathic indication and assimilated it into the medical-social indication of the current § 218a Par. 2 StGB (and which I favored at that time: see ESER, loc. cit. n. 131,

ment upon the physical or mental health of the pregnant woman and the risk cannot be averted in any other way without unduly burdening her,[312] and

2. the aforementioned prerequisites have been stated in writing by a physician other than the one performing the termination and presented to the latter prior to the carrying out of the termination.

(3) If on the basis of medical findings it can be assumed that the child could already remain alive outside the womb, the termination is permissible only if

1. a) continuation of the pregnancy creates a serious risk to the life of the pregnant woman or

   b) on account of extremely grave damage or developmental disorders the child would not survive its birth, and

2. the aforementioned prerequisites have been stated in writing by two medical specialists, who are independent of the physician performing the procedure and who have appropriate qualifications, and submitted to the physician performing the procedure prior to its performance.

§ 4 Mandatory counseling

(1) In order to clarify for herself whether there is an emergency or conflict situation within the meaning of § 3 par. 1, a pregnant woman who wishes to undergo a termination is required to obtain counseling from a qualified counselor in a personal conversation in accordance with the following principles.

1. Counseling serves to protect the unborn life and to care for the pregnant woman. Counseling should enable her to make her own responsible decision in which, in addition to her personal concerns obligation to the unborn life finds due consideration. As part of a comprehensive discussion of the current and future circumstances of her life, all help that is in fact available and that could be of importance in the elimination of the emergency or conflict situation caused by the pregnancy should be presented to her and, if necessary and possible, procured. Counseling should also contribute to the avoidance of unwanted pregnancies in the future.

---

at p. 509) – or whether, in light of experience gathered in the meanwhile, it would not indeed be better, both as an acknowledgment of reality as well as for the sake of clarity, to name explicitly the damage to the child as a possible factor contributing, in the final analysis, to the undueness of the burden on the pregnant woman of a continued pregnancy and, through emphasis of the latter, to counteract the impression that the expected pathology of the embryo, in and of itself, is a sufficient reason to terminate.

[312] Since these prerequisites may also be satisfied in the case of an unlawfully forced pregnancy, an additional criminological indication appears to be unnecessary.

2. Counseling may be conducted by a recognized counseling center or a physician recognized as a counselor in accordance with this provision who will not him/herself carry out the termination.
3. Counseling must take place at least three days prior to the intervention being considered.
4. If the pregnant woman agrees, additional persons are to be incorporated into the counseling process to the extent possible, like, namely, the man whose co-responsibility stems from the conception.
5. At the request of the pregnant woman, the counselor must immediately confirm in a dated writing that counseling has taken place.
6. The [competent] government minister will be empowered to regulate by means of ministerial orders additional details regarding: goals, content and form of counseling; the support available to the pregnant woman, should she take advantage of public and private sources of help for pregnant women, families and mothers and children; public support of counseling centers; as well as the requirements for the recognition of counselors.

(2) In cases of § 3 par. 2 [termination indicated on the basis of the expected grave damage to the child], the pregnant woman must be offered the opportunity to consult with a specialist.

§ 5 Consent

The consent of the pregnant woman in accordance with the following principles is a prerequisite for the performance of a termination:
1. The pregnant woman must consent in writing after consultation with a physician and after being informed of the significance and the risks of the intervention.
2. In addition to the consent of a pregnant woman who, at the time of the intervention is not yet sixteen years old, the consent of [one of] her legal guardian[s] is also necessary. This requirement can be waived only if the counselor within the meaning of § 4 par. 1 No. 2 has confirmed in writing to the physician performing the termination that the participation of her legal guardian[s] would injure in an especially lasting way those concerns of the pregnant woman that are worthy of protection or if, in a case of § 3 par. 2 or 3, the statement of her legal guardian[s] cannot be acquired in time.
3. If the pregnant woman is unable to comprehend the significance and the risks of the termination, a termination may only be undertaken to avert the risk of death or grave damage to the health of the pregnant woman and only with the written consent of her legal guardian[s]. In such cases the

pregnant woman herself must be instructed in a manner commensurate with her abilities.

§ 6 Performance in an appropriate facility

The termination of a pregnancy may only be undertaken in a hospital or in a recognized facility. The [competent] minister will be empowered to regulate by means of ministerial order the requirements that such a facility must satisfy. In so doing, especial care must be taken to insure appropriate medical care for the pregnant woman and to guarantee the reliability of the operator of the facility.

§ 7 Punishability of the non-medical termination of pregnancy

(1) Anyone who terminates a pregnancy without being admitted to the practice of medicine will be punished by imprisonment of up to three years or a fine.

(2) In especially serious cases, the punishment is imprisonment from six months to five years. A case is especially serious if the offender
1. acts without the consent of the pregnant woman
2. recklessly causes the risk of death or grave injury to the health of the pregnant woman.

(3) If the offender acts contrary to the [expressed] intent of the pregnant woman or exploits her lack of capacity, imprisonment is from one year to ten years.

(4) The attempt is punishable.

§ 8 Punishability of the physician

(1) A physician who, in the absence of the fulfillment of the prerequisites of § 3 par. 2, terminates a pregnancy within twelve weeks of conception without the pregnant woman having
1. consented in accordance with § 5,
2. proven that she was counseled at least three days prior to the termination in accordance with § 4, or
3. presented [and explained] her reasons for considering herself to be in an emergency or conflict situation within the meaning of § 3 par. 1
will be punished by imprisonment up to three years or a fine.

(2) The same applies to the case in which after twelve weeks have passed since conception a physician terminates the pregnancy in the absence of the fulfillment of the prerequisites of § 3 par. 2 or 3.

(3) If the offender acts contrary to the [expressed] intent of the pregnant

woman or exploits her lack of capacity, imprisonment is from one year to ten years.

(4) The attempt is punishable.

(5) A physician who despite better knowledge makes an incorrect determination under § 3 par. 2 No. 2 or par. 3 No. 2 will be punished by imprisonment up to two years or a fine.

(6) A physician who performs a termination otherwise permissible somewhere other than in a hospital or a recognized facility, commits a regulatory offense. The regulatory offense can be sanctioned with a monetary penalty of up to DM 10,000.

§ 9 Punishability of the pregnant woman

(1) The pregnant woman is punishable only to the extent that
1. she terminates the pregnancy herself or allows it to be terminated by a third party not admitted to the practice of medicine,
2. prior to the passage of twelve weeks following conception she allows the pregnancy to be terminated by a physician without having obtained counseling in accordance with § 4 at least three days prior to the intervention (punishability in this case applies only if the prerequisites of § 3 par. 2 are not fulfilled) or
3. subsequent to the passage of twelve weeks following conception she allows the pregnancy to be terminated in the absence of the fulfillment of the prerequisites of § 3 par. 2 or 3.

(2) The punishment is imprisonment up to one year or fine. The court can dispense with punishment entirely if, at the time of the intervention, the pregnant woman was under great pressure.

(3) The attempt is not punishable for the woman.

§ 10 The reporting requirement for statistical purposes

A physician who has performed a termination within the meaning of this law has until the end of the current calendar quarter to provide information concerning
1. the reason for the termination,
2. the marital status of the pregnant woman as well as the number of children in her care,
3. the number of previous pregnancies and how they ended,
4. the duration of the terminated pregnancy,
5. the type of intervention and observed complications,

6. the location where the intervention took place and in the event of a hospital stay the duration thereof, as well as

7. the first three digits of the postal code of the pregnant woman's place of legal residence or, if applicable, the foreign country in which the pregnant woman has legal or habitual residence

to the [competent] bureau of statistics. The name of the pregnant woman may not be reported.

§ 11 Right to refuse

No one can be required to participate in the termination of a pregnancy. This does not apply if participation is necessary to prevent the risk to the woman of death or grave injury to health that cannot be averted in any other way.

Appendices

Appendix A: Country Reports   309

Appendix B: Publications   311

APPENDIX A
LIST OF COUNTRY REPORTS

Volume 1: European countries

Austria	1079; *743*
Belgium	383; *667*
Bulgaria	1667; *675*
ČSSR/Slovakia/Czech Republic	
	1667; *787; 803*
Denmark	1383; *683*
Finland	1383; *691*
France	475; *699*
German Democratic Republic	
	325
Germany, Federal Republic of	
	17; *629*
Great Britain	623; *713*
Greece	573
Hungary	1667; *807*
Ireland	759; *721*
Italy	799
Luxembourg	953
Netherlands	991; *735*
Norway	1383; *739*
Poland	1161; *747*
Portugal	1247; *761*
Romania	1325; *767*
Soviet Union/Russia	1551; *771*
Spain	1621; *791*
Sweden	1383; *777*
Switzerland	1483; *783*
Yougoslavia/Croatia	891; *731*

Volume 2: Non-European countries

Algeria	1119
Argentina	1187
Australia	63; *825*
Bahrain	1119
Brasilia	133; *833*
Canada	593; *863*

Chile	1187; *845*
China, People's Republic of	
	213; *837*
Colombia	*845*
Costa Rica	261/1187
Ecuador	1187
Egypt	15/1119
Ghana	335
India	385; *849*
Iraq	425
Israel	463
Japan	537; *857*
Jordan	1119
Kuwait	1119
Lebanon	1119
Libya	1119; *820*
Mali	1297
Mexico	661/1187
Morocco	1119
Nigeria	1297
Oman	1119
Peru	1187; *846*
Qatar	1119
Saudi Arabia	1119; *820*
Senegal	1297
South Africa	729; *871*
Sudan	1119; *822*
Syria	1119
Taiwan	175
Tunisia	897/1119
Turkey	835
United Arab Emirates	1119
United States of America	949; *881*
Uruguay	1187
Yemen	1119; *819*
Zambia	1297; *869*

---

* Numbers in normal script: page numbers of the country report in E/K I or II; numbers in italics: page number of the update in the appendix to E/K III.

APPENDIX B

PROJECT-RELATED PUBLICATIONS BY THE MAX-PLANCK-INSTITUTE
FOR FOREIGN AND INTERNATIONAL CRIMINAL LAW*

ESER, ALBIN/KOCH, HANS-GEORG (Hrsg.): Schwangerschaftsabbruch im internationalen Vergleich. Rechtliche Regelungen – Soziale Rahmenbedingungen – Empirische Grunddaten, Teil 1: Europa, 1744 Seiten, Baden-Baden 1988; Teil 2: Außereuropa, 1353 Seiten, Baden-Baden 1989. Rechtsvergleichende Untersuchungen zur gesamten Strafrechtswissenschaft, 3. Folge, Bände 21.1 und 21.2.

– Schwangerschaftsabbruch im internationalen Vergleich, Teil 3: Rechtsvergleichender Querschnitt – Rechtspolitische Schlußbetrachtungen – Dokumentation zur neueren Rechtsentwicklung, 932 Seiten, Baden-Baden 1999. Rechtsvergleichende Untersuchungen zur gesamten Strafrechtswissenschaft, 3. Folge, Band 21.3.

AHRENDTS, KATHARINA: Bayerischer Abweg im Abtreibungsrecht, Forum Recht 4 (1996), S. 136.

– Einstweiliges Ende des bayerischen Abwegs im Abtreibungsrecht, Forum Recht 4 (1997), S. 139.

ALBRECHT, HANS-JÖRG: Schwangerschaftsabbruch – Empirische Untersuchungen zur Implementation der strafrechtlichen Regulierung des Schwangerschaftsabbruchs, in: A. ESER/G. KAISER/E. WEIGEND (Hrsg.), Zweites deutsch-polnisches Kolloquium über Strafrecht und Kriminologie, Baden-Baden 1986, S. 195-223. – In polnischer Übersetzung: Studia Prawnicze 1985, S. 295-317.

ARNOLD, HARALD/GEISSLER, ISOLDE: Bericht über das Kolloquium 'Die Implementation des reformierten § 218 StGB – Empirische Untersuchungen zu Einstellung und Verhalten von Schwangeren und Ärzten', Zeitschrift für die gesamte Strafrechtswissenschaft 100 (1988), S. 855-870.

ESER, ALBIN: Reform der Schwangerschaftsunterbrechung, Die Medizinische Welt 1971, S. 238-253.

– Schwangerschaftsabbruch in der strafrechtlichen Diskussion, Theologische Quartalsschrift 151 (1971/3), S. 238-253.

– Aspekte eines Strafrechtlers zur Abtreibungsreform, in: D. HOFMANN (Hrsg.), Schwangerschaftsunterbrechung, Frankfurt/Main 1974, S. 117-177.

– Kommentierung der §§ 218-219d (Schwangerschaftsabbruch), in: A. SCHÖNKE/H. SCHRÖDER, StGB, München 17. Aufl. 1975 bis 26. Aufl. 2001.

– Zwischen 'Heiligkeit' und 'Qualität' des Lebens. Zu Wandlungen im strafrechtlichen Lebensschutz, in: J. GERNHUBER (Hrsg.), Tradition und Fortschritt im Recht. Festschrift zum 500jährigen Bestehen der Tübinger Juristenfakultät, Tübingen 1977, S. 377-414.

– Recht und Praxis des Schwangerschaftsabbruchs, Sexualpädagogik und Familienplanung 9 (1981), S. 27-29.

---

* Publications in English are italicized.

Eser, Albin: Schwangerschaftsabbruch im Ausland. Ein rechtsvergleichender Überblick, in: H. Müller/H. Olbing (Hrsg.), Ethische Probleme in der Pädiatrie, München 1982, S. 64-73.

– Konzeptionsverhütung und Schwangerschaftsabbruch bei geistig behinderten Adoleszentinnen aus rechtlicher Sicht, in: H. Müller/H. Olbing (Hrsg.), Ethische Probleme in der Pädiatrie, München 1982, S. 105-123.

– Ärztliches Handeln gegen den erklärten oder mutmaßlichen Willen der Eltern – Juristische Gesichtspunkte, in: H. Müller/H. Olbing (Hrsg.), Ethische Probleme in der Pädiatrie, München 1982, S. 178-187.

– Reform des Schwangerschaftsabbruchs im Strafrecht der Bundesrepublik Deutschland: Entwicklung und gegenwärtiger Stand, in: A. Eser/G. Kaiser/E. Weigend (Hrsg.), Zweites deutsch-polnisches Kolloquium über Strafrecht und Kriminologie, Baden-Baden 1986, S. 123-151. – In polnischer Fassung in: Studia Prawnicze 1985, S. 266-293; in griechischer Fassung in: Poinika Chronika 36 (Athen 1986), S. 545-564; *in englischer Fassung in: The National Review of Criminal Sciences, Kairo 1987, S. 247-287;* in spanischer Fassung in: J.L. de la Cuesta/I. Dendaluze/E. Echeburúa (Hrsg.), Criminología y Derecho Penal al Servicio de la Persona, San Sebastián 1989, S. 719-739.

– *Contraception and Abortion in Mentally Handicapped Female Adolescents Under German Law, in: A. Carmi/S. Schneider/A. Hefez (Hrsg.), Psychiatry, Law and Ethics. Medicolegal Library, Berlin 1986, S. 268-272.*

– *Reform of German Abortion Law: First Experiences, The American Journal of Comparative Law, Vol. 34 (1986), S. 369-383.*

– Neuartige Bedrohungen ungeborenen Lebens: Embryoforschung und 'Fetozid' in rechtsvergleichender Perspektive. Schriftenreihe der Juristischen Studiengesellschaft Karlsruhe, Heft 187, Heidelberg 1990, 74 S.

– Beginn des menschlichen Lebens: Rechtsvergleichende Aspekte zum Status des Embryos, in: Ch. Fuchs (Hrsg.), Möglichkeiten und Grenzen der Forschung an Embryonen, Stuttgart 1990, S. 113-125.

– Zwischenergebnisse aus einem internationalen Vergleich zum Schwangerschaftsabbruch, in: Dokumentation des Workshops: 'Wie geht es weiter mit dem § 218?' der Fraktion der SPD im Deutschen Bundestag, Bonn 1990, S. 11-32.

– Schwangerschaftsabbruch: Zwischenergebnisse eines internationalen Vergleiches, in: S. Heil (Hrsg.), § 218 – Ein Grenzfall des Rechts, Tutzinger Materialien Nr. 68 (1991), S. 63-72.

– Die Wirkung von Fristen und Indikationen, Frankfurter Allgemeine Zeitung Nr. 163 vom 17.7.1991.

– *The Legal Status of the Embryo in Comparative Perspective, in: 9th World Congress on Medical Law, Proceedings, Vol. I, Gent 1991, S. 301-312.*

– Schwangerschaftsabbruch zwischen Grundwertorientierung und Strafrecht – Eine rechtspolitische Überlegungsskizze, Zeitschrift für Rechtspolitik 24 (1991), S. 291-298. – Auch veröffentlicht in: Arzt und Christ, Vierteljahresschrift für medizinisch-ethische Grundfragen 37 (1991), S. 231-246.

– Amenazas a la vida humana en su comienzo: Problemas básicos en la interrupción del embarazo, inseminación artificial y 'reducción de los embarazos múltiples por feticidio' (Bedrohungen menschlichen Lebens an seinem Beginn: Zu Grundsatzproblemen bei Schwangerschaftsabbruch, künstlicher Fortpflanzung und 'Mehrlingsreduktion durch Fetozid'). Cuadernos del Consejo General del Poder Judicial, Jornadas sobre la 'Reforma del Derecho Penal en Alemania', Madrid 1991, S. 5-17.

ESER, ALBIN: Neuregelung des Schwangerschaftsabbruchs vor dem Hintergrund des Embryonenschutzgesetzes. Gedanken zur Vermeidung von Wertungswidersprüchen, in: H. BIELEFELD/W. BRUGGER/K. DICKE (Hrsg.), Würde und Recht des Menschen. Festschrift für Johannes Schwartländer zum 70. Geburtstag, Würzburg 1992, S. 183-198.

– Zur Rechtsnatur der 'Allgemeinen Notlagenindikation' zum Schwangerschaftsabbruch. Kritische Bemerkungen zum Urteil des BayObLG vom 26. April 1990, in: K. GEPPERT/J. BOHNERT/R. RENGIER (Hrsg.), Festschrift für Rudolf Schmitt zum 70. Geburtstag, Tübingen 1992, S. 171-186.

– 'Ärztliche Erkenntnis' und richterliche Überprüfung bei Indikation zum Schwangerschaftsabbruch nach § 218a StGB. Kritische Bemerkungen zum BayObLG-Urteil vom 26.4.1990, unter Berücksichtigung des BGH-Urteils vom 3.12.1991, in: G. ARZT (Hrsg.), Festschrift für Jürgen Baumann zum 70. Geburtstag, Bielefeld 1992, S. 155-181. – Vorveröffentlichung in: Juristenzeitung 1991, S. 1003-1014.

– Gustav Radbruchs Vorstellungen zum Schwangerschaftsabbruch: Ein noch heute 'moderner' Beitrag zur aktuellen Reformdiskussion, in: M. SEEBODE (Hrsg.), Festschrift für Günter Spendel zum 70. Geburtstag, Berlin-New York 1992, S. 152-177.

– Stellungnahmen in der Öffentlichen Anhörung des Sonderausschusses 'Schutz des ungeborenen Lebens' am 14.11.1991, in: Zur Sache – Themen parlamentarischer Beratung: Schutz des ungeborenen Lebens, 1/92, Bonn 1992, S. 243-245; 262-264; 293-294; 318-328; 461-514. – Auch veröffentlicht in: J. BAUMANN u.a. (Hrsg.), § 218 StGB im vereinten Deutschland. Die Gutachten der strafrechtlichen Sachverständigen im Anhörungsverfahren des Deutschen Bundestages, Tübingen 1992, S. 21-69.

– Das neue Schwangerschaftsabbruchsstrafrecht auf dem Prüfstand, Neue Juristische Wochenschrift 1992, S. 2913-2925. – In japanischer Fassung in: The Doshisha Law Review 227 (1992), S. 121-167.

– Aufbruch zu neuem Weg – Halt auf halber Strecke. Erste Einschätzungen zum Schwangerschafts-Urteil des BVerfG vom 28.5.1993, in: Das Urteil zu § 218 StGB – in Wortlaut und Kommentar, Kritische Vierteljahresschrift für Gesetzgebung und Rechtswissenschaft, Baden-Baden, Sonderheft 1/1993, S. 132-139.

– Schwangerschaftsabbruch: Zwischenergebnisse eines internationalen Vergleichs, in: Festschrift für Prof. Dr. Hae-Mock Sonn, Seoul 1993, S. 665-678.

– Strafrechtliche Stellungnahme, in: § 218 Urteil des Bundesverfassungsgerichts – Probleme und Konsequenzen. Gesundheitspolitische Gespräche Schering, Heft 15 (1994), S. 11-14; 30-40; 44-48; 53-55; 59.

– *Abortion Law Reform in Germany in International Comparative Perspective, in: European Journal of Health Law 1 (1994), S. 15-34. – In spanischer Fassung in: Actualidad Penal No. 4, Madrid 1994, S. 55-71; in japanischer Fassung in: The Doshisha Law Review 248 (1996), S. 1-63.*

– Schwangerschaftsabbruch: Reformversuche in Umsetzung des BVerfG-Urteils, Juristenzeitung 1994, S. 503-510.

– Indikationslösung, in: Lexikon für Theologie und Kirche, Band 5, Freiburg 1996, S. 470.

– (unter Mitarbeit von CHRISTOPH HÜLSMANN und HANS-GEORG KOCH): Schwangerschaftsabbruch: Auf dem verfassungsrechtlichen Prüfstand. Rechtsgutachten im Normenkontrollverfahren zum Schwangeren- und Familienhilfegesetz von 1992, Baden-Baden 1994, 120 Seiten.

ESER, ALBIN: Schwangerschaftsabbruch: Rechtlich, in: W. KORFF/L. BECK/P. MIKAT (Hrsg.), Lexikon der Bioethik, Band 3, Gütersloh 1998, S. 267-274.

–   'Wertebewußtsein schaffen'. Ein Gespräch zur Diskussion über die Schwangerschafts-beratung, in: J. REITER (Hrsg.), Der Schein des Anstoßes. Schwangerschaftskonflikt-beratung nach dem Papstbrief, Freiburg 1999, S. 126-135.

–   Auf der Suche nach dem mittleren Weg: Zwischen Fundamentalismus und Be-liebigkeit, in: M. LANGER/A. LASCHET (Hrsg.), Unterwegs mit Visionen. Festschrift für Rita Süssmuth, Freiburg 2002, S. 117-139.

ESER, ALBIN/HIRSCH, HANS A. (unter Mitarbeit von HANS-GEORG KOCH): Sterilisation und Schwangerschaftsabbruch. Eine Orientierungshilfe zu medizinischen, psychologischen und rechtlichen Fragen. Reihe 'Medizin und Recht', Band 10, Stuttgart 1980, 317 Seiten. – Darin als Autor: Sterilisation in rechtlicher und rechtspolitischer Sicht, S. 55-68; Schwangerschaftsabbruch: Der rechtliche Rahmen, S. 105-126; Beratung der Schwangeren: Rechtsgrundlagen und Rahmen, S. 127-136; Indikation zum Schwangerschaftsabbruch, S. 160-170; Sterilisation und Schwangerschaftsabbruch im Ausland, S. 245-249.

ESER, ALBIN/KOCH, HANS-GEORG: Schriftliche Stellungnahme zur Anhörung im Bundesrat über die Neuregelung des Schwangerschaftsabbruchs am 17.4.1991 in Berlin, in: Bundesrat (Hrsg.), Dokumentation 'Neuregelung des Schwangerschaftsrechts'. Öffentliche Anhörung des Ausschusses für Jugend, Familie, Frauen und Gesundheit des Bundesrates am 17. April 1991 in Berlin, Bonn 1991, S. 38-53; 199-202; 259; 282-285.

–   Plädoyer für ein 'notlagenorientiertes Diskursmodell', in: J. BAUMANN/H.-L. GÜNTHER/ R. KELLER/TH. LENCKNER (Hrsg.), § 218 StGB im vereinten Deutschland. Die Gutachten der strafrechtlichen Sachverständigen im Anhörungsverfahren des Deutschen Bundestages, Tübingen 1992, S. 21-79.

–   Schwangerschaftsabbruch: Auf dem Weg zu einer Neuregelung. Gesammelte Studien und Vorschläge, Baden-Baden 1992, 249 Seiten.

GROPP, WALTER: § 218a StGB als Rechtfertigungsgrund: Grundfragen zum rechtmäßigen Schwangerschaftsabbruch, Goltdammer's Archiv für Strafrecht 1988, S. 1-32.

HÄUSSLER-SCZEPAN, MONIKA: Der Arzt als Implementationsträger und Normadressat: Sank-tionsdrohung und Generalprävention im Rahmen der §§ 218 ff. StGB, in: G. Kaiser/ H. Kury/H.-J. Albrecht (Hrsg.), Kriminologische Forschung in den 80er Jahren, Freiburg 1988, S. 43-62.

–   *Abortion from the perspective of the medical profession. An empirical survey of the attitude of gynecological practitioners to abortion and its statutory regulation, in: G. KAISER/I. GEISSLER (Hrsg.), Crime and Criminal Justice, Freiburg 1988, S. 15-30.*

–   Schwangerschaftsabbruch im Urteil der Gynäkologen, Deutsches Ärzteblatt 1988, S. 1011-1014.

–   Arzt und Schwangerschaftsabbruch. Eine empirische Untersuchung zur Implemen-tation des reformierten § 218 StGB. Reihe 'Kriminologische Forschungsberichte', Band 39, Freiburg 1989, 291 Seiten.

HÄUSSLER-SCZEPAN, MONIKA/HOLZHAUER, BRIGITTE: § 218: Gut beraten, Psychologie heute 15 (1988), S. 15-16.

HÄUSSLER-SCZEPAN, MONIKA/HOLZHAUER, BRIGITTE: Die Implementation der reformierten §§ 218 f. StGB. Empirische Untersuchungen zu Einstellung und Verhalten von Ärzten und schwangeren Frauen, Zeitschrift für die gesamte Strafrechtswissenschaft 100 (1988), S. 817-854.

– Beratung nach § 218: Hürdenlauf oder Hilfestellung?, Pro Familia Magazin 1988, S. 22-26.

HEINEMANN, NICOLA: Frau und Fötus in der Prä- und Perinatalmedizin aus strafrechtlicher Sicht, Baden-Baden 2000.

HOLZHAUER, BRIGITTE: Der Verfahrensweg nach § 218 StGB im Licht der Erfahrungen betroffener Frauen, in: G. KAISER/H. KURY/H.-J. ALBRECHT (Hrsg.), Kriminologische Forschung in den 80er Jahren, Freiburg 1988, S. 23-42.

– *Abortion: Attitudes and Decision-Making, in: G. KAISER/I. GEISSLER (Hrsg.), Crime and Criminal Justice, Freiburg 1988, S. 31-48.*

– Schwangerschaft und Schwangerschaftsabbruch. Die Rolle des § 218 StGB bei der Entscheidungsfindung betroffener Frauen. Reihe 'Kriminologische Forschungsberichte', Band 38, Freiburg 1989, 436 Seiten (2., unveränderte Auflage 1991).

HUBER, BARBARA: Termination of Pregnancy Law – An Unresolved Problem of the German Criminal Code of 1975, South African Journal of Criminal Law and Criminology 8 (1984), S. 31-43.

HÜLSMANN, CHRISTOPH: Indikationsfeststellung zum Schwangerschaftsabbruch – eine staatliche Aufgabe? Kritische Bemerkungen zur herkömmlichen Interpretation des BVerfG-Urteils vom 25. Februar 1975, Strafverteidiger 12 (1992), S. 78-86.

– Produktion und Reduktion von Mehrlingen. Aspekte einer Folgeerscheinung medizinisch unterstützter Fortpflanzung aus strafrechtlicher und rechtspolitischer Perspektive. Reihe 'Medizin in Recht und Ethik', Band 27, Stuttgart 1992, 310 Seiten.

– Fetozid: Bemerkungen aus strafrechtlicher Sicht, Neue Juristische Wochenschrift 1992, S. 2331-2338.

– 'Produktion' und 'Reduktion' höhergradiger Mehrlingsschwangerschaften in strafrechtlicher Perspektive, Zeitschrift für Geburtshilfe und Frauenheilkunde 52 (1992), S. 570-573.

– Strafrechtliche Aspekte höhergradiger Mehrlingsschwangerschaften – Zugleich ein kritischer Beitrag zum Embryonenschutzgesetz, Juristenzeitung 1992, S. 1106-1114.

– Produktion und Reduktion höhergradiger Mehrlingsschwangerschaften, in: V. SCHUBERT-LEHNHARDT (Hrsg.), Tagungsmaterialien des Medizin-ethischen Seminars 'Ethik zwischen Anspruch und Wirklichkeit' der Martin-Luther-Universität Halle/Wittenberg vom 27.6.1992.

– Mehrlingsschwangerschaft und Fetozid im Lichte des Strafrechts, Der Frauenarzt 34 (1993), S. 55-61.

JEROUSCHEK, GÜNTER: Lebensschutz und Lebensbeginn. Kulturgeschichte des Abtreibungsverbots. Reihe 'Medizin in Recht und Ethik', Band 17, Stuttgart 1988, 331 Seiten.

KAISER, GÜNTHER: Was wissen wir über den Schwangerschaftsabbruch? Ergebnisse eines empirischen Forschungsprojekts, in: Aus Politik und Zeitgeschichte, Beilage zur Wochenzeitung Das Parlament B 14/90 (1990) vom 30.3.1990, S. 21-31.

KOCH, HANS-GEORG: § 218: Diskussion ohne Ende, Schleswig-Holsteinisches Ärzteblatt 38 (1985), S. 75-76.

– Recht und Praxis des Schwangerschaftsabbruchs im internationalen Vergleich. Rechtsvergleichende Anmerkungen zur aktuellen politischen Diskussion, Zeitschrift für die gesamte Strafrechtswissenschaft 97 (1985), S. 1043-1073.

Koch, Hans-Georg: *Law and Practice of Abortion in an International Comparison, in: The National Review of Criminal Sciences, Kairo 1987, S. 289-328.*
– Schwangerschaftsabbruch und Recht in Europa, EG-magazin 1988, S. 10-11.
– Prävention statt Repression, Der Deutsche Arzt 39 (1989), Nr. 6, S. 10.
– Prävention statt Repression, Schwangerschaftsabbruch und Recht in Europa, Der Deutsche Arzt 39 (1989), Nr. 6, S. 10.
– *German Reunification and the abortion law, Planned Parenthood in Europe 19 (1990), Heft 2, S. 4.*
– Recht des Schwangerschaftsabbruchs – Ein Blick über die Grenzen, in: A. Hauner/ E. Reichardt (Hrsg.), § 218: Zur aktuellen Diskussion, München 1992, S. 39-65 (erschienen 1991).
– Editorial: Neuregelung des Schwangerschaftsabbruchs, Ethik in der Medizin 4 (1992), S. 1-3.
– Stellungnahmen zu Fragen der Neuregelung des Schwangerschaftsabbruchs, in: Zur Sache – Themen parlamentarischer Beratung 1/1992, S. 245-247; 270-271; 285-286.
– Das deutsche Embryonenschutzgesetz vom 13.12.1990, Journal für Fertilität und Reproduktion 2 (1992), Heft 1, S. 21-25.
– Über Schwierigkeiten von Ärzten und Gerichten im Umgang mit § 218 StGB, in: A. Eser/H.-G. Koch (Hrsg.), Schwangerschaftsabbruch: Auf dem Weg zu einer Neuregelung, Baden-Baden 1992, S. 109-118.
– Recht des Schwangerschaftsabbruchs im europäischen Vergleich, in: U. Körner (Hrsg.), Ethik der menschlichen Fortpflanzung. Ethische, soziale, medizinische und rechtliche Probleme in Familienplanung, Schwangerschaftskonflikt und Reproduktionsmedizin. Reihe 'Medizin in Recht und Ethik', Band 26, Stuttgart 1992, S. 207-229.
– Problemstellung zu BGH 1 StR 120/90 (Straf- und strafverfahrensrechtliche Fragen des ärztlichen Schwangerschaftsabbruchs), Medizinrecht 10 (1992), S. 334-340.
– El Control de la Natalidad y el Derecho Penal, Eguzkilore 1992, No. 5 extraordinario, S. 123-131.
– Der Weg in den neuen Einheitsstaat. Zur Diskussion über die Neuregelung des Schwangerschaftsabbruchs im vereinten Deutschland, in: M. Enigl/S. Perthold (Hrsg.), Der weibliche Körper als Schlachtfeld, Wien 1993, S. 190-201.
– Wann beginnt das menschliche Leben? – Rechtliche Überlegungen, Zeitschrift für ärztliche Fortbildung 87 (1993), S. 797-800; dazu Diskussionsbeiträge S. 827 f.; 856; 884; 899; 903 f.; 906 f.; 910 f.
– *Reforming Abortion Legislation in Unified Germany, in: American Institute for Contemporary German Studies (Hrsg.), The Abortion Debate in Transatlantic Perspective, AICGS Seminar Paper Nr. 10, The Johns Hopkins University, Washington D.C. 1995, S. 85-100.*
– Regelungsmodelle im internationalen Vergleich, in: Arbeitsgruppe 'Schwangerschaftsabbruch' (Hrsg.), Hearing zur Neuregelung des Schwangerschaftsabbruchs für die Mitglieder des eidg. Parlaments, die Presse und weitere interessierte Kreise, Bern 1997, S. 4-6; 19; 21-23; 25-27.
Koch, Hans-Georg/Newman, Karen: *Review of the Abortion Legislation in Europe: An Analysis of the de jure and de facto Situation in Europe, Background Document for the Meeting 'From Abortion to Contraception', WHO Kopenhagen 1990, 95 Seiten.*
Koch, Hans-Georg/Tönggi, Stefan: Streitpunkt Abtreibung – wie geht's weiter?, Mannheimer Morgen Nr. 82 vom 9.4.1991, S. 2.

KOCH, HANS-GEORG/VON BAROSS, JOACHIM: Indikationsfeststellung zum Schwangerschaftsabbruch, in: Pro Familia Bundesverband (Hrsg.), Aspekte des Schwangeren- und
Familienhilferechts, Frankfurt 1995, S. 62-74 (erschienen 1996).

KÖPKE, ULF: § 218 StGB: Ein alter Streit auf neuen Bahnen? Zur aktuellen Diskussion des
Schwangerschaftsabbruchs vor dem Hintergrund empirischer Materialien, Zeitschrift
für Rechtspolitik 1985, S. 161-164.

KÖPKE ULF/LIEBL, KARLHANS: Schwangerschaftsabbruch. Empirische Materialien zu den
Erfahrungen mit dem reformierten § 218 StGB, Soziale Arbeit 35 (1986), S. 2-8.

LAMMICH, SIEGFRIED: Grundzüge des neuen tschechoslowakischen Schwangerschafts-
abbruchrechts, WGO-Monatszeitschrift für osteuropäisches Recht 29 (1987), S. 21-
42.

LAMMICH, SIEGFRIED/NAGY, FERENC: A terhességmegszakítás és a magzatelhajtás egyes jogi
illetve büntetőjogi kérdései (Einige rechtliche beziehungsweise strafrechtliche Fragen
der Unterbrechung der Schwangerschaft und der Abtreibung), Magyar Jog 33 (1986),
S. 633-642.

LENZ, KARL-FRIEDRICH: Doitsu rempôsaibansho no dainiji ninshinchûzetsu hanketsu ni tsuite
(Zur zweiten Entscheidung des deutschen Bundesverfassungsgerichts über den
Schwangerschaftsabbruch), Juristo No. 1034 (1993), S. 22-27.

–   Blick in die Zukunft: Schwangerschaftsabbruch, in: J. ARNOLD/B. BURKHARDT/W.
GROPP/H.-G. KOCH (Hrsg.), Grenzüberschreitungen – Beiträge zum 60. Geburtstag
von Albin Eser, Freiburg 1995, S. 341-358.

LIEBL, KARLHANS: Ermittlungsverfahren, Strafverfolgungs- und Sanktionspraxis bei Schwangerschaftsabbruch. Reihe 'Kriminologische Forschungsberichte', Band 40, Freiburg
1990, 189 Seiten.

LIEBL, KARLHANS/BORA ALFONS: Einstellungen zum Schwangerschaftsabbruch. Zur Bedeutung
generalisierter Wertsysteme in Konfliktsituationen, in: H.-W. FRANZ (Hrsg.), 22.
Deutscher Soziologentag 1984, Opladen 1985, S. 451-453.

–   Einstellung zum Schwangerschaftsabbruch. Zur Bedeutung generalisierter Wertsysteme in Konfliktsituationen, Pfaffenweiler 1986, 50 Seiten.

MEYER, JÜRGEN: Verfassungsrechtliche Fragen im Zusammenhang mit dem Schwangerschaftsabbruch, in: Friedrich-Ebert-Stiftung (Hrsg.), Frauenpolitik und aktuelle
verfassungspolitische Fragen, Bonn 1993, S. 9-14.

PAETOW, BARBARA: Bericht über das Kolloquium 'Recht und Praxis des Schwangerschaftsabbruchs im internationalen Vergleich', Zeitschrift für die gesamte Strafrechtswissenschaft 97 (1985), S. 1074-1086.

PERRON, WALTER: Das Grundsatzurteil des spanischen Verfassungsgerichts vom 11.4.1985
zur strafrechtlichen Regelung des Schwangerschaftsabbruchs, Zeitschrift für die
gesamte Strafrechtswissenschaft 98 (1986), S. 287-305.

PETERS, RALF: Der Schutz des neugeborenen, insbesondere des mißgebildeten Kindes. Ein
Beitrag zur Geschichte des strafrechtlichen Lebensschutzes. Reihe 'Medizin in Recht
und Ethik', Band 18, Stuttgart 1988, 290 Seiten.

TALLROTH, PAULINA: Utvecklingen av den tyska abortlagstiftningen i jämförelse med
utvecklingen i Norden (Die Entwicklung des deutschen Schwangerschaftsabbruchs-
rechts im Vergleich mit der Entwicklung in den nordischen Ländern), Nordisk Tidskrift
for Kriminalvidenskab 1 (1997), S. 36-49. – Englische Zusammenfassung S. 85.

WALTHER, SUSANNE: Schwangerschaftsabbruch in den USA: Neuere Rechtsentwicklungen,
Europäische Grundrechte Zeitschrift 19 (1992), S. 45-60.

WALTHER, SUSANNE: *Thou shalt not (But thou mayest): Abortion after the German Constitutional Court's 1993 Landmark Decision*, in: German Yearbook of International Law 36 (1994), S. 385-402.

WALTHER, SUSANNE/HERMES, GEORG: Schwangerschaftsabbruch zwischen Recht und Unrecht. Das zweite Abtreibungsurteil des BVerfG und seine Folgen, Neue Juristische Wochenschrift 1993, S. 2337-2347.

WEIGEND, EWA/ZIELINSKA, ELEONORA: Dopuszczalność przerywania ciąży w świetle orzeczenia niemieckiego Trybunału Konstytucyjnego (Die Zulässigkeit des Schwangerschaftsabbruchs im Lichte des Urteils des Bundesverfassungsgerichts), Państwo i Prawo 48 (1993), Heft 9, S. 70-79.

–   Das neue polnische Recht des Schwangerschaftsabbruchs: politischer Kompromiß und juristisches Rätselspiel, Zeitschrift für die gesamte Strafrechtswissenschaft 106 (1994), S. 213-226.

–   Nowa niemiecka ustawa: Prawna dopuszczalnosc przerywania ciąży. (Das neue deutsche Gesetz: Rechtliche Zulässigkeit des Schwangerschaftsabbruchs), Rzeczpospolita, 29.- 30.7.1995, S. 19.

INDEX

A

abortion opponent 40, 121, 207
abortion pill 37, 107
adoption 170
advertising prohibitions
   see prohibitions against advertising
anonymity 111
ascertaining an indication
   see third-party review
attempt 134
autonomous decision of the pregnant woman
   102
   see also counseling
autonomy of the pregnant woman 6, 33, 126
   conflict in making decision 214
   definition 267
   influence of psychosocial factors 237
   as protected legal value 139
     see also legal values
   self-assessment 224
   'self-determination models' 227
autonomy
   definition 267
   'procreative' ~ 262

B

ban on the practice of medicine 158, 163
   see also physician
balancing test
   see weighing-up process
birth 61, 213, 265
birth control
   see contraception
   see also demographic policy, family plan-
      ning

C

capacity to consent
   see consent of the pregnant woman
child-unfriendliness 4
churches
   see religion and termination of pregnancy
compensation for the costs of termination 123,
   298
   and legislative intent 220

differentiated models 125
uniform model 124
confidentiality 110
confidentiality requirement
   see medical confidentiality requirement
conflict-oriented discourse model
   see regulatory models: emergency-oriented
     discourse model
consent of the partner/of the social milieu 93,
   155
   legal responsibility 275
   psychosocial factors 238
consent of the pregnant woman 88
   alternative to the ~ 91
   capacity to consent 91
   information, informed ~ 92
   involvement of the woman's social milieu
     93
   medically extreme situations 90
   minors 91
   objection of the woman 91
   prerequisites 91
   presumed consent 90
   relevance 90
   right of the partner to object 93
   right of the partner to participate in deci-
     sions on termination 93
   special problems 92
   substitutability 88
   urgent cases 90
constitutional foundations 34
   legislative freedom 246
contraception
   access to contraceptives 167, 182
   as legislative intent 216, 297
   government services 166
   relation to the termination of pregnancy 9,
     212
contraindication
   see indication: contraindication
counseling 45, 95, 101, 227, 274, 285, 297
   on birth control 102
   consequences 105, 155
   content and goals 101
   counseling certificate 105

counseling (cont.)
  counseling persons/institutions 101
  effectiveness of the ~ concept in practice
      287
  functions of physicians 154
  goals 101
  historical development 285
  involvement of third parties 104
  limitation to purely medical aspects 102
  medical ~ 102, 155
  method 103
  as model-building 223
  and prevention 285
  setting of goals 289
  social ~ 102
  subsequent ~ 103
  target group 289
  waiting period 104
  see third-party review, performance re-
      quirements, preliminary proceeding
counseling certificate
  see counseling
counselor
  see counseling
covering of costs of termination
  see compensation for the costs of termina-
      tion
crime statistics 185
crimes against life
  abortion as ~ 27
  killing of newborn 14
  killing of a pregnant woman as termination
      of pregnancy 133
criminal law's role
  'abortion tourism' 236
  'dark area' effect 211, 217, 234
  determining conduct by means of proceed-
      ings 241
  effects of statutory amendmends 234
  influence on the frequency of termination
      231
  influence on moral value system 184, 247
  manipulability of grounds underlying indi-
      cations 235
  psychosocial and socioethical factors 237
criminal prosecution 19, 171
  duties of disclosure see there
  prohibition of use of evidence 174
  prosecutorial discretion 173, 186
  statistics 187
  statute of limitations 173

D
demographic policy 7, 20
  importance 20
  as legislative intent 29, 34, 80
disciplinary codes of conduct
  see physician
discrimination
  see protection from discrimination
documentation
  see performance requirements
double standards 255
duties of disclosure
  analysis of the material collected 111
  goals 111
  members of medical professions 138
  physicians 171
  planned illegal termination 172
  reporting requirements 138, 211
  statistical purposes 138
  suspected illegal termination 138

E
emancipation
  see equality of men and women
equality of men and women 5
  as reform-inducing factor 215
exemptions from punishment 69
  justification 255
  indication see there
  legal nature 71, 111
  material prerequisites 70
  procedural prerequisites 228, 276
      see also third-party review, counseling
expedited proceedings
  see requirement of prompt termination
extramarital relationship 82

F
family
  as protected value 93, 259
family planning 7, 216
  governmental measures 9, 166
  termination of pregnancy in relation to other
      methods of ~ 9
father
  interests of the ~ as protected legal value
      30, 33
  legal responsibility 231, 238, 270
fertilization 41, 47, 71 116, 173

foreign pregnant women 87
    'abortion tourism' 123, 143
    legal claim to performance of termination
        122
freedom of choice and action
    see autonomy of the pregnant woman

G

grounds for reducing punishment
    see legal consequences of a punishable ter-
        mination

H

health of the pregnant woman 32
    relation to indications 278
Hippocratic Oath
    see medical community
historical development of the termination of
        pregnancy
    family planning 7
    reform-inducing factors 215

I

ideological prejudices
    see public opinion
implantation 47, 60, 67
incest *see* rape and incest
indication 6, 72, 224, 241, 278
    age 87
    and progress of pregnancy 78
    contraindication 75, 83, 87
    criminological ~ 75, 81, 122
    embryopathic ~ 75, 79, 122
    ethical ~ *see* indication: criminological
    eugenic ~ *see* indication: embryopathic
    form requirements 83
    itemization 74
    judicial review 224
    medical ~ 75, 77, 119
    medical-social ~ 75, 77
    other ~ 75, 86
    social ~ 75, 83
    terminology 72
indication model
    and time-limit model 224
    discrepancies 282
    influence on conduct 241
information
    see consent of the pregnant woman

information prohibitions
    see prohibitions against advertising
informed consent
    see consent of the pregnant woman
intensity of prosecution 210
international criminal law 143

J

judges' and prosecutors' attitude towards ter-
    mination 215

L

'late term abortion' 266
    see also partial birth abortion
lawfulness of the termination 69, 255, 291
legal claims of the pregnant woman
    compensation for the costs *see there*
    de facto access to termination services 121
    medical indication 119
    more broadly defined indications 120
    narrowly defined indications 121
    to the performance of a permissible termi-
        nation 118
legal consequences of a punishable termination
    139
    grounds for reducing and enhancing pun-
        ishment 142
legal values 3, 30, 31, 53, 255
    balancing of interests 256
    fetus's right to life 41, 248, 259
    health/life of the pregnant woman 41, 259
    honor 41
    human dignity 41
    interests of the father 257
    plurality of interests 245, 256
    pregnant woman's freedom of choice 139,
        267
legislative intent 29
    avoidance of unwanted pregnancies 216
    constitutional foundations *see there*
    demographic policy 34, 80, 245
    plurality of interests 245
    protection of unborn life 245
    government services 166
    social ethics 246
legitimation through procedure 276
liberalization of the termination of pregnancy
    18, 215

M
marketing prohibitions
    see prohibitions against advertising
medical community
    Hippocratic Oath 15
    professional codes of ethics 15
    stance regarding the termination of preg-
        nancy 14, 154,
medical confidentiality requirement 138
medicalization of the termination of pregnancy
    228
mental element 133
method of calculating the duration of pregnancy
    71
Mifegyne 37, 107
    see also 'morning-after pill'
minors 92
'morning-after pill' 60

N
ne bis in idem 147, 163
necessity 112
    see also exemptions from punishment
negligence 134

P
partial birth abortion 107
parties to the termination 135
performance requirements 44, 106
    counseling 45, 95, 285
    determination of indications 97
    documentation 109
    exclusive approval 108
    in-patient vs. out-patient treatment 107
    institutional requirements 106
    and international criminal law 145
    issues of control and sanctioning 108
    lack of procedural provisions 44
    notification 109
    personal requirements 106
    physician 44, 48, 106, 153, 229, 297
    procedural prerequisites 95, 230
    reporting requirements 45, 109
    social indication 86
    support staff refusing 129
    third-party review 44, 95
    trends 96
    type and means of termination 107
permissible termination of pregnancy 69
personality principle 144

physician
    as attorney for the unborn 154
    ban on practice of medicine 158, 163
    determining conduct by means of penal law
        240, 253
    determining conduct by means of proceed-
        ings 241
    disciplinary/professional codes of conduct
        109, 157, 163
    duties of disclosure *see there*
    duty to conduct investigations 99
    heavier punishment 158
    medical community *see there*
    'medicalization' of the termination of preg-
        nancy 228
    own value system 239
    in preliminary proceedings 154
    preparatory and preliminary offenses 164
    privileges 158
    and religious attitudes 214
    ~ requirement for termination
        see performance requirements
    responsibility 270
    sanctions related to deficits in medical ad-
        vice and/or disclosure 162
    sanctions related to failure to comply with
        the 'hospital requirement' 159, 162
    sanctions related to the infringement of sub-
        sequent duties to disclose and report
        163, 171
    sanctions related to the performance of ter-
        minations 157
    sanctions with respect to 'preliminary pro-
        cedure' 159
    special certification 106, 153
    special role 153
'praeterintentional' abortion 134
pregnant womans' attitude towards termination
    212, 237
pregnant woman's right to submit a complaint
    see right to submit a complaint
prejudices
    see public opinion
preliminary proceeding
    see also third-party review
    counseling *see there*
    decision-making instances 155
preparatory acts 164
prevention of implantation 52, 60
preventive measures 164
    counseling as ~ 285

procedural provisions
  see performance requirements
procedural rules
  see also performance requirements
  determining conduct by means of ~ 241
  legitimation through procedure 276
'proceduralization' of the termination 228
professional codes of conduct
  see physician
professional codes of ethics
  see medical community
prohibition of use of evidence
  see criminal prosecution
prohibitions against advertising 165
prohibitions against dissemination of informa-
      tion
  see prohibitions against advertising
prompt termination
  see requirement of prompt termination
proposed regulation 295
protection from discrimination 130
protection of life 259
  equality of born and unborn life 250, 263
  maximum time limit for termination 265
  as a mere principle 261
  weighing-up 259
psychosocial situation of the pregnant woman
      237
public opinion
  ideological prejudices 207
  judges and prosecutors 215
  role of criminal law 231, 236
  social acceptance 210
  social ethics 237
  termination equalized to killing 214
  and unlawfulness of the termination 255
punishability of the termination of pregnancy
      27, 131, 136
  see also exemptions from punishment
  grant of privilege to the pregnant woman
      45, 142, 271

R
rape and incest 82
regulatory models 42
  conflict-oriented discourse model
  see ~: emergency-oriented discourse model
  'counseling model' 228, 298
  criteria for classification 42, 224
  dependence on social mores 228

regulatory models (cont.)
  emergency-oriented discourse model 55,
      228, 295
  graduated indication model 48, 78
  grant of privilege to the pregnant woman as
      criterion for classification 45
  indication model 43, 46, 224, 241
  prohibition model 43, 46, 52, 72
  'self-determination model' 227
  successive time-limit-indication model
    see time limit solution: combined (suc-
      cessive) 'time-limit-indication mod-
      els'
  'time-based exemption on the basis of self-
      determination' 228
  time-bound gradations as criteria for clas-
      sification 42
  uniform model 131
  variety 218
reimbursement of expenses
  see compensation for the costs of termina-
      tion
religion and termination of pregnancy 10
  Anglican Church 13
  Catholic Church 11, 105, 274
  Greek Orthodox Church 13
  Hinduism 14
  influence on the frequency of termination
      182
  Islam 13
  Judaism 13
  physicians 214
  Protestant Churches 12
  secular state 247
reporting requirements
  see performance requirements
  see duties of disclosure
representational principle 145
requirement of prompt termination 108
right of medical personnel to refuse participa-
      tion 127
    see also religion and termination of preg-
      nancy
right to submit a complaint 99
rights of the partner to participate in decisions
      on termination
  see consent of the pregnant woman
Roman law 34
RU 486 see Mifegyne

S

sanctions
  see punishableness of the termination of pregnancy
  see legal consequences of a punishable termination
secular state 247
  see also religion and termination of pregnancy
self-/third-party termination 132
  see also punishability of the termination of pregnancy
  attempted ~ 134, 151
  crime of omission 133
  instruments used to commit the offense 133
  mental element of the offense 133
  modes of commission 133
  parties to the ~ 135
  preparatory acts 164
  reporting requirements
    see duties of disclosure
  setting of criminal penalties 140, 152
self-assessment of the pregnant woman 270, 283, 284
sentencing 187
sex education 168
significance 72
social ethics 246
social system 4, 166
societal changes
  as reform-inducing factors 215
statistics 178, 211, 232
  see also reporting requirements
  crime statistics 185
  dark figures 178
  effect of changes in the law 181
  factors influencing prevalence of termination 182
  frequency of the termination of pregnancy according to the respective regulatory model 180
  frequency of the termination of pregnancy in various countries 179
  judicial ~ and trends in prosecution 187
  scope of unreported cases 178
  sentencing 187
  state of the data 178, 185, 187
  under reporting 178
statute of limitations 173

subsequent counseling
  see counseling
supplementary criminal law 28
'suprastatutory necessity' 112
'symbolic criminal law' 231, 249

T

termination of pregnancy
  definition 57, 134, 219
  international criminal law 143
  scope of substantive coverage 59
  temporal range 60
  terminological evolution 58
termination tourism 123
territorial principle 144
therapeutic abortion 77
third-party evaluation
  see third-party review
third-party review 95, 277, 280
  see also performance requirements
  divergence in attitude 210
  influence on frequency of termination 210
  legal significance 156
  legal significance of ascertaining an indication 156
  by a physician   *see* physician
  qualification of the counselor 98
  reviewability 225
third-party termination
  see self-/third-party termination
time limit model
  see time limit solution
time limit solution 12, 37, 43, 50
  combined (successive) 'time-limit- indication models' 49, 66, 72, 97, 116
  exemption from criminal liability subject to time limits and based on self-determination 54
  ~ and indication model 224
  pure time limit models 50
transparency of the conduct-determining message 252
types of regulations 26

U

unborn life
  personality 263
  right to life 40, 222, 250, 296
  viability 265
unlawfulness of the abortion 255

V

values *see* legal values
value-parity of born and unborn life
   see protection of life
viability of the fetus
   and temporal range of termination 62, 265

W

weighing-up process 223, 245, 257, 262, 267,
    269, 281, 284, 287, 293, 296
women
   discrimination
    see equality of men and women
   position of ~ in society 5, 216
women's attitude towards termination 212, 237
World Medical Association 16